CONTRACTORS AND WAR

CONTRACTORS AND WAR

The Transformation of
US Expeditionary Operations

Edited by Christopher Kinsey and
Malcolm Hugh Patterson

Stanford Security Studies,
An Imprint of Stanford University Press
Stanford, California

Stanford University Press
Stanford, California

Special discounts for bulk quantities of Stanford Security Studies are available to corporations, professional associations, and other organizations. For details and discount information, contact the special sales department of Stanford University Press.
Tel: (650) 736–1782, Fax: (650) 736–1784

Printed in the United States of America on acid-free, archival-quality paper

Library of Congress Cataloging-in-Publication Data

  Contractors and war : the transformation of US expeditionary operations / edited by Christopher Kinsey and Malcolm Hugh Patterson.
    pages cm
  Includes bibliographical references and index.
  ISBN 978-0-8047-6990-7 (cloth : alk. paper)
  ISBN 978-0-8047-6991-4 (pbk. : alk. paper)
    1. Defense contracts—United States. 2. Contracting out—United States. 3. Government contractors—United States. 4. United States—Armed Forces—Procurement.
5. Private military companies—United States. I. Kinsey, Christopher, editor of compilation. II. Patterson, Malcolm Hugh, 1959– editor of compilation.
UC267.C575   2012
355.6'2120973—dc23

                                                                  2012007451

Contents

Acknowledgments

THERE ARE SEVERAL PEOPLE TO WHOM WE ARE BOTH GRATEFUL. WE wish to thank each of the contributors for sharing their extensive knowledge of the subject. We are also indebted to Asher Hildebrand, who helped us navigate the corridors of Congress; and special credit goes to Margaret Bennett and Mark Erbel, both of whom assisted in editing the manuscript. We owe thanks to Geoffrey Burn and his staff at Stanford University Press, and two anonymous reviewers, whose enlightened critiques proved encouraging and valuable. Last, the back cover remarks were provided by prominent individuals who were kind enough to set aside time to examine the manuscript and provide public opinions.

Introduction

Christopher Kinsey and Malcolm Hugh Patterson

1. Developments in US Expeditionary Operations

This book concerns the role of contractors in support of American expeditionary operations. Whether training a receiving state's workforce, providing armed security for US and other nationals, or delivering logistics and technical services, contractors support the full spectrum of US operations. Today these may extend from conventional armed conflict to counterinsurgency; from reconstruction and stabilization deployments to American aid delivered in uncontested circumstances. In Afghanistan, South America, the Middle East, Africa, and elsewhere, the US military focuses on policy objectives while the marketplace supplies much of the support. This is why contractors are now part of the military structure and integral to the point where they have become essential strategic assets. In their absence, most expeditionary operations could not be deployed nor sustained.

This is very different from the Cold War model, in which the military functioned with a far higher high degree of self-sufficiency. Nor is the United States likely to return to even a modest degree of military self-reliance. Such a step is improbable for reasons of entrenched neoliberal economic philosophy,[1] legal obligations arising from statutory requirements,[2] executive policy direction,[3] growing financial constraints as the US economy struggles with prodigious debt,[4] and the momentum of foreign policies predicated on recruitment of personnel by means other than civil and/or military conscription.[5]

Unsurprisingly, self-sufficiency was discarded partly for reasons advanced by contractors. Arguments based on cost, reliability, speed of deployment, and the availability of specialist skills and equipment have proved persuasive. Should stability and reconstruction operations (SROs) become more prominent in US foreign engagement—as seems probable in the present climate—the scope for contractor involvement will grow. A major reason for this is that where America intervenes in this fashion, the utility of military force tends to be limited. Subduing threats to the United States and its interests will necessitate the deployment of personnel in addition to combat troops. And regardless of contractor weaknesses, the federal government is unlikely to abruptly recruit and train sufficient numbers of uniformed and civilian personnel to satisfy future needs. Cost aside, an unpopular conflict may attract few volunteers from a less than receptive populace. Nor should one expect every state plagued by conflict or civil disaster to be stabilized through American intervention. Whether benign or otherwise, current and future US deployments may be dogged by costly and indeterminate outcomes. In that event, deployment of a non-uniformed and mostly non-US presence may reduce political risk.

In one sense, there is little that is new in contract support of American forces on deployed operations. Today's suppliers of goods and services have antecedents that extend back to the sutlers who equipped American revolutionaries in their war against the British.[6] Another formative development of the eighteenth century was the enduring and widely accepted belief that states may be defined in part by their claim to a monopoly on legitimate violence.[7] The precise form of this monopoly has never been static and today a spectrum of private contractors work in and around US deployments across the world. Yet changes over the last twenty years or so have been qualitatively and quantitatively different from the earlier evolution in twentieth-century roles.

One cause was the cut in defense spending as the Cold War began to wane. Consequently, civilians and uniformed military within the Department of Defense (DoD) faced staff redundancies, early retirement, and restricted recruiting. A decline in numbers was followed by a gradual rise in the number of civilians contracted to carry out an expanding range of tasks. This increase in contractors was also spurred by decreasing political will to sustain the various costs of armed conflict. That development was consistent with a broader shift in neoliberal economics and a reduction in government responsibilities as both Republicans and Democrats promised greater efficiency in delivery of public goods. The security of the state no longer enjoyed the extent of immunity from financial constraints applied elsewhere. State security instead became the subject of market ideology, as commercial entities began to perform tasks formerly carried out by civilian and uniformed government employees.

Nor have American governments and US corporations been hindered by debris left in the wake of Cold War political, social, cultural, and legal constraints. Corporations have experimented to their advantage with foreign subsidiaries and cultures. They now pursue business around the world without breaching US trade embargoes or enduring criticism for un-American conduct. The end of the Cold War also saw massive demobilization across the globe and the creation of a large pool of skilled and disciplined ex-military personnel. Proficient foreigners were always likely to attract US interest where their ready availability increased the appeal of lower costs than comparable American labor. The resultant mix of civilian and ex-military third country nationals (TCNs) combined with host-state labor and smaller numbers of Americans has assisted considerably in effective military outsourcing. This occurred at a time of enhanced global communications and trading technologies, while weakening labor unions accompanied fewer constraints on business migration and financial institutions wielded increased influence. Each of these factors permitted goods, services, money, and labor to flow over international borders in a less inhibited fashion.

Simultaneously, training soldiers for armed conflict became more expensive as the revolution in military affairs called for more lengthy and intensive training of American technicians and engineers. One example is the complexity of today's network-centric warfare, which links command, control, communications, computers, intelligence, surveillance, and reconnaissance (C4ISR). The costs of modern warfare have also risen as weapons systems have become more complicated and the skill required to maintain them has increased. This has caused greater numbers of civilians to be located in the operational theater, although in relatively safe locations. The systems they maintain include missiles, helicopters, artillery, tanks and unmanned aerial vehicles; the last deployed by both the US military and American intelligence agencies.[8] The battlefield is being further civilianized through participation of nonmilitary labor in advanced information technology and intelligence collection.[9]

Other opportunities in contemporary support include planning and construction of military bases. This includes building fences, roads, landing strips, power generators, hangars, accommodation, latrines, and mess halls. After construction has been completed, there are further roles in postal services, fuel supply, static and mobile security, laundry, water purification and waste removal, pest control, preparation of foodstuffs, interpreter services, records and inventory maintenance. Logistic support in fact supplies the bulk of contractor revenue. The very large, multi-billion dollar tasks within the Logistics Civil Augmentation Program (LOGCAP) is the most prominent example of commercial sustainment of US expeditionary operations.[10]

2. The Reason for This Inquiry

A convincing anthology usually provides the reader with adequate explanations to two questions: the editors' purpose(s) in investigating the topic at hand, and why the content has been conceived and ordered in a particular manner. In addressing the first query, most readers will be aware that despite some noteworthy commercial success, contractors grapple with substantial and persistent problems. In order to understand the growth, influence, and future of this industry, these matters bear some examination. To answer the second inquiry, the editorial intention is to avoid a thematic approach and instead divide the book into four parts. These draw the reader in a succession of coherent steps that explore different facets of the outsourcing of military responsibilities. In chronological order, these identify the major features; consider a prominent form of US expeditionary engagement; scrutinize some legal issues; then propose desirable changes to public administration. Although each chapter may be read individually to illuminate a particular aspect, the editors are mindful that to explore military outsourcing through one attribute is likely to limit one's understanding. The purpose of this book is to impart a grasp of the subject through the collective application of a range of views and disciplines to a variety of issues.

These aspirations find a niche within vigorous debates over outsourcing and the privatization of security and logistic support. Those debates are concerned with many worthy issues. They range from the substance of evolving taxonomies to the nature of state and corporate control; from legitimacy and ethics to government and corporate financing; from theories of the modern state to definitions of inherently governmental goods and services—and how to keep the latter from private hands. To a greater or lesser degree, discussion of these matters has been a consistent feature in the literature. One can locate these themes in earlier American works in the field—by the likes of Robert Mandel, Peter W. Singer, and Deborah Avant.[11] These issues endure and often carry a normative aspect. Normative argument is not absent from the following pages, but this book is concerned with US government policy and practice. That is why the contributors have properly focused on ends demanded by the American government and the merits in practical means employed to achieve them. How these means are supplied and whether US government ends are fulfilled is a quite distinctive purpose and one without predecessors in book-length form. With this in mind, the editors complete the Conclusion by identifying lessons likely to guide greater operational success in the future.

The reader should also be without doubt as to what is not included and s/he may discern four topics that are absent from the pages that follow. The first is theory. This is a book concerned with US government policy; or more accurately, generating an impetus toward improved policy choices by the US executive, legislature, and bureaucracy. Second, the content is not intended to form an indirect critique of the first and second administrations of President G. W. Bush. Some readers will seek details of moral hazards arising from nepotistic government–contractor relations; the engineering of expanded choices for executive government through a "democratic deficit" as a consequence of extensive contractor deployments; or contractor-sourced covert homicide squads sent to Iraq, Somalia, and Afghanistan. Those readers will find ample information elsewhere.

A third omission is a more comprehensive examination of legal issues. Space constraints oblige the editors to refrain from examining the policy ramifications of litigation in US industrial courts over insurance held by wounded contractors; suits in negligence over contractors' injuries and deaths; and criminal and tortious cases pursued by relatives of foreign civilians killed or injured intentionally or negligently by contractors in the course of their employment. Nor does this book assess quasi-legal codes of conduct or the impact of "good corporate citizenship" measures. By limiting Part III to problems of law and policy, the legal component remains of manageable size. Last, this is not a document preoccupied with armed contractors. They tend to receive most of the public attention and much of the journalistic, legal, and academic commentary. One does not wish to trivialize the more disagreeable aspects of their presence on operations. Yet armed contractors comprise only a small part of the overall labor force and financial costs involved in outsourced support. Accordingly, the editors have sought to focus the academic spotlight on a broader range of contractors and those issues that affect their roles in support of US expeditionary operations.

3. Structure of the Book

The first part begins with a chapter that explains the contracting phenomenon and summarizes current developments in the field. Robert Mandel's succinct review suggests buoyant prospects resulting from tension between continuing global engagement by the United States and limits to American military workforce and budgets. He suggests that contractor influence may help to shape the nature of American expeditionary operations; yet there remains an inadequate bureaucratic grasp of the conditions under which deployment of private contractors makes the most and least sense. In the following chapter, Ryan Kelty and Darcy Schnack hold a sociological prism to views on contractors held by service personnel. These authors plumb the dynamic nature of military identity and plot a change in roles as civilians and their privatized workforce become more involved in battlefield roles. In the third chapter, Renée de Nevers studies the global breadth of contractor deployments and refers to their operations in areas as diverse as Afghanistan, Africa, and Latin America. She puts a case for improved effectiveness in governance and clarity in legal and military authority.

Part II explores three facets of reconstruction and stabilization operations, which is a growth market in the contracting business. In the first chapter, a US Army peace operations expert delivers an illuminating perspective on military expectations of those who provide essential resources to the armed forces. Colonel William Flavin supplies a view as to how contracting should be integrated or nested in the US military's operational and strategic frameworks. He emphasizes the need for improved doctrinal and conceptual guidance and proposes an enhanced operational concept. This relationship between the military and corporate support has become increasingly complex, as it elevates the battlefield prominence of what has until recently been a less conspicuous body of civilians.

The following chapter was written by the chief executive of a prominent NGO. Samuel Worthington explains how reconstruction during counterinsurgency operations creates difficult relations between NGOs (and aid organizations in particular), the US military, and civilian contractors. This is especially likely where these contractors are armed and their behavior jeopardizes the delicate fabric of trust that sustains NGOs in turbulent places. US-based NGOs do not see themselves as an extension of US power; and Mr. Worthington is concerned with the imprudence of US militarization of foreign assistance. The third chapter is a quite different exploration of emerging battlefield complexity: a pessimistic hypothesis that concerns incompatible cultures of risk-taking held by contractors and the US military. Political scientist Kateri Carmola evaluates risks that private security contractors both reduce and escalate through deployments in counterinsurgency operations. She concludes that the organizational risk cultures of contractors do not align with those of the military or the requirements of counterinsurgency warfare more generally.

Part III is divided into topics of a broadly legal nature. Geoffrey Corn begins with a summary of three pressing issues: the status of contractors while accompanying US armed forces in an operational environment; those functions that may be legally transferred to contractors; and the nature of criminal justice remedies attracted by contractor misconduct. The American public has been aware for some time that in Iraq in particular, serious questions have been raised over improper contractor violence and the absence of a functional criminal justice system. In the next chapter, Allison Stanger explains how outsourcing has enabled American policy makers to spend their way out of crises rather than garner support for contingency operations from the American people. Her focus is the Commission on Wartime Contracting (CWC) and the moral and legal hazards that have driven its creation. As a consequence of critical CWC reports, it seems likely that some reforms in US law will follow. Professor Stanger provides her own remedies to address the excesses of what she describes as "free market fundamentalism." The third contribution is by Congressman David Price, who writes on the uncertain and unsatisfactory legal framework attached to US government contractors. He provides a compelling case for an effective criminal justice system that would apply to all contractors deployed on future American expeditionary operations.

Part IV is a review of US administrative structures required to sustain and administer effective contractor operations. Frank Camm begins with the fundamental observation that there have been few attempts to compare the costs or performance of government and contractors where they have provided similar services to deployed military forces. In addressing this perhaps surprising situation, he devises a risk comparison that identifies which circumstances favor government or contractor sources. In the next chapter, Stuart Bowen draws on extensive personal experience in explaining how the reconstruction of Iraq grew from an "adhocracy" in which "no US office had full responsibility for planning, executing, or being held accountable for the rebuilding program." The results were regrettable and burdened the US taxpayer with colossal costs. Mr. Bowen envisages extensive reform of stabilization and reconstruction operations through a range of institutional changes. These are intended to unify overlapping missions and resources; to reorganize those resources and existing structures; and to integrate management into a single agency.

In the third chapter Jacques Gansler and William Lucyshyn examine problems in Department of Defense contracting through three categories of analyses: human capital; policies, processes, and procedures; and information technology. They conclude that future deployments are likely to involve up to 50 percent contractors within the total force. This mix of military, US government civilian employees, and contractors of mixed nationality will require extensive DoD adjustments. These will affect the department's organization, culture, doctrine, and planning.

When studying these chapters, the reader is likely to benefit from clarification in the meaning of several terms. One is "contractor." In the present context, a contractor is an agent who carries out tasks on behalf of a government or corporate principal. Another distinction is between "privatization" and "outsourcing." A persuasive view is that privatization involves the transfer to private contractors of responsibility for planning, organizing, financing, and managing a program. In contrast, outsourcing involves contracting military support services to outsiders while retaining responsibility for these within the military.[12] And "defense logistics" is "the science of planning and carrying out the movement and maintenance of air, sea and land forces."[13]

4. Summary

An increased reliance on the commercial sector generates consequences that extend further than American objectives. This dependence is altering behavior among allies and adversaries, other governments and nongovernment organizations. All of these actors have their own reasons to better adapt to conventional hostilities, counterinsurgency campaigns, and post-conflict stabilization and reconstruction operations. There is little doubt that greater involvement of contractors implies an ongoing transformation in US expeditionary operations, the effects of which will exert both subtle and more apparent influence over the projection of American power.

While other scholars have written on this topic, *Contractors and War* stands alone in that it is the first publication to assemble essays by eminent American scholars drawn from the military, economics, law, an umbrella NGO, the legislature, civilian bureaucracies, and the social sciences. This is a book written by American authors for American readers who seek to improve their understanding of the impact of contractors on US expeditionary operations. The writers have applied collectively formidable knowledge to several of the thornier problems that confront policy makers today. The result is intended to propel debate a little further in constructive directions. Meanwhile, the private sector continues to influence and be influenced by current operations and planning for future deployments.

Notes

1. For a sanguine view on the more positive possibilities of business–government relations in the context of contractor support, see Allison Stanger, *One Nation Under Contract* (New Haven, CT: Yale University Press, 2009), chap. 8.

2. See the US Office of Management and Budget Circular A-76 Fact Sheet at http://oma.od.nih.gov/ms/a76-fair/A-76%20HHS%20Fact%20Sheet.pdf.

3. Christopher Hinton, "Pentagon Still a Cash Cow Despite Budget Cuts," *Market Watch*, April 7, 2009, http.marketwatch.com/story/pentagon-still-a-cash-cow (accessed Dec. 23, 2010). The future for military contractors remains buoyant despite a Pentagon intention to cut contractors "as a percentage of its total workforce to 26% from 39%, and hire up to 30,000 new civil servants over the next five years."

4. Donna Smith and Kenneth Barry, "US Debt to Rise to $19.6 Trillion by 2015," *Reuters*, June 8, 2010, www.reuters.com/article/idUSN08846252010000608 (accessed Dec. 22, 2010).

5. In 2009, there were more contractors than military in Afghanistan, and in Iraq the number of military and contractors were almost the same. See Richard Fontaine and John Nagl, *Contractors in American Conflicts: Adapting to a New Reality* (Washington, DC: Center for a New American Security, Dec. 2009), 7, http.humansecuritygateway.com/documents/CNAS_ContractorsInAmericanConflicts.pdf (accessed Dec. 23, 2010). The 2010 *Quadrennial Defense Review Report* includes contractors within the "total defense workforce" (55–56).

6. For a sound account of how George Washington's revolutionary army was supplied, see J. A. Huston, *Logistics of Liberty* (Newark: University of Delaware Press, 1991).

7. Weber described this claim as essential. See Max Weber, *The Theory of Social and Economic Organization,* translated by A. R. Henderson and T. Parsons (London: William Hodge: 1947), 141, 143.

8. C. Johnson, *The Sorrows of Empire* (London: Verso, 2004), paperback ed., 142.

9. Less well-known than the analytical services offered by American business is the collection of intelligence by manned and unmanned aerial vehicles operated by private firms. See, for example, Airscan, Inc. site, www.airscan.com/about.html (accessed June 11, 2011).

10. LOGCAP was created by the US Army in 1985. Its purpose has been to plan the integration of contractors in support of contingencies and crises, and utilize existing civilian resources in the United States and overseas to augment active and reserve forces. See United States General Accounting Office, *Contingency Operations: Opportunities to Improve the Logistics Civil Augmentation Program,* GAO/NSIAD-97-63 (Feb. 1997), 2.

11. Robert Mandel, *Armies Without States* (Boulder, CO: Lynne Rienner, 2002); P. W. Singer, *Corporate Warriors: The Rise of the Privatized Military Industry* (Ithaca, NY: Cornell University Press, 2003); and Deborah Avant, *The Market for Force* (Cambridge, UK: Cambridge University Press, 2005).

12. W. Mitchell, "Privatizing Defense: Britain Leads the Way," National Center for Policy Analysis/*Brief Analysis* no. 391, www.ncpa.org/pub/ba/ba391 (accessed April 2, 2005).

13. NATO *Logistics Handbook* 1997, 1.

1 THE NATURE OF CONTRACTOR SUPPORT IN FUTURE US MILITARY OPERATIONS

1 Overview of American Government Expeditionary Operations Utilizing Private Contractors

Robert Mandel

1. Introduction

The recent expanded reliance by the United States on private contractors in military operations overseas has reached unprecedented levels, so much so that "the scope of today's wartime contracting dwarfs that of past military conflicts."[1] Indeed, today the United States seems to be totally unable to engage in expeditionary operations without using private contractors: in particular, in 2007, over 190,000 contractors worked in Iraq on US-funded contracts, making the number of private contractors roughly equal to that of American government soldiers; in 2008, the Department of Defense spent around 316 billion dollars on contracted services, about as much as the total amount it spent on weapons systems and equipment; and in 2009, private contractors outnumbered military personnel in Afghanistan and nearly equaled the number of military personnel in Iraq.[2] No longer does the United States even attempt to achieve military self-sufficiency by maintaining enough government troops to fulfill its global security objectives.

This chapter's explicitly conceptual analysis provides an explanation of why the American government chose recently to rely more on private contractors, the controversies surrounding this reliance, arguments identifying the strengths and weaknesses associated with American government use of private contractors, and the future course of private contractors in American expeditionary operations.[3] The central purpose is to provide a deeper and more balanced perspective on well-publicized trends. In the process, this chapter carefully situates the private contractor issue within the broader security context.

2. Motivation for American Government Use of Private Contractors

This escalating use of private contracting has many roots. The supply and demand changes surrounding military personnel after the Cold War, the foreign policy limitations associated with exclusive reliance on government forces, and the reluctance by the government to undertake operations that risk significant citizen casualties have combined to foster a groundswell of interest and activity in this area. Private contractors have been adept recently at realizing and taking advantage of opportunities presented.

One of the pivotal causes is the post–Cold War downsizing of the American military.[4] Since the mid-1990s, "the Department of Defense (DOD) has increasingly viewed contracted support as a 'force multiplier' that supplements existing U.S. force structure capacity and capability":[5]

> The Department of Defense (DOD) has a long history of relying on contractors to support troops during wartime and expeditionary operations. Generally, from the Revolutionary War through the Vietnam War, contractors provided traditional logistical support such as medical care, transportation, and engineering to U.S. armed forces. Since the end of the Cold War there has been a significant increase in contractors supporting U.S. troops—in terms of the number and percentage of contractors, and the type of work being performed. . . . According to DOD, post–Cold War budget reductions resulted in significant cuts to military logistical and support personnel, requiring DOD to hire contractors to "fill the gap."[6]

Between 1989 and 2002, the Department of Defense's total civilian workforce shrunk by 38 percent.[7] Shortages of trained personnel still hamper American expeditionary operations, as the United States has assumed security responsibilities in multiple parts of the world without enough qualified government personnel to support these far-flung responsibilities. The post–Cold War downsizing of government military personnel, which occurred not just within the United States, released onto the global market sizable numbers of people with soldiering skills looking for employment, and thus provided private contractors with ready manpower and an ability to supply requisite services on the battlefield.

At the same time the American military has been downsizing, global disruptions and threats to US interests abroad have appeared to multiply and diversify. The end to the Cold War opened the door to different kinds of foreign threats, including an increasing number of domestic insurgencies, internal civil wars, failing states, the spread of weapons of mass destruction, transnational organized crime, and violent acts perpetrated by transnational terrorists. Emerging threats have been typically covert, dispersed, decentralized, adaptable, and fluid, with threat sources relatively difficult to identify, monitor, target, contain, destroy, and with these sources' past actions not necessarily a sound guide to their future behavior. This pattern reflects "the 'de-massification' of threats in the world," where "a single giant threat of war . . . is replaced by a multitude of 'niche threats'" in which "war will not be waged by armies but by groups we today call terrorists, guerrillas, bandits, and robbers."[8] Many of these dangers are asymmetric threats involving ruthless adversaries that call for strong coercive responses. Because of widespread anti-American sentiments in various parts of the world, the United States or American interests are frequently directly or indirectly a target of these disruptions. So the demand for expeditionary operations to promote or maintain international stability has increased.

Recognition of foreign policy limitations associated with the use of government forces in expeditionary operations also has contributed to private contractor reliance. The inability of the United States to achieve a ground force victory in Vietnam "persuaded a generation or more of American and Western generals that the use of Western and particularly American ground forces in foreign conflicts is a mistake"; indeed, the "mounting human and financial costs" resulting from helping to manage "seemingly intractable civil wars" overseas has created a kind of "intervention fatigue" among Western states.[9] Moreover, "the unanticipated length and complexity of post-conflict operations in Iraq and Afghanistan" provided incentives to move away from reliance on uniformed government soldiers.[10] Particularly in dealing with the elusive security challenges they face today, the use of conventional government military forces alone has not shown itself consistently to be the most efficient and effective way to manage the threat.

In a related manner, casualty aversion helps to explain the increased reliance on private contractors. American political leaders have to some extent become "quite terrified of taking casualties" through interventions overseas, and as a result private contractors have begun to look awfully attractive: several years ago an American ambassador in Europe confessed "that his country could no longer emotionally, psychologically or politically accept body bags coming home in double figures."[11] When a government chooses to outsource to private contractors, the attraction may result from the state bearing little public accountability for undesired consequences, deaths of citizens, or moral and legal dilemmas about the legitimacy of an intervention.[12] Moreover, when the US government wants to restrain its commitment in its international intervention, private security outfits give it a low-risk means to do so. Utilization of private contractors can capitalize on the vast numbers of trained, skilled former military personnel in foreign countries, many of which have depressed economies and have qualified people looking for work. As a result, missions that the United States would like to undertake for political or security reasons that do not warrant the loss of American lives or that do not enjoy substantial domestic political support (in Congress and the public) could then still be undertaken, since public concern would be much lower for the lives of foreign nationals who voluntarily sign a paid contract indicating a willingness to fight and die for American interests. Because the prevailing international security environment fosters considerable ambiguity in prioritizing areas for expeditionary operations, versatility in deployment options—facilitated by private contractors—becomes critical to cope with changing priorities.

3. Controversies Surrounding Private Contractor Use

Controversy surrounds the use of private contractors in recent American expeditionary operations. Areas of debate include (1) the level of corruption within private contractor activity; (2) the money savings (or lack thereof) associated with private contractor activity; (3) private contractors' loyalty and suitability to the security tasks assigned; (4) private contractors' level of adherence to high moral standards; (5) the proper balance between public and private support for expeditionary operations; (6) tensions between private contractors and government military personnel; and (7) the availability of appropriate policy options as alternatives to reliance on private contractors. Participating in this heated discussion are not just academic and policy experts but also members of the mass media and of antagonistic public interest groups.

Unfortunately, the character of this debate is far less than ideal. First, much analysis is polemical, evidencing a preconceived bias for or against the use of private contractors and simply attempting to find evidence supporting this prejudice. For opponents of American use of private contractors, the Blackwater scandal appears to be the primary—and in some cases the only—reference point. Second, many observers talk past each other because of the lack of specificity about what kind of private security in what context is being discussed. Specifically, the use of private contractors by the United States for expeditionary operations differs markedly from the use of private contractors by Third World countries to help with their own security or by international organizations for humanitarian assistance. Third, many analysts prefer to jump right to prescriptions about private contractors without first enhancing understanding of current and future opportunities and dangers. Lastly, many observers are exclusively concerned with the American use of private contractors in Iraq and Afghanistan, without considering the broader implications of articulated critiques beyond these specific ongoing conflict zones.

One key ongoing disagreement surrounds the accusation that military contracting in Iraq and Afghanistan has been "rife with fraud, waste, and abuse."[13] As an example of alleged corruption, an October 2003 Center for Public Integrity study analyzing companies in Iraq and Afghanistan "matched $49 million from 70 companies doing about $8 billion in government business to political contributions that went almost two to one to Republicans over Democrats, President George W. Bush pulling in the most of all."[14] The United States Congress is very worried about oversight and management of Department of Defense private contracting in Iraq, particularly about "a lack of accountability for large sums of money spent for Iraq contracts," due to "the expense and difficulty of managing logistical support contracts" and "questions regarding DOD's ability and capacity to manage such contracts."[15] Deficient contractor management can keep vital support from getting to military troops and promote waste; and deficient contractor oversight can lead to contractor abuses that undermine security objectives.[16] As with any incident of alleged misbehavior, the central bone of contention is how representative or widespread the dysfunctional activity is, and this is difficult to determine due to the lack of relevant reliable data.

A second major debate concerns whether using private contractors saves the American government money. On the surface, the answer would appear to be affirmative, for private contractors are not eligible for pensions, retirement benefits, and long-term health care the way government soldiers are. Popular news coverage has exaggerated the costs of private contractors, especially the salaries paid to contractors, and does not take into account benefits and compensation only regular military personnel—not private contractors—receive.[17] Yet a recent Government Accountability Office report questions this conclusion:

> A key assumption of many of the federal management reforms of the 1990s was that the cost-efficiency of government operations could be improved through the use of contractors. GAO recently reported that sufficient data are not available to determine whether increased service contracting has caused DOD's costs to be higher than they would have been had the contracted activities been performed by uniformed or DOD civilian personnel. GAO recently probed, in-depth, the cost of contractor versus government contract specialists at the Army's Contracting Center for Excellence and found that the Army is paying up to 26 percent more for the contractors as compared to their government counterparts.[18]

Indeed, whether public or private security is more inexpensive may be situational:

> It is not clear that outsourcing of military training saves the U.S. government any money. . . . Studies of privatization have found that cost savings depend on competition. . . . There is often collusion among competing firms, and long-term contracts lead to opportunistic behavior, such as firms bidding low, knowing that they can add on later. Further, the calculated costs of outsourcing rarely take into account the fact that the Pentagon must hire people to police the contractors.[19]

Once again, complexities surrounding private contractors impede gauging their overall value.

A third controversy revolves around the loyalty and task suitability of private contractors. First, about 80 percent of the Department of Defense contracted employees in Iraq and Afghanistan are foreign nationals, who "may not be accountable to any American government authority."[20] Some analysts have accused private contractors of participating in illicit activities, including drug-trafficking, illegal extraction of resources, and even international terrorism:[21] this possibility received some vindication when a Mexican drug-trafficking organization hired mercenaries to train cartel security forces in advanced military tactics and surveillance techniques,[22] and occasionally links emerge between private contractors and all the unruly perpetrators of global privatized violence—transnational criminals, warlords, rebels/

insurgents, and terrorists.[23] Second, "the Rules of Engagement for the military differ significantly from the Rules for the Use of Force for private security contractors."[24] These differences can mean that even an effective private contractor behaving abroad in an unexpected manner can create disruptive ripples. Third, the limited, short-term nature of much private contractor involvement may not match long-term mission needs. Fourth, the net result of heavy Department of Defense reliance on contractors whose mission fit is questionable can be devastating, as it "is developing a growing dependency on contracted services and the PMO [private military organization] industry to fulfill tactical, operational and sometimes strategic needs"[25] to the extent that "many analysts now believe that DOD is unable to successfully execute large missions without contractor support."[26]

Fourth, a critical debate centers on whether the moral and ethical standards of private contractors are high enough. Several analysts feel that the presence of privatized security increases the frequency and severity of human rights violations or other crimes against humanity.[27] Concern frequently arises that "contractors are not subject to the same ethics rules as government even when doing the same job, and the government risks entering into an improper personal services contract if an employer/employee relationship exists between the government and the contractor employee.[28] Suspicions abound that those choosing to work for private contractors may either be scoundrels or—at the very least—possess significantly lower standards of performance or desire to adhere to prevailing norms. This way of thinking would presume that private contractors would often be tempted to consider a situation a "no-holds-barred" carte blanche to do whatever barbarous acts they deem necessary to achieve the objectives for which they are being paid:

> There have been published reports of local nationals being abused and mistreated by some DOD contractors in such incidents as the shooting at Iraqi civilians by private security contractors and the abuse of prisoners at Abu Ghraib prison in Iraq. Local nationals may not draw a distinction between government contractors and the U.S. military, and the abuses committed by contractors may strengthen anti-American insurgents, as evidenced by the public outcry following such incidents.[29]

Much of this debate stems from differing assumptions about the qualifications of private contractors, with observers differing sharply on whether these nongovernmental personnel possess the requisite restraint and discipline to execute assignments appropriately.

A fifth issue of dispute concerns the balance of public and private functions in American expeditionary operations:

> DOD has increasingly turned to contractors to fill roles previously held by government employees and to perform many functions that closely support inherently governmental functions, such as contracting support, intelligence analysis, program management, and engineering and technical support for program offices. This trend has raised concerns about what the proper balance is between public and private employees in performing agency missions and the potential risk of contractors influencing the government's control over and accountability for decisions that may be based, in part, on contractor work.[30]

Government agencies clearly "face challenges in developing an appropriate mix of contractor and government personnel to meet current and future needs."[31] In particular, some observers are concerned that, if too large a proportion of government security responsibilities is outsourced to private contractors, then the American federal government—and by extension the American people—will lose control over its expeditionary operations.

A sixth related disagreement about private contractors is the possibility of tensions erupting between public and private forces. In particular, friction frequently surfaces between private contractors and government army personnel.[32] Some of the problems that have surfaced in this regard relate to the need for clearer communication and expectations—for example, in 2006 several military commanders "said their pre-deployment training did not provide them with sufficient information on the extent of contractor support that they would be relying on in Iraq and were therefore surprised by the substantial number of personnel they had to allocate to provide on-base escorts, convoy security, and other force protection support to contractors."[33] Contrasting underlying logic is often evident when comparing the two sources of these tensions: government security officials may see the private contractors as superfluous, with inferior qualifications and experience, serving in the end only to interfere with rather than to promote safety or to make its enforcement more difficult; while private contractors may assume that the whole reason their services were requested was the incompetence, inadequacy, or ineptitude of government military personnel. Furthermore, "the use of contractors in war, particularly in areas once considered the exclusive domain of uniformed personnel, can have a corrosive effect on warrior ethos—that combination of discipline, selflessness, and cohesion that binds warriors in a collective covenant."[34] There is, for example, a long tradition of military personnel in many countries being more skeptical than others in government about whether nonmilitary people can do the things they do as well as they do. In this way of thinking, expecting these two groups to cooperate harmoniously in the common pursuit of security may be unrealistic.

A final controversy centers on whether policy alternatives outside of reliance on private contractors are realistically available. Some analysts feel contractors are truly the only option:

> Overseas, the government currently has no short-term option but to rely on contractors for every conceivable task that it lacks appropriate staff to fulfill. In Iraq, the military relies on contractor personnel not only for transportation, shelter, and food, but for unprecedented levels of battlefield and weaponry operation, support, and maintenance. Accordingly, defense experts now recognize that without contractors, our military simply cannot project its technical superiority abroad. But highly publicized incidents—whether of prisoner abuse at Abu Ghraib or allegations of the shooting of civilians by the private military company Blackwater—raise fundamental questions regarding both the tasking of contractor personnel and the oversight of their performance.[35]

Given the limited number and mission flexibility of American government military personnel, if a global trouble spot requires speedy coercive outside intervention, there may not be in the short-run feasible options available that would make turning to private contractors superfluous. In the most severe cases of uncontrollable turmoil, privatized contractors may seem to present the only means of restoring order, filling a void where existing government authorities are fearful of treading due to political, military, or financial costs.[36] However, both inside and outside the American government some staunchly believe that innovative thinking could lead to numerous alternative ways of coping with challenges in expeditionary operations.

4. The Case For and Against US Private Contractor Use

Private contractors possess several advantages over government military personnel for execution of American expeditionary operations. These include speed and flexibility, special expertise, execution of tasks for which government military personnel are not the most capable, and freeing up of government personnel for important, sensitive functions that only they can undertake effectively. These advantages are significant but not universal, making the utility of private contractors situationally dependent.

Private contractors often possess great flexibility, an ability to create unique solutions for each case, knowledge about the problem area and operational expertise, business integrity, secure confidentiality, and a generally apolitical nature.[37] Assuming that winning the type of war prevalent today is "less a matter of applying massive force across a wide front as it is of applying intelligent force at carefully selected points,"[38] traditional government-sponsored standing armies may often be less well suited to facilitating this goal than are many private contractors:

> Contractors can provide operational benefits to DOD. Using contractors to perform non-combat activities augments the total force and can also free up uniformed personnel to perform combat missions. Since contractors can be hired faster than DOD can develop an internal capability, contractors can be quickly deployed to provide critical support capabilities when necessary. Contractors also provide expertise in specialized fields that DOD may not possess, such as linguistics. Using contractors can also save DOD money. Contractors can be hired when a particular need arises and be let go when their services are no longer needed. Hiring contractors only as needed can be cheaper in the long run than maintaining a permanent in-house capability.[39]

Private contractors often note that the integrity of their own staff prevents abuse of power, that they are careful in choosing clients that will not use newly acquired capabilities back against the United States, and that in any case the defensive training and advice they give cannot be readily converted to offensive purposes. In the end, "as current and former DOD officials point out, not a single mission in Iraq or Afghanistan has failed because of contractor non-performance."[40]

Indeed, one American army officer explains how these private contractors could effectively relieve government armies of tasks for which they are not the most capable (or eager to undertake):

Just as private security firms are accepted as a positive development, if success-ful in reducing crime, so too are military contractors accepted, if successful in assisting an army to accomplish its missions at a reduced cost. Coinciding with the shrinking size of the world's armies [are] the growing requirements placed upon them. Armies the world over are being asked to perform missions that are outside the traditional mission of defending national sovereignty. As-sisting the nation in the policing of national borders, combating drugs, and humanitarian relief missions are now the everyday missions of armies around the world. What had been traditional police missions now have a mix of po-lice, private security firms and military working in the same arena. With the proliferation of private security firms and military contractors who assist the armies, it is time the US Army begins to consider the implications of operat-ing in an environment where the most capable military force may be a private company, not a government entity.[41]

If companies outside of government can more efficiently and effectively pro-vide security services, in the minds not only of the clients protected by these services but also of the government which outsources them, then why should not these functions be privatized? Following a variant of comparative advan-tage, under such an arrangement the government can provide those security services that it does best while private contractors provide those services that they do best, and the net result can be that those protected can get the best of all possible worlds. Former Deputy Assistant Secretary of Defense for Afri-can Affairs James Woods argues that private contractors operating abroad can help to relieve anarchy and chaos, keep local security disruptions from spreading, and provide sound defense against outside threats.[42] The use of private contractors can thus free up government military personnel for key functions for which these government employees have a particular compar-ative advantage, and at the same time offset ongoing or imminent budget-driven cuts in military force structure.

In contrast, important disadvantages also are associated with the Ameri-can government use of private contractors in expeditionary operations. These disadvantages include interfering with state sovereignty, making force and violence more attractive tools of foreign security policy, conducting foreign policy by proxy, and being unable to achieve long-term peace and stability. As with the advantages, these drawbacks only apply in certain circumstances.

Perhaps the most significant cost associated with American government reliance on private contractors in expeditionary operations is the reduction of state sovereignty and decreasing state capacity to provide security, implicitly altering the social contract between the ruling regime and its citizenry. Tremendous concern has emerged about the cumulative impact of the externalization of security functions, traditionally most cherished by the state:

> While liberalisation and democratisation continue to be sold as the panacea, the state is being virtually hollowed out and little to nothing is left for democratically elected politicians to decide, because the major state functions have long since been externalised. . . . Military functions and security services are only the latest additions to the list of state functions being externalised and often privatised.[43]

It is possible to claim that using private contractors in expeditionary operations ends up, at times inadvertently, becoming the equivalent of conducting foreign policy "by proxy," with the long-standing asset of plausible deniability eliminating the possibility of any sustained and coherent link between foreign policy principles and interventions actually undertaken.[44] In addition to "hollowing out" the state, some specific potential dangers from extensive reliance on private contractors include (1) poor contractor performance; (2) entrance of contractors into specific engagements that they have not anticipated or trained for and are not well equipped to handle; (3) significant unanticipated degradation of the overall security environment in which they operate, where it becomes more physically dangerous or even vulnerable to attacks from adversarial groups; (4) engagement of contractor personnel in unauthorized or unlawful acts, inviting adverse reactions (or lawsuits) from the public, the media, or the government of the host country; (5) protracted delays or competition-related problems in acquiring the contracts, leading to inefficiencies or gaps in coverage; (6) transformation of contractors into targets for hostile intelligence services; and (7) unwillingness of contractors to do the work specified by the government for the amount of money it has budgeted or thinks the job is worth. Considered together, these drawbacks could embarrass a national government that has carefully and deliberately chosen to outsource some of its security functions, highlighting for the entire international community—as well as unsupportive internal factions—the jeopardy that may emerge from this transfer of protection to the private sector.

Reliance on private contractors in expeditionary operations also can make force and violence more readily available as an international policy tool. Private contractors appear to make the resort to force more attractive, and if government military personnel are scarce, even status quo organizations attempting to maintain order within a society might be more prone to resort to coercive solutions if private contractors are readily available. In particular, legitimate questions emerge about whether private contractors can ensure long-term peace and stability within a region, as opposed to a temporary cessation of hostilities as long as armed private peacekeepers are present.[45] Because of the availability of private contractors to all sides in a conflict, an arms-race-like escalation of coercive capabilities by all sides could result, making the predictable workings of stable conflict-preventing deterrence less likely. Military assistance would be in effect for sale on the international marketplace, causing an uncontrolled dissemination of war-fighting skills, lethal arms to be viewed as neutral commodities, and a loss of faith in the official government military establishment.[46] Private contractors may even attract unhappy insurgent groups or feisty rogue states to be used as tools to foment instability.[47] All of these worries revolve around a fear that somehow accountability, controllability, and restraint diminish when private contractors serve as instruments of foreign policy.

5. Future of American Government Use of Private Contractors

Speculating on the future of American use of private contractors in expeditionary operations necessitates considerable caution and even trepidation. Even with the years of private contractor experience in Iraq and Afghanistan, the strategic environment is sufficiently fluid that the decision calculus in this regard could easily change. However, it is neither just a random rolling of the dice nor tight "best-fit" logic that will ultimately determine whether American government officials will choose to utilize private contractors and whether this use of these contractors will have beneficial or detrimental consequences—the intentional choice to use private contractors will incorporate both dispassionate cost-benefit analysis of the value of this instrument and subjective prevailing political passions at the time. Without sustained systematic data on the conditions most conducive to private contractor usage or on the differing projected outcomes from different types of private contractor usage, making the crucial decision in a sound manner about whether, when, and how to use private contractors in expeditionary operations constitutes a real challenge.

Several sea changes could significantly alter current trends in American government use of private contractors in expeditionary operations. If in the future the United States decided to reduce its need to maintain a global military hegemonic presence, then the utility of private contractors would substantially decrease. Unlike during the Cold War, the United States no longer sees that it is in its national interests always to intervene to achieve stability in distant parts of the world, with an increasingly unclear basis for legitimate coercive action due to the uncertain payoff, the high risks of involvement, and murkiness about which side to assist. Many intervention opportunities necessitate a kind of long-term low-intensity involvement in which American government military personnel have never been particularly successful in foreign settings. There exists a pervasive indifference to these foreign predicaments among the American mass public, whose wealth and position cause them to want protection for themselves, despite their questionable loyalty to the state; at the same time, they are reluctant to sacrifice their lives for the protection of others in faraway lands, something that reinforces the move toward private contractors.[48] Furthermore, changes in the regulatory environment could affect the future course of private contractor use in American expeditionary operations: for example, final recommendations from the Commission on Wartime Contracting, commissioned by the 2008 National Defense Authorization Act, could redirect such activities. It is also extremely likely that in future American government use of private contractors in expeditionary operations, the mix of application types may change over time: it seems especially important to distinguish between defensive and offensive uses, between combat use and noncombat uses, and among uses in combat support, humanitarian assistance, and peacekeeping operations.

Despite these constraints on future projections, consensus exists that for the United States "the large-scale employment of contracted support on the battlefield is now all but irreversible."[49] Indeed, the prospects for private contractors participating in American expeditionary operations appear to be quite robust for the foreseeable future:

> Despite increasing scrutiny of the industry and an inevitable decline in demand for most PMO [private military organization] services in Iraq, the industry's long-term outlook remains generally positive. Three principal drivers of PMO market expansion are likely to remain features of the strategic landscape: a concerted effort to reduce military forces and spending, an increase in the number of deployments, and the DOD's use of increasingly

sophisticated weapons systems. Unless the USG [US government] adopts a radically different and more isolationist foreign policy and/or chooses to increase significantly the size of its active duty force, the conditions and drivers that make outsourcing necessary are likely to remain unchanged in the near to mid term. Consequently, the future of contractor-provided expeditionary support is secure in that contractors have locked in a niche that may be too costly, fiscally and politically, for the DOD to fill with existing military capabilities and forces.[50]

The United States seems likely to "continue to be dependent on contractor support to deployed operations," and the private security contractor industry seems likely to "remain healthy, albeit somewhat smaller and with a modified structure, and will become increasingly competitive."[51] The American government will be especially reliant on private contractors when "future wars involve messy insurgencies and attempts to boost host government legitimacy, rather than conventional battles between massed armies," and when the United States attempts "to extinguish support for insurgencies, build the security forces of host governments, expand the capacity to provide services to local populations, create jobs, train civil services, and construct (or reconstruct) infrastructure."[52]

While the impending American withdrawal from Iraq will reduce the need for private contractors there, other areas of American foreign military policy may call for increased private contractor participation. As private military companies continue to become more sophisticated, and an industry shakeout occurs, shedding firms exhibiting less integrity or less effectiveness, the remaining private contractors may possess more long-term legitimacy. As the United States fights—and helps others to fight—against disruptive state and non-state threats, American government military forces may be spread too thin or may not possess the versatility to deal with the full range of emerging challenges. Indeed, in the future, private contractors may actually help to shape the nature of American expeditionary operations. As strategic planning increasingly explicitly incorporates an integral role for private contractors, the changing capabilities and successes of these organizations may affect the kinds of missions the United States feels confident about undertaking.

More specifically, the role of private contractors in American expeditionary operations will likely follow a type of gradient—stronger involvement at the lower end of the scale, especially in the area of administration, logistics, security, technical support; and decreasing involvement as one climbs the slope toward physical hostilities. Noncombat uses in non-offensive situations generally appear to be best for private contractors in the future.

It is the probability of coming under fire that drives the slope—wherever avoidable, US government officials do not want private contractors involved in physical hostilities. These officials might employ contractors in a mission or campaign not because it is desirable but because regular government troops could be in great demand and pulled in different directions, or not in sufficient supply: when high-level decisions are made about how to allocate combat forces among a variety of current operations, a campaign may not get all the troops requested by commanders, and so they would need to augment their forces with private contractors if possible.

Although the long-term prognosis for the global survival and spread of private contractors may be bright, there will be more than a few bumps in the road. Ongoing handicaps still significantly constrain the credibility of this emerging industry. Some private contractors are poorly managed and therefore short-lived; some clients are unable to effectively investigate contractors' credentials; and some security firms do not possess the combination of skills and tools necessary to manage the risks and dangers they confront.[53] Given that private security firms will be competing for a limited number of contracts, the net result may be that their global survival may entail "a difficult balancing act"—particularly for smaller private contractors or those offering direct combat services—since "projects are invariably in war zones or other regions of conflict" where tangible long-term success may be elusive.[54] However, prevailing security forecasts suggest that the kinds of unstable predicaments calling for security privatization are likely to increase, while the ability and willingness of other parties—particularly states and international organizations—to manage the turmoil is likely to decrease.

6. Conclusion

Weighing evident dangers and opportunities, American government use of private contractors in expeditionary operations appears likely to continue to generate mixed security results. The cost effectiveness of government outsourcing tasks to private contractors has proven to be inconclusive when analyzed across the board and no systematically deduced logic or hard evidence appears sufficient to make definitive judgments in this regard. Despite a continuing claim by some analysts that "in an ideal world the state would provide for public safety,"[55] the reality is that public management works better under some conditions and that private management works better under others. Unfortunately, the specific conditions under which government use of private security contractors makes the most and least sense have not as yet been identified, so there needs to be far more definitive understanding than exists today about exactly when private contractors have a net positive or negative impact on international security.

In particular, the United States Government Accountability Office has recently highlighted that government agencies "face challenges in determining what functions and activities can be contracted out and what should be provided by government personnel,"[56] indicating a pressing need for rigorous conditional analysis of this issue. Filling this gap is a critical security priority that seems necessary prior to improving contractor management and oversight. In this regard, certain activities seem logically to be the domain of government employees: "inherently governmental functions include activities that require either the exercise of discretion in applying government authority, or the making of value judgments in making decisions for the government; as such, they are required to be performed by government employees, not private contractors."[57] Although most security challenges today require the exercise of discretion and value judgments, it seems that those predicaments most pivotally dependent on this subtle and subjective decision making—and most vulnerable to devastating backfire effects if things go sour—should rely the most on government employees.

A key question underlying the use of private contractors is whether they indeed thrive on instability. While broadly speaking "instability provides their market," once hired private contractors have the potential to help restore stability: ultimately the impact on instability may boil down to "the lesser of two evils—either running the risk of total state collapse and anarchy against a background of international indifference, or using private actors who have access to the means of coercion in order to halt additional suffering."[58] In this regard, the opportunity costs of turning to private contractors desperately need assessment, including comparing their utility to that of alternatives such as international or regional governmental peacekeeping operations as well as other forms of transnational private intervention.

In evaluating long-term security consequences, it seems useful to identify the worst-case and best-case scenarios for future American government use of private contractors in expeditionary operations. The worst-case scenario would appear to incorporate the following elements: the destruction of a sense of community obligation and the interference with state sovereignty; the magnification of perceived fear among the mass public; the creation of a "might-makes-right" social order; the hollowing out of the state; the proliferation of violence and crimes against humanity and a move away from long-term peace and stability; the corruption of coercive authority and the intensification of friction between public and private personnel; and the use of unsuitable, immoral, and disloyal agents to carry out foreign security policy. In contrast, the best-case scenario for private contractors participating in American expeditionary operations might include the following elements: private contractors would save money, be speedy and flexible, possess special expertise needed for security tasks assigned, make it possible for government military personnel to execute their sensitive tasks more effectively. In this ideal scenario, oversight and accountability would be tight:

> A government workforce with sufficient authority to do a job well and that will be held accountable for its areas of responsibility. Contracting officers will work closely with all military forces and other interagency representatives in their areas of responsibility. They will supervise contracts under a contingency contracting process capable of matching the needs of the force with contractors qualified and equipped to do the job.
>
> The contracting officer and the contractors themselves will be overseen by an integrated, qualified team of auditors and inspectors who provide real oversight and accountability, but who do not interfere with the ability of the contractors to do their jobs. All their work will be part of a system that provides visibility and transparency so that everyone who needs to understand the process and why will have access to the relevant information.[59]

Whether either of these two extreme scenarios actually materializes may depend on the nature of future discussions between private contractors and government officials, especially on whether common agreement can be reached about acceptable standards of behavior and the terms surrounding public reliance on the private sector for security.

In the end, evaluating future changes in and effects of the American use of private contractors in expeditionary operations requires that these changes and effects be placed in the context of future changes in other dimensions of American foreign security policy affecting these overseas military activities. The most salient related future changes appear to be (1) increasing leveraging of foreign military and security forces, with the role of the United States being more for training and provision of support such as weapons, intelligence, and logistics; (2) increasing emergence of threats to the United States that are more covert, transnational, and elusive and that require unconventional modes of interdiction; (3) increasing intractability in international insta-bility challenges, especially those surrounding failing states; (4) increasing American reliance on automated, computerized, and even artificially intel-ligent unmanned units to carry out support tasks during combat operations; (5) increasing inability in modern warfare to distinguish cleanly between civilian and combatant targets; (6) increasing indeterminacy in assessing the points when wars are over or whether wars have successful outcomes; and (7) increasing American reluctance to undertake or sustain foreign military missions that pose the risk of prolonged involvement or indeterminate out-comes.[60] Because the complex security implications of American government reliance on private contractors are deeply intertwined with several other ongoing trends within a fluid security setting, it appears important that any proposed changes in the use, management, or oversight of private contractors be dynamically adaptive and incorporate flexibility to deal with future global security changes.

Without consideration of more creative security thinking to address this growing phenomenon, there is a distinct possibility that efforts to reduce the spiraling anarchic violence within and across societies will actually be thwarted by the expanding use of private contractors in American govern-ment expeditionary operations. Regardless of overall appropriateness, due to misunderstandings, the global proliferation of private contractors is associ-ated with (1) those American government officials employing these contrac-tors thinking less carefully about how integral they are to the overall mission and how significant the security implications of that choice may be; and (2) those foreign societies where these contractors operate sensing ambivalence about the kind of credible commitment signaled by this private security choice. Ultimately, then, a concerted move to systematically reevaluate the conditions under which contractors are most and least likely to fulfill critical security responsibilities appears to be a crucial prerequisite to transforming the American government use of private contractors in expeditionary opera-tions into a truly effective and legitimate enterprise.

Notes

1. James Jay Carafano, *Contracting in Combat: Advice for the Commission on Wartime Contracting* (Washington, DC: Heritage Foundation Backgrounder #2228, Jan. 13, 2009), 1, www.heritage.org/research/NationalSecurity/upload/bg_2228.pdf.

2. Richard Fontaine and John Nagl, *Contractors in American Conflicts: Adapting to a New Reality* (Washington, DC: Center for a New American Security, Dec. 2009), 5, 7, 8, www.humansecuritygateway.com/documents/CNAS_ContractorsInAmerican Conflicts.pdf.

3. Some of this chapter's analysis was inspired by Robert Mandel, *Armies Without States: The Privatization of Security* (Boulder, CO: Lynne Rienner, 2002).

4. Carafano, *Contracting in Combat*, 1–2.

5. Industrial College of the Armed Forces, *Privatized Military Operations* (Fort McNair, Washington, DC: National Defense University, Spring 2007), 1.

6. Moshe Schwartz, *Training the Military to Manage Contractors during Expeditionary Operations: Overview and Options for Congress* (Washington, DC: Congressional Research Service Report for Congress, Dec. 17, 2008), 1.

7. David M. Walker, *DOD Needs to Reexamine Its Extensive Reliance on Contractors and Continue to Improve Management and Oversight* (Washington, DC: Government Accountability Office, Mar. 11, 2008), 24, www.gao.gov/new.items/d08572t.pdf.

8. Alvin Toffler and Heidi Toffler, *War and Anti-War* (New York: Warner Books, 1993), 104, 122; Martin Van Creveld, *The Transformation of War* (New York: Free Press, 1991), 197; Colonel Thomas X. Hammes, *The Sling and the Stone: On War in the 21st Century* (St. Paul, MN: Zenith Press, 2004), 208; and Robert Mandel, *Global Threat: Target-Centered Assessment and Management* (Westport, CT: Praeger Security International, 2008), 11–27.

9. Abdel-Fatau Musah and J. 'Kayode Fayemi (eds.), *Mercenaries: An African Security Dilemma* (London: Pluto Press, 2000), 1–2.

10. Carafano, *Contracting in Combat*, 1–2.

11. Frederick Forsyth, "Send in The Mercenaries," *Wall Street Journal*, May 15, 2000.

12. David Shearer, *Private Armies and Military Intervention* (London: Oxford University Press, International Institute for Strategic Studies Adelphi Paper 316, 1998), 69–72.

13. *Dollars Not Sense: Government Contracting under the Bush Administration* (Washington, DC: United States House of Representatives Committee on Government Reform, June 2006) http://oversight.house.gov/Documents/20060711103910-86046.pdf; Carafano, *Contracting in Combat*, 2; and Fontaine and Nagl, *Contractors in American Conflicts*, 5.

14. Carafano, *Contracting in Combat*, 2.

15. Valerie Bailey Grasso, *Defense Contracting in Iraq: Issues and Options for Congress* (Washington, DC: Congressional Research Service Report for Congress, Aug. 15, 2008), 1, 6.

16. Moshe Schwartz, *Department of Defense Contractors in Iraq and Afghanistan: Background and Analysis* (Washington, DC: Congressional Research Service Report for Congress, Dec. 14, 2009), 3.

17. David Isenberg, "The Good, and Bad, News on Contractors," *Asia Times Online*, April 28, 2009, www.cato.org/pub_display.php?pub_id=10154.

18. David M. Walker, *Defense Acquisitions: DOD's Increased Reliance on Service Contractors Exacerbates Long-Standing Challenges* (Washington, DC: Government Accountability Office, Testimony before the Subcommittee on Defense, Committee on Appropriations, House of Representatives, United States Congress, Jan. 23, 2008), i.

19. Deborah Avant, "The Market for Force: Exploring the Privatization of Military Services," paper presented at the Council on Foreign Relations, Study Group on Arms Trade and Transnationalization of Defense, New York, 1999.

20. Commission on Wartime Contracting in Iraq and Afghanistan, *At What Cost? Contingency Contracting in Iraq and Afghanistan*, Interim Report (Arlington, VA: June 2009), 1–2, www.wartimecontracting.gov/index.php/reports.

21. International Alert, "Use of Mercenaries as a Means of Violating Human Rights and Impeding the Exercise of the Right of Peoples to Self-Determination," unpublished submission to the United Nations Commission on Human Rights, London (Mar. 26, 1999).

22. Douglas Farah, "Cartel Hires Mercenaries to Train Security Forces," *Washington Post*, Nov. 4, 1997, A12.

23. See Robert Mandel, *Global Security Upheaval: Armed Non-State Groups Usurping State Stability Functions* (Stanford, CA: Stanford University Press, forthcoming 2013).

24. Commission on Wartime Contracting in Iraq and Afghanistan, *At What Cost?*, 3.

25. Industrial College of the Armed Forces, *Privatized Military Operations* (2007), 1.

26. Schwartz, *Department of Defense Contractors in Iraq and Afghanistan*, 1.

27. "Philippines: Private Armies, Public Enemies," *Economist* 328 (Aug. 14, 1993): 34.

28. Walker, *Defense Acquisitions*, i.

29. Schwartz, *Department of Defense Contractors in Iraq and Afghanistan*, 16; see also Fontaine and Nagl, *Contractors in American Conflicts*, 17.

30. Walker, *Defense Acquisitions*, i.

31. Walker, *DOD Needs to Reexamine Its Extensive Reliance on Contractors and Continue to Improve Management and Oversight*, 9.

32. Herbert M. Howe, "Global Order and the Privatization of Security," *Fletcher Forum of World Affairs* 22 (Summer/Fall 1998): 4.

33. Walker, *DOD Needs to Reexamine Its Extensive Reliance on Contractors and Continue to Improve Management and Oversight*, 3.

34. Industrial College of the Armed Forces, *Privatized Military Operations* (Washington, DC: National Defense University, Spring 2009), 16, http.ndu.edu/icaf/industry/reports/2009/pdf/icaf-is-report-private-mil-ops-2009.pdf.

35. Steven L. Schooner and Daniel S. Greenspahn, "Too Dependent on Contractors? Minimum Standards for Responsible Governance," *Journal of Contract Management* (Summer 2008): 10.

36. Howe, "Global Order and the Privatization of Security," 5.

37. *Summary of Proceedings*, Defense Intelligence Agency Conference on The Privatization of Security in Sub-Saharan Africa, Washington, DC (July 24, 1998), 1–2.

38. Al J. Venter, "Privatising War," unpublished paper (May 2000), 7.

39. Schwartz, *Department of Defense Contractors in Iraq and Afghanistan*, 2.

40. Fontaine and Nagl, *Contractors in American Conflicts*, 14.

41. Major Thomas J. Milton, "The New Mercenaries—Corporate Armies for Hire" (Springfield, VA: Foreign Area Officer Association, Dec. 1997), www.information clearinghouse.info/article3394.htm.

42. David Isenberg, "Have Lawyer, Accountant, and Guns, Will Fight: The New Post-Cold War Mercenaries," paper presented at the annual national convention of the International Studies Association, Washington, DC (Feb. 19, 1999), 9.

43. Peter Lock, "Military Downsizing and Growth in the Security Industry in Sub-Saharan Africa," http.idsa-india.org/an-dec8-10.html.

44. Ken Silverstein, "Privatizing War," *Nation* 265 (July 28/Aug. 4, 1997): 12.

45. Global Coalition for Africa, "A Consultation on 'The Privatization of Security in Africa,'" unpublished paper, Overseas Development Council, Washington, DC (Mar. 12, 1999).

46. Bruce D. Grant, "U.S. Military Expenditure for Sale: Private Military Consultants as a Tool of Foreign Policy," unpublished paper entered in the 1998 Chairman of the Joint Chiefs of Staff Strategy Essay Competition, Institute for National Strategic Studies, 1998.

47. *Summary of Proceedings*, 1–2.

48. Ibid.

49. Fontaine and Nagl, *Contractors in American Conflicts*, 11.

50. Industrial College of the Armed Forces, *Privatized Military Operations* (2007), 7.

51. Industrial College of the Armed Forces, *Privatized Military Operations* (2009), 11.

52. Fontaine and Nagl, *Contractors in American Conflicts*, 11.

53. James R. Davis, *Fortune's Warriors, Private Armies, and the New World Order* (Vancouver, BC: Douglas & McIntire, 2000), chap. 8.

54. Ibid.

55. Sebastian Mallaby, "Mercenaries Are No Altruists, But They Can Do Good," *Washington Post*, June 4, 2001, A19.

56. Walker, *DOD Needs to Reexamine Its Extensive Reliance on Contractors and Continue to Improve Management and Oversight*, 7.

57. Walker, *Defense Acquisitions*, 3.

58. Jakkie Cilliers and Christian Dietrich, "Editorial Comment: Privatising Peace Enforcement," *African Security Review* 5 (1996).

59. Carafano, *Contracting in Combat*, 6.

60. For elaboration of these tendencies, see Robert Mandel, *Security, Strategy, and the Quest for Bloodless War* (Boulder, CO: Lynne Rienner, 2004); and Robert Mandel, *The Meaning of Military Victory* (Boulder, CO: Lynne Rienner, 2006).

2 Attitudes on the Ground

What Soldiers Think about Civilian Contractors[1]

Ryan Kelty and Darcy Schnack

1. The Civilian–Military Distinction

Military actions, and the individuals who carry out those actions, are often
viewed as separate and distinct from the everyday, mundane civilian society.
The culture that surrounds the military is in many ways uniquely different
from that of its host (civilian) society. Military culture places a high priority
on public service to the extent that normative pressures are placed on both
service members and their spouses (generally wives) to engage in community
activities.[2] The military is intentionally and overtly formal and hierarchical,
and uses uniforms, insignia, decorations, and prescribed language to express
these highly valued aspects of its culture publicly. The military also has a legal
and judicial system separate from that of civilian society: the Uniform Code
of Military Justice (UCMJ). The norms, rituals, rules, and expectations of
life in the military are intentional social constructs that allow those in the
military to plan for and execute actions that are directly antagonistic in many
ways to those adhered to in its ambient society.[3]

The balance between convergence and differentiation between the military and its host society has been debated in the literature since the 1960s.
Janowitz argued that the military should be tightly integrated into the fabric
of its host society. For him, service members should not be separated from
broader society.[4] Conversely, Huntington claimed that the progressively
liberal society was weakening the traditional values and principles of the

military that are necessary for its proper functioning. He argued for clearer and more complete separation of military personnel from civilian society in an attempt to shield its members from the growing dysfunctions of society.[5]

2. What It Means To Be Military

In the broadest sense, the military is the institutionalization of the state's monopoly on violence.[6] Militariness may be measured by the probability of being injured or killed for the common good (i.e., one's country, or even abstract principles such as liberty or sovereignty).[7] If this is taken as the appropriate measure, then our current military is much less military than in prior eras. Technology is a primary reason for the reduced chances among service members of being killed or injured for the common good. Technology has affected this outcome in three ways. First, technology has improved the survivability of American service members through inventions such as Kevlar body armor, improved intelligence capabilities that can detect and monitor dangerous people and weapons, and advances in medical technology to treat injuries sustained by military personnel. Second, the US military's technological sophistication has made deterrence a viable option in most instances, preventing service members from having to engage in conflicts that might otherwise erupt. Third, when conflict is inevitable, the technological sophistication that the US military is able to bring to bear is unparalleled. When combined with decisive battle tactics, this reduces the likelihood of injury and death for US personnel by limiting the duration of conventional threats that are the most taxing in terms of the quantity of injuries and deaths among service members.[8]

On the opposite side of the issue, the types of duties performed by civilians in support of military operations and the changed nature of warfare are argued to have effectively eliminated the distinction between front lines and rear positions.[9] In this respect, civilians appear to be gaining in militariness. Civilians are being integrated with the US military in forward-deployed locations and it is not uncommon for contractors presently in Iraq to have firearms for self-defense. Moreover, and more significant, is that the asymmetric threats presented by the insurgents in Iraq and terror networks worldwide do not discriminate between uniformed military personnel and civilians. In his open videotapes Osama bin Laden stated unequivocally that he and his followers do not differentiate between military and civilian, they are all equally viable targets.[10] The general American public at home, and especially the civilians deployed overseas in support of the military missions, are at risk. This has been made patently clear by the attacks of September 11, 2001; the public desecration of four deceased Blackwater civilian contract employees in Fallujah, Iraq, in March of 2004; and the kidnapping and public beheading (via internet broadcast) of civilian contractors working in Iraq.

Alternately, if militariness is defined by the degree of sacrifice demanded by the institution of the service member, then there is a distinct difference between service members and civilians.[11] Service members and civilians operate under separate legal and judicial systems. Failing to comply with directives from supervisors has very different consequences for the two groups. Whereas the military more or less owns the service member and can coerce physical tasks, extra duty, and even press criminal charges for failing to follow orders, supervisors and employers have much less latitude in dealing with civilian employees who fail to execute directives satisfactorily.

What is military, or militariness, is also influenced by similarities and differences between military personnel and civilians. Increased bureaucratization and rationalization within the military (and society) in the modern era has pushed workers toward specialization. Similarly, technological advances foster specialization among military and civilian personnel, and in this specialization the jobs of service members begin to mirror more closely jobs performed by civilians.[12] Thus, it is not clear where the line is drawn between jobs that constitute inherently military work and those that are nonmilitary, but support the military—or whether this distinction itself is arbitrary and outdated.

Building on Biderman's work, Boëne argued for understanding the military as two different components, the teeth (or combat component) and the tail (or the supply and support component). The actions of those operating in the teeth of the military—i.e., the taking of life and destroying things by military personnel in the name of freedom, democracy, sovereignty—are not rational.[13] To counter this irrationality, there must be structural and normative boundaries surrounding military personnel and the actions they are called on to perform. Even those in the tail (i.e., supply and support), who are not expected to kill people and destroy things in the course of their daily duties, must be prepared to do so. Indeed, should the need arise, service members of all specialties are not only expected to perform such acts, they are duty bound to do so.

Not only are these inherently military acts (i.e., killing people and destroying property in defense of freedom, democracy, sovereignty), they are *uniquely* military acts. This behavior is explicitly prohibited for civilian contractors and Department of Defense civilian employees. In fact, if they were to perform such acts they would forfeit their noncombatant status and any benefits and protections that status might convey.

3. Civilianization of the Military

The civilianization of the military is at the heart of the institutional–occupational model of military organization proposed by Moskos in 1977 and continues to influence conceptualization and research on military organization. The institutional military is one in which soldiers serve in response to a call to duty and honor. Traditional values and norms are paramount in manning the armed forces in an institutional military, shaping the service members into a distinct and cohesive group.[14] By fostering internalization of these values in their constituent members, the military is able to elicit performance and dedication above what might otherwise be expected.[15]

In contrast to the institutional military, individuals in an occupational military are driven by self-interest and the free market.[16] They are externally motivated, especially by monetary compensation. These occupational qualities run counter to the institutional model's emphasis on the collective group's benefit as expressed via values, norms, and internal motivation.

The institutional–occupational model asserts that "the overarching trend within the contemporary military is the erosion of the institutional format and the ascendancy of the occupational model."[17] To be competitive in a market-driven all-volunteer force, the military transformed its policies and manpower models. Changes included adjustments in pay scales, the use of monetary and educational enlistment incentives, marketing campaigns highlighting the specialized training provided by the military, the development of more family-friendly policies, and the increased recruitment and participation of women. All of these changes were a nod to the fact that the military must now compete against the civilian economy for manpower and a recognition that to recruit and retain the best soldiers the organization needs to pay more attention to remaining competitive on highly salient job-related characteristics.

The increasing technological sophistication required of many military specialties has resulted in a greater reliance on private-sector support in order to maintain a cutting edge military.[18] Light noted that outsourcing is motivated by a desire to increase flexibility by targeting qualified labor for specific project goals without carrying long-term costs for training and maintaining personnel (and their families).[19] Economic constraints and personnel caps have also motivated force reductions and base closures. Thus, aside from soldiers, sailors, airmen, and marines perhaps becoming more "occupationally" oriented themselves, there has been a conscious effort to infuse into the military a pure form of occupationally oriented personnel via civilian contractors.[20] Indeed, today America's military cannot function effectively without these contractors.

4. Federal Outsourcing: OMB Circular A-76

The federal mandate driving the movement of jobs performed by federal employees to the private sector is the Office of Management and Budget circular A-76 (OMB A-76), first issued in 1966. This mandate was born from the belief that government should not compete with its citizens. Rather, it should foster a free enterprise economy through contracting business to private industry based on identified needs.[21] Numerous revisions of OMB A-76 over the years have kept outsourcing in the eye of Congress and the federal agencies responsible for its implementation.

OMB A-76 tasks the government with identifying any and all possible government-operated commercial activities, performing a cost-benefit analysis of all permissible jobs, and shifting the work to private industry whenever the work can be done as well or better at less cost.[22] The goals of outsourcing mandated through OMB A-76 include increased effectiveness and efficiency of an organization's operations, greater organizational flexibility, and increased cost savings.[23]

A weakness of OMB A-76 is that it focuses on economic outcomes generally to the exclusion of social outcomes. Social outcomes may indirectly affect the dependent variables of interest, and should be of concern to stakeholders. Akerlof and Kranton examined the effects of pecuniary versus social identity motivators in military and civilian settings. They found that increasing employees' identification with the organization (and thereby internalizing its goals and practices) has positive effects on employees' production, net of pecuniary incentives.[24] This work is in the relatively new, but rapidly expanding tradition on transaction cost economics. This field of economics focuses on the costs of "making exchange or the indirect production expenses" through motivation (i.e., motivating specialized interest agents to align their interests) and coordination (e.g., obtaining and coordinating production input, measurement costs) of expenses.[25] In short, transaction cost economics focuses on the social-psychological factors affecting production costs. Akerlof received the 2001 Nobel Prize in economics for his work in this area. It would seem prudent for the military's organizational outcomes related to OMB A-76 to include social-psychological as well as economic outcomes.

5. The OMB A-76 Process in the Military

The OMB A-76 directive has met with varying levels of support and execution by presidential administrations over the years. The Reagan administration used OMB A-76 extensively, whereas the Clinton administration invoked it only sparingly.[26] The George W. Bush administration pushed for increased privatization of government jobs via OMB A-76. This push is especially evident in the DoD. President Obama has initiated a review of OMB competitive sourcing process with emphasis on the Department of Defense.

Examples of defense-related commercial activities targeted by OMB A-76 competitions include, but are not limited to: engineering, installation, operation, maintenance, and testing for communications systems, missile ranges, satellite tracking and data acquisition; radar detection and tracking; and operation of motor pools, vehicle and aeronautical operation and maintenance, and air/sea/land transportation of people and supplies.[27] Civilian contractors are employed in stateside locations, overseas maintenance depots, on deployed naval ships, and in forward-deployed positions during peacekeeping and combat operations.

There is a clear sense that military leaders are looking to utilize contractors so that uniformed personnel can increase their time and energy focusing on the core mission of the military: fighting and winning America's wars. Lt. Col. Bill McNight, Chief of the 9th Reconnaissance Wing Manpower and Organization Office, voices this goal of the US military: "We want to apply our resources most directly to war fighting because that's what we do."[28]

6. Effects of Civilian Contractor Integration on Service Members

Despite the ubiquity and growing proportion of civilian contractors engaged in the US wars in Afghanistan and Iraq, there has been little empirical examination of the effects this manpower strategy has had on service members who work alongside contractors. Kelty and Segal found that social comparisons with civilian contractors and civilian mariners had significant negative effects on soldier and sailor retention attitudes, respectively. These negative effects were not direct, but rather operated indirectly through their impact on job satisfaction and organizational commitment.[29]

Kelty and Smith examined racial, gender and marital status differences in soldiers' attitudes toward contractors, as well as social comparisons with contractors. They found more agreement than divergence in attitudes across these social categories. Among differences, Hispanic soldiers viewed contractors more negatively than did non-Hispanic soldiers, and white soldiers were significantly more likely than black soldiers to view contractors as relatively advantaged over soldiers. Neither attitudes toward contractors nor level of contact with contractors significantly impacted retention, but social comparisons were observed to negatively impact intent to remain in service indirectly through satisfaction and commitment.[30] These data have small sample sizes of women, Hispanics, and African Americans, so results should be viewed cautiously.

A cross-national comparative study of attitudes toward military employment found that a minority of officers agreed that civilianization and outsourcing in the military enhances operational effectiveness.[31] Only 16 percent of British officers agreed that civilian outsourcing benefited the military, with slightly higher numbers of Canadian (20 percent) and German (24 percent) officers voicing support. South African officers had a more positive view of civilian integration (43 percent stating it enhanced military effectiveness), though the author notes that civilianization and outsourcing in the military is in its infancy in this country. This study of mid-level officers included a single variable related to civilian contracting. This important work should motivate additional studies to examine a more robust suite of variables related to outsourcing and their effects on readiness and retention.

A final study conducted by Kelty using data from National Guard soldiers recently returned to the eastern seaboard from a 15-month deployment at a military detention facility demonstrated that negative social comparisons with contractors have direct negative impacts on perceived unit cohesion and general attitudes toward contractors. Soldiers' general attitudes toward contractors did not significantly impact perceived unit cohesion, though the total indirect effect of general attitudes toward contractors on retention was significant. Views of contractors that are more positive increase intention to remain in service.[32] As in previous studies, the effect of social comparisons on retention attitudes was significant, but only indirectly through perceived unit cohesion, job satisfaction, and organizational commitment.

These four studies are consistent in demonstrating that the integration of civilian contractors is having negative impacts on retention attitudes. Civilian integration in the military has been shown to produce feelings of relative deprivation among service members (via negative social comparisons), as well as negatively impacting job satisfaction, commitment to military service, and perceived unit cohesion and operational efficiency. This chapter provides information on general attitudes toward civilian contractors across several dimensions in an effort to better understand soldiers' general experiences with and thoughts about contractors. One important contribution of the data presented here is that it combines two different data sets that allow for a more robust assessment of attitudes toward civilian contractors by race, ethnicity, and gender, which to this point has been a challenge.

7. Methodological Notes

The data presented in this chapter were collected from two Army combat arms units; one infantry (n = 348) and one combat aviation unit (n = 191).[33] The infantry battalion sampled in this study was located in the southeastern United States. At the time it was surveyed (in the summer of 2006) the battalion had recently returned from a 12-month deployment in Iraq. During their deployment these infantry soldiers worked with contractors whose specializations ranged from mechanics who repaired their armored vehicles, to computer technicians, to private security who secured the forward operating base on which these soldiers were stationed.

The Army combat aviation squadron was stationed outside of the continental United States and was surveyed in the winter of 2005, but it was not in a combat theater. The civilian contractors who worked with this squadron performed duties that were previously done by uniformed Army personnel.

The integration of civilian contractors with this squadron was well established, having been initiated well before any of the current military or civilian personnel arrived on post. The contracting organizations working with the squadron do change over time, however. Surveys included the following definition to focus and contextualize respondents' responses to contractor related questions:

> For this survey "civilian contractors" are defined at those civilians who are either organically attached to military units (e.g., mechanics, IT specialists) or those who operate as private security forces (e.g., Blackwater security personnel) in support of the U.S. military. For this survey the term "civilian contractors" does not refer to the more general unskilled support personnel who cook, clean, and maintain physical grounds who are not working directly with military units.

Social comparisons and attitudes toward contractors were operationalized using a multiple-item scale. The social comparisons scale includes 16 items[34] that were modeled on Crosby's *Working Women and Relative Deprivation* and Segal's analysis of the military and the family as greedy institutions.[35] The literature on job satisfaction was used to inform additional job-related characteristics that are identified as most salient by workers and likely to be used by respondents as points of comparisons with civilian contractors. Respondents rated their attitude on a five-point Likert-type scale ranging from "Much Greater for Myself" to "Much Greater for Civilian Contractors," with a neutral midpoint. Several items were reverse coded for analysis so that higher values equate to more positive social comparisons for soldiers.

Soldiers' attitudes toward contractors[36] was measured using 15 items that refer to both salient characteristics of civilian coworkers brought into the "total force" (e.g., level of commitment, expertise, work ethic), and many that refer specifically to the espoused benefits offered by proponents of federal outsourcing (e.g., organizational flexibility, cost savings, improving morale, freeing soldiers up to perform core military duties).[37] Response categories range from "disagree strongly" to "agree strongly" using a six-point Likert-type scale. Scale reliability for this measure is strong, indicating the various items are tightly clustered around a common underlying construct.[38]

Single-item measures were used to assess several additional experiences with and attitudes toward civilian contractors. Soldiers were asked how much contact they had with contractors during their current assignment. Responses

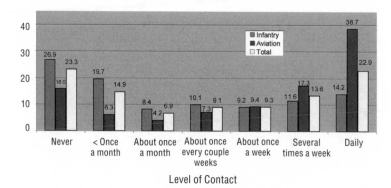

FIGURE 1. Soldiers' Level of Contact with Civilian Contractors (n=537)

to this item ranged from never to daily using a seven-point scale. Service personnel were also asked to rate the attractiveness of working as a civilian contractor after leaving the service using a five-point Likert-type scale ranging from "very unattractive" to "very attractive." Attitudes about whether soldiers view contractors as part of the total force were measured using a Likert-type scale ranging from "strongly disagree" to "strongly agree."

8. Soldiers' Exposure to Contractors and the Allure of Working as a Contractor

Initial analyses focused on descriptive data examining soldiers' level of contact with contractors (Figure 1). A quarter of the soldiers in the infantry unit reported never working with a contractor during deployment, with another 2 percent saying they did so less than once a week. This contrasts sharply with the soldiers in the aviation unit where nearly 40 percent indicate working with contractors on a daily basis. This discrepancy is attributed to the highly localized work space in the combat aviation unit—the hangar—where most soldiers worked and where the contractors worked side-by-side with many of them, in comparison to the more variable work conditions experienced by the infantry unit. The structure and duties of the infantry unit did not create the same interaction opportunities with contractors.

A plurality of soldiers (43.6 percent) report that they do not have any friends who have left the Army to become a civilian contractor, though 20 percent report five or more friends have separated to become contractors (Figure 2). Taken together, approximately two-thirds of the soldiers surveyed

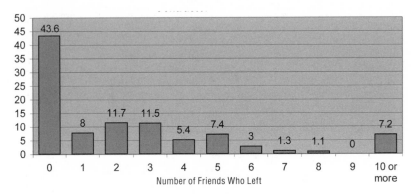

FIGURE 2. Number of Friends Who Have Left to Become Contractors (n=536)

indicate that they have at least one friend who has left the Army to work as a civilian contractor. Of those who know friends who have left to become a contractor, most knew two or three friends who have done so.

Two measures related to access to employment as a civilian contractor were analyzed; whether a soldier had ever been solicited by a contracting firm and whether he/she knew where to go to apply for a job at a contracting firm. Results indicate that 18.5 percent of the soldiers surveyed have been actively solicited to work as civilian contractors. Conversely, a small majority of soldiers (52.2 percent) reported that they knew where to go to apply for a job as a civilian contractor.

Soldiers' attitudes toward working as civilian contractors once they separate from the Army are presented in Figure 3. Soldiers are overwhelmingly positive in their attitude about potentially working as a civilian contractor; 70.1 percent say it is either an attractive or very attractive option. Later in this chapter we will examine soldiers' comparisons with civilian contractors, which will provide insight into why such a high proportion of soldiers report positive attitudes toward working as a contractor.

The proportion of soldiers (18.5 percent) who reported being solicited by contracting companies contrasts sharply with the 70 percent of soldiers who report that they find employment as a contractor to be an attractive or very attractive option. These data indicate that there appears to be more interest among soldiers to work as a contractor post-service than there is recruitment interest by those who represent the various contracting firms. We recognize that this gap may vary across different samples of military

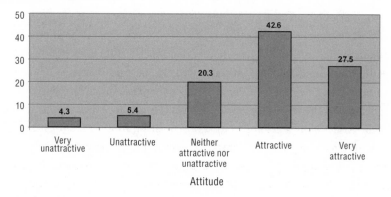

FIGURE 3. Soldiers' Attitudes toward Becoming a Contractor (n=538)

personnel depending on factors such as expertise with technology, proportions of women and racial minorities, command climate of unit, experiences with the military, and family constraints.

9. Soldiers' Attitudes toward Contractors

Soldiers' general attitudes toward contractors are summarized in Table 1. Focusing on both the means and distributions, accounting for negatively worded questions, we observe that 12 of the 16 items indicate positive views toward contractors. Soldiers indicate that they enjoy working with contractors; that contractors make the Army more efficient, effective, and flexible; that contractors are not believed to negatively impact morale or cause increases in service separation among soldiers; and that use of contractors frees soldiers up to perform core duties. Additionally, they report that contractors are not less committed than soldiers to doing a good job; they are equally motivated as soldiers to do a good job; contractors perform at comparable levels of expertise as soldiers; and that they are impressed by the abilities of the contractors with whom they work. The only negative attitudes soldiers expressed toward contractors are that they disagree that contractors are more cost effective than soldiers, and that they disagree that contractors work as many hours and as hard as soldiers. Soldiers' attitudes are essentially neutral regarding the statement, "The Army should not use its personnel to perform duties that the civilian work force can do just as well."

Another question asked of soldiers focused on how soldiers view contractors in the overall schema of military effort. Soldiers were asked whether they thought civilian contractors are members of the US military's "total force."[39] The distribution of soldiers' attitudes on this question is skewed to the left, with nearly two thirds (63.4 percent) reporting that they consider contractors as part of the total force at some level (Figure 4). Thus, it appears that a majority views both groups as working toward military mission success in an integrated, dependent relationship. Even so, soldiers report important differences between groups. These are symptomatic of the distinct nature and conditions of work performed by each group; an understanding of differences due to symbolic and tangible realities associated with things such as the military oath, the military uniform, and wearing a flag on one's uniform; and the legal differences that guide the actions of each group.

Additional analysis revealed that aviation unit soldiers are significantly more likely than infantry unit soldiers to view contractors as part of the total force.[40] Examinations of the effect of sex and race on attitudes toward contractors as part of the total force failed to produce significant results, indicating that neither race nor sex impacts soldiers' view of contractors as part of the total force. Years of service with cut points at both five and ten years also fail to significantly affect soldiers' views toward contractors as part of the total force.

10. Social Comparisons with Contractors

Examination of soldiers' social comparisons with contractors reveals broad perceptions of relative deprivation for soldiers in relation to their civilian contractor coworkers. Nine items are reported to be squarely in favor of contractors. Compared to soldiers, contractors are perceived to be paid more, to assume less risk of personal injury, to enjoy greater autonomy in their jobs, to be less controlled by their employer, to have fewer negative impacts on family happiness, to enjoy better relations with coworkers, to have greater freedom to negotiate their terms of employment, to be better cared for by their employer, to spend less time away from their families, and to work fewer hours per day. Contractors are viewed as on par with soldiers for task variety in their job, quality of leadership in their organization, gaining a feeling of accomplishment from their work, and having leadership support to facilitate completing work. There were no items on which soldiers reported having a resounding

TABLE 1. Soldiers' General Attitudes toward Civilian Contractors

N	Item	Mean	St.d. Dev.	(1) Strongly Disagree	(2) Disagree	(3) Disagree Somewhat	(4) Agree Somewhat	(5) Agree	(6) Strongly Disagree
						Percent			
538	As a soldier in the U.S. Army, I am uncomfortable working with civilian contractors*	2.97	1.59	19.7	30.3	13.4	13.6	15.8	7.2
538	Civilian contractors allow the Army to operate more effectively	4.47	1.17	2.6	4.6	8.4	29.4	37.2	17.8
537	Civilian contractors are important because they free-up soldiers to train for and perform real war-fighting duties	4.41	1.26	3.0	7.3	8.2	27.6	35.4	18.6
537	Civilian contractors increase the efficiency of the Army	4.40	1.15	1.9	5.4	11.2	30.0	35.8	15.8
537	I would prefer not to work with civilian contractors*	2.39	1.41	31.7	33.5	13.6	10.8	6.0	4.5
536	Civilian contractors decrease morale of Army personnel*	2.37	1.29	28.4	36.6	15.5	11.9	4.9	2.8
538	By having soldiers work alongside civilian contractors performing comparable duties, it encourages soldiers to leave the service*	3.89	1.53	8.4	13.8	12.5	29.9	16.9	18.6
530	Civilian contractors are less expensive to employ than soldiers	2.36	1.31	33.0	28.1	18.5	13.2	4.9	2.3
535	The Army should not use its personnel to perform duties that the civilian work force can do just as well as soldiers	3.44	1.51	11.0	19.3	21.9	21.3	15.1	11.4
535	The use of civilian contractors increases the flexibility of the Army in striving to achieve its core missions	4.36	1.14	2.2	6.0	7.7	35.9	33.6	14.6
537	Civilian contractors work just as long as soldiers	2.77	1.50	26.1	23.1	18.6	17.1	10.2	4.8
536	Civilian contractors work just as hard as soldiers	3.21	1.57	20.0	16.4	18.1	21.1	17.2	7.3
536	Civilian contractors are less committed to the work they perform than soldiers*	2.96	1.33	13.2	27.2	28.2	17.0	10.1	4.3
490	Civilian contractors perform at least to the same level of expertise that I do	4.05	1.40	5.9	10.4	13.3	28.4	27.1	14.9
490	Civilian contractors are less motivated than I am to do a good job*	2.97	1.29	12.7	27.3	26.5	22.0	7.1	4.3
488	I am impressed by the abilities of civilian contractors	4.23	1.30	4.1	7.2	12.7	29.5	30.3	16.2

*Negatively worded item; disagreement indicates positive attitude toward contractors. Scale ranges from 1 (Strongly Disagree) to 6 (Strongly Agree).

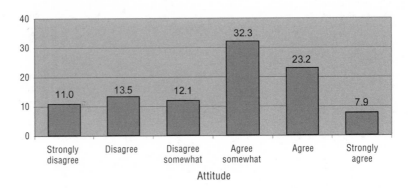

FIGURE 4. "I consider civilian contractors to be members of the US military's total force" (n=535)

advantage over contractors, though benefits and feeling one's work makes a contribution to society slightly favor soldiers over contractors.

11. Who Thinks What about Contractors?

A series of analyses were conducted to test whether soldiers' attitudes toward and experiences with contractors were dependent on various social structural characteristics. Analysis of soldiers' attitude toward contractors (using scale mean) by number of years served and military unit (infantry versus combat aviation) produced significant findings.[41] The attractiveness of employment as a civilian contractor depends on years of service among soldiers in the combat aviation unit, but not among soldiers in the infantry unit.[42] Among the combat aviation soldiers surveyed, those with more than four years of service were significantly more likely than those with fewer than four years of service to state that working as a contractor was either an unattractive or very unattractive option. Part of this difference could be due to self-selection among those who chose to re-enlist, whereas those who may have found contracting more favorable may have separated from service to pursue this option after their first term of enlistment.

Additionally, soldiers' attitudes toward working as a civilian contractor are observed to be dependent on race.[43] African American soldiers reported significantly more positive attitudes toward working as contractors than did white soldiers. This finding is consistent with prior research suggesting that African Americans who serve have a stronger orientation than other groups

TABLE 2. Soldiers' Social Comparisons with Civilian Contractors

N	Item	Mean	Std. Dev.	Much Greater for Myself	Greater for Myself	About Equal for Both	Greater for Contractors	Much Greater for Contractors
						Percent		
530	Pay	4.51	0.77	1.1	2.1	4.3	29.2	63.2
529	Benefits	2.98	1.11	7.8	27.0	36.7	16.6	11.9
533	Level of risk of personal injury*	2.12	1.07	37.1	25.9	28.5	5.1	3.4
534	Freedom to make decisions about how a job is done	3.88	0.99	3.4	4.7	21.9	41.0	29.0
532	Task variety within one's job	3.08	1.12	9.4	19.0	37.4	22.9	11.3
532	Promotion opportunities based on merit	3.05	1.13	7.5	25.9	33.8	19.9	12.8
533	Quality of leadership in the organization	3.11	1.07	7.3	18.9	40.0	22.5	11.3
531	Organizational control over employee behavior*	2.60	1.25	24.1	26.0	24.7	16.8	8.5
531	Negative impacts on family members' happiness*	2.14	1.10	35.8	28.2	26.2	5.5	4.3
533	Satisfying relations with co-workers	3.20	0.88	3.8	10.3	57.4	19.5	9.0
532	Freedom to negotiate employment contract	4.28	0.83	0.9	2.1	12.8	36.8	47.4
532	Degree to which the organization cares for employees	3.48	1.04	3.2	11.8	38.5	26.7	19.7
533	Requires one to spend time away from their family*	2.03	1.09	42.8	22.3	28.0	3.0	3.9
534	Gaining a feeling of accomplishment from one's work	3.04	0.96	7.1	13.1	57.3	13.3	9.2
533	Feeling that one's work makes a contribution to society	2.85	0.93	10.1	15.0	61.4	6.8	6.8
534	Time spent working per day*	2.08	1.18	40.3	30.9	16.1	6.2	6.6

*Negative item; responding "much greater for myself" indicates perceptions of relative deprivation. Scale ranges from 1 (much greater for myself) to 5 (much greater for contractors).

toward building human capital through military service for the purpose of transferring those skills and knowledge into successful civilian careers.[44] Given the dramatic increase in the use of contractors by the military, the strong attraction to transitioning to work as a contractor among African Americans appears to be a logical continuation of prior trends. A higher propensity toward working as a contractor among African American soldiers may also have implications for racial representation in the higher ranks, though this remains an empirical question beyond the scope of our data.

Additionally, desire to work as a civilian contractor was also evaluated with respect to military unit membership (infantry vs. combat aviation), sex, marital status (married vs. not married), and presence of children as dependents. No significant relationships were identified.

Analyses examining soldiers' level of contact with contractors by military unit, sex, and race indicate that significant dependent relationships exist only by military unit and race. Combat aviation unit soldiers were observed to work with contractors with much greater frequency than infantry unit soldiers.[45] White soldiers reported working with civilian contractors with significantly higher frequency than did African American soldiers.[46] No meaningful difference exists between male and female soldiers' level of contact with contractors in these units.

Analyses to determine if being solicited to work as a civilian contractor depends on soldiers' unit membership (infantry or aviation), sex, and race failed to produce significant results. It would appear that solicitation to work as a contractor is an equal opportunity prospect in relation to these three variables.

Examination of whether having knowledge of where to go to apply for a civilian contracting position is dependent upon soldiers' military unit, sex, and race revealed significant relationships for each set of variables tested. Infantry unit soldiers and African American soldiers are much more likely than aviation unit soldiers and white soldiers to know where to go to apply for civilian contracting work.[47] The test of whether knowledge of where to go to seek employment as a contractor is dependent on one's sex (male or female) approached significance,[48] suggesting women are more likely than men to understand where to go to seek work as a civilian contractor.

12. Predictive Models

The final analyses presented in this chapter include two multiple regression models to determine significant predictors of soldiers' interest in working as a civilian contractor and attitudes toward civilian contractors.

Table 3 presents the variables used in a predictive model to understand which factors are important in motivating soldiers' interest in working as a civilian contractor. The model presented explains a significant amount of variance in soldiers' attitudes toward working as a contractor.[49] Three variables surface as significant predictors of whether or not soldiers desire to work as a contractor. First, soldiers who have at least one friend who has separated from the service to work as a contractor report significantly higher levels of attraction to working as a contractor than do soldiers who do not have any friends who have separated from service to work as contractors.[50] Second, African American soldiers are significantly more likely than white soldiers to want to work as a contractor.[51] The third, and strongest predictor of soldiers' intent to work as a contractor is their general attitude toward contractors, measured by the attitudes toward contractors scale. Results indicate that the more favorable soldiers are toward contractors the more likely they are to want to join their ranks when they leave the Army.[52] The remaining variables did not have enough power to demonstrate significant predictive ability in determining soldiers' interest in working as civilian contractors.

Examination of predictors of soldiers' general attitudes toward contractors revealed four significant variables (Table 4).[53] The more that service personnel feel they are better off compared to contractors, the more favorable are their attitudes toward contractors.[54] The longer a soldier has served, the more negative is her/his view of contractors.[55] Higher levels of contact with civilian contractors correspond with soldiers having more positive opinions of these contractors.[56] Finally, Hispanic soldiers are significantly more negative in their view of contractors than are non-Hispanic soldiers.[57] All other variables tested failed to demonstrate significant predictive power in this model.

Taken together, the results of both predictive models fail to show an effect of sex (men vs. women) on attitude toward contractors. Though race does affect which soldiers are more inclined to view working as a contractor in more positive terms, race is not observed to be a significant factor in motivating general attitudes toward contractors. The reverse is true for the effects of ethnicity: Non-Hispanics have more positive attitudes toward contractors than do Hispanics, though ethnicity is not found to play a

TABLE 3. Predictors of Soldiers' Interest in Working as Civilian Contractors

	Significant Predictor Variables	Non-Significant Predictor Variables
1.	Have friends who left military service and now work as contractors	Level of contact with contractors
2.	Race	Age
3.	Attitudes toward contractors*	Sex
4.		Number of children
5.		Ethnicity
6.		Number of household moves in career
7.		Number of family separations in last 12 months
8.		Years served[†]
9.		Years remaining in service obligation[†]
10.		Marital status (married vs. not married)
11.		Education
12.		Intention to remain in Army for a career
13.		View contractors as part of total force

*scale mean; [†]measured in months

significant role in whether a soldier is likely to view working as a contractor as a favorable post-service employment option. Other important "non-findings" include no measurable impact of time remaining in service, education, or family status on either predictive model. It does not appear that the closer one gets to completing his or her military service obligation produces different attitudes toward contractors and contracting as an employment option. Presence of spouse and children does not appear to be a motivating factor to desire employment as a contractor, nor influence soldiers' attitude toward contractors in general.

13. Making Sense of It All

There are several take-aways that emerge from the data presented in this chapter. The first is that general attitudes toward contractors suggest that many of the motivations offered for moving increasingly to outsourcing are perceived to be working as anticipated (efficiency, effectiveness, flexibility, releasing soldiers for core military duties). There is also a clear perception that the use of contractors is not meeting the mission on anticipated cost savings and soldiers struggle with issues of relative deprivation in comparing

TABLE 4. Predictors of Soldiers' General Attitudes toward Civilian Contractors

	Significant Predictor Variables	Non-Significant Predictor Variables
1.	Social comparisons with contractors*	Race
2.	Years of military service†	Sex
3.	Level of contact with contractors	Number of children
4.	Ethnicity	Marital status
5.		Education
6.		Years remaining in military service obligation†
7.		Intent to serve a career in military at enlistment
8.		Length of family separation in last 12 months
9.		Have friends who left military service and now work as contractors

*scale mean; †measured in months

benefits and risks between service members and contractors. In particular, differences in pay, autonomy, risk of personal injury, time spent working, and negative impacts on family surface as important areas contributing to feelings of relative deprivation. Though it should be expected that military and civilian personnel would have differences on important job characteristics, military leaders should note those aspects that are contributing most to negative feelings among soldiers and, where possible, take steps to reduce the discrepancy. In general these findings touch greatly on leadership issues, no more so than the finding that more soldiers reported that contractors have higher-quality leadership than do service personnel.

Second, our data suggest that soldiers view contractors with a fair bit of ambivalence. Two-thirds of soldiers view contractors as part of the "total force," whereas a solid third of soldiers disagree. Other indicators of ambivalent attitudes include more than a third of soldiers stating they are uncomfortable working with contractors, a majority disagreeing with the statement that the Army should not use military personnel if civilians can do the job just as well, two-thirds agreeing that integrating contractors has negative impacts on retention, and more than a quarter questioning the motivation, commitment, and skill of contractors. There appears to be an important disconnect between how contractors are categorized by the Department of Defense as "force multipliers" and as part of the "total force" and how soldiers view them.

The ambivalence expressed by soldiers also speaks, in part, to the contested institutional-versus-occupational orientation of service personnel. It may be that this ambivalence is further support for the argument that our soldiers serve as pragmatic professionals, combining elements of both selfless service and a need to make a living and support one's family (monetarily and with one's physical presence). Ambivalence may also stem from the convergence of functions between civilian and military personnel in many cases, yet relatively distinct differences persist (and are amplifying) with regard to structural differences in employment (chain of command, legal systems, etc.), risks, and compensation packages.

Third, Hispanic soldiers are significantly more negative in their assessment of contractors than non-Hispanic soldiers and African American service members are significantly more likely than whites to want to work as contractors. One cannot help but wonder what effect this may have on the racial/ethnic composition of the military in years to come, especially with African American enlistment already at record low levels in recent decades. To the extent that it is desirable for our nation's military to reflect those whom it protects and defends, this will be an important issue to track in the years to come.

Fourth, some soldiers were quick to point out that the success of the mission depends on the contribution of contractors. Others argued that this merely reflects current organizational practices, but that it need not be this way. In other words, there does appear to be some distinction between recognizing that contractors can do work that is critical to the mission, versus stipulating this point and asking whether they *should* be doing this work.

Finally, the data presented in this chapter offer only an initial insight into the dynamics of integrating civilian contractors with soldiers in operational units. Future research needs to examine the effect of this integration in other contexts, to include noncombat arms units and the other military service branches. In addition, the current findings are all derived from enlisted service personnel. Attitudes of officers, who represent a different level in the organization of the military, will be an important addition to this field of research.

Notes

1. The ideas expressed in this chapter are those of the authors and not necessarily those of the United States Military Academy, the United States Army, or the Department of Defense. This research was supported by funding from the Center for Research on Military Organization at the University of Maryland and the Faculty Development Fund at the United States Military Academy.

2. Margaret C. Harrell, "Army Officers' Spouses: Have the White Gloves Been Mothballed?" *Armed Forces and Society* 28, 1 (2001): 55–75, at 59–62.

3. Bernard Boëne, "How 'Unique' Should the Military Be? A Review of Representative Literature and Outline of a Synthetic Formulation," *European Journal of Sociology* 31, 1 (1990): 3–51, at 11–20; Samuel P. Huntington, *The Soldier and the State: The Theory and Politics of Civil–Military Relations* (New York: Vintage Books, 1957).

4. Morris Janowitz, *The Professional Soldier: A Social and Political Portrait* (New York: Free Press, 1960), 31–36.

5. Huntington, *The Soldier and the State*, 460–66.

6. Peter Lassman and Ronald Speirs (eds.), *Weber: Political Writings* (New York: Cambridge University Press, 1994), 309–69, at 310–11.

7. Albert Biderman, "What Is Military?" in Sol Tax (ed.), *The Draft: A Handbook of Facts and Alternatives* (Chicago: Chicago University Press, 1967), 122–37, at 128.

8. Victor David Hanson, *The Western Way of War* (New York: Oxford University Press, 1989).

9. Deborah Avant, "What Are Those Contractors Doing in Iraq?" *Washington Post*, May 9, 2004, B1, B5.

10. At the most extreme, the Cold War that continues in Asia represents the ultimate in equal opportunity risk of death and injury across the military–civilian spectrum should the government of North Korea target Alaska with a nuclear weapon.

11. Biderman, "What Is Military?" 132–33.

12. Ibid., 124; Boëne, "How 'Unique' Should the Military Be?" 4–11.

13. Boëne, "How 'Unique' Should the Military Be?" 13–15.

14. Charles C. Moskos, "From Institution to Occupation: Trends in Military Organization," *Armed Forces and Society* 4, 1 (1977): 41–50, at 42–44.

15. Charles C. Moskos and Frank Wood, "Introduction," in Charles C. Moskos and Frank R. Wood (eds.), *The Military: More Than Just a Job?* (Washington, DC: Pergamon-Brassey's International Defense Publishers, 1988), 15–26, at 18.

16. Moskos, "From Institution to Occupation," 43.

17. Ibid., 44.

18. Charles C. Moskos, "Toward a Postmodern Military: The United States as a Paradigm," in Charles C. Moskos, John Allen Williams, and David R. Segal (eds.), *The Postmodern Military: Armed Forces after the Cold War* (New York: Oxford University Press, 2000), 14–31.

19. Paul C. Light, *The True Size of Government* (Washington, DC: Brookings Institution Press, 1999), 4–6.

20. Moskos, "Toward a Postmodern Military," 21.

21. OMB Circular A-76, "The Performance of Commercial Activities," 1999, www .whitehouse.gov/omb/circulars/ a076/a076.html (accessed Feb. 15, 2003).

22. Ibid.

23. Light, *The True Size of Government*, 102; P. W. Singer, *Corporate Warriors: The Rise of the Privatized Military Industry* (Ithaca, NY: Cornell University Press, 2003), 63. The revised OMB A-76 (1999) states that it is US government policy to achieve economy and enhance productivity in providing federal services for the American people. Competition through free markets, it argues, improves quality of goods and services, increases economy, and enhances productivity. Though not stated in the OMB A-76 circular explicitly, former President Bush's FY2002 management plan recognized that social consequences should be considered as part of the outcome goals. Cf. George W. Bush, *The President's Management Agenda*, 2002, www.whitehouse.gov/omb/budget /fy2002/mgmt.pdf (accessed Feb. 25, 2004), 13.

24. George A. Akerlof and Rachel E. Kranton, "Identity and the Economics of Organizations," 2003, www.wam.umd.edu/~rkranton/identityandorganizations.pdf (accessed Jan. 5, 2005).

25. Encycogov, "Decomposing Costs into Transaction Costs and Production Costs," 2005, ww.encycogov.com/B11ResearchTraditions/TCE/Exhi_1DecomposeTC. asp (accessed Mar. 7, 2005).

26. Light, *The True Size of Government*, 148–49.

27. OMB Circular A-76, "The Performance of Commercial Activities."

28. Lt. Col. Bill McNight, quoted in Daniel Witter, "Beal May Add Civilian Positions: Study Finds Converting Military Jobs Could Save Money," 2003, www.ysedc .org/news_articles/ 2003/Beale_ may_add_civilian_positions.htm (accessed Oct. 14, 2004).

29. Ryan Kelty and David R. Segal, "The Civilianization of the U.S. Military: Army and Navy Case Studies of the Effects of Civilian Integration on Military Personnel," in Thomas Jäger and Gerhard Kümmel (eds.), *Private Military and Security Companies: Chances, Problems, Pitfalls, and Prospects* (Wiesbaden: VS Verlag für Sozialwissenschaften, 2007), 213–39, at 233.

30. Ryan Kelty and Irving Smith, "'Racial, Ethnic and Gender Differences in Soldiers' Attitudes toward Civilian Contractors," paper presented at Defense Equal Opportunity Management Institute's 6th Biennial EO/EEO Research Symposium, Cocoa Beach, FL, Jan. 2007.

31. Lindy Heinecken, "Discontent within the Ranks? Officers' Attitudes toward Military Employment and Representation—A Four-Country Comparative Study," *Armed Forces and Society* 35, 3 (2009): 477–500, at 487.

32. Ryan Kelty, "Citizen Soldiers and Civilian Contractors: Soldiers' Unit Cohesion and Retention Attitudes in the 'Total Force,'" *Journal of Political and Military Sociology* 37, 2 (2009) : 1–27.

33. Samples sizes for the various analyses may differ from these totals due to item non-response on some items.

34. Alpha = .75.

35. Faye J. Crosby, *Working Women and Relative Deprivation* (New York: Oxford University Press, 1982); Mady W. Segal, "The Military and the Family as Greedy Institutions," *Armed Forces & Society* 13, 1 (1986).

36. Respondents were not asked what specific jobs contractors performed in working with their units, rather they were instructed to keep in mind the definition of civilian contractor used for the study (presented in a prior paragraph) when responding to survey items. In addition, on the social comparison scale, they were instructed to make comparisons with contractors who perform the same or comparable duties as themselves.

37. Bush, *The President's Management Agenda*, 14; Light, *The True Size of Government*.

38. Alpha = .87.

39. The 2010 *Quadrennial Defense Review* refers to the *Total Defense Workforce*, comprising three distinct groups: military personnel, Department of Defense civilian personnel, and civilian contractors. See *Quadrennial Defense Review*, 2010, www.defense.gov/qdr/QDR%20as%20of%2029JAN10%201600.pdf (accessed Feb. 9, 2010).

40. $\chi^2 = 11.490$, p<.05. Traditional significance levels begin with a p-value of .05 or lower.

41. This analysis used four years as the cut point for military service as a proxy for first-term enlistment versus those who are in successive enlistments. Though this is not ideal, it does provide insight into the underlying motivation of this analysis, which is the effect that experience in the organization has on soldiers' desires to work as contractors.

42. $\chi^2 = 10.903$, p<.01.

43. $\chi^2 = 10.498$, p<.05.

44. David R. Segal and Mady W. Segal, "America's Military Population," *Population Bulletin* 59, 4 (2004): 1–40, at 20.

45. $\chi^2 = 59.803$, p<.001.

46. $\chi^2 = 24.867$, p<.001.

47. unit $\chi^2 = 4.821$, p<.05; race $\chi^2 = 4.720$, p<.05.

48. This test produced a p-value = .07. P-values that approximate a .05 value may be interpreted as approaching significance. $\chi^2 = 3.217$, p = .07.

49. Model statistics: $r^2 = .12$, F = 2.108, p<.01.

50. ß = .136, p<.05.

51. ß = ?.138, p<.05.

52. ß = .231, p<.001.

53. Model Statistics: $r^2 = .074$, F = 2.021 p<.05.

54. ß = ?.159, p<.01.

55. ß = ?.120, p<.05.

56. ß = .2.631, p<.01.

57. ß = ?2.700, p<.01.

3 Looking Beyond Iraq

Contractors in US Global Activities

Renée de Nevers

1. Introduction

The US military has relied on contractors to an unprecedented extent in the Iraq conflict that began in 2003. As the US presence in Iraq winds down and its activities in Afghanistan expand, it is worth considering how lessons learned in Iraq relate to continued US reliance on contractors in contingency operations, and more broadly in support of US foreign policy goals.

The expansion of the contractor workforce to support contingency operations in Afghanistan and Iraq outpaced the government's ability to manage it properly. Rebuilding sufficient oversight capability will be a slow process. But planning for future contingency operations needs to be more cognizant of the oversight issues from the outset, as military planners recognize. Particular attention should be given to assessing the appropriate role for private military and security companies (PMSCs), to ensure that their actions do not harm broader US and allied policy goals in the regions where they are working. Moreover, whether relying on contractors or civil servants, the US should strive to maintain an appropriate balance between civilian and military actions in its foreign policy activities. The author briefly examines some of the key lessons relevant to contracting from the US experience in Iraq. She will then assess the state of US reliance on contractors in Afghanistan, Africa, and Latin America.

2. The Lessons of Iraq

The military's increased reliance on contractors grew out of a desire to downsize the military after the Cold War and pressures to privatize government functions. Downsizing clashed with the expanded set of missions that the military was being asked to do in the 1990s, however, and the gap was increasingly filled by contractors.[1] The Iraq contracting experience suggests that three key areas deserve particular attention: oversight, legal and military authority over contractors in war zones, and the PMSC effect.

(a) Oversight

A central lesson from Iraq is that government oversight over contractors in the field is essential.[2] The occupation that followed the 2003 Iraq invasion was characterized by serious management problems as well as waste, fraud, and abuse by contractors. Much of this was caused by heightened dependence on contractors, the dearth of available contract officers and civilian contract employees, and poor planning.[3] To be sure, most contractors sought to fulfill their contractual obligations responsibly. But the post-invasion chaos and the absence of experienced contracting officers made it difficult for the Department of Defense (DoD) and other agencies to utilize reliable contractors well, and to distinguish between them and "those whose *ad hoc* operations and lack of experience pointed to failure."[4]

Failures of accountability and oversight of contracting activities correspond to the broader failure to plan adequately for the post-invasion occupation of Iraq. The establishment of the Special Inspector General for Iraq Reconstruction (SIGIR) in 2004, to conduct audits, inspections, and criminal investigations of reconstruction efforts, both expanded oversight over contractor activities and highlighted the serious problems caused by the scarcity of experienced contracting officers.[5]

Beginning in 2007, the US Congress introduced several bills to improve oversight of contracting in Iraq.[6] Many of these measures sought simply to ensure that both Congress and the executive agencies comprehended the scope of contracting underway, and who was doing what.[7] In the National Defense Authorization Act of 2008 (FY2008 NDAA), Congress also required greater coordination by DoD, the State Department, and USAID on contracting in Iraq and Afghanistan, including keeping track of contractors in both of these countries, and addressing PMSC hiring practices, rules of engagement, and coordination with the military in these conflict zones. The 2008 NDAA also established a Special Inspector General for Afghanistan (SIGAR), to conduct the functions SIGIR fulfills in Iraq. This position was established six years after US and NATO activities there began, which points to the dearth of oversight previously. The first inspector general was appointed in June 2008, but the office grew slowly due to inadequate manpower and resources.[8]

The need for stronger contracting oversight at multiple levels is now widely accepted. But agencies have struggled to increase oversight, and there are still too few oversight officers in the field, as well as in the agencies employing contractors.[9] In 2009, the DoD set up a Joint Contracting Command and increased acquisition personnel in Iraq and Afghanistan.[10] It has been working since early 2009 to increase the size of its acquisition workforce, but this will take time.[11] Moreover, improved contracting oversight is needed across many agencies, not only DoD.[12]

(b) Legal and Military Authority for Contractors in War Zones

A second lesson is that ensuring military authority over, and legal accountability of, civilian contractors in conflict zones, especially PMSCs, is essential. This became especially urgent after the September 2007 shooting in Nisoor Square. Several contractors employed by Blackwater Worldwide to provide security for State Department personnel killed seventeen Iraqis in central Baghdad. Both the Iraqi government and the US military determined that the Blackwater action was an unprovoked attack. This incident illuminated military commanders' and the DoD's uncertainty about their authority over PMSCs, and raised questions about PMSC accountability under criminal law.[13]

Concerns about the scope of existing laws governing contractors led to expansion of the Military Extraterritorial Jurisdiction Act (MEJA) in 2007, to cover contractors working for any overseas mission.[14] Congress also revised the Uniform Code of Military Justice (UCMJ) in 2006 to ensure that military commanders could exercise greater control over contractors on the battlefield. The State Department guidelines for personal security details were also revised, and the US government is examining what activities should be considered "inherently governmental" and not be outsourced to private contractors.[15]

Accountability also requires attention to the problems that contract employees may confront. Contract employees may have been denied recourse in cases of sexual assault, for example,[16] and contractors and their families have also faced significant obstacles in seeking to get health coverage or insurance benefits for injuries or death while working for companies in Iraq and Afghanistan.[17] Congress has taken up legal remedies to such problems, but it remains to be seen if the planned reforms will be sufficient.[18]

(c) The PMSC Effect

Finally, the US experience in Iraq illuminates the mismatch between the numbers of PMSC employees and the attention they receive relative to the larger universe of contractors supporting US war efforts. Only 11 percent of the more than 100,000 contractors in Iraq were providing security services in 2009, and numbers are probably similar in Afghanistan.[19] Until recently, little attention was given to the significant change in military reliance on contractors in contingency operations.[20] But to the degree that contractors have gained notice, the focus has been overwhelmingly on PMSCs.

One of the core lessons highlighted in the SIGIR's assessment of US reconstruction efforts in Iraq is that "security is necessary for large-scale reconstruction to succeed."[21] Not only DoD, but other government agencies, international organizations, and private groups working in Iraq and Afghanistan have long been forced to hire PMSCs to protect their employees and projects. PMSCs have expanded dramatically to meet this increased need for security. Most of the reportage about PMSC activities has been negative, however. There have been numerous allegations of contractors deliberately shooting civilian bystanders and Iraqi government employees, but no contractors have been convicted for killing civilians in Iraq.[22] Several of the Blackwater employees implicated in the September 2007 Nisoor Square shootings were indicted in US courts, but the charges were dismissed in December 2009 due to errors on the part of prosecutors in making their case.[23] The negative coverage of PMSCs matters because this may have affected attitudes toward contractors in general, at a time when the US military cannot operate overseas without them. Moreover, this could feed anti-American sentiment in the region, with negative repercussions on the US mission in Afghanistan and beyond.[24]

3. Contractors in Afghanistan

Although Afghanistan was relatively calm for the first few years after the US intervention that ended Taliban rule and displaced Al Qaeda's leadership, the security environment there has been worsening since 2006. This has complicated reconstruction activities there, with some reconstruction efforts abandoned, and increases in the security costs of others. The United States and

NATO gradually increased the number of troops in Afghanistan from 1,300 US troops at the end of 2001 to roughly 130,000 US and allied forces as part of the International Security Assistance Force (ISAF) in Afghanistan at the end of 2011.[25]

Reliance on contractors in Afghanistan continues to climb as well, with a 40 percent increase in the number of contractors in the country to a total of 104,101 in September 2009.[26] These numbers are likely to rise along with the troop increases announced by President Obama in November 2009. The contractor presence in Afghanistan may also be protracted, given expectations about stability and ongoing reconstruction needs.[27] The bulk of the contractors in Afghanistan are doing logistics and reconstruction work, and most are locals; 78,430, or 75 percent of the total number of contractors are Afghans, with 16 percent third country nationals, and 9 percent US citizens.[28]

As noted earlier, the DoD and other agencies have struggled with contract oversight problems in Afghanistan. SIGAR's formation should improve oversight, and the Commission on Wartime Contracting in Afghanistan and Iraq recently opened an office in Afghanistan, to ensure that it can better fulfill its reporting and oversight mission to Congress.[29] Both of these should help prod the agencies working in Afghanistan to improve their own oversight mechanisms, but staffing problems mean that this will be a slow process. Additionally, project costs have increased as security concerns have escalated.

Three factors about the contracting experience in Afghanistan may have a notable influence on Western efforts there: the "Afghan First" program, training of the Afghan police and army, and PMSCs. The Afghan First program, adopted in March 2006 and reaffirmed several times, emphasizes hiring Afghans. Indeed, the ratio of local to foreign contractors in Afghanistan is much higher than in Iraq. This was initially an effort by the Combined Forces Command–Afghanistan (CFC-A) to expand opportunities for local economic development in Afghanistan, by encouraging the hiring of Afghans and favoring Afghan products and services where they are available. The program was endorsed by the United Nations at the 2006 London donors' conference for Afghanistan.[30] The Afghan First program is also intended to bypass the usual stipulation that aid dollars be "tied" to hiring of donor country goods and services. Over $1 billion was spent on contracts with Afghan companies in 2006 as part of this program.

In March 2007, the Afghan First program shifted emphasis from hiring Afghans to training programs, in order to increase local capacity and skills.[31]

Afghanistan's labor force is primarily made up of unskilled laborers and the country also has a highly educated workforce of doctors and lawyers, but little in between. This effort to improve Afghanistan's workforce capacity has been underscored several times. US military forces in Afghanistan spent about $1 billion on contracts with Afghan companies in 2008 and this figure was expected to double in 2009. In November of that year, the US ambassador to Afghanistan Karl Eikenberry announced the adoption of an Afghan First program by the US embassy.[32]

The Afghan First program reflects the very different economic and political circumstances between Afghanistan and Iraq. Although the Iraqi economy was decimated by decades of war and economic sanctions, its population was relatively well-educated and a skilled labor force and bureaucracy existed. However, the United States established the Coalition Provisional Authority (CPA) to govern Iraq after the US invasion in March 2003. The CPA banned the Ba'ath Party associated with Saddam Hussein's rule and removed those having Ba'ath Party backgrounds from upper-level positions in all government institutions. The CPA also disbanded the Iraqi Armed Forces. Both measures helped fuel the insurgency that debilitated Iraq for several years, and made US agencies leery of hiring Iraqis due to questions of trust. In contrast, Afghanistan's population is largely illiterate, and thirty years of war destroyed what economic base the country had. It has been easier to hire locals in Afghanistan because those hiring did not need to worry about hiring Ba'athists by mistake, and Afghanis have worried less about the security consequences of working for outside agencies and organizations.[33] Hiring locals has also been part of an explicit "hearts and minds" campaign intended to build trust and support for coalition activities; this is also seen as a way to improve both immediate security concerns and the longer-term success of reconstruction projects in Afghanistan.[34]

Some observers have suggested that the Afghan First policy may have partially hindered rather than helped reconstruction and development efforts. Foreign contractors often pay better salaries than Afghans can make by setting up their own companies or working for the government, which appears to have led skilled workers to take unskilled jobs with contractors.[35] From the contractor's perspective, local hires provide cost savings and bring useful local knowledge.[36] But this creates a dynamic also found in regions where nongovernmental organizations and aid agencies are active; these organizations often attract the best workers away from local and government jobs

because they pay better, making it harder for the state to build its governing capacity. The Afghan government's concern about this problem was evident in the restrictions it placed on hiring former military and police officers
unless they could provide evidence of their honorable discharge from their
state positions in early 2010. Policemen have been quitting their jobs to work
for better paying PMSCs.[37]

A second critical element of the US strategy in Afghanistan is the assumption that Afghan security forces will gradually take over responsibility for
the country's security. Training of both the Afghan National Army (ANA)
and Afghan National Police (ANP) has been a major US policy priority for
several years. Much of the military and police training has been outsourced
to contractors. Military Professional Resources Incorporated (MPRI) began
working with the DoD in October 2002 to assess the needs of Afghanistan's
security forces, and since then it has provided training and mentoring in
areas ranging from defense planning, force and personnel management, to
logistics and disaster response for the ANA, the Afghan Ministry of Defense,
and the Department of the Interior.[38] DynCorp has provided training and
mentoring of the ANP since 2003. The police training program was run by
the State Department until January 2010, although Congress delegated funds
for this purpose only to the DoD beginning in 2005. These funds were then
transferred to the DoS, and the program was jointly overseen by both agencies. Oversight responsibility for the program was supposed to revert to the
DoD early in 2010, in recognition that Afghani police need training that more
closely resembles military training due to increased security concerns and the
deteriorating counterinsurgency operation.[39] But this shift was also intended
to eliminate the program's problematic dual chain of command. The shift to
DoD was postponed, however, due to a protest filed by DynCorp regarding its
exclusion from new contract competitions.[40]

Both contractor representatives and US government officials emphasize
the benefit derived from continuity in training and mentoring programs
supplied by contractors in Afghanistan. Military personnel are often in the
country for twelve months, and contracting oversight personnel are sometimes in country for only three to six months. In contrast, contract employees
are often in their positions for years and some MPRI personnel have been
in Afghanistan since 2002. This not only helps sustain the training mission,
but also helps build trust with Afghan counterparts.[41] Employees with long
experience in the country and region are also more likely to bring cultural

awareness to their work, which both government and corporate personnel consider essential.

Contractors also contribute to the training mission by expanding the workforce available for this task. The US military has been fighting two wars since 2003, and the Afghan mission struggled until recently to get enough manpower and supplies for its operation.[42] Contractors thus were essential to US and NATO efforts to train the Afghan army and police. Indeed, the US continues to struggle to get troop contributions it considers sufficient for the training mission from its NATO allies.[43] The US military and Afghan Interior Ministry shifted to sending some police officers abroad for training in mid-2010, in part to address this problem.[44]

However, the police training program has exhibited serious problems, and has failed to build a well-trained Afghan police force. In 2008, a Government Accounting Office (GAO) report determined that although the US had spent about $6.2 billion on training and equipment for the ANP, of 433 police units evaluated, none were fully capable of conducting missions on their own. Seventy-seven percent of the units were not capable at all, and 16 percent of supposedly active units were not formed or not reporting for work.[45] Serious questions were raised at that point about corruption among existing police forces, and the padding of police rolls by senior officers and ministry officials in order to receive the salary payments for additional employees.[46] More recent reports note that only 30,000 of the 170,000 Afghans trained since 2003 remain in the police force.[47] Concerns have also been raised about the ANA's abilities after years of US and NATO training, and some observers have criticized MPRI's advice to the Ministry of Defense for failing to hand over responsibility to Afghans after several years.[48]

These training failures have been attributed to the quality of contractor-provided training. In 2006, DynCorp's training efforts were condemned as failing to produce trained police able to carry out routine tasks. In the same year DynCorp itself was criticized for being unable to account for equipment and personnel associated with a $1.1 billion contract. Moreover, independent experts and Afghan government officials have criticized the quality and experience of the personnel DynCorp hired as trainers and mentors.[49]

In spite of serious criticisms of its performance, DynCorp has been awarded a succession of contracts to train the Afghan police.[50] This points to one of the concerns raised about outsourcing in the security arena. Privatizing government functions is generally viewed as likely to be more efficient and cost effective if it occurs with competitive bidding and if contractors are allowed flexibility in fulfilling their contracts. But governments frequently limit competition because they place a higher value on reliability.[51] This appears to be particularly pertinent to contracting in war zones. Moreover, once contracts have been awarded, the contract-holding firm gains advantages in future rounds of bidding, and vendors can exploit this advantage to raise prices or reduce the quality of the services they provide.[52] Finally, the problems of insufficient oversight detailed earlier have plagued the Afghan training contracts, and this will not be solved overnight. This matters because police training is fundamental to the US/NATO mission.

Third, heightened attention to PMSCs has increased scrutiny of their misdeeds, and some incidents in recent years suggest that PMSC oversight and management remains inadequate. This could have negative consequences for US efforts in Afghanistan and elsewhere. One example is the controversy over sexual misconduct, mistreatment of support staff, and alcohol abuse by ArmorGroup North America (AGNA) employees hired to guard the US embassy in Kabul in the fall of 2009, which brought to light long-standing concerns about AGNA's performance. This example is important not only because of the evidence it presents of behavior likely to damage US policy goals, but also because it illustrates the problems caused by the State Department's legislative mandate to accept the lowest bid to fill security contracts. The Commission on Wartime Contracting has noted that this does not allow the State Department to take into account other factors such as experience and quality. The State Department had sought since 2007 to address performance problems with AGNA, including its failure to provide sufficient security guards, and guards who could communicate in English with embassy staff. The company also failed adequately to train and equip its employees as specified under the terms of its contract, to the point that State Department officials feared that "the security of the US Embassy in Kabul is in jeopardy."[53] In addition to the contract mandates, whistleblowers who had earlier worked for AGNA asserted that the company's priority had been to cut costs and ensure profits, rather than to ensure the embassy's security.[54]

Continued State Department reliance on Xe Services (Blackwater Worldwide) and its subsidiaries has also complicated ties in the region as Blackwater's reputation has eroded. In 2009, two employees of a Blackwater subsidiary were accused of murdering Afghan civilians, and two others were among the victims of a suicide attack on a CIA facility in Khost, Afghanistan.[55] The former brought renewed questions about Blackwater employee behavior and whether the company tolerates or encourages overly aggressive tactics; the latter raised concerns about what missions are being performed by Blackwater for the CIA, particularly as CIA director Norman Panetta sought to end the CIA's ties to the company.

More generally, continued reliance on Blackwater in Afghanistan and, apparently, Pakistan, has roiled tensions in both countries over US intentions. Some Pakistani groups believed to be responsible for the rash of suicide bombings in Pakistan in the fall of 2009 disavowed responsibility for specific attacks that had led to strong public condemnation, and instead blamed these on Blackwater USA.[56] This may seem ludicrous in Washington. But the fact that the CIA hired Blackwater for some covert operations in Afghanistan and Pakistan, and the general tendency to believe conspiracy theories in Pakistan, make this claim potentially very damaging to US efforts in South Asia. Indeed, Afghan president Hamid Karzai announced that foreign private security companies would have to leave Afghanistan in two years during his second inaugural speech in November 2009, an indication of the government's concern about these companies' behavior.[57]

Contractors in Afghanistan thus present a different picture than those in Iraq. The bulk of them are doing reconstruction work, as in Iraq, and most employees are Afghan, which may help contribute to the overall mission. But PMSCs continue to dominate attention, and their activities have engendered ill will for the international effort, even though many PMSC employees are Afghans, and work for Afghan-owned companies. Finally, questions remain about whether the United States and its allies can train Afghan security forces to competency in a reasonable time frame. There do not appear to be alternatives to private trainers, at least in the short run. Once the United States has withdrawn more troops from Iraq, it may be able to increase the number of trainers dedicated to the Afghan mission, but this remains to be seen; forces are stretched, and developments in Afghanistan in the meantime will be critical.

4. Contractors in Africa

US activities in Africa represent another arena in which contractors are likely to flourish. Indeed, some observers see Africa as the future for contractors. US reliance on contractors in Africa is not new; rather, the United States has relied on the private sector to support a variety of missions there for many years, including military training and providing support for peacekeeping operations. Industry trade representatives argue that the private sector plays a critical role in peacekeeping support, and that many missions in Africa could not operate without private logistical support.[58]

Two elements of US strategy are relevant to the question of contractors in Africa: the AFRICAP contract managed by the State Department, and AFRICOM, the military's African command. AFRICAP is the State Department's Africa Peacekeeping program, and it funds security assistance activities in Africa. It is similar in structure to the Army's LOGCAP contract in that AFRICAP involves selecting a small group of companies to compete for particular task orders over a several-year period, within a guaranteed range of payment. The most recent AFRICAP covers a 5–year period, and is a $1.5 billion indefinite delivery/indefinite quantity contract. AFRICAP was established in 2003, though little attention was paid to this move at the time due to US operations in Iraq. When the contract was re-competed in 2008, its stated objectives were to enhance regional peace and stability in Africa through training programs for African armed forces with particular focus on peacekeeping and conflict management and prevention, as well as logistics and construction activities in support of peacekeeping and training missions.[59] The most recent contract was awarded in September 2009 to four companies: PAE Government Services, AECOM, DynCorp International, and Protection Strategies Incorporated. One of the first contracts awarded under AFRICAP went to DynCorp. PAE and DynCorp had previously provided logistical support for peacekeeping in Sudan, and DynCorp had trained infantry and non-commissioned officers for Liberia's new army.[60] Under the new contract, Dyn-Corp will provide operations and maintenance support for the Liberian army.

Contractors will also play a central role in AFRICOM, the new US military command for Africa that was established in 2007. Prior to this, the continent was divided between three separate military commands. AFRICOM's stated purpose is "to build strong military-to-military partnerships" with states in Africa. Additionally, AFRICOM aims to help African countries better address the threats they face by improving African military capacity, and doing more to bolster peace and security there.[61] Unlike other regional combatant commands, AFRICOM expects to rely on partnerships that extend across different branches of the US government, and one of its deputy commanders is a former diplomat. This interagency structure, which includes

State Department and USAID personnel as well as military staff, is intended to ensure that US assistance in Africa remains broader than military training.[62] AFRICOM does not plan a permanent military presence in Africa, and initial resistance delayed discussion of establishing a headquarters in Africa. Indeed, the US military has sought to dispel the view that AFRICOM was established primarily to fight terrorism and to counter China's growing presence in Africa. AFRICOM currently maintains a Combined Joint Task Force in the Horn of Africa, based in Djibouti, and it has established liaison offices in eleven countries.[63]

Many of the tasks AFRICOM is currently undertaking in Africa have been delegated to contractors in the past. Since its inception, AFRICOM has awarded contracts for training, air transport, information technology, and public diplomacy. It is worth noting that General William E. Ward, AFRICOM's first Combatant Commander, stated bluntly in January 2010 that AFRICOM does not use "private military contractors."[64] This reflects longstanding concerns in Africa about mercenaries, and the perceived linkages between mercenaries and the early private military companies.[65] It is important to note, however, that many of the companies contracting with AFRICOM and AFRICAP fall within the broad rubric of PMSCs.

Several concerns have been raised by the US's activities in Africa and its reliance on contractors there. One is the balance between civilian and military activities. While AFRICOM is seen as a good step because it affirms Africa's importance to the United States, there may be too much emphasis on the military side. Indeed, although AFRICOM is intended to be an interagency command, this structure is unique, and questions have been raised about how well it will work in practice, given imbalances in budgets and staff. Planning for the interagency command was undertaken primarily by the DoD, and it has had to revise initial plans to allocate up to a quarter of the command's positions to other agencies because few agencies could or would provide sufficient staff, due to personnel shortages. Thus, in 2008, only 13 of 1,304 staff positions were filled by representatives of agencies other than the DoD.[66] In 2009, the DoD hoped this number would increase to 52 of 1,356 positions.[67]

Oversight concerns have also been raised with regard to the State Department's AFRICAP contract. Although the State Department claims significant successes with some of the training programs it has funded, the GAO found in 2008 that State lacked the capacity to evaluate these programs' effectiveness in training peacekeepers or instructors; moreover, participants in some of its training programs were not screened for improper past conduct, with the consequence that some of those trained were later identified as having committed human rights abuses.[68]

A final concern is simply the effect of US police and military training programs in Africa. According to the Strategic Studies Institute of the US Army, "every armed group that plundered Liberia over the past 25 years had its core in these U.S.-trained AFL (Armed Forces of Liberia) soldiers."[69] The current DynCorp training of Liberian forces, and similar programs in other African countries, may in the long run create elite units that governments cannot afford to support economically, which might lead these forces to take matters into their own hands. This underscores the need to balance military training activities with broader aid packages.

Many of the contractors active in Africa are PMSCs. These companies work not only for the US government, however; they also work for African governments, private companies, especially in the extractive industry, and NGOs. MPRI, for example, recently contracted with the government of Equatorial Guinea to improve its maritime security. The goal is to establish a central surveillance network and operations center based in Equatorial Guinea within three years, which will improve not only that country's security but also regional stability, according to MPRI.[70] Notably, this project complements AFRICOM's central goal of enhancing maritime security capacity in the region.[71]

More broadly, PMSCs are affecting economic growth in Africa. One estimate suggests that the private security industry—meaning employees ranging from mall guards to industrial site security—is the largest source of employment in some parts of Africa.[72] PMSCs have also sought recruits in several African states for employment in Iraq in particular.[73] Some governments have objected to this recruitment. Namibia expelled two recruiters working for the Special Operations Consulting-Security Management Group in 2007, and the South African government passed legislation in November 2007 that would make it a crime for any South African citizen to work in a conflict zone without government permission. This law could have broad repercussions, because roughly 2,000–4,000 South Africans are believed to be working in Iraq and another 800 serve in the British military.[74] Moreover, the bill's wording could apply to humanitarian workers in conflict zones as well as the intended targets—mercenaries—which indicates the difficulty of designing legislation specifically for PMSCs.[75]

The large role played by private security in Africa illustrates a dearth of government capacity to provide protection to local economic activities. At the same time, some scholars have suggested that PMSC employment of "third country nationals" such as Africans could have negative long-term effects for the employees' home states. In a pattern similar to the hiring of locals by PMSCs in Afghanistan and elsewhere, this could lead to the hollowing out of state armies as soldiers seek more lucrative contracts, and reliance on private companies may threaten the state's monopoly over violence.[76]

5. Contractors in Latin America

Contractors have supported US foreign assistance policies in Latin America for decades. These policies have been dominated since at least 2000 by anti-narcotics and counterterrorism efforts.[77] Two pieces are notable: Plan Colombia, begun in 2000, and the 2007 Merida Initiative.

Plan Colombia is the central element of a broader counterdrug initiative focusing on the Andean region, which is the source of virtually all the cocaine that reaches the international market. The program has two central aims: to reduce drug production in Colombia, and to strengthen Colombian security forces to better secure the state against the range of threats it confronts.[78] Although the US spent $6.1 billion on Plan Colombia between 2000 and 2008, the program has failed to slow drug production there. However, the training of the military and police has led to security improvements, the second policy aim.[79]

To achieve this goal, the US government provided equipment and training by both US troops and civilian contractors to Colombian police and military forces. Roughly half of the military aid to Colombia is spent on private contractors, through contracts administered by DoD and the State Department. It is unclear how many contractors are active in Colombia. In 2004, Congress set a ceiling on the number of US troops in Colombia at 800 and on contractors at 600, and the State Department suggests that the current US presence is about half of those figures.[80] Finding accurate data on contractors' roles in Colombia is difficult, because many of the foreign military sales contracts through which contractors are hired are opaque.[81] Indeed, some estimates from the early 2000s suggest that DynCorp alone had between 300 and 600 contractors working in Colombia on a contract to provide support for aerial drug eradication and surveillance.[82] The US Congress mandated in

2005 that programs in Colombia be "nationalized" to reduce the US role and costs there. This led to a reduction in contractors that is expected to continue, suggesting that Colombia will present at most a modest market for contractor services. The future may lie in Mexico.

The Merida Initiative is a US–Mexico agreement on US assistance to Mexico and central American states to combat the growing drug trade and the accompanying increase in violence in Mexico in particular. As with Plan Colombia, a central goal has been to disrupt drug trafficking activities by providing equipment and training to Mexican security forces. Under the Obama administration, focus shifted to place greater emphasis on improving both security and trade conditions at the US–Mexico border, and supporting civil society in Mexico.[83] As with Plan Colombia, contractors are likely to play a large role in implementing the Merida Initiative. The US Congress authorized about $1.3 billion for aid to Mexico as part of this initiative between 2007 and 2009, with additional funding for Central America.[84] Most of this money must be spent either by the US government on equipment or to hire US contractors.

Government reliance on contractors for each of these initiatives has raised similar concerns. To begin with, the use of contractors in Plan Colombia was seen as a way to circumvent congressionally mandated limits on US military personnel and the tasks they were authorized to undertake.[85] Additionally, US military units were forbidden by Congress from working with Colombian units that could not be certified as free from human rights violations, but these constraints did not apply to contractor activities. Finally, in these areas, as elsewhere, contracting reduces the transparency of government policy.

A final area in which contractors could play a significant role in Latin America is in efforts to rebuild Haiti after the January 2010 earthquake devastated the capital, Port au Prince. The US government pledged $1.15 billion in aid as part of an international effort substantially to rebuild Haiti's infrastructure and bureaucracy.[86] Much of this work will be contracted to NGOs, international organizations, and private companies.

6. Conclusion

Absent major policy changes, contractors will continue to play a significant role in US policy, both in contingency operations and in other arenas. The Iraq experience, and to a lesser degree, experience in Afghanistan, have illuminated the dangers of overreliance on contractors without effective oversight. The government is working to correct this problem in two ways: by building up the oversight workforce, and by reevaluating which functions can appropriately be outsourced, and which are inherently governmental. But both of these will take time and resources, particularly if it is determined that some currently outsourced missions should return to government. And planning for future contingency operations must incorporate attention to oversight issues from the outset, as military planners recognize.

Both Afghanistan and Iraq have shown that greater clarity is needed regarding the accountability of contractors under domestic and international law, and protection of contractor employees' rights, and those with whom contractors come into contact. The US government is slowly moving to ensure that all contractors it employs overseas fall under US legal jurisdiction. Other states that rely heavily on contractors will also need to ensure their jurisdiction over their contractors. And states in which contractors are operating must also ensure that their laws address the challenges raised by contractors in country. Given the uncertainties that are likely to endure regarding the status and accountability of contractors working overseas, particularly PMSCs, international efforts to build voluntary governing frameworks can play a positive role. But these mechanisms are only likely to be effective if they have broad support among states that hire or export contractors. A Swiss government–ICRC effort to develop an international code of conduct for PMSCs is a good example; the Montreux Document on which the draft code builds was supported by only seventeen states.[87] This included states that have both relied most heavily on PMSCs and that host the major companies, notably the United States and the UK. But for such a code to have global reach, it needs greater international support.

Greater attention needs to be paid to how contractors fulfill their contracts, and what this means for the countries in which they are working in support of US policy. While hiring locals can be a useful part of a "hearts and minds" campaign by providing employment, it can also weaken the governing structures of the states that the United States and its allies are trying to support. Finding an appropriate balance will be difficult. Additionally, training programs may create forces that are too expensive for local governments to maintain. This has implications for the sustainability of these programs absent external support. This may create potential for unrest if military and police forces come to expect payments that the local government cannot provide.

Over the last twenty years, there has been a tendency to turn to the military to take on foreign policy tasks that other government agencies no longer have the capacity to do—and many of these tasks have subsequently been outsourced. Greater attention is needed to ensure that the face the United States presents to the world is not solely military or outsourced. The United States needs to strive to maintain an appropriate balance between civilian and military activities in its foreign policy.

Notes

1. Carl Coneta, *An Undisciplined Defense: Understanding the $2 Trillion Surge in US Defense Spending*, Project on Defense Alternatives (Cambridge, MA: Commonwealth Institute, Jan. 2010). See also P. W. Singer, *Corporate Warriors: The Rise of the Privatized Military Industry* (Ithaca, NY: Cornell University Press, 2003).

2. SIGIR, *Hard Lessons: The Iraq Reconstruction Experience* (Washington, DC: US Government Printing Office, 2009), 334.

3. As one example, DoD contract transactions increased by 328 percent between 2000 and 2009, but the staff responsible for reviewing contractor purchasing at the Defense Contract Management Agency (DCMA) declined from 70 in 2002 to 14 in 2009. Commission on Wartime Contracting in Iraq and Afghanistan, *Defense Agencies Must Improve Their Oversight of Contractor Business Systems to Reduce Waste, Fraud, and Abuse*, CWC Special Report 1 (Sept. 21, 2009), www.wartimecontracting .gov/index.php/reports (accessed Feb. 7, 2010).

4. SIGIR, *Hard Lessons*, 334. See also Dina Rasor and Robert Bauman, *Betraying Our Troops: The Destructive Results of Privatizing War* (New York: Palgrave Macmillan, 2007).

5. On SIGIR's work, see www.sigir.mil/Default.aspx (accessed Jan. 28, 2010).

6. Jennifer K. Elsea and Nina M. Serafino, *Private Security Contractors in Iraq: Background, Legal Status, and Other Issues*, CRS Report for Congress, RL 32419 (July 11, 2007), 33–36.

7. The DoD acknowledged early that year that it did not know how many contractors were working for it. Moshe Schwartz, *Department of Defense Contractors in Iraq and Afghanistan: Background and Analysis* (Washington, DC: Congressional Research Service Report for Congress, 7-5700, Dec. 14, 2009), 4.

8. Bruce Falconer, "Afghanistan: Oversight AWOL?" *Mother Jones*, July 16, 2009, http://motherjones.com/politics/2009/07/afghanistan-oversight-awol (accessed Dec. 28, 2009).

9. Ibid.

10. Schwartz, *Department of Defense Contractors in Iraq and Afghanistan*, 14.

11. *Quadrennial Defense Review Report* (Washington, DC: Department of Defense, 2010), 93, http.defense.gov/qdr/images/QDR_as_of_12Feb10_1000.pdf (accessed Feb.

25, 2010); Hearing Transcript, "Hearing to Receive Testimony on Afghanistan," U.S. Senate Committee on Armed Services Hearings (Dec. 2, 2009), 42–43, http://armed-services.senate.gov/Transcripts/2009/12%20December/09-65%20-%2012-2-09.pdf (accessed Dec. 29, 2009).

12. SIGIR, "Long-Standing Weaknesses in Department of State's Oversight of DynCorp Contract for Support of the Iraqi Police Training Program," SIGIR Report 10-008 (Jan. 25, 2010).

13. Peter Spiegel and Julian E. Barnes, "Gates Moves to Rein In Contractors in Iraq," *Los Angeles Times*, Sept. 27, 2007; Robert Gates, "UCMJ Jurisdiction over DoD Civilian Employees, DoD Contractor Personnel, and Other Persons Serving with or Accompanying the Armed Forces Overseas during Declared War and in Contingency Operations" (Mar. 10, 2008), http.justice.gov/criminal/dss/docs/03-10-08dod-ucmj.pdf (accessed Nov. 21, 2009).

14. Josh Meyer and Julian Barnes, "Congress Moves to Rein in Private Contractors," *Los Angeles Times*, Oct. 4, 2007.

15. The White House, "Memorandum: Government Contracting" (Mar. 4, 2009), http.whitehouse.gov/the_press_office/Memorandum-for-the-Heads-of-Executive-Departments-and-Agencies-Subject-Government/ (accessed Feb. 11, 2010).

16. A notable example is the case of Jamie Leigh Jones, an employee of Kellogg, Brown and Root, who alleges that shortly after her arrival in Iraq in 2005 she was drugged and raped by fellow employees. KBR has disputed her claim and her right to sue. Chris McGreal, "Rape Case to Force US Defence Firms into the Open," *Guardian*, Oct. 15, 2009.

17. T. Christian Miller, "Injured Abroad, Neglected at Home: Labor Dept. Slow to Help War Zone Contractors," *ProPublica*, Dec. 17, 2009, http.propublica.org/feature/labor-dept-slow-to-enforce-defense-base-act-for-contractor-care-1217 (accessed Dec. 31, 2009); T. Christian Miller, "Contractors in Iraq Are Hidden Casualties of War," *ProPublica*, Oct. 6, 2009, http.propublica.org/feature/kbr-contractor-struggles-after-iraq-injuries-1006 (accessed Dec. 31, 2009); T. Christian Miller, "Sometimes It's Not Your War, But You Sacrifice Anyway," *Washington Post*, Aug. 16, 2009.

18. Cynthia Dizikes, "Senate Passes Franken Amendment Aimed at Defense Contractors," MinnPost.com, Oct. 6, 2009, http.minnpost.com/stories/2009/10/06/12247/senate_passes_franken_amendment_aimed_at_defense_contractors (accessed Dec. 29, 2009); T. Christian Miller, "Labor Department, Congress Plan Improvements to System to Care for Injured War Contractors," *ProPublica*, Oct. 13, 2009, http.propublica.org/feature/congress-plan-improvements-to-system-to-care-for-injured-war-contractors-10 (accessed Dec. 31, 2009).

19. Moshe Schwartz, *The Department of Defense's Use of Private Security Contractors in Iraq and Afghanistan: Background, Analysis, and Options for Congress* (Washington, DC: Congressional Research Report for Congress, 7-5700, R40835, Sept. 29, 2009).

20. Contractors are barely mentioned in some of the best-known analyses of the Iraq conflict since 2003. See, for example, Thomas Ricks, *Fiasco: The American Military Adventure in Iraq, 2003 to 2005* (New York: Penguin, 2007); Bob Woodward, *Plan

of Attack (New York: Simon and Schuster, 2004). One book that does discuss the early role of contractors is Rajiv Chandrasekaran, *Imperial Life in the Emerald City* (New York: Vintage Books, 2006).

21. SIGIR, *Hard Lessons*, 331.

22. Steve Fainaru, "Four Hired Guns in an Armored Truck, Bullets Flying, and a Pickup and a Taxi Brought to a Halt: Who Did the Shooting and Why?" *Washington Post*, April 15, 2007; Bill Sizemore, "Iraq Killing Tracked to Contractor Could Test Laws," *Virginian-Pilot*, Jan. 11, 2007; Sudarsan Raghavan and Josh White, "Blackwater Guards Fired at Fleeing Cars, Soldiers Say," *Washington Post*, Oct. 12, 2007. One contractor in Iraq was convicted on charges related to child pornography. Jennifer K. Elsea and Nina M. Serafino, *Private Security Contractors in Iraq: Background, Legal Status, and Other Issues* (Washington, DC: Congressional Research Service, 2007), 19.

23. The US government appealed this ruling in January 2010. Del Quentin Wilber, "U.S. Appeals Ruling in Blackwater Case That Involved a Baghdad Shooting," *Washington Post*, Jan. 30, 2010.

24. Declan Walsh, "Blackwater Operating at CIA Pakistan Base, Ex Official Says," *Guardian*, Dec. 11, 2009.

25. International Security Assistance Force, "About ISAF: Troop Numbers and Contributions," http.isaf.nato.int/troop-numbers-and-contributions/index.php (accessed Jan. 16, 2012).

26. Schwartz, *Department of Defense Contractors in Iraq and Afghanistan*, 12.

27. Christopher Shays, "Opening Statement, Contractor Training of Afghan Security Forces," Commission on Wartime Contracting Hearing (Dec. 18, 2009), 3, http.wartimecontracting.gov/docs/hearing2009-12-18_transcript.pdf (accessed Feb. 7, 2010); Mark Landler, "U.S. Envisions a Continuing Civilian Presence in Afghanistan and Pakistan," *New York Times*, Jan. 21, 2010.

28. Schwartz, *Department of Defense Contractors in Iraq and Afghanistan*, 13.

29. "Wartime Contracting Commission opens offices in Iraq and Afghanistan to support its work," CWC-NR-19 (Jan. 26, 2010), http.wartimecontracting.gov/index.php/pressroom/pressreleases/120-cwc-nr-19 (accessed Feb. 8, 2010).

30. Scott Gomer, "Coalition Boosting Business Opportunities with 'Afghan First,'" Combined Forces Afghanistan Press Release #060411-03 (April 11, 2006), www.peacedividendtrust.org/en/data/files/download/News/Coalition%20boosting%20business%20opportunities%20with%20Afghan%20First.pdf (accessed Dec. 27, 2009); "United States Emphasizes Local Purchasing in Afghan Market," US Embassy Kabul Press Release 107/2006 (April 9, 2006), http://kabul.usembassy.gov/pr040906.html (accessed Dec. 31, 2009).

31. Thomas J. Doscher, "'Afghanistan First' Program Shifts Focus to Training," *American Forces Press Service* (Mar. 14, 2007), www.defense.gov/news/newsarticle.aspx?id=3361 (accessed Dec. 27, 2009).

32. Karl Eikenberry, "Afghan First" (Nov. 11, 2009), http://kabul.usembassy.gov/speech_111109.html (accessed Dec. 31, 2009).

33. Elizabeth Newell, "Contractors Welcome Military Surge in Afghanistan," *Government Executive* (Feb. 3, 2010), www.govexec.com/story_page.cfm?articleid=44531 (accessed Feb. 11, 2010).

34. "Statement of Admiral Michael G. Mullen . . . before the Senate Armed Services Committee," US Senate Committee on Armed Services Hearings (Dec. 2, 2009), http://armed-services.senate.gov/statemnt/2009/December/Mullen%2012-02-09. pdf (accessed Dec. 31, 2009); Richard Owens, "Remarks Submitted for the Roundtable Regarding Business Perspectives on United States Agency for International Development Reconstruction and Development Contracts in Afghanistan before the Senate Committee on Homeland Security and Governmental Affairs Subcommittee on Contracting Oversight" (Feb. 2, 2010), http://hsgac.senate.gov/public/ index.cfm?FuseAction=Hearings.Hearing&Hearing_id=c8de2f28-290d-447b-92a4-9cf5939e05a7 (accessed Feb. 15, 2010).

35. Hearing Transcript, "Hearing to Receive Testimony on Afghanistan," US Senate Committee on Armed Services Hearings (Dec. 2, 2009), http://armed-services. senate.gov/Transcripts/2009/12%20December/09-65%20-%2012-2-09.pdf (accessed Dec. 29, 2009), 37–38; Steve Rennie, "Afghanistan to Regulate Private Security," *Toronto Sun*, Jan. 26, 2010. It has also been pointed out that Taliban may pay better than the police force. Donald Ryder, "Statement before the Commission on Wartime Contracting" (Dec. 18, 2009), 7, www.wartimecontracting.gov/index.php/hearings /commission/hearing20091218 (accessed Feb. 11, 2010).

36. Doug Brooks, "Think Globally. Hire Locally," *Journal of Peace Operations* (Nov./Dec. 2009).

37. Walter Pincus, "Contractor Hirings in Afghanistan to Emphasize Locals," *Washington Post*, Dec. 7, 2009; Steve Rennie, "Afghanistan to Regulate Private Security," *Toronto Sun*, Jan. 26, 2010; Matthew Green, "Afghan Drive to Stop Poaching of Police Recruits," *Financial Times*, Jan. 25, 2010.

38. "Testimony of Richard C. Nickerson, Program Manager, MPRI . . . before the Commission on Wartime Contracting in Iraq and Afghanistan," Dec. 18, 2009, www .wartimecontracting.gov/index.php/hearings/commission/hearing20091218 (accessed Feb. 11, 2010).

39. Kenneth P. Moorefield, "Risks and Challenges Associated with ANSF Training Contracts," Hearing of the Commission on Wartime Contracting, Dec. 18, 2009, 18, www.wartimecontracting.gov/index.php/hearings/commission/hearing20091218 (accessed Feb. 11, 2010).

40. Christine Spolar, "Military Training of Afghan National Police Mired in Contract Dispute," *Huffington Post Investigative Fund*, Feb. 22, 2010, http://huffpostfund. org/stories/2010/02/military-training-afghan-national-police-mired-contract-dispute (accessed Feb. 23, 2010).

41. "Testimony of Richard C. Nickerson," 6.

42. "Statement by Major General Richard P. Formica . . . to the Commission on Wartime Contracting," Dec. 18, 2009, 3, www.wartimecontracting.gov/index.php /hearings/commission/hearing20091218 (accessed Feb. 11, 2010).

43. Adam Entous, "U.S. Makes Urgent Appeal to NATO on Afghan Training," *Reuters*, Feb. 4, 2010, http://af.reuters.com/article/worldNews/idAFT-RE6133JO20100204 (accessed Feb. 15, 2010).

44. Greg Jaffe, "Program Aims to Rebuild Afghan Police Force, Repair Its Image," *Washington Post*, Mar. 12, 2010.

45. Charles Michael Johnson, Jr., *U.S. Efforts to Develop Capable Afghan Police Forces Face Challenges and Need a Coordinated, Detailed Plan to Help Ensure Accountability*, GAO Report GAO-08-883T (June 18, 2008), 7.

46. Ibid., 7–8.

47. T. Christian Miller, Mark Hosenball, and Ron Moreau, "$6 Billion Later, Afghan Cops Aren't Ready to Serve," *Newsweek*, Mar. 20, 2010.

48. C. J. Chivers, "Marines Do Heavy Lifting as Afghan Army Lags in Battle," *New York Times*, Feb. 20, 2010.

49. James Glanz, David Rohde, and Carlotta Gall, "Afghanistan: The Reach of War; US Report Finds Dismal Training of Afghan Police," *New York Times*, Dec. 4, 2006.

50. Pratap Chatterjee, "Policing Afghanistan: Obama's New Strategy," *CorpWatch*, Mar. 23, 2009, www.corpwatch.org/article.php?id=15328&printsafe=1 (accessed Feb. 11, 2010).

51. Deborah Avant, "Think Again: Mercenaries," *Foreign Policy* (July/Aug. 2004).

52. Trevor L. Brown, Matthew Potoski, and David M. Van Slyke, "Managing Public Service Contracts: Aligning Values, Institutions, and Markets," *Public Administration Review* (May/June 2006): 326.

53. *Lowest-Priced Security Not Good Enough for War-Zone Embassies*, Commission on Wartime Contracting in Iraq and Afghanistan Special Report 2 (Oct. 1, 2009), www.wartimecontracting.gov/index.php/reports (accessed Nov. 17, 2009), 4.

54. Richard Lardner, "Ex-managers: Security Firm Cut Corners at Embassy," *Washington Post*, Sept. 10, 2009.

55. James Risen, "Former Blackwater Guards Charged with Murder," *New York Times*, Jan. 7, 2010; Sheryl Gay Stolberg and Mark Mazzetti, "Suicide Bombing Puts a Rare Face on CIA's Work," *New York Times*, Jan. 7, 2010.

56. Robert Mackey, "Taliban Blame 'Blackwater' for Pakistan Bombings," *New York Times News Blog*, Nov. 17, 2009, http://thelede.blogs.nytimes.com/2009/11/17/taliban-blames-blackwater-for-pakistan-bombings/?scp=1&sq=blackwater%20pakistan&st=cse (accessed Nov. 20, 2009).

57. Richard Beeston, "Karzai: Private Security Companies Will Leave Afghanistan within Two Years," *Times Online*, Nov. 19 2009, www.timesonline.co.uk/tol/news/world/Afghanistan/article6922760.ece (accessed Nov. 23, 2009).

58. Doug Brooks and Jennifer Brooke, "AFRICOM and the Role of the Private Sector," *Africa Journal* (Fall 2007).

59. *AFRICAP Program Re-Compete*, US Department of State (Feb. 6, 2008), www.fbo.gov/index?s=opportunity&mode=form&tab=core&id=4fbad7bde428a5595aca7bfe3cdbc02d&_cview=1 (accessed May 6, 2010).

60. "DynCorp International Wins $20 Million AFRICAP Task Order in Liberia" (Jan. 28, 2010), http.benzinga.com/press-releases/b103570/dyncorp-international-wins-20-million-africap-task-order-in-liberia (accessed Feb. 2, 2010); David Isenberg, "Back to Africa," United Press International, May 30, 2008, www.cato.org/pub _display.php?pub_id=9436 (accessed Dec. 31, 2009).

61. *Actions Needed to Address Stakeholder Concerns, Improve Interagency Collaboration, and Determine Full Costs Associated with the U.S. Africa Command*, GAO Report GAO-09-181 (Feb. 2009).

62. David McKeeby, "New Africa Command Will Promote Security, Spur Development," *USINFO* (Nov. 15, 2007), www.africom.mil/getArticle.asp?art=1579&lang=0 (accessed Feb. 19, 2010); Stephanie Hanson, "U.S. Africa Command," Council on Foreign Relations Backgrounder (May 3, 2007), www.cfr.org/publication/13255/ (accessed Jan. 31, 2009). See also Isenberg, "Back to Africa."

63. *Actions Needed to Address Stakeholder Concerns*, 12, 24.

64. Aidan O'Donnell, "Africom's General Ward Interviewed by Radio France Internationale," *U.S. AFRICOM Public Affairs* (Jan. 8, 2010), www.africom.mil/get Article.asp?art=3845 (accessed Jan. 12, 2010).

65. The so-called "Wonga Coup," which involved South African mercenaries in an attempt to overthrow the government of Equatorial Guinea, is only the most recent example. Adam Roberts, *The Wonga Coup* (New York: Public Affairs, 2007).

66. Mark Malan, "Testimony before the Subcommittee on National Security and Foreign Affairs, Committee on Oversight and Government Reform, House of Representatives" (July 23, 2008), www.refintl.org (accessed Dec. 31, 2009).

67. *Actions Needed to Address Stakeholder Concerns*, 5.

68. *Peacekeeping: Thousands Trained But United States Is Unlikely to Complete All Activities by 2010 and Some Improvements Are Needed*, GAO Report GAO-08-754 (June 2008).

69. As quoted in Isenberg, "Back to Africa."

70. "L-3 Awarded Maritime Security Work in Equatorial Guinea" (Feb. 24, 2010), www.mpri.com/esite/index.php/content/news_archive/ (accessed April 12, 2010).

71. *The Military Balance 2010* (London: Routledge, for the International Institute for Strategic Studies, 2010), 288.

72. Mauricio Lazala, "Private Military and Security Companies and Their Impacts on Human Rights in Contexts Other Than War," Business and Human Rights Resource Center (Jan. 2008), www.havenscenter.org/files/Lazala%20Paper_0 .doc (accessed April 6, 2010).

73. Stephanie Hanes, "Private Security Companies Look to Africa for Recruits," *Christian Science Monitor*, Jan. 8, 2008.

74. Nathan Hodge, "Army for Hire," *Slate Magazine*, Aug. 31, 2006; Len Le Roux, "South African Mercenary Legislation Enacted," Institute for Security Studies (Jan. 21, 2008), http.issafrica.org/blog/2008/01/iss-today-south-african-mercenary.html (accessed Feb. 29, 2008).

75. Sarah Percy, *Regulating the Private Security Industry* (London: International Institute for Strategic Studies, 2006), 30–32; Michael Peel and Alec Russell, "South Africa Mercenary Law Attacked," *Financial Times*, May 29, 2007.

76. Deborah Avant, "The Implications of Marketized Security for IR Theory: The Democratic Peace, Late State Building, and the Nature and Frequency of Conflict," *Perspectives on Politics* 4, 3 (Spring 2006): 507–28.

77. Connie Veillette, Clare Ribando, and Mark Sullivan, "US Foreign Assistance to Latin America and the Caribbean," CRS Report #RL32487 (Jan. 3, 2006), 2.

78. These threats include terrorist organizations, drug traffickers, and paramilitary groups.

79. Government Accountability Office, *Plan Colombia: Drug Reduction Goals Were Not Fully Met, But Security Has Improved*, GAO Report GAO-09-71 (Oct. 2008), 15.

80. "US–Colombia Defense Cooperation Agreement," US State Department Press Release (Oct. 30, 2009), www.state.gov/r/pa/prs/ps/2009/oct/131134.htm (accessed April 26, 2010).

81. Marina Caparini, "Licensing Regimes for the Export of Military Goods and Services," in Simon Chesterman and Chia Lehnardt (eds.), *From Mercenaries to Market* (Oxford: Oxford University Press, 2007), 166.

82. Singer, *Corporate Warriors*, 208.

83. Clare Ribando, "Mérida Initiative for Mexico and Central America: Funding and Policy Issues," CRS Report #7-7500 (April 19, 2010), 1–3.

84. Ibid., 6.

85. Singer, *Corporate Warriors*, 209.

86. Mary Beth Sheridan and Colum Lynch, "$5.3 Billion Pledged Over 2 Years at UN Conference for Haiti Reconstruction," *Washington Post*, April 1, 2010.

87. "The Montreux Document" (Sept. 17, 2008), www.eda.admin.ch/etc/media lib/downloads/edazen/topics/intla/humlaw.Par.0056.File.tmp/Montreux%20Document.pdf (accessed Dec. 28, 2009).

II RECONSTRUCTION AND STABILIZATION OPERATIONS

A Market Growth Area

4   The Elephant in the Room

William J. Flavin

1. Introduction

Contractors have become an enduring and essential part of US national security. Though contracting has always existed, its reach today encompasses a breadth and depth unseen before. Contractors support the Departments of State and Justice, USAID, and the Department of Defense, and in many parts of the world they are the face of the United States. They now provide the backbone for logistical support and maintenance of our armed forces and augment service and joint staffs. They develop and run military war games, write concepts and doctrine, and conduct research in support of departments and combatant Commands. They have assumed a significant role as instructors, from the undergraduate Reserve Officers' Training Corps (ROTC) level to the more senior service and joint schools.

Contractors comprise over half of the whole-of-government participation in current operations in Afghanistan and Iraq. Today, the character of modern conflict and the structure and resources of the agencies of the US government require a level of expertise and engagement that necessitates contracting; therefore, contracting has a significant impact on how the US government conducts its operations in support of national strategic goals. But much of the focus of the Congress, the American public, and the military itself has been on the issues of waste, fraud, abuse, legality, and overall management rather than on how contracting affects the national strategy of the United States. Contracting should be nested in operational and strategic frameworks as outlined by the *Quadrennial Defense Review* (QDR) and recent military and interagency doctrine. This chapter will address how contracting should be nested in these frameworks. It will examine the critical need for contract support in the new operational environment, discuss the lack of doctrinal and conceptual guidance, identify some of the issues and challenges, and propose a way ahead.

2. The Contemporary Environment and Whole-of-Government Approach

The US military will in the future be called upon to conduct a wide range of missions combining offensive and defensive approaches with stability tasks to address what the US Army and Joint Forces Command call "the contemporary operating environment." This operating environment is characterized by weak and failing states that will require an international array of economic, diplomatic, and military resources to establish or sustain stability. The US military will have to integrate with other agencies, international organizations, nongovernment organizations, and the peoples and governments of the affected countries. Military commanders are therefore likely to encounter a broad array of private contractors, employing many nationalities, under contract to a plethora of governments and organizations. Not all of these will share the same culture, goals, or values. All of them will become essential to address problems in a coherent framework.[1]

Field Manual (FM) 3-07 describes the whole-of-government framework for dealing with this environment. This framework is based on reducing the drivers of conflict and instability and building local institutions' capacity to generate sustainable peace, security, and economic growth. Conflict transformation is at the heart of this framework and focuses on converting the dynamics of conflict into processes for constructive, positive change. This is a process that reduces the means and motivations for violent conflict by focusing on the drivers of conflict while developing more viable, peaceful alternatives for the competitive pursuit of political and socioeconomic aspirations.[2]

There are five related aspects to successfully transforming conflict: first, assessing the situation to properly understand the drivers of conflict and underlying grievances and focusing efforts on them; second, achieving a comprehensive approach to build the requisite unity of effort; third, ensuring the legitimacy of the effort that underpins the operation; fourth, strengthening the host nation through capacity building; and last, conducting all of this under a rule of law that establishes the path. Contracting support must operate inside this framework for an operation to be a success. In particular, contractors should understand core grievances and sources of social and institutional resilience as well as drivers of conflict and mitigating factors so that they can focus on diminishing those drivers and developing sustained capacity. They need to accept the comprehensive approach that integrates the cooperative efforts of the departments and agencies of the US government, inter-government and nongovernment organizations, multinational partners, and private-sector entities to achieve unity of effort toward a shared goal. They need to continuously support the legitimacy of the operation because with legitimacy comes the support of the people. Contractors should be concerned with creating an environment that fosters host-nation institutional development, community participation, human resources development, and strong managerial systems. This must be accomplished under the rule of law that sets a path by providing the local populace with the confidence that they will be treated fairly and justly and can participate in a government that is accountable to them under the law. This forms the groundwork for legitimacy that is central to building trust and confidence among the people, upon which a stable state will develop.[3]

3. US Capacity and Capability to Achieve Success

The US Army doctrine lays out the tasks that the commander and staff must consider to achieve the conflict transformation described above. The Army's tasks are based on the essential goals of the Department of State's post-conflict reconstruction: security, justice and reconciliation, humanitarian assistance and social well-being, governance and participation, and economic stabilization and infrastructure. The military recognizes that civilian actors are better capable of carrying out most of the core tasks with the military in support. From a military perspective, the challenge is determining which of the whole-of-government tasks it should undertake, how those tasks should be prioritized and sequenced, and how to transition those tasks to either the host nation or other nonmilitary agencies.[4]

While this is understood, civilian agencies and military structures lack the capacity to provide the full range of skills needed to be successful in a stability operation. A study by the RAND Corporation has identified the lack of civilian and military capacity to perform these stability tasks and the need for the United States to project a US government civilian rather than military face in support of US foreign policy.[5] Yet there is little slack or flexibility in the civil capacity of the US government. Unlike the military, the civilian organizations are fully committed all the time. They have no excess capacity in training and preparation for emerging crises. Because every operation will be unique, requirements will differ. Trying to recruit, hire, retain, and maintain expertise across this wide range on the government books has not proved feasible. The only way to obtain quick response and reliable expertise is to contract. The development of in-house civil and military expertise in the US government will take time. And there is no certainty that the appropriate capacity or capability will be available when needed and in the quantity required. As the contracting business has expanded, talent has shifted from military, academic, and government agencies toward contractors. Now the only place some of the expertise exists is in the private sector

4. Advantages of Contracting

Many contractors use local nationals and can now provide critical knowledge of terrain, culture, language, social and political structures as well as specialized skills in the stability sector. The burden is on the contracting agency to ensure that this knowledge is present and appropriate. This is especially the case if the contracting agency is directly supporting the host nation and its institutions. It is incumbent on the contracting agency to take the time to insist on getting that expertise. The military and the other agencies of government must also be prepared to handle this contracting. As the Gansler Report of November 2007 has stated, neither the Army nor other federal agencies were prepared to transition to an expanded contracting approach that, in the wake of Iraq and Afghanistan, increased their contracting work load by over 600 percent. These organizations need a cultural transformation on how to appropriately use contracting to accomplish their mission.[6]

Contracting agencies can provide the US government with more flexible options than can be achieved inside the federal system. Contractors will use best business practices that will emphasize the most efficient and effective methods, processes, and activities to accomplish the task. Contracts can be quickly adapted to changing circumstances and packages of expertise can be tailored to meet situations to provide economy of force and force multiplier functions, if done properly. As needs become apparent—as they will in the fluid moments of a post-conflict stability operation—the US government can reach back, and using the correct contracting vehicle, obtain and apply the expertise needed. USAID has recognized this for years and the majority of its efforts are provided through implementing partners, be they private enterprise or NGOs.

One example of contracting in an "economy of force" situation was the response of the Economic Community of West African States (ECOWAS) to Liberia in 2003. It was in the US interest to stabilize the situation in Liberia, but global commitments limited what the United States could do directly. Additionally, the goal was to develop local capacity to deal with local situations. "The West African troops that were used for this operation were trained by private companies, flown to Monrovia by private companies, and once in Liberia were transported, based and supported locally by private companies."[7]

Another example, from Iraq, illustrates the flexibility of contracting in thinking outside normal ways of conducting business. Mr. Sam Miess worked for a private sector US/Iraqi joint venture company. A significant portion of his assignment involved developing static site and mobile security support teams for a commercial cellular phone conglomerate. Initial infrastructure construction included transmission towers and switching sites in metro Baghdad and Al Anbar Province, as well as several smaller regions licensed by the Iraqi Ministry of Communications in metropolitan areas of Karbala, An Najaf, Al Hillah, and Al Basra. This assignment included supervision of some 1,500 Iraqi personnel assigned to site security, personnel security escorts, and convoy security operations in these tasks. The security tempo of operations included over a hundred daily personnel and convoy security missions, achieving some eleven months of safe transits for Iraqi and Egyptian engineers and technicians in southern Iraq, metro Baghdad, and Al Anbar Province. He considers that the significant factor in the success in Al Anbar Province was the hiring of four resident sheiks. They served as local/provincial security consultants and provided a large, reliable cadre of guards (of over 150 personnel) and leased vehicles. The drivers operated in a low-profile mode from the eastern edge of Al Anbar Province and metro Baghdad to the westernmost reach of the cellular phone transmission towers installation project. This was possible because of the thorough vetting and hiring process.

In support of the rollout projects by the commercial cellular telephone conglomerate, security teams enabled large numbers of ten-to-twelve-day road assignments. These effected construction of the cellular phone transmission towers and switching stations along two major highways within the Euphrates River Basin to the respective border stations adjoining Syria and Jordan. These assignments were necessarily accomplished without any visible presence or involvement of Coalition forces operating in these areas. It was Mr. Miess's assessment that should the cellular phone construction and development have been linked in any noticeable manner to Coalition forces' activities, the results could have been disastrous. Hostile elements—insurgents and criminals—would have targeted the Coalition resources, convoys, and activities. Yet, in contrast, projects perceived to be normal commercial activities often escaped attack. A determining factor in these successes was clearly the advice of the four resident sheiks. These efforts were a recurring "win-win," contributing directly to key infrastructure development, and provided reliable employment for Iraqi nationals who in turn supported over ten thousand immediate family members.

5. Disadvantages of Contracting

Several factors can make contracting inflexible. Unlike in the case above, some practices use multiple agencies, multiple contractors, and multiple flows of money. These practices confuse unity of effort, obscure accountability, and can undercut legitimacy. A RAND study on training the Iraqi security forces illustrated such a practice. Without using the normal processes established for security assistance, no less than five US government agencies mixed and combined funds in creative ways using implementing contractors that produced a less than efficient and effective outcome.[8]

Contractors work for money and are interested in maintaining their hold on their contract even if it might not meet the client's needs or has ceased to embody best business practices. This can be counterproductive as it will have a direct effect on the people and the government of the host nation, thus affecting development of capacity and legitimacy. The struggle over training the Afghanistan police is a case in point, where various agencies squabbled over who should have the lead and what the outcomes should be. The Department of State contracted with DynCorp, a Virginia-based organization that previously contracted to train police in the Balkans and Haiti using former

US police officers and sheriffs. Afghanistan was a more challenging job than had been anticipated because the contract was under-resourced and limited in scope, a functional police system definition did not exist, and the Department of State short-staffed its contract-monitoring office in Afghanistan, limiting its ability to oversee and manage. The Department of Defense was not satisfied with the police that were certified as trained and local communities rejected them.

The Department of Defense decided to take over police training in the fall of 2009. General Richard Formica, commander of the Combined Security Transition Command–Afghanistan, sought to avoid a lengthy bidding competition. The general suggested folding the police training mission into an existing anti-drug and counter-terrorism program overseen by the US Army's Space and Missile Defense Command. Bids were limited to companies already under contract to the missile command, effectively excluding DynCorp. In the end only two firms bid: Northrop Grumman and Xe Services (formerly known as Blackwater). DynCorp filed a formal protest in December 2009. The Government Accounting Office accepted the company's appeal on March 24, 2010, and the contract with DynCorp was extended through July 2010 as the office continues to review the appeal. In February 2010 the State Department and DoD inspectors general issued a joint audit saying that the DynCorp program did not provide the Afghan police "with the necessary skills to successfully fight the insurgency and therefore hampers the ability of the [US military] to fulfill its role in the emerging national strategy."[9] While the debate, protests, and appeals proceed, what is the effect on Afghanistan? This should have been a comprehensive security sector reform package dealing with the police problem in a holistic way. It should have been synchronized with other aspects of rule of law in an appropriate social, cultural, and political context. It instead ended up dysfunctional and the system for fixing the matter is also dysfunctional.

The Afghan National Police (ANP) problem is an example of the lack of an operational concept for the employment of contractors in support of stability operations. Security sector reform (SSR) is a key operational outcome that should be planned, executed, and managed by the combined whole-of-government team in theater from the beginning. This program must support the overall legitimacy of the mission and the legitimacy of government processes. The ANP program jeopardizes those key constructs. SSR must be a line of effort supporting a major mission element in the whole-of-government plan. Contracting support needs to fit into that context as to its place, duration, and outcome. Unfortunately, our current doctrine offers little guidance to thinking conceptually about outcomes and the contractor role in those outcomes. The current military doctrine has few suggestions on how planning, preparation, execution, and management of a combined military and contractor operation should proceed.

6. The Current Concept for Employing Contractors

A great deal of attention has been paid to the proper oversight of contractors and ensuring compliance with their statements of work but little has been written about how contractors should be employed at the strategic or operational level. Both the Joint Counterinsurgency and Army operational-level manuals focus on sustainment and logistical support but do not describe how contracting can be used to support the larger operational concept. The manuals, however, come close to providing some guidance. They state that commanders need to be able to influence contractors' performance and contractors should be considered an extension of the agencies they support. The writers of the counterinsurgency manuals realize that DoD is only one of many in the operational area that will be contracting and urge commanders to identify the contractors working in their area, determine the nature of their contract and what the accountability mechanisms are, and figure how to coordinate.[10]

Contractors have been identified in several ways but none are useful in determining how they can best be deployed. Peter Singer divides contractors into military provider firms that provide direct support; military consulting firms that advise and train; and military support firms that provide supplemental military services. The International Peace Operations Association categorizes contractors as logistical and support companies, private security companies, and development and security sector reform companies.[11] US Army FM 3-100-21 *Contractors on the Battlefield* defines three types of contractors: theater contractors, who provide goods, services, and minor construction to meet the immediate needs of the commander; external contractors, who provide a variety of combat and combat service support; and systems contractors, who provide support to Army weapons, vehicles, and command and control systems.[12]

Another taxonomy focuses on whether the contractor is replacing key functions that should inherently be part of a government institution. A great deal of thought and effort has been put into determining which functions are inherently governmental and which are not. US law has sought to protect the core functions of the US government. Although there is a consensus that government legitimacy and accountability require that certain functions remain in governments' purview, there is no consensus as to what those exact functions are. Fontaine and Nagl (2009) write that "the U.S. Code uses the term [contractor] 15 different times; DoD requires over 120 pages to describe inherently governmental activities; and Federal Acquisition Regulation list 17 different examples."[13]

7. A Proposed Operational Concept for Contracting

Figuring out whether a function is inherently governmental or what type of contractor one is dealing with is not helpful for commanders or diplomats trying to put together and manage an operation that achieves US national strategic objectives. It is more useful to focus on the effects that contractors have on the operational environment. Whether the effects are direct or indirect should determine who should be doing the task, how it is to be done, how it is to be controlled, and how it is to be evaluated. Those effects can be indirect or direct.

(a) Indirect Contracting Effects

Indirect contracting effects are those that are coincidental to the purpose of the contract. If the contract's focus is on directly supporting the force with logistics, maintenance, base support, base construction, staff augmentation, and general housekeeping, then the effects on the operational environment will be secondary and a consequence of the original contract. Within the Department of Defense, anywhere from 75 percent to 90 percent of all contracting falls into this category. For other US government departments the percentage may be reversed or closer to even.

These types of tasks lend themselves to contracting and free soldiers, sailors, airmen, and marines to focus on planning and managing military power in support of the mission. The mechanisms that have been developed as a result of several investigations and boards—notably the Gansler Report in 2007—seem sufficient to establish policy while planning, integrating, and managing "indirect" contracting. Implementing actions by DoD included establishing the Joint Contingency Acquisition Support Office (JCASO), and co-locating fourteen joint operational contract support planner (JOCSP) positions with select combatant commands to improve operational contract support. The JCASO and JOCSP can also be leveraged to assist in planning, integrating, and managing contractors. Additional organizations and boards have been established for Afghanistan and Iraq to facilitate contracting.[14]

Although the purpose of this contracting is to support the force or agency, the effects on the operational area may be significant. As the framework above suggests, the purpose of the intervention is to develop local capacity while diminishing the drivers of conflict. The way that indirect contracting is carried out can assist or hinder the accomplishment of the mission objective. Just the presence of a large logistical military footprint in a country can alter the operational environment. If the command has not completed an in-depth assessment as the framework requires, then it will be operating in the dark and executing support contracts that will counteract what comprehensive development programs are trying to achieve. Displacement of local capacity or alteration of socioeconomic factors needs to be considered when building a large US footprint in a country.

In support of the 1994 Unified Task Force (UNITAF) deployment to Somalia, the United States established its support function in Mogadishu with no assessment of how this would affect the local social and economic situation in the country. Young Somali males were encouraged by the prospects of employment by the United States and moved into the city. Few of them were hired. The result was that they left their traditional clan areas, and the influence of clan elders, and became unemployed, shiftless, and desperate elements in the city. Here, warlords such as Mohammad Farah Aidid could prey upon them. The US military force was unaware that the presence of its support base and the lure of filling contracts were having a destabilizing social impact.[15]

Problems can also be more subtle and influence ideas and attitudes and affect the legitimacy of the operation. In both Iraq and Afghanistan rumors have been started at various times that the US command was contracting local men to work in the dining facilities, forcing devout Muslims to handle pork. Many of the workers were third country nationals, some of whom were also Muslim. Additionally, the many Muslim contractor employees who were secretaries and support staff ate at these dining facilities where the menu usually included forbidden fare. The "all American food" served at the dining facilities by the contractor not only provided evidence for the propagandist but also failed to build the local capacity that the mission was all about.[16]

Mechanisms have been established that should resolve some of the issues described above. A contract support integration plan is usually drafted by the command's logistical staff contracting personnel. Its purpose is to define key contract support integration capabilities necessary to execute subordinate joint task force's contract support integration requirements. These include command and control (C2) relationships, cross-functional staff organization (e.g., board, center, and cell) requirements, theater business clearance policies, and the like. The plan allows the joint force to define, vet, and prioritize its contracting requirements. This will be supplemented by the "contract management implementation plan." This plan is focused on government obligations under the terms and conditions of the contract to provide support (e.g., accountability, force protection, and government furnished equipment [GFE] to contractor personnel). The plan includes developing policies and procedures required to ensure proper integration of contractor personnel into military operations. These vehicles can provide appropriate guidance, but they must not be thought of as simply logistical support documents under the full purview of the J4 staff section.[17] Additionally, the recently published *Joint Forces Command Handbook on Contracting* offers recommendations and considerations for balancing contracting best practices with operational needs.

(b) Direct Contracting Effects

Direct contracting affects the host government, elites, and the people of the country and can exert immediate and long-term impact. The purpose of this contracting is to interact directly with the locals to produce an effect that supports mission accomplishment. Examples are training, educating, and advising host-nation military, paramilitary, and police forces; training, educating, and advising all ministries of the government, both national and local; conducting security sector reform that includes reform of penal, judicial, and legal codes as well as disarming, demobilizing, and reintegrating combatants into civil society; assisting in intelligence operations including interrogations; providing security forces both static and mobile in support of the movement and delivery of people and goods; and establishing and managing command, control, and communication centers. These tasks are most likely to require armed contractors and they are the contractors most likely to use deadly force. All of these activities directly advance the US mission in theater and therefore must be handled differently from the indirect contracting listed above.

Direct contracting must not be seen as substituting for a lack of US government capacity or capability in key areas. It must be seen as complementary. Therefore the US government must increase or develop capability based on a sound assessment of what portion of these tasks need a US government presence and what portion can best be conducted by contractors. The Civilian Response Corps (CRC) and Civilian Expeditionary Workforce (CEW) are initiatives by the government to increase that civilian capacity and they must take contracting into account.

(c) An Overarching Concept

In determining the composition and focus of contract support, we need to look at the framework outline above and ask the following five questions to develop the optimal combination of contract and government action that will accomplish overall objectives.

(i) How can contracting increase the short and long-term capability and capacity of the host nation and lead to ultimate host-nation ownership? This effort must focus foremost on building effective, legitimate, and resilient states. The ultimate responsibility for the stabilization and reconstruction process belongs to the host nation. This means all efforts of both the US government and its contractors must assist the host-nation government and civil society to ensure that they lead and participate in both planning and implementation. Utilization of formal and informal host-nation processes and structures builds ownership. The key issue is how to meet immediate needs yet also build long-term capacity. There is a tradeoff between relying on private contractors or US government agencies to meet the immediate needs of the population and thereby reduce the risk of instability, and laying the more time-consuming groundwork for state institutions to deliver essential services and strengthen the legitimacy and effectiveness of a nascent democracy. The other concern is determining what tasks should be contracted and what tasks need to remain in the hands of US government agencies. The USAID *Handbook on Governance* warns that contracting can lure talent away from the host-nation government and undermine host-nation agencies. Those responsible for contracting need to consider the long-term consequences of short-term actions.[18]

The tendency in Iraq and Afghanistan has been to contract US or third country nationals as an immediate solution to obtain stability. In June 2009 nearly 88 percent of contractors in Iraq and Afghanistan were third country nationals. Only 8 percent were local and the rest were US citizens. These figures were only for the contractors under DoD contract. This imbalance can create long-term issues for transitioning to host-nation ownership. The above example of cell phone protection provided a local option early on through the creative use of contracting. However, short-term needs must not cloud long-term goals. The operation must be carefully structured to avoid creating dependencies or retarding local contracting just to get things done immediately. Yet because of a need to get things done promptly, the trend is not to contract locally. From June 2008 to September 2009 the number of Iraqi contractors dropped by 57 percent while the number of US contractors increased. In January 2009 General Raymond Odierno issued a memorandum stating the need to employ more Iraqis to strengthen the economy and eliminate poverty. The percentage of Iraqis increased from 12 percent to 18 percent by September 2009, although this was still below the June 2008 level. This is a good trend.[19]

Increasing host-nation ownership requires a long-term commitment and continuity on the part of the contractor and US government agencies. Contractors should be able to nurture relationships and maintain records to sustain a long-term program. Short tours and the demands of military assignments get in the way of long-term relationships. In a two-year period in Afghanistan one contractor had to work with seven US/ISAF mentors working in the Afghan Ministry of the Interior. The military personnel were constantly rotated and reassigned, which inhibited cohesion and rapport building so essential to any credible mentoring and advisory role. On the other hand, there have been disputes among subcontractors who have terminated their contracts early. The first group of contractors assigned to protect Afghanistan's (then) new president Hamid Karzai resigned en masse at the end of the first rotation over a dispute with the parent company over vacation pay. It is therefore critical that the US government have transparency over contractors and examine their track record to optimize their effects.[20]

The division between what should be a US government face versus a contractor face must be determined by the outcomes. It is a US objective to instill a concept of democratic governance that is responsive to the needs of the people. A US government face in key advisory positions sends a message different from that conveyed by a contractor face, even if that contractor is a subject matter expert. There must be a collaborative approach and a determination as to what messages need to be sent to achieve the effect desired. A combination of current federal employees and contracted personnel providing expert assistance can work well to instill ideas of democratic control. It becomes difficult to convince local governors, chiefs of police, and politicians in Afghanistan not to hire their own illegal and unlicensed PMSCs when the United States leads by example in its dependence on such organizations. In his research paper on police training, Dennis Keller concluded that the US government must develop its in-house capability to train police to ensure continuity and provide training in non-permissive environments.[21]

One aspect sometimes overlooked in the rush to apply US government or contractor solutions is private-sector investment. The USAID handbook on post-conflict economic development states that "After security and macro-economic policies, the business enabling environment is the most important element for encouraging and sustaining growth."[22] Key issues include dealing with constraints and restrictions, fostering a supportive legal environment, ensuring stability, and understanding and responding to local demand by encouraging private investment rather than a quick fix using military or DoD contracted assistance. The trade-off that must be considered is immediate need versus long-term solutions. The following is an example.

> Post-conflict Liberia lacked capacity to provide power from the national grid, but private suppliers of electricity using privately-owned generators have served homes and small enterprises without legal sanction. Although less efficient and more expensive, such unregulated electricity generation was a very effective solution to the immediate problem of scarce electrical power. Reliance on informal-sector providers should be strongly encouraged and even legally recognized until local or national power supply capacity can be restored. At that point, larger producers offering lower costs can recapture customers from the less efficient producers. This pragmatic approach serves business by reducing the risk of inconstant electricity supply. It also creates a more business-friendly environment by permitting small-scale manufacturing and services to continue operating.[23]

(ii) Does contracting sustain the legitimacy of the host nation's governance and the legitimacy of the intervention force? Acts performed by contractors have directly affected the legitimacy of US operations in both Afghanistan and Iraq both positively and negatively. Local populations may see contractors as agents of the US government and therefore as a reflection of the policies of the US government. The effect is not just on the host country, but also

on international and US audiences.[24] For example, where service provision is contracted to a non-host-state actor, this carries the risk that the host government, both central and regional, will be perceived as having failed to provide services. This is why contract support and advice to government agencies can undercut the legitimacy of an operation striving to achieve host-nation ownership. Examples are foreign development of security forces, military and police. Peter Singer describes such a case in Papua New Guinea (PNG), where the government's security forces were unable to cope with an unstable situation on the island of Bougainville. In 1997, the PNG government hired a London-based private military contractor named Sandline International to bring order to the island. Instead, the company intervention caused a civil–military crisis because the population felt the government had abandoned its responsibilities. The legitimacy of the government and its security forces was compromised, causing countrywide instability.[25]

Use of third country nationals to the exclusion of locals must be managed so that it does not jeopardize legitimacy. The nationalities employed may also be a sensitive issue. The host-nation government cannot be seen to be selling out to third country nationals and not providing employment for its own people. Major-General Darryl Scott, former head of the Joint Contracting Command Iraq/Afghanistan, attempted to award over 75 percent of funds to host-nation contractors who encouraged the use of host-nation subcontractors.[26]

The manner in which contractors carry out their jobs can also adversely affect the legitimacy of an entire intervention. This is critical in fighting an insurgency as abuses committed by contractors—including those working for US agencies other than DoD—can strengthen anti-American insurgents. Many high-profile reports of private security contractors (PSCs) acting irresponsibly have concerned contractors working for the Department of State.[27] A recent US court decision dismissed the case against former Blackwater employees involved in the Nisoor Square incident in Baghdad during September 2007. Such incidents not only erode the legitimacy of US operations, but also the legitimacy of the Iraqi government. Even if these incidents are rare in the entire contracting effort, it only takes one or two such episodes to create a strategic problem.[28]

On the other hand, contractors can increase the legitimacy not only of the operation but also of the host-nation government by supporting host-nation ownership by placing a local face on projects, and backstopping the host-nation in areas in which it is weak, without the appearance of US government or military forces' involvement. An example was the security and movement of construction cranes from Jordan to Baghdad in 2007. The requirement was to transport safely six oversized construction cranes from a commercial shipyard in Aqaba, Jordan, to Baghdad and deliver them to the Iraqi Ministry of Housing and Construction. These oversized cranes required loading and transport on the largest available low-boy trailers, which moved at a top speed of 25 km/hr day and night. The convoy security planning and execution required careful coordination with the donor nation, the crane manufacturer, and the commercial corporation on behalf of the donor nation, as well as careful timing and implementation of the convoy transits.

Convoy security teams at times exceeded 75 personnel in twenty or more vehicles for each of the two convoys containing three cranes each. Again, these unique, very high-profile convoys were successful because of contracting through and with locals. The added benefit in this particular case was that a contractor was able to perform a specific service that was clearly outside the scope of US/Coalition security forces—since participation by US/Coalition resources would have significantly raised the risk of attack and failure. In this case, the area of operations expanded to a neighboring state. The contractors were not as constrained as government and Coalition partners, but were well suited to meld with the Theater /Coalition objectives and opportunities in the region. The contractors encouraged normal economic growth and trade and enhanced the legitimacy of local solutions.[29]

(iii) Can contracting diminish the drivers of conflict?   Contracting can diminish the drivers of conflict. Contract support is more able to think outside the box than military or US government agencies. Contractors have various flexible means to enhance capabilities for dispute resolution and support institutional and social resilience to transform conflict. This can allow grievances to be addressed through a system of justice that confronts impunity and develops opportunities to live in communities that have mechanisms for peaceful resolution of conflict. USAID has been using contracting in this area for years and partnering with such organizations as the US Institute of Peace through its centers for mediation and conflict resolution, centers for innovation, and centers for post-conflict peace and stability operations.

Success requires assessments to determine whether contractors are addressing drivers of conflict. Useful measures of effectiveness (MOEs) must be tied to stability and counterinsurgency goals—especially population-centric ones. Outcomes must be measured, not just inputs and outputs. *Inputs* refer to such elements as the amount of money and labor used to build a project. *Outputs* are the first-order results of an assistance program and include such examples as trained police officers and soldiers, functional courthouses, and refurbished prisons.[30] While helpful in some ways, they tell us little about the strategic effect of contracting efforts. Consequently, *outcomes* refer to conditions that directly affect the population.

> Outcomes are not what governments and international institutions do, but rather represent the consequences of their efforts. Without the ability to measure performance, policymakers lack an objective method for judging success and failure in ongoing crises, making midcourse corrections more difficult.[31]

(iv) Does contracting support a comprehensive approach to the problem? This presents the greatest challenge given that contractors are not in the military chain of command and that DoD is only one of many contracting entities in the operational area. Two improvements are required. One is to establish a central organization as the focal point for all US agencies contracting for an operational area. The other is the full integration of contracting in the military decision-making process and interagency planning framework.

Training police is a prime example of different organizations, different money streams, and different approaches that have not led to a comprehensive approach to achieve a desired effect. This was evident in both Iraq and Afghanistan. In the 1950s and 1960s, USAID was the sole agency managing police training. It had an in-house capacity of 590 trainers, which was sufficient to ensure a comprehensive approach. This is no longer the case. In current operations, police training as depicted in Figure 1 is a confusing, disconnected process.

The Department of State's International Narcotics and Law Enforcement Affairs (INL) contracted directly with DynCorp International to procure 690 international police liaison officers (IPLOs) to provide assessment, training, and mentoring for Iraqi police in the field. INL also funded the Department of Justice's International Criminal Investigative Training Assistance Program (ICITAP), which then contracted Military Professional Resources, Inc. (MPRI) to provide 192 international police trainers (IPTs), who provide assistance to Iraq's police training academies. INL also funded 143 border enforcement advisors, 123 of whom were provided by an INL contract with

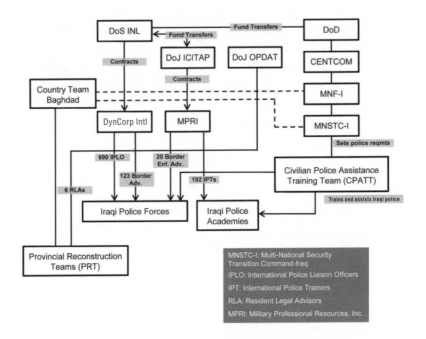

FIGURE 1. US Police Training and Assistance in Iraq

NOTE: This diagram is based on information available as of April 2007. Given the very ad hoc and fluid nature of the organization of the US footprint in Iraq, many of the relationships and numbers of police advisors contracted certainly have changed since then. Other civilian corporations in addition to DynCorp Intl and MPRI likely have received contracts for police training as well. There are undoubtedly other agencies and fund sources involved in some sort of police training not reflected in this diagram, as the situation is so complex it is difficult to identify and capture all police assistance and training in one diagram. The purpose of this diagram is not to provide a complete and precise layout of all police training in Iraq, but rather to illustrate some of the key funding and staffing relationships to demonstrate the complexity, interagency nature and cross-agency funding involved in US police assistance and training in Iraq.

SOURCE: Dennis E. Keller, *U.S. Military Forces and Police Assistance in Stability Operations: The Least Worst Option To Fill the U.S. Capacity Gap* (Carlisle, PA: PKSOI, April 2010), 17.

DynCorp, and 20 of whom were provided by an ICITAP contract with MPRI. The Department of Justice's Overseas Prosecutorial Development Assistance and Training (OPDAT) provided seven resident legal advisors (RLAs) to Iraq as of February 2008. Six RLAs were deployed to Provincial Reconstruction Teams (PRTs) in Iraqi provinces, with the seventh RLA in Baghdad.

The interagency arrangement is that the Civilian Police Assistance Training Team (CPATT)—a multinational advisory team—and Multi-National Security Transition Command–Iraq (MNSTC-I) set overall requirements for the civilian security development mission, whereas Multi-National Forces–Iraq (MNF-I) exercises operational control over international police liaison officers (IPLO) and international police trainers (IPT) supplied by INL and ICITAP, and ICITAP and INL manage and oversee contracts with service providers such as DynCorp and MPRI.

Clearly, there needs to be a central organization in the operational area that can be the focal point for all US government contracting as well as a touch point for coordinating with other contracting operations of other nations. This organization needs to be fully staffed, trained, and provided with the tools necessary not only to be a focal point for planning, but also for oversight and management across agencies. The need for such an organization has been identified for some time. The Special Inspector General for Iraq Reconstruction has called for such an organization in his report *Applying Hard Lessons*.[32]

The latter report also recommends developing an integrated planning and budgeting process so that all agencies of government can approach contracting in a holistic manner. This should help eliminate stovepipes and encourage uniform contingency contracting practices across all agencies.[33] Differences in planning approaches have proven to be an obstacle in the past. The purpose of various working groups spawned by National Security Presidential Directive (NSPD) 44 and the Interagency Planning Framework developed by the State Department Office of the Coordinator for Reconstruction and Stabilization (SCRS) was to resolve this problem by providing a framework. Their intention was that all government agencies could plan in a collaborative way using a similar approach. However, the Special Inspector General's report stated that "Although some improvements in the interagency planning process have been made since the 2007 GAO report, civilian agencies still lack sufficient capacity to develop and implement integrated plans for stability and reconstruction operations (SROs)."[34]

In the military, planning and management of contractors is most often associated with logistical functions and included in an annex to plans and orders. Since February 2006, DoD guidance has called for the integration of an operational contract support annex called Annex W into combatant command operational plans. According to a March 2010 GAO report, progress has been slow. The planners have largely assumed that this is the realm of the logistics community and therefore have not included these considerations in the base plan.[35] Direct contracting needs to be considered part of the joint operational functions that can provide effects in the operational space. Making "provisions for contracting management during planning"—as Army doctrine suggests—is insufficient. Contracting must be considered as another system that needs to be synchronized, integrated, and fused in accordance with the commander's intent. Contracting must be part of the single unifying concept of operations.

To accomplish these goals, contractors must be invited to become part of the operational planning group and integrated into the management of operations. Contractors who have direct influence in the operational area must be integrated as part of the seamless fabric of the operation. Trust and mutual understanding will be the cornerstone of the relationship. Although legally commanders can only exercise management control through supervisors employed by the contractor, the contract needs to specify that these supervisors are an integral part of the planning and control processes. This includes ensuring that contract activities are part of the common operating picture. This is not unlike operating with allied military forces. Initiatives to create a common operating picture have been tried in Iraq and Afghanistan but have not proved satisfactory. The US government has not been able to use an agreed whole-of-government planning and management system.[36]

Contractors can have different and often convoluted chains of command inside themselves. They are responsible to the entity that contracts them but may subcontract the work several times. Understanding who has responsibility to perform the contracted tasks can be a challenge. At least 135 companies have subcontracted on US government contracts in Iraq between 2003 and 2008.[37] The responsible contractor must be clear when anticipating direct contracting effects. There is a need for a contracting center and an essential requirement for a clear delineation of responsibilities and authorities—or in military parlance, a common operating picture. The authors of the Center for a New American Security working paper on contractors make the point that the military commander must go out of his/her way to determine a common contractor operating picture. This should include not only contractors who work for the US government, but also those who work for multinational partner governments, NGOs, and international organizations that have contracted security services in the past several years.

This will require knowing the basics: how many contractors are in a particular battle space, who and where they are, and what they are doing; how their responsibilities mesh with the authorities and responsibilities of American government personnel; and how operational plans incorporate contractors into the array of forces in play.[38]

(v) Is the combination of contracting and US government agency actions conducted in accordance with the rule of law? Peter Singer has identified private military firms as essentially an unregulated global industry. Yet operating within the rule of law is one of the basic tenets for a successful stability operation. There have been several initiatives such as the Montreux Document that have attempted to clarify the legal status of private military and security companies.[39] Legality and legitimacy go hand in hand, so the need to get something done immediately cannot overshadow the need to be well within international and local legal limits. This is especially the case with security and intelligence functions. Contractors must follow the legal authorities of the host-nation government as negotiated during periods of post-conflict confusion. They cannot be seen as being outside of these norms lest the legitimacy of both the host-nation government and the operation itself be compromised. An example is the Nisoor Square Incident. On September 16, 2007, Blackwater (now Xe Services) guards shot and killed 17 Iraqi civilians in Nisoor Square, Baghdad. The fatalities occurred while a Blackwater personal security detail (PSD) was escorting a convoy of US State Department vehicles en route to a meeting in western Baghdad with United States Agency for International Development (USAID) officials. This matter caused both the Iraqi and US governments to inquire into the legality and oversight of Blackwater's operations in Iraq. The Iraqi government called for justice and a review of the licensing of such organizations operating in Iraq. A US judge's decision to dismiss all charges against Blackwater defendants in January 2010 sparked outrage in the Arab world. There were bitter protests in Iraq, threats of legal action, and protests that these contractors were operating beyond legal oversight.[40]

States where private military firms are operating, such as Colombia, Afghanistan, and Iraq, are beginning to exercise their regulatory authority. That some states have weak regulatory authorities is not an excuse for taking advantage and using gaps. Companies operating transnationally can often avoid domestic regulations. Perceptions are a key factor. At a minimum, contractors should protect human rights and follow international human rights conventions. Accountability and transparency will go a long way to reassure clients and communities that they are supporting the emergent rule of law in post-conflict countries.[41]

8. Conclusion

Contracting is necessary to achieve goals in the new international security environment. Direct or indirect effects of contracting should be considered when determining who should be doing a task, how it is to be done, how it is to be controlled, and how it is to be evaluated. To ensure success, contracting needs to be fully nested in the goals and processes of the US government and synchronized and integrated into an overall stability operations framework. Contracting should not be considered a substitute for a lack of government capacity and capability, but part of a comprehensive approach to achieve US strategic objectives.

Glossary

Anbar Awakening Council: a movement started among the Sunni tribes in Anbar Province in 2005. Also known as the Sons of Iraq, the council became an ad hoc armed force across the country. Council salaries were initially paid by the US military and more recently by the Iraqi government as it attempted to integrate council members into government ministries and security forces. The council is credited with helping turn the tide of the insurgency in 2006.

capacity building: the process of creating an environment that fosters institutional development and strengthening of managerial systems. Capacity building is supported by appropriate policy and legal frameworks.

FM (Field Manual): published by the US Army Publishing Directorate, FMs contain detailed information and procedures of importance to soldiers serving in the field.

DoJ (Department of Justice): an executive department of the government of the United States established in 1870 with the Attorney-General at its head. The relevant act supplied the DoJ with control over all criminal prosecutions and civil suits in which the US has an interest. The DoJ has become the world's largest law office and is the primary agency for enforcement of US federal law.

DoS (Department of State): the US federal executive department responsible for international relations. The DoS was created in 1789 and was the first executive department to be established. DoS carries out functions similar to the foreign ministries of other states.

ICITAP: Department of Justice International Criminal Investigative Training Assistance Program.

IRFF2 (Iraq Relief and Reconstruction Fund 2): a fund created by the Emergency Supplemental Appropriations Act for the Defense and Reconstruction of Iraq and Afghanistan. The fund supplemented the Iraq Relief and Reconstruction Fund for which Congress had earlier appropriated $18.4 billion for the rebuilding of Iraq in Public Law 108-106.

ISFF (Iraqi Security Force Funding): a Department of Defense–administered program that permits the Multi-National Security Transition Command-Iraq (MNSTC-I) to provide assistance to the Iraqi Security Forces (ISF).

legitimacy: the popular acceptance of the authority of a governing regime or law. Legitimacy derives from three considerations: identification with government, based on history, culture and ideology; protection of the population (security); and the provision of essential services (e.g., economic opportunity).

P/INL (Department of State Bureau of International Narcotics and Law Enforcement Affairs): plays a role in police training.

QDR (Defense Quadrennial Review): a legislatively mandated review of the Department of Defense (DoD) strategy and priorities. The QDR sets a long-term course for the DoD as it assesses threats and challenges faced by the nation. The QDR re-balances DoD's strategies, capabilities, and forces to address today's conflicts and tomorrow's threats.

ROTC (Reserve Officers' Training Corps): a college-based, officer-commissioning program. Predominately in the United States, the ROTC produces officers for all branches of the US Armed Forces except the Coast Guard.

SSTR: security, stability, transition and reconstruction.

TITLE 10: the US law that identifies military organization and military powers, personnel, training and education, service supply and procurement for all branches of the service—Army, Navy and Marine Corps, Air Force and Reserve components.

UCC (Unified Combatant Command): A US joint military command composed of forces from two or more services and having a broad and continuing mission. A UCC is organized either on a geographical basis (i.e., an area of responsibility) or on a functional basis. A UCC (formerly known as a COCOM) is led by a combatant commander (CCDR) formerly known as a regional "commander-in-chief" (CINC). A CCDR is either a four-star general or admiral. The Unified Command Plan (UCP) is updated annually and can modify areas of responsibility or combatant command alignments or assignments. As of January 2008, there were ten Unified Combatant Commands specified in Title 10 and the latest annual UCP. Six have regional responsibilities and four have functional responsibilities.

USAID (United States Agency for International Development): the US government agency primarily responsible for administering civilian foreign aid. It was created by an executive order signed by President John F. Kennedy in 1961 to implement development assistance programs in areas authorized by Congress in the Foreign Assistance Act of 1961. USAID is an independent federal agency that receives its overall foreign policy guidance from the US Secretary of State. It supports economic growth, agriculture and trade; health and democracy; and conflict prevention and humanitarian assistance.

USG (United States government): the federal government of the United States established by the United States Constitution. The USG shares sovereignty over the United States of America with governments of individual US states. It dates from 1790 and is considered to be the first modern national federation.

Notes

1. Joint Forces Command, *Joint Operating Concept 2010* (Norfolk, VA, Feb. 2010) 17, 67; HQ Department of the Army, *Stability Operations FM 3-07* (Washington, DC: US Department of the Army, Oct. 2008), 1–3.

2. FM 3-07, 1–3, 1–6.

3. FM 3-07, 1–2 to 1–10. Beth Ellen Cole, *Guiding Principles for Stabilization and Reconstruction* (Washington, DC: US Institute for Peace, 2009), 7.

4. Office of the Secretary of Defense, *Quadrennial Defense Review Report 2010* (Washington, DC, 2010).

5. Thomas S. Szayna, Derek Eaton, James E. Barnett II, Brooke Stearns Lawson, Terrence K. Kelly, and Zachary Haldeman, *Integrating Civilian Agencies in Stability Operations* (Santa Monica, CA: RAND, 2009).

6. Commission on Army Acquisition and Program Management in Expeditionary Operations, *Urgent Reform Required: Army Expeditionary Contracting* (Washington, DC: Department of the Army, Oct. 31, 2007), 11, 18, 22.

7. Doug Brooks and Gaurav Laroia, "Privatized Peacekeeping," *Business & Economics* (Summer 2005): 123.

8. Szayna et al., *Integrating Civilian Agencies in Stability Operations*, 65.

9. Christine Spolar, "Military Training of Afghan National Police Mired in Contract Dispute," *Huffington Post Investigative Fund* (Feb. 22, 2010), http.huffingtonpost.com/2010/02/22/military-training-of-afgh_n_471519.html (accessed April 2, 2010); T. Christian Miller, Mark Hosenball, and Ron Moreau, "The Gang That Couldn't Shoot Straight," *Newsweek* on-line (Mar. 19, 2010), www.newsweek.com/id/235221 (accessed April 2, 2010).

10. U.S. Joint Chiefs of Staff, *Joint Operations JP 3-0* (Washington, DC: JCS, Feb. 13, 2008), III-34; U.S. Joint Chiefs of Staff, *Counterinsurgency Operations JP 3-24* (Washington, DC: JCS, Oct. 5, 2009), IV-4.

11. Volker Franke, *Security by Contractor: Outsourcing in Peace and Stability Operations, Case Study 1* (Washington, DC: Center for Complex Operations, National Defense University, 2010), 5, 6, outlines the different taxonomies.

12. HQ Department of the Army, *Contractors on the Battlefield FM 3-100-21* (Washington, DC: US Department of the Army, Jan. 2003), 1–3.

13. Richard Fontaine and John Nagl, *Contractors in American Conflicts: Adapting to a New Reality* (Washington, DC: Center for a New American Security, Dec. 2009), 13.

14. Joint Forces Command, *Handbook for Private Security Contractors in Contingency Operations*, (Suffolk, VA: JFCOM, Feb. 23, 2010), chap. 3.

15. Walter Clarke, Deputy Chief of Mission, US Embassy, Somalia during Operation Restore Hope, and Mark Walsh, District Administrator in Baidoa, Somalia, for UNOCHA, interviewed by the author in 2000 at the Peacekeeping Institute, Carlisle Barracks, PA, USA, where all three were employed.

16. Rajiv Chandrasekaran, "Excerpt: Imperial Life in the Emerald City: Inside Iraq's Green Zone" (Oct. 10, 2007), linked from Media Bistro Home page at www.mediabistro.com/articles/cache/a8798.asp (accessed April 2, 2010); and author's interviews in Afghanistan, 2002.

17. J4 – Integrates logistics planning and execution in support of joint operations to drive joint readiness, maximize the Joint Force Commander's freedom of action, and advise the Chairman of the Joint Chiefs of Staff on logistics matters. It works across the myriad of organizations in the logistics Community of Interest (COI) including the Office of the Secretary of Defense, the Services, the Combatant Commands, the industrial base, and multinational and interagency partners. See Joint Forces Command, *Handbook for Private Security Contractors in Contingency Operations*, chap. 3.

18. Office of Democracy and Governance, Bureau of Democracy, Conflict, and Humanitarian Assistance, *USAID Guidance For Democracy and Governance Programming in Post-Conflict Countries* (Washington, DC: USAID, Feb. 2009), 14.

19. Joint Forces Command, *Handbook for Private Security Contractors in Contingency Operations*, chap. 3; Moshe Schwartz, *Department of Defense Contractors in Iraq and Afghanistan: Background and Analysis* (Washington, DC: Congressional Research Service, Dec. 14, 2009), 11; Moshe Schwartz, *The Department of Defense's Use of Private Security Contractors in Iraq and Afghanistan: Background, Analysis, and Options for Congress* (Washington, DC: Congressional Research Service, Dec. 19, 2010), 8.

20. Sam Miess, "A Contractor on the Battlefield: Observations and Opportunities" (Carlisle, PA: PKSOI), unpublished research paper 22; Renée de Nevers, "Private Security Companies and the Laws of War," *Security Dialogue* (Oslo: International Peace Research Institute, 2009), 176, http://sdi.sagepub.com/cgi/content/abstract/40/2/169 (accessed April 5, 2010).

21. Dennis E. Keller, *U.S. Military Forces and Police Assistance in Stability Operations: The Least Worst Option To Fill the U.S. Capacity Gap* (Carlisle, PA: PKSOI, April 2010), 18. These institutional shortfalls in US capacity for police training were identified by a State Department official at the Conference for Building Capacity in Stability Operations: Security Sector Reform, Governance, and Economics, jointly sponsored by AUSA, CNA, and PKSOI, Washington, DC, April 6, 2009.

22. Office of Economic Growth, Bureau for Economic Growth, Agriculture and Trade, *A Guide to Economic Growth in Post-Conflict Countries* (Washington, DC: USAID, Jan. 2009), 58.

23. Ibid, 60.

24. Fontaine and Nagl, *Contractors in American Conflicts*, 17.

25. P. W. Singer, *Corporate Warriors: The Rise of the Privatized Military Industry* (Ithaca, NY: Cornell University Press, 2003), chap. 12.

26. Ibid, 17.

27. Schwartz, *Department of Defense Contractors in Iraq and Afghanistan*, 3.

28. David G. Savage, "Judge Throws out Blackwater Guards' Charges in Iraqi Deaths," *Los Angeles Times*, Jan. 1, 2010, http://articles.latimes.com/2010/jan/01/nation/la-na-blackwater1-2010jan01 (accessed April 5, 2010).

29. Miess, "A Contractor on the Battlefield," 6.

30. First, second, and tertiary effects of actions are used to understand the implications of actions. Some changes are induced by an initial set of actions (first order effects), others because the initial set of actions creates effects (second order), and so on. The Joint Publication 1-02 *Department of Defense Dictionary of Military and Associated Terms* uses this terminology in relation to pre-planned options that allow responses to expected changes in the operating environment.

31. Seth G. Jones, "Stabilization from the Bottom Up," Testimony before the Commission on Wartime Contracting in Iraq and Afghanistan (Washington, DC: Feb. 5, 2010), 6; C-Span http://cspan.org/Watch/Media/2010/02/22/HP/A/29827/Wartime+Contracting +Commission+Examines+Stabilization+in+Iraq+and+Afghanistan.aspx.

32. Special Inspector General for Iraq Reconstruction, *Applying Iraq's Hard Lessons to the Reform of Stabilization and Reconstruction Operations* (Washington, DC:

Feb. 2010), 18; United States Department of State and the Broadcasting Board of Governors, Office of the Inspector General, *Report of Kabul Embassy Inspection Afghanistan # ISP-I-10-32A, February 2010* (Washington, DC: Department of State, Feb. 2010).

33. Stovepipes in this context refers to rigid funding allocations that allow hoarding of funding for one organization or division over another. This can cause redundancy and inefficiency.

34. Special Inspector General for Iraq Reconstruction, *Applying Iraq's Hard Lessons*, Part II, 13; William Nash et al., *Improving U.S. Post-Conflict Capabilities: Report of an Independent Task Force* (New York: Council on Foreign Relations, 2005).

35. US Government Accountability Office, *Warfighter Support: DOD Needs to Improve Its Planning for Using Contractors to Support Future Military Operations* (Washington, DC: GAO, Mar. 2010), 4, 20.

36. HQ Department of the Army, *Mission Command: Command and Control of Army Forces FM 6-0* (Washington, DC: US Department of the Army, Aug. 2003), 5–23; Hon. Christopher Shays, Co-Chairman, Commission on Wartime Contracting, "An Urgent Need: Coordinating Reconstruction and Stabilization in Contingency Operations," Testimony before the Commission on Wartime Contracting, Feb. 10, 2010 (Washington, DC, transcript), 2; Col. George Franz, Lt. Col. David Pendall, and Lt. Col. Jeffery Steffen, "Command's Information Dominance Center Fuels Comprehensive Operations," *SIGNAL Magazine*, www.afcea.org/signal/articles/templates/Signal_Article_Template.asp?articleid=2250&zoneid=292 (accessed April 5, 2010).

37. De Nevers, "Private Security Companies and the Laws of War," 177.

38. Fontaine and Nagl, *Contractors in American Conflicts*, 14.

39. International Committee of the Red Cross, *The Montreux Document: On Pertinent International Legal Obligations and Good Practices for States Related to Operations of Private Military and Security Companies during Armed Conflict* (Geneva, 2009).

40. James Risen, "Interference Seen in Blackwater Inquiry," *New York Times*, Mar. 2, 2010, www.nytimes.com/2010/03/03/world/middleeast/03blackwater.html (accessed June 1, 2010).

41. James Cockayne and Emily Speers Mears, *Private Military and Security Companies: A Framework for Regulation* (New York: International Peace Institute, Mar. 2009). See 3, 8, for discussion of the lack of transparency.

5 Sharing the Same Space

The Evolving Relationship between US NGOs, Battlefield Contractors, and US Armed Forces

Samuel A. Worthington

1. Introduction

Armed forces, private contractors, and the personnel of international non-profits, commonly known as international nongovernmental organizations (NGOs), can find themselves operating in the same hostile environments in places like Iraq and Afghanistan. Just how well these communities understand and effectively relate to each other in a challenging shared space has a direct impact on their missions and, from the NGO perspective, on the safety of their staff. US-based NGOs are advancing a dialogue with the US military to clarify and reinforce that they are global development and humanitarian actors in their own right. US-based NGOs are independent actors with distinct missions unrelated to shifting US foreign policies, and do not see themselves as force extenders or even as an extension of US smart or soft power.

Nor should the US NGO community be confused with US government contractors. Private contractors, from security firms to other for-profit development actors, also operate in complex conflict environments. These contractors further complicate the work of international NGOs and, at times, actually make their operational environment less secure. Even if some NGOs accept US government grants to carry out their work, there are important distinctions between contractors and nonprofits based on the missions, staffing, program approaches, funding, and relations with local populations. This chapter reviews the evolution and current state of relations among US NGOs, private contractors, and the US military in undertaking humanitarian and development work abroad in close proximity to one another. In failing to understand and support the role of US NGOs, the growing role for the military in relief and development projects has resulted in increased tensions among development actors and with local communities overseas, reduced security for NGOs, growing US government reliance on for-profit contractors, and less effective, less sustainable development projects.

2. How International NGOs Approach Their Work

Every day, a myriad of diverse US-based NGOs deliver programs in countries and communities around the world. They work to promote development, fight poverty, and reduce human suffering. Their ranks include humanitarian NGOs that help those fleeing or caught up in war. Because US NGOs have worked in war zones for decades, they have successful and proven methods of designing programs, building relationships with communities, and functioning in complex, often-hostile environments. US NGOs carry out significant humanitarian programs separate from US government-funded efforts, using resources raised from other governments, UN agencies, and primarily private sources, including the American public. In fact, the entire US NGO community raised $11.8 billion in private funding in 2008.[1] With this support, US NGOs are exploring best practices, adhering to international standards, advancing partnerships with other international NGOs, and helping communities that are often not reached by US diplomats and development officials. Humanitarian NGOs form a community whose members often engage local civil society in countries at war as they serve the needs of vulnerable people or displaced populations.

As the largest coalition of US-based NGOs focused on the world's poor and most vulnerable people, InterAction represents a diverse group of US NGOs with programmatic expertise in a wide range of areas including disaster response, protection and promotion of human and other rights, aid to refugees and the displaced, hunger and food security, health, agriculture, gender equity, climate change, the environment, and urban poverty. Collectively, as one of the largest global aid donors, InterAction members recognize that complex global challenges are interconnected. They engage a wide number of other development actors such as national governments, USAID, the World Bank, UN agencies, and other multilateral institutions, and—in some circumstances—the US military.

International NGOs work through and in partnership with local community-based groups and local governments, and the vast majority of their in-country staff are local citizens. The face of the typical aid worker employed by a US NGO is a local one. US NGOs often maintain a long-term presence in communities—well past the life of any one project—to develop trust, increase knowledge, and improve results. At the same time, they have a global reach that spans both developing and industrialized countries. The largest of these global NGOs have experience working at scale. With high public profiles, reputations for strong financial management and global operations, and a proven commitment to mission, these organizations often attract the bulk of private donations and are acknowledged leaders in the field. Many US NGOs use these private donations to fill the gaps where the host government lacks the capacity to provide basic services in order to ensure that healthy livelihoods are sustained within that country. It would be a mistake to think of US NGOs solely as alternative social service providers, or as contractors simply implementing the wishes of a donor government. These organizations realize the value of government-distributed services and are committed to both the needs of the local population and to building the capacity of host governments.

The work of NGOs is driven by a set of common values and, by necessity, NGOs are committed to independence. US NGOs do not implement the policies of donor governments except to the extent the policy coincides with their own policies. They do not provide political, economic, or military information for purposes other than to serve strictly humanitarian ends. They have to strike a delicate balance between local community groups or civil society, which may be opposed to the policies of their government, and as implementing partners to donors interested in strengthening a national government. Like the military, NGOs subscribe to a strict set of principles and standards of behavior. For NGOs these are based on the *Code of Conduct for the International Red Cross and Red Crescent Movement and Non-Governmental Organizations in Disaster Relief.*[2] This code of conduct binds signatories to key principles:

The Humanitarian Imperative: Every human being has the right to humanitarian assistance when affected by a natural or man-made disaster;

Independence: NGO staff must not knowingly allow themselves to be used by governments or other groups for non-humanitarian purposes; and

Impartiality: Assistance is provided according to need, without regard to race, religion, nationality, or political affiliation.

NGOs are also guided by the principle of "Do No Harm," which requires the humanitarian community to ensure that it minimizes any negative ripple effects of its activities. It is crucial that humanitarian assistance projects be designed in a way that does not exacerbate the conflict or tensions that are present in the program environment. For example, improperly designed food aid distributions can result in beneficiaries becoming the targets of violence or theft. Distribution sites and methods must be carefully scrutinized to ensure that food can be distributed fairly and equitably and that it can be transported and stored with minimal risk to the recipients. Equally, it is possible to design projects that bring communities together to achieve common goals, such as rehabilitating markets or health facilities that serve several communities that might be at odds with one another. By supporting the communities to design and carry out mutually beneficial projects, NGOs can promote joint project "ownership" that can lead to better communications among participant communities.

Many US NGOs got their start responding to humanitarian crises and that capacity remains a core competency. They quickly and effectively leverage large amounts of private resources to save lives and address basic needs when an emergency occurs. They have played a leading role in the creation of global norms for humanitarian action, such as the Sphere Project standards,[3] and in improving the quality of the transition from relief to recovery and long-term development. As part of a recent study by the Hauser Center for Nonprofit Organizations at Harvard University, NGO leaders and senior staff, funders, and scholars concurred on the following distinctive attributes that are important for this discussion.[4]

(a) US NGOs are at the forefront of "what works," seeding and replicating innovations in services and service delivery to improve the lives of the poor. Their approach—based on reciprocity and grounded in the participation of the poor themselves in designing and delivering programs—has underscored the importance of cultural sensitivity in program design and shaped best practices in development.

(b) US NGOs play an important role in strengthening civil society in developing countries. NGOs help create, strengthen, and expand the efforts of local NGOs through training, mentoring, and providing access to funding and global expertise. By helping local communities organize themselves to set priorities, meet social needs, and urge their governments to use public funds effectively, international NGOs aim to play a significant role in improving the accountability, transparency, and responsiveness of local and national governments.

(c) US NGOs act as conduits for sharing knowledge and innovation. NGOs, because of their long presence in many developing countries, are important vehicles for sharing ideas across borders and adapting successful approaches to other places. As a link to outside influences and expertise, they help build the capacity of local NGOs and governments to improve their results.

To a large extent how NGOs approach their work is defined by their missions to save lives, to do no harm, to protect the least fortunate, and to improve the well-being of the poor. It is also shaped by decades of experience that confirm what works, how to ensure acceptance and ownership of a program and lasting results, and importantly how not to put the lives of their staff and partners at greater risk. The ability of professional NGOs to operate in war zones is shaped by competencies that in many ways are as highly developed as those found in the military.

3. Sharing Humanitarian Space

The relationship between the US NGOs and private contractors operating in war zones ranges from one of little or limited contact, to one marred by real concerns that continue to cause significant challenges to the NGOs' operational environments. Some parts of the contractor community, notably firms that provide equipment maintenance or engineering support to the Department of Defense (DoD), have little contact with US NGOs. For-profit contractors with strong development missions often provide an important range of services similar to those offered by US NGOs. At times these contractors and NGOs work together to deliver programs funded by the US Agency for International Development (USAID). For-profit contractors that deliver development-focused contracts adopt program objectives and goals that are identical to those of their financial supporters and they are often closely identified as institutions committed to deliver services for USAID or other US government agencies. These firms often operate as a direct extension of the US government, their primary stakeholder.

The practices of other private contractors, such as private security contractors or private organizations that work closely with US intelligence services, are of real concern to NGOs. Private firms that work in communities where NGOs operate may take actions that increase the distrust of local governments and populations. This can significantly hinder the ability of NGOs to work safely in complex operational environments. This is because these private actors are often armed but do not wear uniforms, without which they are not easily identifiable as different from the NGO community. It is very easy for the local population to see armed foreign actors and their actions as typical of the entire international community working in that area, so any misbehavior or threatening perception attributed to private security firms is also attributed to the NGO community. The blurring of lines between private contractors and US NGOs may be one of the factors that have increased the number of attacks on NGOs and deaths within the humanitarian community.

Private contractors' approach to their programs is shaped by the time frame of a contract and an interest to effectively deliver services on time and make a profit. NGOs take a different approach. They generally make a long-term commitment to a situation, often with their own resources, acquire a deep understanding of local societies, employ largely local staff, and design projects with community participation and cultural sensitivity to ensure sustainability. US-based NGOs also take care to demonstrate cultural sensitivity in war-torn countries. NGOs know how to recognize and support effective indigenous solutions or recommend tested approaches to complex humanitarian challenges. They can involve local groups and hire locally, and do so much more efficiently than governments or the US armed forces or contractors that choose to employ American or foreign labor. US NGOs operate in a multilateral context with the local host government taking the lead and, when local institutions are not functioning, with the UN. The primary operational driver for all international NGO humanitarian and development efforts is the central role of a local community and its willingness to design, shape, and "own" the program. We have seen the strength of this approach in many complex war environments, including in Afghanistan. In 2009, an InterAction member was operating in Helmand Province in Afghanistan on a project to improve local agricultural productivity. All of its vehicles were stolen by the local Taliban forces. After a direct intervention by local tribal leaders the vehicles were returned to the NGO's staff. The tribal leaders wanted "their agricultural program" to continue and in this case had the influence to resolve the matter.

US government efforts to advance a counterinsurgency strategy and win "hearts and minds" to meet a primary goal of US foreign policy is at odds with, and can seriously hinder, the efforts of an NGO focused on the humanitarian and longer-term development needs of a local community or vulnerable population. While often sharing the same goals as US development policy, as a non-state actor, and a private nonprofit entity, an NGO's independence from US foreign policy goals is often critical to its ability to deliver programs. In a conflict environment, whether the US military has a mission that is at odds or aligned with an NGO's people-focused mission, the result is often the same: the humanitarian space and NGO access and ability to operate are compromised. Moreover, the military generally lacks specialized humanitarian and development expertise. Quick-impact projects and other force protection activities motivated by security objectives often undermine sustainable development projects and relationships built by NGO workers over years or decades. Well-intended projects may have negative consequences and are often unsustainable due to the military's short-term goals and high turnover.

One example illustrates the point. The isolated desert town of Nema, 1,100 kilometers from the Mauritanian capital Nouakchott, has a new US-funded health clinic. The clinic sits abandoned. The local population cannot access the clinic because the Ministry of Health cannot support its operation. The Ministry of Health was not consulted before construction began; funds to build the clinic came from the DoD and Special Forces soldiers coordinated the construction through the Mauritanian Ministry of Defense. While a critic might say the soldiers should have coordinated with USAID, there is no USAID office in Nouakchott; there is no USAID presence in all of Mauritania with which the soldiers could coordinate their activities.[5] The story of the Nema medical clinic is as much about the diminished civilian capacity of US foreign assistance as it is about the increased militarization of aid.

Short-term, "quick-impact" projects typically implemented for security purposes tend to be unsustainable because they address the symptoms of poverty, as opposed to its underlying causes. Such projects do not usually encourage community ownership and participation, which are essential for addressing the long-term needs of beneficiaries. In our experience, these projects often restrict the access of NGOs, undermine the development process by failing to promote sustainability, and even hinder the mission of preventing further conflict. Blurring of boundaries between civilian and military actors in the field has heightened insecurity for NGO staff, local partners, and beneficiaries and has thus restricted access to the communities served.

The US military should not consider US NGOs as "force extenders" or assume their cooperation and must leave development and humanitarian response efforts to US civilian agencies and NGOs as much as possible. US NGOs recognize that communication with military actors is mutually beneficial when conducted in a neutral space, and guidelines exist to help improve NGO–military relations when they operate in a common space. Although the InterAction–DoD Guidelines apply in hostile and potentially hostile environments, they are useful in any complex environment where the Western military is present. The US armed forces should focus on their mandate and their strengths, including security sector reform, maritime security, and military-to-military training in civilian protection and HIV/AIDS. However, when the US military does engage in humanitarian and development activities, its involvement should be approved, led, and coordinated by civilian agencies. The military should develop clearly specified security and developmental objectives before implementing any assistance project and should regularly monitor progress towards achieving these goals.

4. NGO Safety

Diminishing security is a major factor that shapes the evolving US NGO–US military–US contractor relationship. Sadly, humanitarian workers are at times directly targeted in today's world. In 2008, 260 humanitarian aid workers were killed, kidnapped, or seriously injured in violent attacks. This toll is the highest in the last twelve years of tracking, and has risen most dramatically in the past three years. The 2008 fatality rate for international aid workers exceeds that of UN peacekeeping troops and the 155 American soldiers killed that year in Afghanistan.

Instead of using weapons or armed guards for their security, NGOs rely on an "acceptance" model that rests upon perceived impartiality and the trust of the communities in which they work. In conflict situations, NGO staffs, who as mentioned above are primarily local,[6] are careful to keep their distance from the military and its private contractors and limit their contact to discussions on how to address civilian needs. This is not an expression of hostility to or lack of respect for the US military and its role, but instead is a necessary security measure. NGOs use a security approach that depends on community acceptance and working in an impartial manner while adhering to other humanitarian principles, including working independently from political and military actors and providing aid based on need and not affiliation with parties to a conflict, ethnic or other groups.

Contractors that work closely with the US military or intelligence services often deliver services and social programs accompanied by private armed security firms. US NGOs seeking an often elusive degree of neutrality in war zones need to manage the perception of a local population that is influenced by the practices, both positive and negative, of the private contractor community. When private contractors working with a very different approach to security become indistinguishable from the US military or intelligence services, their actions can decrease the security of US NGOs. Other belligerents do not see the line between the independent NGO working with a local population on a humanitarian mission and a private agency delivering a contract that is part of a US counterinsurgency strategy.

In very challenging environments InterAction members must establish themselves as neutral and independent actors to remain functioning humanitarian organizations. Indeed, in order to collaborate most effectively with local communities, most US NGOs do not hire major security firms or carry guns or other weapons. This acceptance model, while clearly under pressure, has limited the fatality rate of InterAction member organization staff to around one person killed each year for every 5,000 employees around the world. The vast majority of the lives lost are local staff working in or near conflict zones. Impartiality combined with community ownership makes any attack on a project, or on an NGO staff, an attack on the community itself.

As NGO immunity decreases, humanitarian NGOs are being forced to adapt their security approaches. The acceptance model is being challenged on multiple fronts. Whether it is the direct targeting of NGOs by radical groups, or the shrinking of neutral humanitarian space by private contractors and the US armed forces, the safety of NGO staff in war zones continues to deteriorate. Assailants appear to be motivated by politics (opposed to what NGOs do and/or what international NGOs represent) or greed (NGOs have assets they want). According to the Humanitarian Policy Group, violent incidents against humanitarian workers that were judged as politically motivated rose from 29 percent of the known total in 2003 to 49 percent in 2008.[7] Aid groups are now being attacked because they are perceived as Western or in partnership with

Western governments and militaries, even though the majority of NGO staff is local or national and dedicated to helping their families and fellow citizens and developing or reconstructing their own countries.

Local staffs working for an NGO are now seen as legitimate targets and the result can be horrific. Some groups even appear to be targeting aid organizations *because* they are providing aid. Just after my tenure at Plan USA ended, that global organization's Mansehra, Pakistan, field office was targeted by terrorists using a coordinated attack with small arms, hand grenades, and explosives. Four local staff lost their lives and eight more were injured in the attack. Reasons attributed for the attack included the fact that Plan ran educational programs for girls and employed women. The funerals for the local staff drew large numbers of mourners. This year in the same region, World Vision was the target of an attack that killed seven local staff. Most attacks or threats do not make the news. NGOs typically take the precaution of not publicizing security incidents, in part to avoid rewarding the attackers with publicity or endangering the lives of hostages. This was the case for another InterAction member specifically targeted in recent years for providing health services to women on the Afghanistan/Pakistan border. It has suffered hostile attacks that have gone unpublicized.

In response to these increased security threats, InterAction members have developed and adopted minimum standards for security systems and reached an accord with the United Nations called "Saving Lives Together," which formalizes UN-humanitarian NGO security cooperation efforts.[8] Wars in Afghanistan and Iraq followed by periods of widespread insurgency or unrest have led the US NGO community to conclude that too much proximity to the US military increases the likelihood of such attacks. This, in turn, led to negotiations between US NGO leaders and senior officers of the US military and the development of formal guidelines for how NGOs and the military can coexist in hostile areas. The exercise that produced these guidelines is discussed in a later section.

5. The Evolving US NGO–US Armed Forces Relationship

The NGO community is used to operating in areas in which various militaries or armed groups are active. Many US NGOs routinely work alongside UN peacekeeping missions in nations recovering from war. In Afghanistan,

NGOs work near NATO forces, including US and foreign militaries. Just how this relationship evolves will shape the nature of the humanitarian enterprise. It is a relationship that is increasingly founded on mutual respect and the recognition that an ongoing dialogue between the US military and US NGOs is essential. However, tensions continue as government officials—in Congress and the executive branch—who do not know or appreciate the NGO approach call for US NGOs to work closely with the US military and for the US military or private contractors to undertake tasks that could be better performed by civilian agencies. From the NGO perspective there is the need to affirm "humanitarian space"—the ability of NGOs to gain access to and help populations in need. In complex environments where both the military and NGOs are active, that vital humanitarian space continues to shrink. Without clear boundaries, in complex conflict environments where the military, private contractors, and NGOs are active, NGOs no longer have the acceptance of the local population and the security they need to operate.

NGO–military dialogues have occurred in many different contexts, and have achieved differing degrees of success. In the early years of the Afghanistan and Iraq conflicts, there was a great deal of confusion about the roles of the various actors on the ground. NGOs that had been working with local communities for decades were suddenly finding US military forces in their humanitarian space. Armed soldiers visited NGO project sites without prior notice, intelligence officers dressed as civilians or riding in white vehicles sought to blend in with expatriate aid workers, private contractors engaged in security operations harmed the local population, and soldiers approached community leaders with large sums of money to carry out short-term projects with little or no prior consultation. NGOs feared that the local population would fail to distinguish between civilian and military personnel and projects. Indeed, some armed groups ascribed political motivations to the NGOs and tried to block their activities, sometimes violently.

After a number of serious security incidents, the leadership of several InterAction members asked for a meeting with the Department of Defense to discuss the increased risk for their field staff. In March 2005, a number of CEOs met with flag officers from the Office of Secretary of Defense and the Joint Chiefs of Staff to discuss how the US military and the US NGO community could engage in a dialogue to improve the military's understanding of the NGO and UN roles in Afghanistan and Iraq. They wanted to determine how the military and NGOs might continue to work in the same geographic

areas without undermining the NGOs' ability to access vulnerable populations or carry out their work. The United States Institute for Peace (USIP)
agreed to facilitate this NGO–military dialogue and participants from the US
NGO community, DoD, USAID, and the State Department thus formed the
Civil–Military Working Group.

The USIP Civil–Military Working Group's first major task, aside from providing a general forum for learning, was to create guidelines that would suggest a set of "rules of behavior" for both the US military and NGOs to follow
when in non-permissive environments, as well as a set of procedures for communication between the two communities. In July 2007, after months of work,
the *Guidelines for Relations between US Armed Forces and Non-Governmental
Humanitarian Organizations in Hostile or Potentially Hostile Environments* was
approved by the deputy secretary of defense and the InterAction board of directors. Work began in earnest to ensure that these guidelines were included in
pre-deployment briefings for personnel of both US NGOs and the US military
and incorporated in US military doctrine. The USIP Civil–Military Working
Group was invited to review the US Army Stability Operations Field Manual
(FM 3-07) and substantive comments from the humanitarian community
(NGOs, UN, and others) were incorporated into the final document. Since
2008, a similar process on the subject of "Inter-organizational Coordination
during Joint Operations" (JP 3-08) brought together representatives of US government civilian agencies, NGOs, UN agencies, and others to ensure that each
new version of the doctrinal publication reflected the learning and output of the
various civil military dialogues, including the US NGO–military forum.

The *Guidelines for Relations between US Armed Forces and Non-
Governmental Humanitarian Organizations in Hostile or Potentially Hostile
Environments* has become one of the InterAction website's most popular
downloads.[9] Divided into two parts, the publication provides recommended
guidelines and processes. The recommendations for the military include the
following key points:

- Consistent with military force protection, mission accomplishment,
  and operational requirements, the US armed forces should wear
  uniforms or other distinctive clothing to avoid being mistaken for
  NGO representatives.
- Arrange visits to NGO sites in advance, respect NGO views on the
  bearing of arms within NGO sites, give NGOs the option of meeting

with armed forces personnel outside military installations for information exchanges.

- Avoid interfering with NGO relief efforts directed toward segments of the civilian population that the military may regard as unfriendly, and respect the desire of NGOs not to serve as implementing partners for the military in conducting relief activities.

- Additionally, the military should not display NGO logos on any military clothing, vehicles, or equipment[10] and should not describe NGOs as "force multipliers," "partners" of the military, or in any other fashion that could compromise their independence and their goal to be perceived by the population as independent.

The *Guidelines'* recommendations for NGOs are just as critical and shape the behavior of humanitarian NGOs working in war zones. Among other points they include the following requirements:

- NGOs should use their own logos on clothing, vehicles, and buildings. When security conditions permit, NGOs should make prior arrangements for visits to military facilities/sites, should minimize their activities at military bases that might compromise their independence, and should limit travel in military armed forces vehicles to the extent practical.

- NGO personnel should not wear military-style clothing. Protective gear, such as helmets and protective vests, ought to be distinguishable in color and appearance from US armed forces items.

- NGOs should not have facilities co-located with facilities used by US armed forces personnel.

- The guidelines also state that NGOs may, as a last resort, request military protection for convoys delivering humanitarian assistance, take advantage of essential logistics support available only from the military, or accept evacuation assistance for medical treatment or to evacuate from a hostile environment.[11]

The *Guidelines* also provides a framework for communication between US NGOs and the US military. This option for communication and information sharing is often essential to both parties. For example, to the extent feasible, NGO liaison officers should participate in security briefings conducted by US armed forces to share unclassified information. This information may concern security conditions, operational sites, locations of mines and unexploded ordnance, humanitarian activities, and population movements. NGOs will provide information to the military insofar as it facilitates humanitarian operations and the security of staff and local personnel, and liaise with military commands to avoid conflicts between military and relief operations. US forces will provide military assistance to NGOs for humanitarian relief activities *in extremis* when civilian providers are unavailable or unable to do so. One recognizes that such assistance will not be provided if it interferes with higher-priority military activities.

Finally, the *Guidelines* offers recommendations covering procedures for NGO–military dialogue during contingency planning for Department of Defense relief operations in a hostile or potentially hostile environment; NGO and military access to each other's assessments of humanitarian needs; and NGO liaison with combatant commands engaged in planning military operations in hostile or potentially hostile environments. It also identifies possible organizations that could serve as a bridge between NGOs and US armed forces in the field such as USAID's Office of Military Affairs, the State Department's Office of the Coordinator for Reconstruction and Stabilization (S/CRS), and the UN's Humanitarian Coordinator. Progress has been made and the ongoing dialogue is educating the military that NGOs are key stakeholders in their own right. With better management at the strategic level these efforts can result in improved instructions to NGO and military personnel at the operational and tactical level in the field. If successful, this ongoing dialogue will help shape a military doctrine that recognizes the independent role of US NGOs, not as force extenders but as legitimate global actors.

6. Increased Militarization of US Aid

One driver for the need to clarify the separation between NGOs and the armed forces is a shift in Washington in how foreign assistance is allocated. Since September 11, 2001, there has been a growing militarization of foreign assistance with resources moving toward the DoD. Only in the past three years have resources been invested in USAID, but certainly not at the expense of DoD funding. DoD's share of US Official Development Assistance has increased dramatically as have its relief, development, and reconstruction assistance. This has been implemented through programs such as Section 1207 aid for the purpose of funding stabilization projects,[12] the Commander's

Emergency Response Program (CERP), and the Combatant Commander's Initiative Fund. Both of the latter are highly flexible funding sources for carrying out projects through the activities of troops on the ground and soldiers working out of heavily fortified government bases guarded by the military. Outside of capital cities, these bases are staffed by interagency personnel called Provincial Reconstruction Teams or PRTs. There has been a growth in defense funding for the military in coordination with private contractors for relief, reconstruction, and development purposes. Most US NGO leaders would prefer to see these tasks funded in the international assistance rather than the defense part of the federal budget and administered by civilian agencies. Secretary of Defense Robert Gates has stated that "America's civilian institutions of diplomacy and development have been chronically undermanned and underfunded for far too long—relative to what we traditionally spend on the military, and more important, relative to the responsibilities and challenges our nation has around the world."[13]

Secretary Gates first emerged as one of the strongest advocates for increased civilian-led development funding in 2007. At that time, Gates warned of the "creeping militarization" of US foreign policy and called on US leaders to increase the State Department's funding. "One of the most important lessons of the wars in Iraq and Afghanistan is that military success is not sufficient to win," said Gates, delivering the annual Landon Lecture at Kansas State University.[14] The US military has shouldered much of the burden of the lack of US government civilian expertise, Gates said, adding that US civilian agency efforts in Iraq and Afghanistan—such as the creation of the interagency provincial reconstruction teams—had been done "ad hoc and on the fly in a climate of crisis." He has subsequently called for developing "a permanent, sizeable cadre of immediately deployable experts with disparate skills" integrated with the US government, private sector, and institutions of foreign countries that receive assistance.

The secretary of defense's warning has echoed throughout the Washington, DC–based development community. In an article published in August 2008 and directed toward the new administration, Sheila Herrling and Steven Radelet of the Center for Global Development stated that as aid to Afghanistan, Iraq, and other "frontline" states such as Jordan and Pakistan has increased, responsibilities for oversight of these assistance programs has shifted to or been shared by DoD. This has resulted in increased fragmentation of aid programs across the US government.[15] Even as DoD grew into a major development funder in recent years, USAID—once one of the premier foreign assistance agencies in the world—weakened. The size of its staff decreased to less than half of what it was fifteen years ago. Recent reports from the RAND Corporation and the Government Accountability Office, as well as numerous media accounts, speak of the lack of appropriately trained officials and vacant language-specific positions at US embassies around the world, and the consequences of those shortfalls. Inexperienced US diplomats instead of seasoned professionals or aid experts frequently fill positions in conflict zones. The diminished US government civilian capacity led the military to fill a perceived vacuum.

Today, USAID operates to a certain degree as a contracting agency, dependent on the work of private firms, with only limited ability to provide strong input to US policies and programs in countries that are top foreign policy priorities, such as Pakistan. The Obama administration has promised changes to strengthen and elevate development. Important staffing capacity is being added at USAID and Rajiv Shah, the new administrator, is a frequent guest at the White House and inter-agency National Security Council meetings. Yet, USAID no longer operates as an independent agency and instead is increasingly managed as an annex of the Department of State. The US government's development efforts are now inextricably tied to US foreign policy, a direction that has given prominence to presidential initiatives launched by the Bush and Obama administrations in the areas of HIV/AIDS, malaria, global health, and food security. At the same time, however, development work in South Asia has become increasingly comingled with counterinsurgency security aims, largely delivered by for-profit contractors.

As a general rule, experienced civilian agencies, especially USAID with its professional development and humanitarian staff, are best placed to support effective development, humanitarian assistance, and reconstruction activities that address the needs of the poor. USAID is currently trying to shift away from the privatized aid model of past decades and, if implemented, its dependence on private contractors should decrease.[16] Whether these shifts toward less privatization by USAID and the State Department will result in increased humanitarian space for NGOs to operate is unclear. In countries that are strategically important to the United States, a counterinsurgency policy that includes services through private contractors is likely to continue. Given that the role of DoD in foreign aid is unlikely to decrease in the near future, the US military must demonstrate the utility of specific development, humanitarian, and reconstruction activities it undertakes to advance security interests. DoD should monitor and evaluate its own development and humanitarian activities according to international standards and best practices, including how such activities impact the poor in local communities and their relationship with US NGOs.

7. Evolving and New Challenges

How the US military relationship with the US NGOs evolves over time and particularly in war zones will continue to face significant challenges. It is, however, important to recognize that the US military does have an important role to play in humanitarian relief and to a lesser extent in development efforts. In large-scale natural disaster emergencies, such as the recent Haiti earthquake and in the aftermath of the 2004 tsunami in Aceh, Indonesia, the US military often plays a crucial role in disaster response by providing logistical resources, air and marine transport capabilities, and engineering services. In such settings, relations and operational norms between the military and NGOs have become increasingly routine. Three months after the Haiti earthquake, I witnessed a massive feeding program run by Catholic Relief Services (CRS). With troops from the 82nd Airborne Division observing, between 5 to 20 meters away hundreds of volunteers from the Pétion-Ville Club/Golf Delmas camp worked in shifts to help CRS staff provide one month's ration of food to 60,000 people. Everyone knew their role, from the author of a "no guns" sign over the NGO offices to important security provided by troops watching the operation.

Yet when humanitarian and development efforts are delivered under the auspices of national security logic or a counterinsurgency doctrine the results are often problematic. Even the US Army Field Manual No. 3-24 states that counterinsurgency "operations can be characterized as armed social work."[17] When US armed forces were asked by President George W. Bush to lead the humanitarian intervention after the war in Georgia, NGOs experienced a wide range of complications. In post-conflict and disaster settings, NGOs, the UN, and other customary actors employ a well-developed coordination infrastructure that expedites the delivery of services to the distressed population. The US military showed limited interest in working with the UN humanitarian coordination infrastructure and the US NGOs kept on getting mixed messages as to who was in charge. Even more problematic was that most "aid" provided by the military was in the form of Meals Ready to Eat (MREs). US NGO claims that they were neutral held little sway as the NGOs brought MREs through Russian checkpoints and ran into significant challenges. The development and humanitarian role for DoD to eventually adopt within the US government is still under much debate. Whatever the outcome, the creeping militarization and contractorization of US aid raise significant concerns among international NGOs.

The effectiveness of the Department of Defense and its contractors as a development actor remains very much in question. Even after years of programs in Iraq and Afghanistan, DoD does not appear to have a methodology for measuring the effectiveness of its development and humanitarian activities. Twenty-first-century best practices and sensibilities require that we assess the community's needs for the type and placement of buildings and for goods and services, including education and skill development. The military lens is necessarily different and often cannot be the same as the lens through which US civilian aid workers and the NGO community view their tasks. The unfortunate result can be unusable buildings that feed the very "hard" feelings that the military's diligent work was intended to transform.

For NGOs one of the greatest challenges to their relationship with the US government has been recent attempts by the government to track NGOs in war zones and to require that NGOs gather intelligence on their staff and partners. These unilateral incursions into NGO space are seen as necessary anti-terror efforts. Of primary concern is the new Partner Vetting System (PVS) and the Synchronized Pre-Deployment and Operational Tracker (SPOT). Both systems may decrease the ability of US NGOs to work in complex operational environments and if fully implemented have the potential to mar their relationship with various US government agencies, including with the US military.

Though it has not yet been implemented, the PVS would affect every organization that applies for USAID and US State Department funding working around the world. It would require US organizations and their sub-grantees to turn over private information concerning their officers and employees to the US government, to be vetted against a classified list of terror suspects maintained by the Terrorist Screening Center. According to the language in the proposed regulation, USAID partner organizations will have to vet every person on their boards of directors and every staff member, including both American citizens and foreign nationals. This system will negatively impact life-saving humanitarian programs and will jeopardize the lives of American foreign aid workers abroad. Since the information collected under the PVS could be shared with other agencies for law enforcement purposes, the system will almost certainly create the perception that US NGOs are collecting sensitive information on behalf of US law enforcement and intelligence agencies. This will undoubtedly increase the risk of violence that the employees of US NGOs already face around the globe. The consequences of USAID's implementation of the PVS will cripple US humanitarian and development programs in places like Iraq, Afghanistan, Pakistan, and the Horn of Africa. The PVS will undermine the ability of NGOs to partner effectively with communities, especially in potentially hostile environments.

SPOT is broader, more ambitious, and therefore even more problematic to US NGOs. SPOT was originally conceived as a centralized information database to assist the Department of Defense in "planning force protection, medical support, personnel recovery, and logistics support of contractors who accompany the US Armed Forces."[18] In July of 2008, SPOT was accepted as the common database in a memorandum of understanding (MOU) signed by the Department of Defense, Department of State, and USAID and was expanded to include grants with them for services in "an area of combat operations." The implications of SPOT are troubling to the US NGO community. First, the SPOT database requirement that NGOs provide detailed personal information for a military database on both their international and local staff poses legal difficulties arising from privacy protections of host-country and third-party governments and undermines working relationships built on trust with local communities and civil society organizations.

Second, as the system is owned and maintained by DoD with its contents subject to interagency information-sharing and intelligence gathering operations, SPOT fails to consider some significant implications for, and special challenges to, US NGOs, which are dedicated to working as neutral actors in the field. SPOT blurs the distinction between civilian-led humanitarian and development activities and US military operations and creates a perception that NGOs are closely associated with the military and US intelligence agencies. NGO managers collecting the data may also feel that their personal security will be compromised if they are perceived to be agents of US intelligence and law enforcement agencies or the US military, whereas security contractors may not object to the collection of such data. As the relationship between the US military and NGO community evolves, it remains imperative to continue civilian–military dialogues to promote common interests and mutual respect.

8. Conclusion

A complex global environment often drives the US armed forces and US NGOs to share a common space in volatile and dangerous environments. In these conflicts, contractors often serve as adjuncts to the military or US government agencies and their modes of operation often make it unclear as to whether they are part of the military, the US government, or an NGO. All of these actors implement programs or operate in war zones, often driven by similar operational cultures but with significantly different missions, language, and approaches. While this chapter has focused on tensions, it is important to acknowledge the similarities between NGOs and the US armed forces. Both face the prospect of losing colleagues and both have developed professional operating standards to work in challenging environments. Recognition of these similarities has led to a degree of mutual respect, which has formed the foundation for an ongoing dialogue. It is a dialogue that has led to operational guidelines that define aspects of the relationship but which, in many ways, the US NGO community does not have the staffing resources to advance or make operational.

However, with different understandings of basic language and tactical concepts and the complicating factor of contractors, misunderstandings at the operational field level are bound to occur. The US military understands the term "humanitarian assistance" quite differently than the NGO community, and this is often a source of confusion between the two communities. For NGOs humanitarian assistance is a precise term focused on needs-based assistance in a relief setting. For the military it includes the gamut of relief, reconstruction, and development efforts, but focused on short-term gains and not on expressed need. With such different starting points, even with agreed upon guidelines in place, the US NGO community does not have the capacity to educate an officer operating in a theater so that s/he understands an NGO's role and why US NGOs need to be treated differently than contractors.

In many places, NGOs have had staff on the ground far longer than the armed forces. US NGOs with a long-term established presence have inevitably gone local and become part of the surrounding culture. The face of a US NGO operating in Darfur or Afghanistan is a Darfuri or Pashtun aid worker. The challenges to this local face are very real in conflict zones. A US military-led Provincial Reconstruction Team (PRT) convoy recently put lives at risk by forcing a van off the road in Afghanistan. It was not apparent to the US military that the van had been filled with Afghans who included the leadership of an important US NGO-led development effort. NGOs' reliance on an acceptance model where they operate as part of a community is an approach that goes far beyond security needs. Local ownership is in many ways at the heart of the principles that guide international NGOs. The principles of impartiality and independence are intimately tied to the effectiveness and ability of US NGOs to function in war zones. In many ways how the US military and its contractors relate to the NGO community has a direct impact on the ability of NGOs to deliver programs.

This long-effective NGO model is now increasingly at risk as illustrated by increasing deaths, kidnappings, and threats to humanitarian workers. Add to this volatile mix the increased funding for development delivered by the US military in combat zones, the moves in Washington to "vet" NGO workers to meet US intelligence and anti-terror needs, and the undesirable effects of some contractor conduct. As a consequence, the NGO worker is placed at greater risk. The guidelines and conversations happening now must be broadened and enhanced, with the US armed forces showing greater willingness to understand and respect the role of US NGOs. The US NGO community in turn must reach out to all parties in conflict zones. National security imperatives and efforts to save lives can coexist if NGOs have the space to operate.

Notes

1. Hudson Institute Center for Global Prosperity, *Index of Global Philanthropy and Remittances*, 2010, www.hudson.org/files/pdf_upload/Index_of_Global_Phil anthropy_and_Remittances_2010.pdf.

2. InterAction, *US Civilian-Military Guidelines* (Washington, DC, July 2007).

3. www.sphereproject.org (accessed Sept. 7, 2010).

4. Sherine Jayawickrama and Neil McCullagh, *What Makes International NGOs Distinctive? Contributions, Characteristics, and Challenges* (Cambridge, MA: Hauser Center for Nonprofit Organizations, Harvard University, Oct. 26, 2009).

5. *MD*, InterAction, Aug. 2009.

6. InterAction members have over 13,000 staff in Afghanistan. Approximately 1 percent are expatriates.

7. Abby Stoddard, Adele Harmer, and Victoria DiDomenico, *Providing Aid in Insecure Environments: 2009 Update*, HPG Policy Brief 34 (Humanitarian Policy Group, April 2009), 5.

8. IASC Security Task Force (Nov. 22, 2006), www.reliefweb.int/telecoms/intro /wgetminutes/Saving%20Lives%20Together.pdf.

9. http.interaction.org/document/interaction-us-civilian-military-guidelines-july-2007.

10. This does not preclude the appropriate use of symbols recognized under the law of war, such as a red cross, when appropriate. US armed forces may use such symbols on military clothing, vehicles, and equipment in appropriate situations.

11. Provision of such military support to NGOs rests solely within the discretion of the US military forces and will not be undertaken if it interferes with higher-priority military activities. Support generally will be provided on a reimbursable basis in accordance with applicable US law. InterAction does have a formal relationship with the United Nations called "Saving Lives Together" that requires UN forces to help and evacuate US NGO personnel in a manner similar to UN staff.

12. This program is referred to as Section 1207 in reference to the section of the *Defense Authorization Act* of FY 2006 where it was first introduced and authorized.

13. July 15, 2008, US Global Leadership Campaign Tribute Dinner.

14. Remarks as Delivered by Secretary of Defense Robert M. Gates, Manhattan, Kansas (Nov. 26, 2007), www.defense.gov/speeches/speech.aspx?speechid=1199.

15. The largest increases by far have been for Iraq, which received $11.2 billion in 2005 and $4.7 billion in 2006 (including about $4 billion in debt relief). Aid to Iraq accounted for nearly a third of all US foreign assistance during those two years. Funding for Afghanistan reached $1.3 billion in 2005 and $1.4 billion in 2006, making it the second largest recipient of US assistance. See Sheila Herrling and Steven Radelet, "Modernizing U.S. Foreign Assistance for the Twenty-first Century," chap. 10 in Nancy Birdsall (ed.), *The White House and the World: A Global Development Agenda for the Next U.S. President* (Washington, DC: Center for Global Development, 2008), www.cgdev .org/content/publications/detail/16560/ (accessed: Sept. 7, 2010). Steve Radelet currently works as a development specialist in the secretary of state's office and Sheila Herrling is a member of the Millennium Challenge Corporation's senior leadership team.

16. Remarks by Dr. Rajiv Shah, administrator, USAID, "Reinventing USAID to Meet 21st Century Development and Security Challenges," National Press Club (Washington, DC, June 18, 2010). Similar remarks have been made about Department of State reform: Remarks, Secretary of State Hillary Rodham Clinton, "On Development in the 21st Century," Center for Global Development, Washington, DC (Jan. 6, 2010), 7, 12.

17. *Counterinsurgency*, US Army Field Manual 3-24, A-7, sect. A-45: 298.

18. "What is SPOT?" M67004-10-R-0003, Attachment #2: http.neco.navy.mil/ synopsis_file/M6700410R001310-R-0013_-_Atch_2_Contingency_Ops_(SPOT).doc (accessed: Sept. 7, 2010).

6 PMSCs and Risk in Counterinsurgency Warfare

Kateri Carmola

Blackwater operated in Afghanistan without sufficient oversight or supervision and with almost no consideration of the rules it was legally obligated to follow. . . . Even one irresponsible act by contractor personnel can hurt the mission and put our troops in harm's way.

Senator Carl Levin, Chairman of the Senate Armed Services Committee, February 23, 2010[1]

I got [sic] sidearms for everyone . . . We have not yet received formal permission from the Army to carry weapons yet but I will take my chances.

Blackwater subsidiary VP Brian McCracken in an email to staff in Afghanistan, November 2008[2]

1. Introduction

Nearly ten years into the wars in Afghanistan and Iraq, the widespread use of private military and security companies (PMSCs) by the US military and other agencies continues unabated, despite many questions raised about their presence. The precise number of the firms employed, and the number of people they employ, remains indeterminate. Congressional committees, think tanks, and the military itself have worked to classify and evaluate the firms and their proper role, as the military tries to rethink its overall strategy and tactics on the ground in these conflicts. In this context, are these companies a part of a risk reduction strategy or are they a risky business? Five years after Frank Camm and Victoria Greenfield first published their RAND study assessing "the comparative risk of contractors on the battlefield" the question remains: do PMSCs reduce risk or increase risk? Or do they do both simultaneously?[3]

The fatal shooting in May 2009 of two Afghan security guards by members of the Paravant Security team provides a good example of risky behavior in the name of risk reduction. The two men were shot and a third injured in the midst of a drunken brawl by two security contractors who had been illegally armed. Their weapons had been taken with company—but not Afghan government—permission from an Afghan Army weapons depot. The incident inflamed anti-American sentiment in the region. In the aftermath, it was discovered that Paravant had decided that it needed weapons despite the lack of approval or permits. Paravant was hired to reduce the risks to those whom the company was guarding, while also trying to reduce risks to company employees. Yet the company heightened operational risk in the counterinsurgency campaign.

In this chapter I argue that the organizational risk cultures of PMSCs do not align with that of the military, nor with the needs of counterinsurgency warfare, despite the fact that these companies are hired in order to reduce certain risks that I will specify below. Counterinsurgency warfare attempts to support existing governments to create legitimacy, security, and trust within the borders of a state. The strategy required, as General Petraeus repeatedly reminds readers of the newest Army *Counterinsurgency Field Manual,* is "varied and adaptive," requiring a "mosaic approach" that is "multifaceted and flexible" and in which "coordination and communication" must replace the traditional military posture of "command and control."[4] Those engaged in counterinsurgency warfare attempt to gain control of an area by defeating an enemy insurgent group militarily *and* politically, by building—or rebuilding—the legitimacy of a new or weakened central government, as it also tries to establish security for the people.

Counterinsurgents aim to win the support of people (their "hearts and minds") caught in a civil war, and to provide security and services to people who often have no experience of these things. Counterinsurgency warfare thus ostensibly relies on the creation of trust in, or at least the reliability of, the central government; it replaces risk and insecurity with trust and security.[5] Counterinsurgency warfare combines three ideas that have come and gone in the last two decades: the idea of "humanitarian war," nation-building, and low-intensity conflict. As Celeste Ward notes, "[counterinsurgency warfare] is on the verge of becoming an unquestioned orthodoxy" and it has become the "new COIN of the realm."[6]

PMSCs operate in the midst of these campaigns in many ways. But this chapter will focus on security contractors who perform three types of tasks—security contractors who work as bodyguards, as convoy security guards, and as CIA contractors on the ground. They are often armed, mobile, and integrated into the larger mission. Their presence adds a level of complexity into an already complex environment. They also introduce types of organizations whose risk cultures are misaligned with those of the military. The addition of these types of security contractors into this complex COIN environment—an environment already populated by a dizzying array of multi-national, multi-agency, multi-service, civilian, military, governmental and nongovernmental actors on the ground—only exacerbates the clash of organizational cultures with very different understandings of both risk and regulation.

In order to make this argument I will explain how PMSCs are embedded in the risk industry in both concrete and abstract ways. I will then show how their organizational profiles clash with the demands of counterinsurgency warfare. Finally, I will compare the organizational cultures of risk and regulation that define the regular military and PMSCs, to demonstrate how contracts are ineffective risk management tools in the specific environment of the complex war zone.

2. PMSCs and the Risk Industry

Risk, strictly defined, is an idea that enables a certain kind of rational approach to the possibility of danger, accidents, and things going wrong. Decision making in all kinds of areas—finance, personal relationships, public policy, and on the battlefield—is now seen as something to be structured through a series of questions about risks and benefits, and how to minimize one while maximizing the other. The formal process of risk management almost always includes some sort of follow-up: What happened? How could it have gone differently? What did we learn? Organizations often have specific processes associated with this reassessment.[7] Importantly, these processes usually include a way in which blame can be allocated. For many theorists of the "risk society," risk management is just a peculiarly modern method for managing blame, and enabling a story to be told about what went wrong.[8]

This way of thinking has become an emblem of modernity, a "new lens through which to view the world," as risk scholar Bridget Hutter recently put it.[9] Although it can certainly be argued that risk management tools allow for a more rational approach to assessing dangers, their usefulness is limited. Risk management rubrics tend to privilege certain kinds of information over others, especially information that can be calculated, or "rationally" assessed, and this, as many scholars have pointed out, can result (paradoxically) in "risky decision making."[10] And sometimes, excessive thinking about risks can lead to risk averseness and prevent action altogether. It can also lead to a false sense of security, and can give organizations the impression that what is in fact incalculable and uncontrollable has been controlled.[11] In the military, debate about risk has taken on a new urgency as the institution tries to transform a risk-averse culture into one that is capable of carrying out the demands of counterinsurgency warfare.

PMSCs are embedded in this world. They are part of what has been called a "risk industry," or those businesses that offer to analyze and minimize, in this case, security risks. Practically speaking, many PMSCs work as consultants with insurance agencies that provide political and terrorism risk insurance to large multinational corporations, nongovernmental organizations, and employees of the media. For instance, Fox News journalists in Iraq were guarded by security guards provided by a British PMSC named AKE. AKE (Andrew Kain Enterprises Ltd.) is a security and risk management company based in Hereford, UK, but with a branch office housed in the same building as political risk insurance giant Lloyd's of London. AKE's own in-house insurance agents advertise that they offer "preferential terms" for the insurance policies taken out by those guarded by their AKE's bodyguards.[12] Many PMSCs began primarily as risk consultants, and then expanded their profile to include the provision of armed security teams. These firms advise clients about avoiding risks, and supply the necessary risk reduction practices to lower insurance premiums.[13]

The second way in which PMSCs play a role in the "economy of risk" is more abstract. These firms are part of what scholars have called "risk transfer warfare," wherein certain kinds of risks that the military is unable to take are outsourced to other groups or organizations.[14] The political risks of casualties are minimized when contractor casualties are not officially reported. And especially in counterinsurgency operations, where military members must expose themselves to more risks, and in which any casualties are harder to justify politically, outsourcing casualties makes sense. PMSCs can bear the risk of casualties precisely because of their organizational risk culture, and the way that culture attracts, or accepts, risks that the military sheds or needs to avoid.[15] I will detail this in Section 3 below. Less obviously, contractor crimes—which include fraud and bribery as well as murder, detainee abuse, and destruction of property—do not get attributed to the military per se; the risks of blame and legal liability are seemingly offloaded onto PMSCs. But because of the multiple layers of unclear regulations that apply to them, detailed below, PMSCs seem to offer a limited liability option: they look able to accept certain risks—and blame—that the military cannot, precisely because it is so difficult to prosecute them for the crimes they do commit.[16] As part of this risk transfer, PMSCs are useful as organizations that have an organizational risk profile that, as I will explain, can better absorb the risks associated with casualties and crimes.[17]

PMSCs are thus embedded in the risk society in both a practical and more abstract—but no less significant—fashion: they are prominent members of the risk industry, working as risk consultants and analysts, as well as providing risk reduction in the form of security details and bodyguard work. More abstractly, they serve as organizations whose profile invites the transfer of certain risks associated with counterinsurgency warfare: the risk of casualties and the risk of lawless behavior.

The practical question remains, however: do PMSCs help or harm the military's counterinsurgency efforts? In the remaining pages, I argue that today's counterinsurgency campaigns introduce a new way of thinking about military victory, and that this new conception exaggerates the differences between organizations with different risk postures, making PMSCs all the more risky insofar as they harm the overall mission of those they are contracted to support. In the next section I analyze the relatively new restatement of counterinsurgency doctrine and practice, and see what kinds of risk cultures are demanded by such a doctrine. After that I will turn to analysis of the contrasting organizational cultures of the military and the PMSC industry.

An organizational risk posture results from the combination of four distinct things: the *cultural attitude* toward risk in general, the specific *type of organization* used to carry out the task (including the accountability or liability structures embedded in it), the *environment* in which the task will be carried out, and the overall *mission*. Given the environment of counterinsurgency warfare, the organizational structure of PMSCs may allow certain risks to be offloaded onto them, but this practice undermines the stated mission of these campaigns. Below I explain how.

3. Risk and Counterinsurgencies

The wars in Iraq and Afghanistan are both now properly termed counterinsurgency campaigns. Although counterinsurgencies, including the US war in Vietnam, have a long history of Western involvement, they are wars fraught with contradiction and complexity. They have become the new face of what a decade ago was called "humanitarian" warfare, with efforts to bring peace, stability, legitimacy, and aspects of a functioning state to areas controlled by insurgents acting on a host of their own competing goals (though usually resolutely anti-American). In Iraq, there were at least four broad types of insurgents: Ba'athist former military men who fought a guerrilla campaign against the United States and its allies in the immediate aftermath of the invasion; transnational insurgents, often affiliated with Al Qaeda, and willing to terrorize or recruit locally; sectarian militias fighting against each other and occupying forces; and home-grown insurgents, loosely affiliated by opposition to the United States and a weak Iraqi government. In Afghanistan, the insurgents come from various Taliban and Taliban-affiliated warlords, mixed with some transnational elements, and financed, in this case, by a thriving trade in illegal narcotics. Broadly speaking, Iraq has seen a more urbanized insurgency, while Afghanistan's is more rural.

In both cases, the US and NATO strategy over time has gradually moved toward a fully articulated strategy of minimizing civilian casualties, working with the host-nation population to build a centralized military and police force, and attempting to extend the benefits of the centralized state to suspicious and peripheral provinces. The task is Sisyphean, and the mixture of actors on both sides makes it truly complex. There are US and UK and NATO forces of all types, civilian diplomats and intelligence officials, reconstruction agencies such as USAID and the US Army Corps of Engineers, hundreds of NGOs of all nationalities, and most importantly for this chapter, a wide array of armed private security contractors.[18] As the 2006 *Counterinsurgency Field Manual* stresses, these kinds of wars require an organizational mentality that emphasizes "coordination and cooperation" over "strict command and control."[19] The manual stresses "new management" principles, such as "flexibility and reassessment," and urges that there be a large degree of judgment and decision making given to the individual officers on the ground.[20] This general attitude toward risk on the battlefield is reflected even in the Defense Department's own understanding of its broader mission. The *2010 Quadrennial Defense Review*, published in February 2010, repeatedly stressed the need for individual judgment and flexibility when managing risk.[21]

> Effectively managing risk across such a vast enterprise is difficult; the range and volume of component activities and competencies defy simple identification, categorization, and aggregation of risk. Moreover, *a dynamic security environment requires the Department to be flexible and diminishes the value of formulaic risk assessments.* Taken together, the challenges associated with measuring risk and performance relegates the use of quantitative metrics to an important but supporting role: in any risk assessment, DoD necessarily *places a premium on informed judgment at all echelons of command.*[22]

Although there are references in the *Counterinsurgency Field Manual* to the need for a robust show of strength, especially on roads and in convoys (see below), COIN soldiers are meant to repeatedly demonstrate that they are not risk averse, that they are willing to sacrifice safety in order to build credibility with local forces. And although the telling acronym seems to stress the ability to buy or rent the loyalty of the local population, the emphasis is often on building long-term personal relationships and partnerships, with as little corruption as possible.

There is enormous controversy about the possibility of success for counterinsurgencies. Military scholar Edward Luttwak recently referred to counterinsurgency warfare as a form of "military malpractice," since no current military is politically able to do what is really necessary to defeat a popularly backed insurgency: out-terrorize the population who supports them, or move to their country permanently and administer it as, essentially, a colony (or both).[23] In addition, and as Luttwak notes early in his critique, there are plenty of ways of governing that do not include popularly supported rule; and many governments that the United States helps are hardly a picture of legitimacy and transparency. The authors of the *Counterinsurgency Field Manual* may admit as much, but nevertheless paint a picture of a possible way forward by helping a national government establish popular and democratic legitimacy by building roads, hospitals, schools, and hosting elections.[24] Although this chapter is not about the risks associated with counterinsurgency campaigns (of which there are many), the sheer complexity of the endeavor and a lack of clarity about the end state are the shifting grounds upon which any contractor involvement will occur.

PMSCs are involved as part of the "total force" in Afghanistan and Iraq in a number of different ways, but for present purposes I will focus on three of their roles: as providers of convoy security, as bodyguards, and as CIA contractors. In the first case, many security contractors are merely extensions of the need to contract out logistics: they are hired to guard convoys of equipment and supplies being trucked into the country. Their mission is simple: guard the enormous amount of material necessary for the war. In the *Counterinsurgency Field Manual*, convoy security necessarily receives a lot of attention, but not only as a means of resupplying the forces: convoys draw the attention of insurgents, and so the space around them becomes one of the most manageable aspects of combat, no matter who is providing the security:

> Combat logistic convoys should project a resolute ("hard and prickly") image that suggests they will not be an easy ("soft and chewy") target. Combat logistic convoys project their available combat power to the maximum extent possible, as would any other combat convoy or patrol. Under these conditions, logistics units—*or anyone else involved in resupply operations*—provide a detailed intelligence preparation of the battlefield.[25]

The case study provided in the manual makes it clear that convoy security is considered the frontline in counterinsurgencies. Taken from Vietnam, it describes the changes made to convoy security provided by a military transportation group that was ambushed as it was on its way to resupply an infantry division. In the aftermath of a devastating attack, certain steps were taken to protect the convoy and engage any insurgents: the truck cabs were armored, and security guards, provided with mounted machine guns, were provided for nearly every vehicle. This resulted in "a change of thinking" that "converted convoy operations from *unglamorous defensive activities into valuable opportunities to engage insurgents offensively.*"[26] Contractors in Iraq and Afghanistan who are hired to do defensive security thus find themselves, by virtue of the nature of their tasks and by admission by the military itself, engaged in offensive operations on the frontline of a counterinsurgency campaign. And despite military logistics units, the *Counterinsurgency Field Manual* makes it very clear that many of the most essential convoy security tasks, especially those that "promote economic pluralism because they rely the most on HN [host nation] employees and vendors" will be provided by contractors "in support of US forces."[27]

The second type of task performed by PMSCs is bodyguarding, or the provision of "personal security details," as they are called. These bodyguards provide "close protection" to a huge range of people throughout a war zone: Afghan officials, US civilian employees from USAID or the State Department, journalists, NGO workers, businessmen, and anyone who can pay for mobile security as they travel around. These bodyguards range in type, but those from the most well known firms—such as Blackwater, DynCorp, or Triple Canopy—are hired through the State Department's Worldwide Personal Protective Services contract, managed by the Bureau of Diplomatic Security. Bodyguards can be from a wide array of backgrounds, including local host country nationals, third country nationals, and (much better paid) American, UK, or South African contractors. The State Department describes the situation as follows:

> Over the past ten years, the Bureau of Diplomatic Security has become increasingly involved in providing protective services for high-level U.S. officials and certain designated foreign leaders in several areas of the world. . . . The return of a democratic government in Haiti in October 1994, the continual turmoil in the Middle East, and the post-war stabilization efforts by the U.S. Government in Bosnia, Afghanistan, and Iraq are all types of world events that require priority deployment of Contractor protective services teams on *a long-term basis*. The Bureau of Diplomatic Security is unable to provide protective services on a long-term basis from its pool of Special Agents, thus outside contractual support is required for *emergency protective requirements stated on extremely short notice*.[28]

PMSC bodyguards are clearly a potentially lethal part of the "total force" in COIN operations. Their profile fits that of a paramilitary team: which includes high-level security clearances (sometimes granted in an expedited manner), their armor and weaponry, their ability to use deadly force (within standard operating procedures), and their ability to call in "counter-assault teams" and "long range marksmanship teams" when necessary.[29] And yet their organizational risk profile, as I argue below, does not align with the wider counterinsurgency mission as a whole.

The third type of PMSC involvement in counterinsurgency—in the intelligence gathering realm—has received a lot of press recently. Contractors are hired by the CIA and other intelligence agencies to gather intelligence on the ground in Afghanistan and Pakistan, analyze that intelligence, and sometimes to interrogate detainees. In the immediate aftermath of 9/11, and as CIA bureau chief Robert Grenier vividly described it, a shortage of manpower forced the CIA to use contractors, often former CIA members who volunteered their help, and quickly formed companies to organize themselves. These initial firms then expanded their reach, and have now become embedded in the core mission tasks of the agency.[30] The risks here are similar: their unclear legal status means that any potential crimes cannot be easily prosecuted; their admixture into the US intelligence community has opened up the risk of reputational harm to an industry already tarnished by revelations of secret prisons, torture, and renditions.

In these three specific ways—convoy security, bodyguard work, and intelligence gathering—PMSCs are doing inherently governmental work that often requires high levels of armor and weaponry, security clearances, and a "hard prickly" image willing to engage possible insurgents. Practically speaking, counterinsurgency warfare places a high demand on exactly what these firms can provide: the ability to move material for reconstruction through highly insecure and actively hostile areas, the presence of civilian and nongovernment officials in need of close protection, and the gathering of intelligence at all levels. And as I argued in the preceding section, certain risks can be transferred onto PMSCs that are the types of risks that need to be avoided in this kind of warfare.

What are the risks of relying on PMSCs in a counterinsurgency environment? Three broad risks are mentioned repeatedly in military and policy documents: operational risk, legal risks, and reputational risk. The last two are especially problematic given the emphasis on legitimacy and host-nation support in counterinsurgency. Camm and Greenfield's 2005 RAND study that aimed to assess "comparative risk" in the decision to use PMSCs, uses the military's own risk assessment "matrix" as a decision-making model about when and how the presence of PMSCs will harm a mission. The risks assessed were twofold: the loss of "command and control" over contract forces, especially in "chaotic battlefield conditions," and in the midst of complex transitions after the end of a conflict; and the legal complexities posed by the unclear status of PMSCs.[31] Later, in 2007, Camm and Greenfield followed up this study with a report that once again stressed the inherent problems of relying on PMSCs, given that their behavior is dictated by a contract, whose parties may include what they termed a "cast of thousands."[32] While they admit that merely switching to the military to carry out a specific complex task is not always possible, they continue to note that "ambiguous roles and responsibilities," amid a chaotic environment, will lead to an overall increase in risks. These points are backed up by other scholars and military studies.[33] The *Counterinsurgency Field Manual* makes a similar point about the legal risks associated with PMSCs. It stresses that providing the proper legal support will be nearly impossible given the wide but vague array of legal tools and orders.

> Modern COIN operations involve many DoD [Department of Defense] civilians as well as civilian personnel employed by governmental contractors. The means of disciplining such persons for violations differ from the means of disciplining uniformed personnel. These civilians may be prosecuted or receive adverse administrative action. Presumably, this means that their contract will be terminated by the United States or contract employers. DoD directives contain further policy and guidance pertaining to U.S. civilians accompanying our forces in COIN.[34]

Recently, the UK government commissioned a "Tiger Team" report on contractor support operations, wherein PMSC members, along with academics and policy makers from the Ministry of Defence and the Foreign Commonwealth Office, put together a series of findings about the increasing reliance of the UK military on contractor support of all types.[35] This report echoes the concern over the legal and reputational risks of a high degree of reliance on contractors, given the ad hoc manner in which this reliance is created, the lack of trust between government and PMSCs, and the requirement that contractors be covered by the military's own force protection standards. This last point is a large operational risk, and the report dwells on its ramifications: the Ministry of Defence advised non-armed PMSCs to subcontract with additional security-providing PMSCs, rather than rely on the government's forces for security or for extraction in an emergency, and this caused considerable protest. The report ends with a recommendation for new set of guidelines "to address potential complications over compliance with a number of the current contractual obligations and wider implications and potential legal risk of contracting PMSCs."[36]

    In addition, researchers have named a number of additional risks, mainly associated with the need of COIN to project an image of legitimacy and concern for the civilian population amid a chaotic and insecure environment. Initially, the large drain of highly skilled members of national militaries recruited to PMSCs negatively affected their ability to recruit and retain highly qualified replacements. Currently, casualties among contractors often place undue risks of evacuation and treatment on the military, tasked with protecting our own regardless of their status.[37]

The biggest problem, however, is simpler: PMSCs add to the chaos of the operational environment and counterinsurgency policy, which is already one of extreme complexity. Their organizational profile contradicts the stated goals of a strategy that emphasizes state control over private militias, rule of law over the quasi-legitimate and the unclearly regulated. Repeatedly, the *Counterinsurgency Field Manual* emphasizes the necessity for partnership and coordination amid a new array of mixed (joint) services, multinational military partners, host countries, and hybridized public–private partnerships.

In other words, the idea of better partnerships, laterally among multinational militaries, and vertically between government principals and contractors and subcontractor agents, is a dangerously optimistic one. This is clearly so, given the real needs of counterinsurgencies, and especially, as the next section will detail, the problems of competing organizational cultures. Our tools to manage complexity are woefully inadequate. And in the specific case of PMSCs and the military, as I argued above, the problem is especially acute since their missions are entwined, but their organizational cultures are defined in direct opposition to each other.

4. Organizational Risk Postures

It seems obvious that most organizations and individuals want to avoid failure, disaster, or accidents. Risk theorists also remind us that risks are essential for all action: too much risk averseness means that nothing will happen. There is a real benefit to certain kinds of risk and some organizations adapt to the risks they take in order to manage or mitigate them, while allowing for, and explaining, others they are prepared to accept. Organizational risk postures are composed of all the attitudes, processes, and cultures that surround decisions about future actions, and provide contexts for the choices (and mistakes) made.[38] Compare, for instance, the risk posture of the Belgian peacekeeping forces deployed by the United Nations in Rwanda in 1994, and extracted as genocide engulfed the nation, after ten of their members were brutally killed. Their mission or mandate was defined as peacekeeping, which ruled out engagement in battle. The environment was chaotic and overwhelming, there was no official UN mandate for any change in their risk-averse posture, and the Belgian government was worried about the political blame if any more of them should be killed. They have remained infamous for not taking enough risks to do what they could during the genocide. In contrast, Executive Outcomes put forward a plan to move into Rwanda in order to halt the genocide and establish safe havens for victims. They were willing to take on the risk, but as no state or international organization offered to pay them for their services, they could not take the risk.[39]

The military, as the principal, is risk averse, while a PMSC, as its agent, is more tolerant of certain kinds of risk. Some of this risk toleration could potentially be helpful for COIN operations. But most of the time, these misaligned risk cultures are dangerous, and only add to the chaos while on the ground and in making judgments back home. How can we clarify the differences? Recall that an organizational risk posture results from the combination of four distinct things: the *cultural attitude* toward risk in general, the specific *type of organization* used to carry out the task (including the accountability or liability structures embedded in it), the *environment* in which the task will be carried out, and the overall *mission*. The 2005 RAND study referenced above spoke directly to the problem of the competing risk cultures of the military and PMSCs.

> Lessons of the past clearly point out the tenuous relationships forged between the warrior and the contractor. These new relationships will have to be built upon *shared risk* and a sense of mission. . . . This *tolerance for risk and the establishment of trust and security* is a challenge for the DOD.[40]

Since that time, researchers have continued to note the lack of alignment in the risk cultures of contractors and soldiers in both directions: at times contractors are too risk averse, and at other times they do not treat the same risks—for instance the risk of alienating the civilian population—as seriously as the military.[41] In other words, the supposed partnership is fraught with risk cultures that are misaligned: different organizations and individuals possess different "risk postures," i.e., attitudes about how much risk is acceptable, even encouraged.

Bridget Hutter's research at London School of Economics' Center for the Analysis of Risk and Regulation has focused on a shift from as she terms it, "government to governance," and the way in which this shift prioritizes risk evaluations as a method of regulation.[42] She notes that the larger background shift away from public toward contracting out to private companies paralleled a move away from a "command and control" model for regulation toward what she calls a *hybridized* model, which mixes a private firm's own self-regulation processes, often mediated by industry groups, with outside auditors or consultants. These multiple levels work together to gather information used in decision making, set standards for review and evaluation, and monitor actions, and hopefully modify them. These "risk regulation regimes" translate into a governance and accountability structure that then allows (or disallows) and justifies certain actions and decisions.

In simple principal–agent terms, the military has a certain risk posture, based on its own public, state-based profile, and it has to justify its decisions in certain specific (and public) ways: there are governmental auditors and inspectors general, there are congressional hearings, and other basic methods of democratic accountability. Intelligence organizations like the CIA are a few steps removed from this kind of public accountability, but still relatively accountable to some members of government. PMSCs are simultaneously contracted agents of the military, subject to the demands and goals of their firms. They are thus subject to a hybrid regulatory regime, composed of public auditors, industry self-regulatory bodies, shareholders, and in many cases, as mentioned earlier, private insurance agencies.

How does this translate into a risk posture on the ground? First, because of the narrow scope of the contracted mission, success (and therefore more contracts) is more achievable despite risks taken. For instance, even after the Nisoor Square massacre, in which Blackwater contractors guarding State Department officials were accused of killing seventeen civilians in what they termed a defensive maneuver, the company did not suffer adverse effects, since it was able to fire its employees, rename the company, and argue that it had done the job well, "not losing a single individual we were contracted to protect in the many years" of work. (In contrast over forty Blackwater employees have died on the job.) Its basic risk posture is out of line with that of the military.

But there is a second problem, only revealed by the fact that in situations of extreme and many-layered risk, reliance on risk rubrics or risk regimes in general is dangerous, even if contractors have to do it as a part of their contract. Formal risk regimes used as tools of governance or decision making prevent a certain kind of holistic judgment and thus subvert the real aims of counterinsurgency. They tend to diminish the agency of individual actors, and prevent the kind of networked, nuanced, and personal approach that marks the "coordination and communication" of a counterinsurgency. As journalist James Risen noted recently, they prevent the innovation and creativity, agency and autonomy that distinguish members of a "profession" from strict "command and control" organizations.[43]

The military has been risk averse because it is subject to very clear regulatory regimes, and because its overall mission is much wider, strategically and politically, rather than narrowly defined, and private. It is the product of a social contract, not a business contract. In contrast, contractors can take risks, because of their much less clear, hybrid, matrix-like, and evolving regulatory regimes. Regardless of whether or not this situation was set up on purpose, risk is easily transferred from one organization to another. This risk transfer has the potential to be positive. Special operations forces have similar operational leeway at times, but only if they are not hamstrung by an overly risk conscious command.[44] Special operations forces and CIA members, however, are squarely within the "governmental agent" category. If their own activities are constrained by too much consciousness of risk, then they will outsource their risk to other, less risk-averse organizations. And as these organizations accept this risk—as bodyguards, convoy security, and spies for hire—they paradoxically augment the risk of the mission as a whole, with its larger goals (which may or may not be attainable, see section above) of establishing the rule of law and a democratically elected and popularly supported nation-state.

The risk postures of organizations involved in Afghanistan and Iraq run along a continuum from risk averse to risk tolerant to risk embracing. Those organizations that embrace risk do so because their loose or evolving regulatory structure enables them to act in this manner. This, however, increases the risk to the overall mission.

5. Conclusion

The global financial crisis of the last few years has focused our attention on the dangers of an over-reliance on risk reduction rubrics in complex situations. In the banking industry, insurance and hedges on high-risk securities ended up increasing the risk attached to the very thing they were meant to control. In a situation eerily similar to that of PMSCs, investors bundled murky financial instruments into packages (collateralized debt obligations) whose value was extremely difficult to assess. In order to mitigate the exposure to these "known unknowns," banks hedged their bets through insurance policies (credit default swaps) and relied on the assurances offered by complex risk modeling tools to calm fears of the "unknown unknowns."[45] In the end, an irrational overreliance on complex and murky financial positions led to a near financial meltdown, and a return to reliance on two more trusty sources of risk management, simple solid commodities, for instance gold, and the government. The banking system was bailed out by the government, whose backing had enabled the risks to be taken in the first place. The story is not that new and government has long been the risk reduction tool of choice. Despite the era of deregulation, the cycle of risk tends to move back toward the use of government and the state in general as the ultimate risk manager.[46]

Will we see a similar trend in the area of PMSCs, whose murky high-risk status, bundled in the midst of complex securities makes them seem a lot like the high-risk loans in the mortgage industry? Will the government and military step back in and either "in-source" their jobs, or find new, stronger ways to centralize their regulation? At the beginning of this chapter, I argued that PMSCs were organizationally enabled, so to speak, by the risk averseness of the military: they were created for certain "dirty" or problematic risks to be transferred onto organizations whose negative outcomes are deniable. If this disparity of risk postures remains the case, then the status quo will also remain in place. If it does not remain, then the only thing that could in the future unify disparate organizations (public and private, civilian and soldier, risk-averse and risk-embracing) is the receding importance of organizational structure. This could be replaced by a much more informal arrangement wherein the "superstructure" of a common mission, and the "substructure" of individual actors who share a common background (former military, former CIA, former police, etc.) align to produce a strong enough culture that could supersede the disparate and seemingly opposed cultures of business and the military. This emerging shadowy world of public private partnerships in counterinsurgency operations would be very hard to analyze and understand, and my sense is that it would have very little staying power, since it would be built on personal relationships that would coalesce and disband quickly.

And since the success of counterinsurgency stands or falls on the creation of some kind of legitimate, long-lasting, and true partnership between a people and its security forces (as well as those who work to create its security forces in the first place), the stakes are very high, and more complexity and more weakly tied relationships will not help. Counterinsurgency warfare may be one of the cases where the late modern propensity for evolving and protean organizations, governed by contracts (that demonstrate the need for trust to be created through legalistic and impersonal means) simply cannot work.

Notes

1. Senator Carl Levin, Opening Statement, Senate Armed Services Committee Hearing on Contracting in a Counterinsurgency: An Examination of the Blackwater-Paravant Contract and the Need for Oversight, US Congress (Feb. 24, 2010), www .cnas.org/node/4168 (accessed Mar. 1, 2011).

2. Full text available in supporting documents for Levin, ibid.

3. Frank Camm and Victoria A. Greenfield, *How Should the Army Use Contractors on the Battlefield?* (Santa Monica, CA: RAND Corporation, 2005).

4. David H. Petraeus and James H. Amos, *Counterinsurgency Field Manual* (Washington, DC: Headquarters, Department of the Army, 2006), sections 1.15, 1.37, 1.155.

5. Ibid., sections 1.113ff.

6. Celeste Ward, "The Pentagon's Obsession with Counterinsurgency," *Washington Post*, May 17, 2009.

7. The US military's Center for Army Lessons Learned at Fort Leavenworth is a prime example of this kind of an organizational structure. Many organizational theorists judge organizations by exactly these internal structures for adaptation and "learning," and the *Counterinsurgency Field Manual* stresses the need for exactly this kind of adaptive learning. see Petraeus and Amos, *Counterinsurgency Field Manual*, introduction.

8. See, for instance, Mary Douglas, *Risk and Blame: Essays in Cultural Theory* (New York: Routledge, 1992).

9. Bridget M. Hutter, *The Attractions of Risk-Based Regulation: Accounting for the Emergence of Risk Ideas in Regulation* (London: London School of Economics, Centre for Analysis of Risk and Regulation, Mar. 2005), 1.

10. See especially Bridget Hutter and Michael Power (eds.), *Organizational Encounters with Risk* (Cambridge, UK: Cambridge University Press, 2005), 7.

11. This is one of the central arguments of the recent bestseller *The Black Swan*. See Nassim Nicholas Taleb, *The Black Swan: The Impact of the Highly Improbable* (New York: Random House, 2007), e.g., xi, 77.

12. See http.akegroup.com (accessed on Mar. 5, 2011); Kateri Carmola, *Private Military Contractors in the Age of New Wars: Risk, Law and Ethics* (London: Routledge, 2010), 64–66.

13. Well-known companies include Control Risks Group, Olive Group, Triple Canopy, and Armor Group. Their offerings might include "defensive driving courses," required by many humanitarian agencies, or practical strategies to avoid conflict or escape hazards.

14. See Martin Shaw, *The New Western Way of War* (Cambridge, UK: Polity Press, 2005); Mikkel Vedby Rasmussen, *The Risk Society at War: Terror, Technology and Strategy in the Twenty-First Century* (Cambridge, UK: Cambridge University Press, 2006).

15. And they are often very willing to take these casualties. See Christopher Spearin, "Private, Armed and Humanitarian? States, NGOs, International Private Security Companies and Shifting Humanitarianism," *Security Dialogue* 39, 4 (2008): 363–82, at 373.

16. For a record of these crimes, see Human Rights First, *Private Security Contractors at War: Ending the Culture of Impunity* (New York: Human Rights First, 2008).

17. Although this point is tangential to the main purpose of this chapter, it is worth pointing out that the transfer of risk and blame onto PMSCs enables the military to seem, in contrast, more legitimate. Mary Douglas, who pioneered the study of what is now called "the risk society," argued that the social benefit of focusing on certain risks and dangers over others served the social purpose of strengthening institutions in decline or in need of redefinition. In this case, PMSCs serve the convenient function of being organizations against which the regular military can be contrasted: compared to PMSCs, the military (or the CIA, or the US State Department) can be seen as more honorable, lawful, and legitimate. Douglas looked specifically at groups or categories or organizations that were deemed polluting, or contaminating, which in her analysis meant usually that they were merely "out of place," or confusing to the accepted categories. The "threat" posed by these organizations was exaggerated in order to provide a focus for another group's faltering foundations.

PMSCs fit into this aspect of the "risk economy" as well. As "protean" organizations, they combine different organizational cultures—those of the military, the corporate firm, and the humanitarian nongovernmental organization—into a new hybridized entity that resists easy classification, and thereby resists accountability in the most basic sense: it is hard to give an account of them. This protean quality makes them seem dirty, polluted, tainted, murky, and generally less legitimate, which is exactly how they continue to be defined, despite the best efforts of their defenders. See Carmola, *Private Military Contractors in the Age of New Wars*; Mary Douglas, *Purity and Danger: An Analysis of Concepts of Pollution and Taboo* (New York: Praeger, 1966); and Mary Douglas and Aaron B. Wildavsky, *Risk and Culture: An Essay on the Selection of Technical and Environmental Dangers* (Berkeley: University of California Press, 1982).

18. For the purposes of this chapter I refer only to armed private security contractors. They are the tip of the iceberg, so to speak, constituting only about 20 percent of all of those who would fit under the category private contractor.

19. Petraeus and Amos, *Counterinsurgency Field Manual*, foreword and repeated throughout.

20. Ibid. Partly this is a reflection of the continual attempt to define the profession of soldiering in an all-volunteer professionalized military. But the stress on individual judgment as a measure of risk is also part of the effort on the part of counterinsurgency theorists to push back against a military that has felt too hemmed in by a risk-averse organizational mentality.

21. The contrast between the language used in the 2006 and 2010 Quadrennial Defense Reviews is striking. In 2006, the "long war" is described in language that imitates a modern business enterprise: the DoD is a "business enterprise" and must be "responsive to stakeholders" and provide the "best value to the taxpayer"; see Department of Defense, *Quadrennial Defense Review Report* (Washington, DC: US Department of Defense, 2006), 63. The risk management plan includes "enterprise goals" and "corporate focus areas" (70). Contractors are the fourth member group of the "Total Force," along with active duty military, reserve units, and members of the civilian intelligence agencies (75). The whole thing has the stamp of Donald Rumsfeld's DoD, and it begins with a quote from him, dated September 10, 2001, wherein he seems to set the stage for the spirit of the report. "[The new DoD] demands agility—more than today's bureaucracy allows. And that means we must recognize another transformation: the revolution in management, technology and business practices. Successful modern businesses are leaner and less hierarchical than ever before. They reward innovation and they share information. They have to be nimble in the face of rapid change or they die" (63).

22. Department of Defense, *Quadrennial Defense Review Report* (Washington, DC: US Department of Defense, 2010), 112 (my emphasis).

23. Edward Luttwak, "Dead End: Counterinsurgency Warfare as Military Malpractice," *Harper's Magazine* (Feb. 2007). This was a truth Machiavelli stressed again and again in *The Prince*. He was deeply aware himself of how a city state like Florence felt toward ostensible occupiers like the pope's armies or the French, and he noted that the only way to keep down "a people who was used to being free" was to destroy them completely, or else move to their country, intermarry, and occupy the area for the long term. See Niccolò Machiavelli, *The Prince* (Chicago: University of Chicago Press, 1985), 21.

24. Petraeus and Amos, *Counterinsurgency Field Manual.* e.g., section 2.6. In addition, the by now infamous PowerPoint presentation is a perfect example of the problem of establishing legitimacy. It purports to describe the strategy of how to move a skeptical Afghan populace away from active or passive support of the insurgents and toward active support of the US and Afghan government forces. Instead, it is a monument to the misuse of PowerPoint. See ibid., appendix.

25. Ibid., section 8.19 (my emphasis).

26. Ibid., section 8.18.

27. Ibid., section 8.52.

28. Quoted from "Specification Section" of the Blackwater, Triple Canopy and DynCorp contract with the US State Department from 2007; available under a Freedom of Information Act request by United Press International and viewed on Nov. 19, 2010 at http://r.m.upi.com/other/12216818791223.pdf.

29. Ibid., 18. Although unclear, it seems that these are contracted forces.

30. In a talk given at the International Spy Museum on June 30, 2010, Robert Grenier noted that Congress mandated budget caps for regular employees, but money was available for "emergency spending" for contractors hired "on short notice but for

a long-term basis" as noted above with diplomatic security providers. And although the contracts under which they are hired seem to imply that the situation is an ad hoc emergency measure, the length of time of current contracts belies this notion.

31. Camm and Greenfield, *How Should the Army Use Contractors on the Battlefield?*, 25ff., especially 27.

32. Victoria A. Greenfield and Frank Camm, "Contractors on the Battlefield: When and How? Using the US Military's Risk Management Framework to Learn from the Balkans Support Contract," paper presented at Proceedings of the Fourth Annual Acquisition Research Symposium, Naval Postgraduate School (May 16, 2007), 195.

33. Industrial College of the Armed Forces, *Final Report: Privatized Military Operations* (Fort McNair, Washington, DC: National Defense University, 2006); Alan Kochems, "When Should the Government Use Contractors to Support Military Operations?" Backgrounder (Washington, DC: Heritage Foundation, May 19, 2006); James Cockayne, "Make or Buy? Principal–Agent Theory and the Regulation of Private Military Companies," in Simon Chesterman and Chia Lehnhardt (eds.), *From Mercenaries to Market: The Rise and Regulation of Private Military Companies* (Oxford: Oxford University Press, 2007), 196–216.

34. Petraeus and Amos, *Counterinsurgency Field Manual*, appendix D-26.

35. UK Ministry of Defence, *Contractor Support to Operations: Tiger Team Final Report*, (Mar. 16, 2010), 23 para. 34.

36. Ibid., 23.

37. On this, see Lt. Col. Redman's comments in Christopher Kinsey, *Private Contractors and the Reconstruction of Iraq: Transforming Military Logistics* (London: Routledge, 2009), 106–7.

38. For instance, one researcher compared the risk posture of NASA's Space Shuttle program in and around the *Challenger* disaster with the Federal Aviation Authority's training of air traffic controllers. Each organization has developed a culture of risk and responsibility. In the first case, this enables a culture of trial and error, when disasters are often composed of unknown features with no historical antecedents. In the case of federal air traffic control, there is a culture in which disasters are averted through a finely tuned interaction of multiple actors trained to deal with each deviation from expectations according to a rigid protocol. See Diane Vaughn, "Organizational Rituals of Risk and Error," in Bridget Hutter and Michael Power (eds.), *Organizational Encounters with Risk* (Cambridge, UK: Cambridge University Press, 2005), 33–66, at 41.

39. On this case, and the political risk calculations associated with using PMSCs to intervene in humanitarian emergencies, see Malcolm Hugh Patterson, *Privatising Peace: A Corporate Adjunct to United Nations Peacekeeping and Humanitarian Operations* (New York: Palgrave Macmillan, 2009), 53.

40. Camm and Greenfield, *How Should the Army Use Contractors on the Battlefield?*, 174, quoting Col. David Mailander, "Battlefield Contractors: Assessing the Benefits and Weighing the Risks," unpublished paper (Carlisle Barracks, PA: US Army War College, 2002).

41. Sarah K. Cotton et al., *Hired Guns: Views about Armed Contractors in Operation Iraqi Freedom* (Santa Monica, CA: RAND Corporation, 2010), 28ff.

42. Hutter, *The Attractions of Risk-Based Regulation*, 3.

43. Phone conversation, July 22, 2010.

44. On the risk averseness of Special Operations Forces in general, see Kateri Carmola, "Outsourcing Combat: Force Protection and the Externalization of War Crimes," *International Journal of Politics and Ethics* 3, 1 (Feb. 2003): 113–34, at 118.

45. I am not alone in seeing the connections between counterinsurgency warfare and the recent financial crisis. David Segal, writing in the *New York Times* op-ed pages on April 30, 2010, used the notorious military PowerPoint slide depicting COIN strategy in Afghanistan to argue that we have moved from an era of complicated problems to ones that are more than that: they are complex. Complicated tasks require that people learn specific skills and do them well, like being a good surgeon. In contrast, complex tasks like running a health-care system require a different set of skills, because the problems and challenges keep changing and the system is "filled with thousands of parts and players, all of whom must act within a fluid, unpredictable environment." See David Segal, "It's Complicated: Making Sense of Complexity," *New York Times*, April 30, 2010, op ed.

46. See especially David A. Moss, *When All Else Fails: Government as the Ultimate Risk Manager* (Cambridge, MA: Harvard University Press, 2002), e.g., 52.

III LEGAL ASPECTS OF FUTURE
   US OPERATIONS

7 Contractors and the Law
Geoffrey S. Corn

1. Introduction

During the past decade there has been a rapid expansion of civilian support to the US armed forces. This trend has pushed civilian contractors ever closer to functions traditionally reserved for military personnel. Driven by a variety of policy, political, and practical factors, it has become a truism that the United States can no longer plan or execute military operations without this robust civilian augmentation.

Civilian support to armed forces in the field, however, is nothing new. The practice of relying on civilians to perform functions in support of the armed forces is as old as the US military itself, and built on a tradition established by the forces of the British Crown. What is new, however, is the sheer magnitude of and dependence on the civilian support function. As force levels dropped through the late 1980s and 1990s, the Department of Defense (DoD) sought to exploit the availability of contracted civilian support to maximize

---

Parts of this chapter were previously published in Geoffrey S. Corn, "Bringing Discipline to the Civilianization of the Battlefield: A Proposal for a More Legitimate Approach to Resurrecting Military Criminal Jurisdiction over Civilian Augmentees," *Miami L. Rev.* 62 (2008): 491; and Geoffrey S. Corn, "Unarmed But How Dangerous? Civilian Augmentees, The Law of Armed Conflict, and the Search for a More Effective Test for Permissible Civilian Battlefield Functions," *2 J. Nat'l Security L. & Pol'y* (2008): 257.

the "tooth-to-tail" ratio for the military component of the force mix. This produced the inevitable effect of not only expanding the presence of civilians in the battle space, but also pushing these civilians into roles and functions tending closer to the traditional military end of the operational function spectrum. Adding to this effect is the reality that the nature of modern warfare has made it increasingly difficult to clearly distinguish between "combatant" and "noncombatant" functions in the contemporary battle space.

Another significant distinction between the use of civilian augmentation in the past and the current trend is transparency of contemporary military operations. Defined by the concept of "the CNN effect," the virtual compression of time and space in relation to military operations has rendered actions even at the lowest tactical level strategically significant. It has simply become axiomatic that events that occur on the battlefield today are subject to a degree of public and political scrutiny that would have been unimaginable in the past. This scrutiny is in large measure driven by an assessment of legality—the focal point for defining the legitimacy of military action. As a result, there has been an increasing tendency to scrutinize the role and behavior of civilian contractors through the lens of law.

This focus has revealed three primary legal issues related to the use of civilian contractors. The first is determining the status of contractors while accompanying armed forces in an operational environment. The second is determining those functions that are legally permissible to assign to contractors. Finally, the reality that contractors may commit misconduct requires an understanding of the legal provisions available for holding these civilians criminally accountable for their behavior. Each of these issues involves complex equations of both law and policy. In many respects, some of the uncertainty associated with addressing these issues is the result of a failure of law to keep pace with the speed of civilianization. However, it has become increasingly apparent that both Congress and the DoD understand the risk associated with legal uncertainty, an understanding that has produced a significant effort to better define the legal framework for the use of contractors. It is this framework that will be the subject of this chapter.

2. Contractor Status: Civilian, Combatant, or Hybrid?

Defining the status of individuals in an area of active military operations is the essential first step in determining their scope of permissible conduct, whether they can be attacked by an enemy, and the legal regime that dictates their treatment upon capture. With the ubiquitous presence of contractors in the modern battle space, each of these consequences of status is as important today as it has ever been.

The principal authority for determining contractor status is the law of armed conflict (LOAC). In order to enhance the protection of the civilian population, the LOAC permits the deliberate attack of only lawful military objectives. To give effect to this rule, it was necessary to define persons who qualify as lawful military objectives and persons who do not. In 1977, The Additional Protocol I to the Geneva Conventions of 1949 (AP I) codified this definition (considered a codification of then existing customary international law by most experts).[1] According to the combined effect of Articles 43 and 50 of this treaty, there are only two categories of individuals in armed conflict: combatants and civilians.

According to AP I, combatants—who as a result of that status are the lawful objects of deliberate attack—are individuals who upon capture qualify for status as prisoners of war pursuant to Article 4 (A) (1), (2), (3) and (6) of the Geneva Convention Relative to the Treatment of Prisoners of War (GPW) and Article 44 of the Protocol.[2] Each of these categories addresses individuals who take part in hostilities. Not all individuals who qualify for POW status are considered combatants. The more significant of two exceptions to this POW/combatant relationship is the category of civilians who accompany the armed forces at GPW Article 4(A)(4). The second category is civilians who provide maritime and aviation support at GPW Article 4(A)(5). Although both categories of civilians are POWs upon capture, they are excluded from the definition of combatant by operation of Article 50 of AP I, which includes in its definition of civilian these categories of individuals who qualify for prisoners of war status, thereby excluding them from the definition of combatant.

This is of profound significance for two reasons. First, by excluding civilians who accompany the armed forces from the definition of combatant, AP I establishes that these civilian support personnel are not by virtue of their function tantamount to combatants or even some "quasi" combatant characterization. Second, because only combatants qualify as lawful military objectives, excluding these individuals from the definition of combatant indicates that they are not to be considered lawful objects of attack. Instead, for purposes of immunity from deliberate attack, these individuals are simply civilians who benefit from a presumptive immunity.

Accordingly, within the combatant/civilian dichotomy, civilian contractors are, at least for purposes of being made the object of attack by an enemy, civilians. This does not, of course, mean that harming a civilian contractor is a conclusive violation of the LOAC. Two qualifiers to this presumptive immunity from attack operate to produce the conclusion that inflicting harm upon civilian contractors can, under the proper conditions, be consistent with their status as civilians.

The first qualifier is derived from the rule that the LOAC does not prohibit inflicting injury on civilians, only doing so deliberately. The reality that civilian contractors may be harmed by the incidental or collateral effects of an attack against a lawful military objective without violating the LOAC operates as a practical qualifier to their immunity from being made the object of deliberate attack. In fact, the role of civilian contractors that places them in immediate proximity of lawful military objectives renders their risk of becoming the collateral victims of lawful attacks almost inevitable. The knowing but nondeliberate infliction of such harm on civilian support personnel is an unfortunate but accepted incident of warfare. Only when he or she believes that such incidental injury will be excessive in relation to concrete and direct military advantage anticipated from attacking the proximate military objective must a commander forego attacking the military objective. As a result of this rule, it is clear that immunity from attack is not analogous to immunity from harm. Perhaps even more importantly, the voluntary commingling of civilian contractors with military personnel in and around military objectives renders it highly unlikely that an attacking commander would cancel an attack based on the risk of incidental injury to these civilians. In essence, while by their function civilian contractors do not become combatants, they do voluntarily assume the obvious risk associated with their presence in support of military operations that tempers the prohibitory effect of the proportionality rule.

The second qualifier is the same qualifier applicable to all civilians: direct participation in hostilities divests the civilian of the presumptive immunity from being made the deliberate object of attack. This qualifier reveals that the immunity afforded to civilians from being made the object of attack is presumptive and not conclusive. According to Article 51(3) of AP I—the same provision that establishes civilian immunity—the immunity afforded to civilians ceases for "such time as they take a direct part in hostilities." Accordingly, any civilian, including a contractor, who engages in conduct falling within the definition of direct participation in hostilities (or more precisely conduct that is perceived by an opponent to fall into that category) can be made the lawful object of attack for such time as that civilian engages in such conduct. Although there is significant contemporary debate on precisely what qualifies as direct participation in hostilities, there is virtually no debate that if a civilian function so qualifies, it results in a loss of immunity from attack.

It is critical, however, to understand that even when a civilian becomes the lawful object of attack by virtue of direct participation in hostilities, this does not in any way alter status upon capture. In other words, direct participation in hostilities is a rule of consequence, not status, because it produces the loss of immunity consequence but does not transform the civilian into a combatant for purposes of status upon capture. Status is dictated by the GPW, which as noted above includes civilians accompanying the armed forces in the field within the definition of prisoner of war. Accordingly, unlike other civilians, who benefit from a presumption against preventive detention upon capture by an opposing armed force, civilian contractors are subject to the same presumptive detention justification that allows for the preventive detention of their combatant counterparts.

This status upon capture, however, is a unique aspect of the treatment of civilian contractors. Pursuant to the LOAC, both civilians and combatants are subject to lawful preventive detention by an opposing armed force. However, there is a fundamental difference between the authority to detain combatants as opposed to civilians. The authority to preventively detain captured combatants is presumptive, with no requirement to make an individual determination of actual necessity. Thus, once an individual is determined to fall within the prisoner of war qualification criteria of the GPW—the same criteria used by AP I to define combatants—preventive detention authority is automatic. In contrast, civilians benefit from a presumption against preventive detention. According to the Geneva Convention Relative to the Protection of Civilian Persons in Time of War (GCC), the preventive detention of civilians under the control of an enemy power is justified only for reasons of imperative security and only as a measure of last resort.[3] Thus, unlike their counterparts, civilians may not be detained based on a presumption, but only based on an individual determination that the presumption against detention has been rebutted because detention is the only feasible means to protect the security of the detaining power.

Civilian contractors, however, are unique in this respect. Although classified as civilians, contractors and other "Persons who accompany the armed forces" are subjected to the same presumptive preventive detention authority applicable to combatants. This is the consequence of falling within the definition of prisoner of war in the GPW. However, as noted above, AP I established that this does not indicate that these civilians are combatants. Instead, they fall into an interesting twilight zone: like all other civilians, they are immune from being made the deliberate object of attack; and like their combatant counterparts, a capturing enemy is authorized to prevent them from returning to their function for the duration of hostilities.

3. Authorized Functions

This anomaly between civilian contractors' status for purposes of targeting versus detention is an important foundation for determining the scope of permissible contractor functions. Because contractors are considered civilians and not combatants, it is generally recognized that they are prohibited from performing functions that would be inconsistent with this status. However, as with so many issues of LOAC implementation, the devil is in the proverbial details of defining what functions fall beyond the scope of permissible civilian support, or even what test should be applied to make such a determination.

Traditionally, legal experts have resorted to the direct participation in hostilities rule to define the limits on permissible civilian functions. Starting from the premise that taking a direct part in hostilities is inconsistent with civilian status, this method of analysis essentially transformed a rule of consequence into a rule of prohibition. Simply stated, because the LOAC establishes that direct participation in hostilities by a civilian results in a loss of immunity from attack, it was presumed that authorizing civilian contractors to perform functions producing this consequence would amount to a violation of the LOAC, and therefore was prohibited.

This analytical approach suffered from two defects. First, not all experts agreed that transforming a rule of consequence into a rule of prohibition was supported by the law. Nothing in the International Committee of the Red Cross Commentary to the direct participation in hostilities rule indicates that engaging in such participation is illegal. Instead, the Commentary focuses exclusively on the consequence of such activity, namely the loss of immunity from attack. Although some states seem to accept this proposition, there remains a lack of international consensus that such conduct violates the LOAC. There is also, however, an additional defect, one that is far more significant: the lack of clarity on what functions amount to direct participation in hostilities. Because there is no consensus on where to draw this "direct participation" line, relying on this rule as a standard for determining the limits of permissible civilian support functions has produced substantial uncertainty and may have even invited an increasingly expansive role for such civilians.

Even starting with the premise that civilian contractors are prohibited not only from engaging in, but more importantly from being tasked to perform functions that amount to direct participation in hostilities, this standard is only as effective as the ability to define what qualifies as direct participation. It is true that there is almost universal consensus that core combatant functions—functions associated with the application of combat power to kill or disable an enemy—fall within this definition. Thus, no one would seriously assert the propriety of using contractors to serve as infantrymen or fire artillery. However, difficulty in reliance on this standard arises with each step away from the direct application of combat power. And, because civilian contractors are moving toward core combatant functions from the periphery, this creates increased uncertainty as to what functions they are and are not permitted to assume.[4]

The impact of this uncertainty has been especially significant with regard to intelligence activities, armed security services, and provision of highly technical support to combat equipment. Each of these functions is essential for facilitating the delivery of combat power against an enemy, yet each is at least somewhat removed from the final step in the process of such delivery, what Major General Charles Dunlap (the Assistant Judge Advocate General of the Air Force) has called the "kill chain."[5] Civilianizing performance of these functions has revealed the inherent weakness of the direct-participation standard.

In response to this uncertainty, the DoD now relies on an alternate approach to defining permissible contractor functions: the "inherently governmental function" test (IGF). DoD Instruction 1100.22 establishes the process for force development planning (called "workforce mix" by the Instruction).[6] This process is intended to ensure that requisite manpower capabilities are available to meet the needs of anticipated missions. In order to plan for uniformed force requirements, it is obviously necessary to assess which functions may be performed by civilians. Thus, this force development Instruction has by necessity incorporated a potentially more effective standard for creating a legally sound military/civilian manpower mix.

The foundation of this Instruction is that only government employees may perform inherently governmental functions. Accordingly, the Instruction prohibits the use of contracted support to provide the manpower for these functions. Thus, IGF becomes the controlling standard for determining permissible and impermissible civilian contractor functions. An IGF is defined as:

> a function that is so intimately related to the public interest as to mandate performance by Government employees. These functions include those activities that require either the exercise of discretion in applying Government authority or the making of value judgments in making decisions for the Government.[7]

This excerpt reveals that the focus of the IGF assessment is not synonymous with the focus of the direct-participation test: the proximity to hostilities or the narrowly focused question of whether the function will cause immediate harm to an enemy. Instead, the IGF standard focuses on the nature of the discretion associated with the function. While it is probably true that this IGF analytical approach suffers from many of the same shortcomings of the direct participation in hostilities test—most obviously the potential varying interpretations of the meaning of "inherently governmental"—it does represent one substantial improvement over the direct-participation test: it is flexible enough to address functions beyond the direct application of combat power.

This flexibility is increasingly essential to address the difficult question of how far civilianization may legitimately extend in contemporary military operations. In an era when collection of intelligence can often be more critical to mission accomplishment than application of combat power, and when technology facilitates the employment of that combat power from remote locations thousands of miles from the battle space, simply focusing on causing immediate harm to an enemy is an under-inclusive analytical focus for making the civilianization assessment. The IGF test seems to respond to this reality with a focus that attempts to distinguish functions that involve the type of discretion that should be reserved only for individuals with a direct obligation of loyalty to the nation from those that need not require such a link.

This more flexible approach is reflected in Appendix B to the Burman Policy Letter, which actually identifies a wide array of functions that may in accordance with the IGF standard be civilianized. Most of the functions designated as nongovernmental are uncontroversial. For example, use of civilian contractors to provide combat service support (such as cooking, cleaning, equipment repair and maintenance, supply management) would be permissible under either the direct-participation test or the IGF test, and is a historic role for civilians in support of military operations. However, several functions expose how difficult it has become to draw the line between permissible and impermissible civilianization.

One prime example is the use of civilian contractors to perform armed security services. The fact that these individuals are armed and granted authority to employ force in self-defense or defense of others is considered by many an indication that they are impermissibly performing combatant functions. However, such use is authorized in accordance with the IGF test under the limited circumstances of providing security in support of stability and support operations.[8] This is most likely the result of a conclusion that in such a context the use of force authority granted to such civilians is far less expansive than that granted to their military counterparts. Unlike military personnel, armed security contractors are authorized to employ force for very limited purposes, namely self-defense and defense of others in response to an actual or imminent threat of violence. Accordingly, in the context of stability support operations their authority is limited to responding to threats that are presumptively unlawful.

There is no explicit indication that the IGF test is intended either to depart from existing LOAC requirements or operate as an indication that the US is attempting to redefine the law related to permissible civilian functions. However, because the use of armed civilian security personnel is consistent with this policy, it could be viewed as having just such an effect. Whether the LOAC permits civilians to use force to defend themselves or others against unlawful force or violence in an armed conflict is a difficult issue that lacks definitive resolution. Irrespective of the propriety of such uses of force by civilians, it seems clear that an enemy force would consider the arming of civilians as evidence that these civilians were taking a direct part in hostilities, a conclusion that would be perceived as inconsistent with the LOAC. For the armed civilian security guard captured by such an enemy, this could result in war crimes liability for engaging in unlawful belligerency. Thus, while the IGF policy may be intended to closer align US manpower and civilian employment policy with the LOAC, by endorsing the use of armed civilians in the context of armed conflict it is also pushing civilians toward functions historically reserved for members of the armed forces.

Another example is the use of civilian contractors to support the employment of unmanned aerial vehicle (UAV) operations. It might be tempting to conclude that any civilian participation in this "kill chain" is impermissible because the final link in the chain involves attack on enemy operatives. However, by dissecting specific aspects of such operations, the IGF functions are limited to the decision-making process to engage enemy personnel and the actual engagement. Launch, recovery, and technical support for the use of the UAV asset is not considered an IGF precisely because such activities do not involve the type of discretion reserved for government actors.

The list of functions subject to permissible civilianization follows this general model. It, and the IGF test it is derived from, are intended to provide more clarity and predictability for force planners and operational decision makers than the direct-participation standard. While it seems clear that this approach will not eliminate all uncertainty related to determining the permissible scope of civilianization, it should provide a standard that if applied in good faith will reserve for military personnel the type of functions involving an exercise of discretion that complies with the LOAC. If this is indeed the effect, it will go a long way in drawing a logical line in the sand between contractor support functions and core combatant functions.

4. Disciplinary Options for Contractor Misconduct

Accountability for misconduct on the battlefield is a critical aspect of credible military operations. Accountability contributes to good order and discipline, maintenance of goodwill with the local population, and the perception of legitimacy with the American public. It is therefore unsurprising that the armed forces of the United States have always been subject to a specialized military criminal code, and that military lawyers have served in the armed forces since the creation of the Continental Army in 1775. What may be surprising is that civilians supporting the armed forces have also been subject to military criminal justice since the inception of the nation. This reflects the historic recognition that like their military counterparts, civilians accompanying the armed forces must also be subject to accountability for their criminal and disciplinary infractions.

This also reflects another reality: for as long as the United States has fielded armed forces, civilian support personnel have been associated with these forces in operational areas, and have been recognized as an essential component of military operations.[9] Often referred to as "sutlers" or "camp-followers," these civilians historically provided essential logistical support.[10] As noted above, this required that civilians be subject to military jurisdiction while they were associated with the armed forces.[11] This jurisdiction was based on the perceived necessity of vesting military commanders with authority to impose disciplinary and criminal sanctions on these civilians, an authority considered essential to the maintenance of good order and discipline in the military unit.[12]

Jurisdiction over civilian support personnel was established by the Continental Congress as far back as the Revolutionary War, in a predecessor to the Uniform Code of Military Justice (UCMJ).[13] Colonel William Winthrop described this jurisdiction in his seminal treatise on military law:

> All retainers to the camp, and all persons serving with the armies of the United States in the field, though not enlisted soldiers, are to be subject to orders, according to the rules and discipline of war." [Article 63 of the Articles of War], which, with some slight modifications, has come down from our original code of 1775, which derived it from a corresponding British article, has always been interpreted as subjecting the descriptions of persons specified, not only to the orders made for the government and discipline of the command to which they may be attached, but also to trial by court-martial for violations of the military code. Protected as they are by the military arm, they owe to it the correlative obligation of obedience; and a due consideration for the morale and discipline of the troops.[14]

This jurisdiction was invoked routinely to prosecute a wide variety of both common-law and military offenses committed by civilians.[15] World War II provided some of the most interesting examples of the use of this jurisdiction.[16] Civilians were tried not only for common-law offenses that other civilians might be prosecuted for outside the military, such as assault and larceny, but also for offenses unique to the military, such as desertion.[17] Although this military law was modified significantly following World War II in order to bring military criminal law in line with the expectations of credible justice—a process that led to the UCMJ—jurisdiction over civilian support personnel remained intact. As a result, civilian support personnel were subjected to trial by court-martial in every war in our nation's history through the conflict in Vietnam.

The ability to use military law to hold civilians accountable for misconduct in the context of military operations was radically altered in 1970. In the case of *United States v. Averette*, the United States Court of Military Appeals, or COMA (the highest appellate court for the armed forces, which is today called the Court of Appeals for the Armed Forces), ruled that the jurisdiction over civilians accompanying the armed forces established by Congress by the UCMJ could only be properly invoked during periods of formally declared war.[18] Because the conflict in Vietnam was not a declared war, but authorized only by a Joint Resolution of Congress, Averette's prosecution for conspiracy to commit larceny while in Vietnam had been invalid and his conviction was overturned.[19]

This decision could have been appealed to the United States Supreme Court, and based on the earlier decision of that Court in the case of *Reid v. Covert*,[20] there was a strong possibility that the COMA decision might have been reversed. However, perhaps as a result of the general anti-military mood that existed at that time, the government did not pursue an appeal. As a result, for the next thirty-six years military jurisdiction over civilians was an effective nullity. Although the *Averette* opinion left open the possibility that this jurisdiction might be exercised in the context of a declared war, the extremely remote possibility that Congress would ever again formally declare a war created an operative assumption that civilians would never again be court-martialed.

As will be discussed below, this assumption was invalidated in 2006 by an amendment to the UCMJ. However, before addressing that amendment and the accordant resurrection of military jurisdiction over civilian contractors (and other civilians accompanying the armed forces during military operations), the void created by the *Averette* opinion and the congressional response to this void must be addressed.

Until 2006, Congress never seriously considered amending the UCMJ to offset the impact of the *Averette* decision.[21] Congress's apparent willingness to accept COMA's nullification of jurisdiction over civilians was likely attributable to a variety of factors. Perhaps most significant was that during this period there was no real theater of active combat operations to implicate the need for such jurisdiction.[22] During the peak of the Cold War, the US military was principally a "forward deployed" force, with large numbers of military and associated civilian personnel stationed in countries with well-developed legal systems.[23] Status agreements generally governed the presence of these forces, with designation of jurisdiction a key component.[24] Under most of these agreements, US personnel—both military and civilian—were subject to the concurrent jurisdiction of the host nation and of the United States.[25]

For military personnel, this meant that an act of criminal misconduct that violated both host-nation law and the UCMJ could be prosecuted in local courts or by court-martial.[26] Offenses that violated only the UCMJ fell under the military's exclusive jurisdiction. But for civilians associated with the force (including family members), the grant of concurrent jurisdiction to the United States in such agreements was essentially a nullity, because no US court was vested with the jurisdiction to try such offenses.[27] Instead, when civilians committed criminal misconduct that violated the UCMJ and host-nation law, they would in fact be subject to the exclusive jurisdiction of the host nation.[28] Although this method of dealing with civilian misconduct did not always satisfy the concerns of US commanders, and although in some cases this method produced arbitrary results, it was generally accepted as an effective accommodation of interests.

This all began to change with the end of the Cold War. That event led to two primary developments that sparked concerns over the lack of viable US jurisdiction over civilians supporting the operations of the armed forces abroad. First, the armed forces underwent a major downsizing.[29] As part of this process, the US military became increasingly reliant on the support of civilian contractors to augment military operations and perform functions previously performed by the much larger Cold War force.[30] As noted by one author:

> The startling growth in the ratio of contractors compared to active duty service members during overseas deployments demonstrates the policy in practice. During the Gulf War in 1991, slightly more than five thousand contractors helped support half a million troops. In the Balkans, from 1995 to 2000, contractors actually outnumbered active duty forces by three thousand civilian personnel. With approximately 138,000 service members currently serving in the Iraqi Campaign (a number that has remained fairly static over the last three years), an American Bar Association report estimates that there are about thirty thousand U.S. contractors operating in Iraq, or "about 10 times the ratio during the 1991 Persian Gulf conflict." When foreign workers actively engaged in the reconstruction and oil work are added to the government contractor mix, the numbers swell as high as 50,000 to 75,000. If we recall from evidence introduced earlier that fewer than ten thousand civilians supported over half a million troops in Vietnam, the phenomenon's picture is complete.[31]

Perhaps more important than the requirement to use civilians to enhance the "tooth-to-tail" ratio was the second development: the US military began to conduct an increasing number of expeditionary military operations. These ranged from the full-scale combat operation of the first Iraq war, to a wide array of peacekeeping operations in locations such as Bosnia, Kosovo, Haiti, and Somalia.[32] These two changes in the nature of the armed forces and the missions they were routinely conducting converged to produce a new military/civilian paradigm in which the civilian component was a constant and increasingly essential part of military operations in locations where reliance on the host-nation criminal justice system to address civilian misconduct was never a viable option.

This soon led to concerns that US civilians were effectively immune from criminal sanctions for their misconduct, regardless of how egregious that misconduct might be.[33] The only real response available to commanders for such misconduct was to terminate the civilian-employment relationship with the military and request that the civilian be removed from the operational area.[34] How could the command maintain credibility when a civilian associated with the unit (even if not technically subject to the authority of the commander) committed a serious criminal offense, such as murder or rape of a local national? What impact would it have on the morale of the military force when they realized that a double standard exists as the result of their being subject to court-martial for misconduct while their civilian counterparts were effectively immune? How could a commander ensure compliance with his or her obligations under the laws of war if a civilian committed a war crime and the commander had no meaningful disciplinary option to respond?

In the mid-1990s, during the height of the "peacekeeping" era, these concerns led Congress, working with the DoD and the Department of State, to address the issue of criminal jurisdiction over civilian support personnel.[35] One option available to Congress, and perhaps the easiest option, would have been to amend the UCMJ to make it explicit that the jurisdiction of the military code was not, as the COMA had ruled, limited to periods of declared war. Congress, however, did nothing to alter the post-*Averette* status quo. Nor did the DoD ever recommend such a course of action.[36]

Instead, Congress chose to enact legislation establishing federal criminal jurisdiction over civilian support personnel who commit serious criminal misconduct outside the jurisdiction of the United States: the Military Extraterritorial Jurisdiction Act (MEJA). MEJA made applicable to civilians accompanying the armed forces overseas (irrespective of the nature of the mission or operation) those offenses applicable to any civilian in the Special Maritime or Territorial Jurisdiction of the United States.[37] Accordingly, these civilians became liable for all offenses with specific extraterritorial application contained in Title 18 of the United States Code, including civilian-type offenses such as homicide, sexual assault, larceny, and arson.[38] Congress did not specify how to implement this statute, delegating that task to the Secretary of Defense.[39]

Unfortunately, the good intentions associated with the creation of the MEJA never really produced analogous results. Since enactment, the MEJA has not been particularly effective.[40] It was not until 2005 that the DoD finally published an implementing instruction.[41] But perhaps more problematic is that as implemented, the statute relies on US Attorneys to "accept" cases referred to them from an overseas-military command.[42] This procedure alone makes it unsurprising that there has not been a strong appetite for prosecuting civilians for MEJA violations. Furthermore, the overall complexity of initiating, coordinating, and managing prosecutions of the MEJA also undoubtedly contributes to this lack of appetite.[43] The several MEJA cases that have been prosecuted do, however, indicate that if applied MEJA can be effective in responding to civilian criminal misconduct.[44]

During this period Congress passed the War Crimes Act (WCA), which also established federal criminal jurisdiction over civilians accompanying the armed forces.[45] Unlike the MEJA, this statute was not motivated primarily by the concerns related to civilian misconduct.[46] Nonetheless, the statute subjects any US national to federal criminal jurisdiction for the commission of certain war crimes.[47] Thus, if it were established that a civilian was a US national and engaged in a defined war crime, the WCA would provide federal criminal jurisdiction over the individual and the offense.

As a result of these developments, the jurisdictional landscape related to civilian support personnel came to be understood by military practitioners as follows: first, although the UCMJ applied extraterritorially, prosecuting civilians for violation of the Code was not a viable command option to respond to civilian misconduct; second, when deemed appropriate, and in response to misconduct that fell within a defined offense of Title 18 of the United States Code, the commander could initiate a process by which the case would be referred to the Department of Justice for prosecution in the United States;[48] third, in the rare case where the alleged misconduct qualified as a war crime, the commander could also refer the case to the Department of Justice for prosecution pursuant to the WCA.

With more than 100,000 civilian contractors associated with military operations in Iraq, this methodology came under increasing scrutiny.[49] This scrutiny was most significant in relation to civilian contractors performing armed security functions or involved in the interrogation of detainees. Reports of detainee abuse, and even killings, by such civilians led human-rights advocates to demand a more robust civilian-accountability structure.[50] Nonetheless, as is reflected in the 2005 Instruction implementing MEJA,[51] the DoD continued to work within this new jurisdictional paradigm, and did not call for the resurrection of military criminal jurisdiction over civilians.

This jurisdictional paradigm was suddenly and radically changed in October of 2006, when Congress passed the John Warner National Defense Authorization Act for Fiscal Year 2007.[52] The amended law included hundreds of provisions related to the armed forces. Although apparently not solicited by the DoD, inserted among these provisions was the following amendment to the UCMJ:

> SEC. 552. CLARIFICATION OF APPLICATION OF UNIFORM CODE OF MILITARY JUSTICE DURING A TIME OF WAR.
>
> Paragraph (10) of section 802(a) of title 10, United States Code (article 2(a) of the Uniform Code of Military Justice), is amended by striking "war" and inserting "declared war or a contingency operation."[53]

With this amendment, Congress resurrected military criminal jurisdiction over every civilian working for, with, or perhaps even in proximity to the armed forces in Iraq, Afghanistan, and other locations designated as "contingency operations" by the secretary of defense. By amending the jurisdictional article of the UCMJ to read "declared war or a contingency operation,"[54] Congress nullified the *Averette* interpretation of the Code that required a formally declared war to trigger the jurisdiction. Because virtually every conflict or non-conflict military operation falls under the expansive definition of "contingency operation,"[55] this amendment effectively made the extraterritorial jurisdiction of the UCMJ coextensive for military and civilian personnel.[56]

Based on the author's discussions with a number of individuals within the military-legal community, this amendment came as a complete surprise to the DoD.[57] To date, the military services have responded cautiously to this revised jurisdiction over civilians,[58] (although there has been one civilian tried and convicted by the US Army pursuant to this amendment to the UCMJ). This is not surprising, for this resurrection creates tremendous uncertainty. This uncertainty stems from two principal concerns: first, which civilians fall within the definition of "accompanying the force"? Since the amendment does not limit the applicability of the statute to US nationals, this is a question that turns on functional association, and not nationality. And second, will the extension of military/criminal jurisdiction to civilians under this amendment withstand constitutional scrutiny?—a question potentially complicated by the fact that the statute can be applied to non-US nationals.[59]

These concerns are exacerbated by the simple reality that virtually all of the jurisprudence related to these questions is decades old. Nonetheless, if this jurisprudence provides a baseline from which to interpret the scope of this provision, the answer to the question regarding who falls into the jurisdictional net is potentially quite broad.[60] During both the First and the Second World Wars, a number of cases addressed the predecessor provision of this jurisdiction grant in the Articles of War.[61] These decisions held that civilians "accompanying the force" included not only civilian employees of the armed forces and contractors working for the armed forces, but also US civilians whose employment with the armed forces had been terminated but who remained in the theater of operations.[62] This expansive understanding of military jurisdiction over civilians "accompanying the force" was confirmed during congressional hearings on enactment of the UCMJ, when the Assistant General Counsel for the DoD asserted that even Red Cross workers and journalists could potentially fall under the jurisdiction established over civilians by the Code.[63]

It is difficult to conceive of a CNN journalist being charged and tried by a court-martial in Iraq simply because he happened to be in the same operational area of US forces. It is equally difficult to conceive of a US military commander pursuing such a course of action. But this extreme example highlights the uncertainty that perhaps lies behind the caution in invoking this jurisdiction by the military services. This example is also useful as it suggests that the object of this amendment to the UCMJ was not to achieve such an extreme result. Instead, a more logical object was likely responsible: the desire to enhance the ability of military commanders to control and discipline civilian contractors integrally related to their units and missions.

It has long been recognized that the military justice system is intended to serve two distinct yet intrinsically connected functions: achieving justice and contributing to the good order and discipline of the military unit.[64] It is this latter purpose that has been so significant in justifying the continuing central role of military commanders in the military justice process. Unlike civilians, or even officers in most foreign military systems, US commanders are vested with enormous authority over the disposition of allegations of misconduct.[65] This authority extends to charging decisions, nonjudicial diversions, the level of court to select, the decision to send a case to trial; and the authority to approve, mitigate or set aside a court's findings or sentence or both.

Commanders are entrusted with this power because to maintain good order and discipline within a unit misconduct must be addressed promptly in a manner that responds to the interests of the military command. It is therefore not surprising that as the numbers of civilians associated with military units in theaters of active operations has increased, the desire to subject them to command disciplinary authority has also increased. It is also completely plausible that the recent resurrection of military jurisdiction might indeed contribute to good order and discipline both by providing a more efficient criminal response to civilian misconduct and by enhancing the sense of equity among members of the uniformed force already subject to such jurisdiction. The key question, however, is not whether this provision is efficient or effective, but whether such increased efficiency in responding to civilian misconduct justifies a deprivation of fundamental constitutional rights in a criminal proceeding.

This implicates the second area of uncertainty related to the resurrection of military jurisdiction over civilians: can it withstand constitutional scrutiny? This is an extremely complex question that will likely ultimately be resolved by the federal courts, and perhaps even the Supreme Court. The complexity stems from one opinion that provides ammunition for both proponents and critics of the resurrection. In the seminal Supreme Court decision of *Reid v. Covert*,[66] the Court struck down as unconstitutional a sister provision of the UCMJ that extended military jurisdiction over civilians associated with the armed forces while overseas but not in a theater of active military operations—locations where the US based its "forward deployed" military. According to the Court, subjecting these civilians to military trial violated the fundamental trial rights guaranteed to them by the Constitution, such as the right to trial by a jury of peers and the right to indictment by a grand jury.

This aspect of the decision calls into question the constitutionality of trying by military courts civilians accompanying the armed forces during contingency operations. In fact, this was a major factor in COMA's reasoning in the *Averette* decision. However, in the *Reid* opinion the Supreme Court also distinguished the use of military courts to try civilians in the context of active combat operations. According to the Court, it was not at all clear that trial of civilians by military courts in that limited context would also violate a civilian's fundamental constitutional rights.

This uncertainty will almost certainly lead to future challenges to the resurrection of military jurisdiction over civilians. Thus, the final chapter to this story is yet to be written. It is, however, clear that by amending the UCMJ, Congress has finally placed this unresolved issue in the proverbial playing field.

5. Conclusion

It would be naive to think that the role of civilian support to military operations will subside or even level off in the foreseeable future. Instead, the ubiquitous presence of civilians in the operational area is a fact; a fact that must be managed from both a policy and legal perspective. Legality, however, must be the fundamental foundation of any policy treatment of this trend. The failure to provide policy makers with clear parameters of legality related to the employment, status, and accountability of civilian support personnel creates a genuine risk to both the effectiveness of the support function and the overall perception of legitimacy of operations. It is therefore essential that those responsible for the development and implementation of this law appreciate the reality of the need for civilian support, and how the law must evolve to provide the clarity so essential to the effective use of this support.

Notes

1. The 1977 *Protocol I Additional to the Geneva Conventions*, Dec. 12, 1977, reprinted in 16 I.L.M. 1391.
2. *Geneva Convention Relative to the Protection of Civilian Persons in Time of War* (Aug. 12, 1949), 6 U.S.T. 3516, 75 U.N.T.S. 287.
3. Ibid., 6 U.S.T. 3516, 75 U.N.T.S. 287, at Art. 78.

4. Geoffrey S. Corn, "Unarmed But How Dangerous? Civilian Augmentees, the Law of Armed Conflict, and the Search for a More Effective Test for Permissible Civilian Battlefield Functions," 2 *J. Nat'l Security L. & Pol'y* (2008): 257.

5. Maj. Gen. Charles J. Dunlap, Jr., "America's Asymmetric Advantage," *Armed Forces Journal* (Sept. 2006), www.armedforcesjournal.com/2006/09/2009013.

6. Department of Defense, Instruction No. 1100.22, *Guidance for Determining Workforce Mix* (Sept. 7, 2006) (Incorporating Change 1, April 6, 2007).

7. Alan V. Burman, Office of Management and Budget, to the heads of Executive Departments and Agencies, "Inherent Government Functions" (Sept. 23, 1992), Policy Letter 92-1, http.whitehouse.gov/omb/rewrite/procurement/policy_letters/92-1_092392.html.

8. Department of Defense, Instruction No. 1100.22, enclosure 2, *Guidance for Determining Workforce Mix* (Sept. 7, 2006) (Incorporating Change 1, April 6, 2007).

9. Samuel Eliot Morison, *The Oxford History of the American People* (New York: Oxford University Press, 1965), 367 (noting the crucial role played by civilians in aiding Lewis and Clark's expedition in 1804); Wm. C. Peters, "On Law, Wars, and Mercenaries: The Case for Courts-Martial Jurisdiction over Civilian Contractor Misconduct in Iraq," *BYU L. Rev.* (2006): 376 ("Civilians have accompanied American military forces in the ranks, in the field, and at post, camp, and station since the War of Independence.").

10. William Winthrop, *Military Law and Precedents*, 2nd ed. (Washington, DC: War Department, 1920), 98–99.

11. Ibid., 98.

12. Thomas G. Becker, "Justice on the Far Side of the World: The Continuing Problem of Misconduct by Civilians Accompanying the Armed Forces in Foreign Countries," *Hastings Int'l & Comp. L. Rev.* 18 (1995): 280 ("As part of an extensive 1920 revision of the Articles of War, Congress recognized a need to control and discipline the many civilians accompanying our expeditionary forces and thus adopted Article 2(d).").

13. The First Continental Congress adopted the Articles of War in June, 1775. Article LXIII allowed military officials to employ punitive measures against both soldiers and "independent company." See 2 Library of Congress, *Journals of the Continental Congress*, 1774–1789 (1905): 121.

14. William Winthrop, *Military Law and Precedents*, 98. For an excellent discussion of the history of military jurisdiction over civilians, see Peters, "On Law, Wars, and Mercenaries," 376–84.

15. David A. Melson, "Military Jurisdiction over Civilian Contractors: A Historical Overview," *Naval L. Rev.* 52 (2005): 294–302.

16. Michael E. Guillory, "Civilianizing the Force: Is the United States Crossing the Rubicon?" *A.F. L. Rev.* 51 (2001): 118; Melson, "Military Jurisdiction," 289–93.

17. Melson, "Military Jurisdiction," 289–94, 307.

18. 19 C.M.A. 363 (1970).

19. Ibid.

20. 354 U.S. 1, 5 (1957).

21. Section 802(a)(10) of the UCMJ was not modified until section 552 of the *John Warner National Defense Authorization Act for Fiscal Year 2007.*

22. After the termination of US military involvement in Vietnam, US defense efforts once again returned to preparation to fight the Soviet threat. This period was marked by a "rebuilding" of the armed forces and revisions of US military doctrine to prepare for such a contingency. During this period, most US forces operating outside the United States were forward deployed to mature theaters of operations pursuant to status-of-forces agreements, such as allied countries in Western Europe and the Far East. Actual combat operations between 1973 and 1991 were characterized by short duration with minimal need for a robust civilian-augmentee presence. 2 U.S. Army Ctr. for Military History, *American Military History* (2005): 251–83 (addressing the evolution of the US Army during the Cold War).

23. Ibid.

24. US Army Judge Advocate General's Legal Center and School, *Operational Law Handbook*, John Rawcliffe and Jeannine Smith, eds. (Judge Advocate General's Legal Center & School, U.S. Army, Charlottesville, VA, 2006): 383–84 [hereinafter, Operational Law Handbook] (explaining the jurisdictional scheme of the North Atlantic Treaty Alliance Status of Forces Agreement).

25. Agreement under Article IV of the *Mutual Defense Treaty between the United States of America and the Republic of Korea, Regarding Facilities and Areas and the Status of United States Armed Forces in the Republic of Korea*, July 9, 1966, United States Treaties and Other International Agreements 1677, pt. 2: art. XXII, 2(a) [hereinafter Mutual Defense Treaty].

26. Operational Law Handbook: 383–84; Mutual Defense Treaty: art. XXII, 2(a).

27. Operational Law Handbook: 137–38; Michael N. Schmitt, "War, International Law, and Sovereignty: Reevaluating the Rules of the Game in a New Century: Humanitarian Law and Direct Participation in Hostilities by Private Contractors or Civilian Employees," *Chi. J. Int'l L.* 5 (2005): 516.

28. According to the Operational Law Handbook (136):

Contractor employees are not subject to military law under the UCMJ when accompanying U.S. forces, except during a declared war. When a contractor is involved in criminal activity, international agreements and the host nation's laws take precedence.

29. P. W. Singer, "Outsourcing War," *Foreign Affairs* (Mar./Apr. 2005): 119, 120.

30. Ibid., 123; Schmitt, "War, International Law, and Sovereignty," 517.

31. Peters, "On Law, Wars, and Mercenaries," 382–83.

32. Rebecca Rafferty Vernon, "Battlefield Contractors: Facing the Tough Issues," *Pub. Cont. L.J.* 33 (2004): 369.

33. Thomas G. Becker, "Justice on the Far Side of the World," 277–78 (describing how the son of a US serviceman stationed in Japan got off easy by being convicted of

involuntary manslaughter, even though the son stabbed to death another US service-man's son); Joseph R. Perlak, "The Military Extraterritorial Jurisdiction Act of 2000: Implications for Contractor Personnel," *Mil. L. Rev.* 169 (2001): 98–99. According to Perlak:

> With court-martial jurisdiction effectively removed by the courts, it devolved to Congress to come up with a legal scheme that would fill the gap. From the very outset in 1957, up to the present day, no court has ever questioned the ability of Congress to do exactly that. Federal criminal laws with extraterritorial effect have existed for years. Likewise, jurisdiction over land under military control or put to military use within the United States has existed under the special maritime and territorial jurisdiction of the United States. However, because this jurisdiction has no extraterritorial effect, there have been conspicuous gaps. Courts have employed a rule of statutory construction providing a presumption that a law does not have extraterritorial effect unless there is clear congressional intent to make it so.

(Citations omitted)

34. Operational Law Handbook: 135–36; Perlak, "The Military Extraterritorial Jurisdiction Act of 2000" ("There is an existing scheme of control, however, based on contract terms and parameters of performance.").

35. Perlak, "The Military Extraterritorial Jurisdiction Act of 2000," 99–100.

36. Peters, "On Law, Wars, and Mercenaries," 372.

37. 18 U.S.C. § 3261 (2000); Perlak, "The Military Extraterritorial Jurisdiction Act of 2000," 99–100.

38. Perlak, "The Military Extraterritorial Jurisdiction Act of 2000," 98–99.

39. 18 U.S.C. § 3266(a), which provides:

> The Secretary of Defense, after consultation with the Secretary of State and the Attorney General, shall prescribe regulations governing the apprehension, deten-tion, delivery, and removal of persons under this chapter and the facilitation of proceedings under section 3265. Such regulations shall be uniform throughout the Department of Defense.

40. Peters, "On Law, Wars, and Mercenaries," 386 ("The tens of thousands of con-tractors who have served or are currently serving in the Iraqi campaign have either scrupulously avoided any meaningful misconduct, or government efforts to address those crimes are either lacking or simply ineffective in practice."); ibid. at 391 ("federal prosecutors have yet to employ MEJA for any alleged misconduct of civilian contrac-tors arising from their actions during the Iraqi campaign.").

41. Department of Defense, Instruction No. 5525.11, *Criminal Jurisdiction over Civilians Employed By or Accompanying the Armed Forces Outside the United States, Certain Service Members, and Former Service Members* (2005), www.dtic.mil/whs/directives/corres/pdf/552511p.pdf [hereinafter Instruction No. 5525.11]; Peters, "On Law, Wars, and Mercenaries," 391.

42. Instruction No. 5525.11: 6.2.2.1. This paragraph provides:

When a Military Criminal Investigative Organization is the lead investigative organization, the criminal investigator, in order to assist the DSS/DOJ and the designated U.S. Attorney representative (once the DSS/DOJ has made the designation), in making a preliminary determination of whether the case warrants prosecution under the Act, shall provide a copy of the Investigative Report, or a summary thereof, to the Office of the Staff Judge Advocate of the Designated Commanding Officer (DCO) (as defined in enclosure 2) at the location where the offense was committed for review and transmittal, through the Commander of the Combatant Command, to the DSS/DOJ and the designated U.S. Attorney representative. The Office of the Staff Judge Advocate shall also furnish the DSS/DOJ and the designated U.S. Attorney representative an affidavit or declaration from the criminal investigator or other appropriate law enforcement official that sets forth the probable cause basis for believing that a violation of the Act has occurred and that the person identified in the affidavit or declaration has committed the violation.

43. For example, the implementing instruction requires coordination between the responsible military command and the host nation; the responsible military command and the Department of Defense General Counsel; the Department of Defense General Counsel and the Department of Justice; the Defense Criminal Investigation Service and the Department of Justice; the Department of Justice and the US Attorney in whose venue the case lies (ibid.).

44. Department of Justice, "Former Ft. Campbell Soldier Indicted in Iraqi Civilian Death," news release (Nov. 2, 2006), http://louisville.fbi.gov/dojpressrel/pressrel06/iraqideaths110206.htm (discussing the indictment of a former soldier under MEJA for the rape and murder of an Iraqi girl); "Abu Ghraib Contractor Sentenced for Child Porn," *MSNBC.com* (May 25, 2007), www.msnbc.msn.com/id/18866442/ (discussing the MEJA-based prosecution of a civilian-network administrator working for the armed forces at the Baghdad Central Confinement Facility in Abu Ghraib).

45. 18 U.S.C. § 2441(a) (2000) ("Whoever, whether inside or outside the United States, commits a war crime . . . shall be fined under this title or imprisoned for life or any term of years, or both, and if death results to the victim, shall also be subject to the penalty of death.").

46. The primary motivation for the War Crimes Act was to fulfill US obligations to implement the four Geneva Conventions of 1949. These treaties include articles obligating state parties to provide domestic legislation for the prosecutions of treaty violations. See H.R. REP. 104-69, at 3–4 (1996). This report indicates that:

> Despite ratifying the Geneva conventions, the United States has never enacted legislation specifically implementing their penal provisions. This was felt to be unnecessary, that existing United States law provided adequate means of prosecution. The Senate Committee on Foreign Relations stated that:
>
> > The committee is satisfied that the obligations imposed upon the United States by the "grave breaches" provisions are such as can be met by existing legislation enacted by the Federal Government within its constitutional powers. A

review of that legislation reveals that no further measures are needed to provide effective penal sanctions or procedures. . . .

A review of current federal and state law indicates that while there are many
instances in which individuals committing grave breaches of the Geneva conventions may already be prosecuted, prosecution would be impossible in many other
situations.

Ibid. (footnote omitted) (quoting *Geneva Conventions for the Protection of War
Victims: Hearing Before the S. Comm. on Foreign Relations*, 84th Cong., 1st Sess. 27
[1955]). Although ratified in 1954, it was not until 1996 that the United States met this
obligation to enact such legislation. The *War Crimes Act*, as amended, establishes federal criminal jurisdiction over any US national who violates certain provisions of the
law of war. This jurisdiction provides an effective gap filler to reach members of the
armed forces who commit war crimes but who separate from the armed forces before
discovery of the offense (military jurisdiction ceases to apply on discharge from the
armed forces). But the jurisdictional language is broad enough to reach any US resident who violates the applicable law-of-war obligations to include civilian augmentees. *Military Commissions Act of 2006*, Public Law 109-366, § 6(b), *U.S. Statute at large*
120: 2600, 2633, to be codified at 18 U.S.C. § 2441.

47. U.S. Code Annotated 18 § 2441(b) (West 2007).

48. Instruction No. 5525.11: 5.1. The Department of Defense also declared that:

Although some Federal criminal statutes are expressly or implicitly extraterritorial, many acts described therein are criminal only if they are committed within
"the special maritime and territorial jurisdiction of the United States," or if they
affect interstate or foreign commerce. Therefore, in most instances, Federal criminal jurisdiction ends at the nation's borders. . . . Similarly, civilians are generally not subject to prosecution under the UCMJ, unless Congress had declared
a "time of war" when the acts were committed. As a result, these acts are crimes,
and therefore criminally punishable, only under the law of the foreign country
in which they occurred. However, there have been occasions where the foreign
country has elected not to exercise its criminal jurisdiction and the person goes
unpunished for the crimes committed. . . .

The Act and this Instruction are intended to address the jurisdictional gap
in U.S. law regarding criminal sanctions, as applied to civilians employed by
or accompanying the Armed Forces outside the United States, members of the
Armed Forces, and former members of the Armed Forces, including their dependents. It does not enforce a foreign nation's criminal laws and, as such, does not
require that the person's actions violate the foreign nation's laws and applies even
if the conduct may be legal under the foreign nation's laws. The jurisdictional
requirement is that the conduct be in violation of U.S. Federal laws. When, however, the same conduct violates the Act and the laws of the foreign nation, the
Act provides for consideration of existing international agreements between the
United States and the foreign nation.

Ibid., 2.4–2.5.

49. Daniel Bergner, "The Other Army," *New York Times*, Aug. 14, 2005, magazine, sec. 6; Jonathan Finer, "Security Contractors in Iraq Under Scrutiny after Shootings," *Washington Post*, Sept. 10, 2005; Nathan Hodge, "Army Chief Notes 'Problematic' Potential of Armed Contractors on the Battlefield," *Defense Daily*, Aug. 26, 2005; David Washburn and Bruce V. Bigelow, "In Harm's Way: Titan in Iraq," *San Diego Union-Tribune*, July 24, 2005.

50. Paul Tait, "Shooting Shines Light on Murky World of Iraq Security," *Reuters*, Sept. 18, 2007, www.reuters.com/article/worldNews/idUSL1882490620070918 ("Iraq has vowed to review all local and foreign security contractors, described by critics as mercenaries who act with impunity, after a shooting incident involving U.S. firm Blackwater on Sunday in which 11 people were killed."); Amnesty International U.S.A., "Corporate Accountability in the 'War on Terror,'" www .amnestyusa.org/War_on_Terror/Private_Military_and_Security_Contractors/page .do?id=1101665&n1=3&n2=26&n3=157 (accessed Jan. 19, 2008).

51. Instruction No. 5525.11.

52. *John Warner National Defense Authorization Act for Fiscal Year 2007*, Pub. L. No. 109-364, 120 Stat. 2083 (2006).

53. Ibid. § 552 (bold omitted).

54. Ibid.

55. 10 U.S.C. § 101(a)(13) (2000).

56. Geoffrey S. Corn, "Bringing Discipline to the Civilianization of the Battlefield: A Proposal for a More Legitimate Approach to Resurrecting Military Criminal Jurisdiction over Civilian Augmentees," *Miami L. Rev.* 62 (2008): 491.

57. There is no legislative record indicating this amendment responded to a request by the Department of Defense.

58. For example, an Air Force Judge Advocate General's Talking Paper on the amendment includes the following:

> Amended Article 2(a)(10) broad enough to include embedded journalists and foreign employees of contractors
>
> · Manual for Courts-Martial does not separately address prosecution of civilians in detail, except Analysis of R.C.M. 202 in Appendix 21, A21–11
> · DoD GC representative first addressed with Joint Service Committee on 1 Feb 07
> · *One possibility, non-binding criteria/guidance to exercise such jurisdiction sparingly*

Air Force Judge Advocate General's Office, Talking Paper on Article 2(a)(10), UCMJ (on file with author) (emphasis added).

59. According to Peters, this concern was actually expressed by the Department of Justice in relation to the development of MEJA:

> Similar language was proposed as an amendment to the UCMJ through the Fiscal Year 1996 Department of Defense (DOD) Authorization Act. The Department of Justice (DOJ) determined that it was likely an amendment to Article 2(a) (10) of the UCMJ, extending courts-martial jurisdiction over civilians during

contingency operations in armed conflict, presented possible constitutional problems and therefore did not support that portion of the proposed amendment.
Telephone Interview with John De Pue, former Senior Trial Attorney, Counterterrorism Section, Criminal Div., U.S. Dep't of Justice (Apr. 7, 2005). Mr. De Pue was
the DOJ representative on the panel that considered the amendment.

Peters, "On Law, Wars, and Mercenaries," 374 n23.

With regard to the applicability to non-US nationals, while *Reid v. Covert* stands
for the proposition that US constitutional rights apply globally, it is not clear that this
precedent is fully applicable to nonresident aliens. Instead, it is conceivable that a
reviewing court could apply a more limited range of constitutional protections to such
defendants. For example, in *United States v. Verdugo-Urquidez*, 494 U.S. 259 (1990), the
US Supreme Court held that nonresident aliens with no meaningful connection to
the United States are not protected by the Fourth Amendment's prohibition against
unreasonable search and seizure when conducted outside the United States. Accordingly, it is not absolutely certain that a reviewing court would even consider the right
to trial by jury and indictment by grand jury applicable to such defendants.

60. Melson, "Military Jurisdiction," 289 ("Military jurisdiction over civilians
reached an unprecedented and expansive limit [during Word War II].") see Corn,
"Bringing Discipline to the Civilianization of the Battlefield."

61. *Hines v. Mikell*, 259 F. 28, 29–30 (4th Cir. 1919); *McCune v. Kilpatrick*, 53 F. Supp.
80, 84 (E.D. Va. 1943); *In re Di Bartolo*, 50 F. Supp. 929, 930 (S.D.N.Y. 1943); *Ex parte
Jochen*, 257 F. 200, 203 (S.D. Tex. 1919); *Ex parte Falls*, 251 F. 415, 415–16 (D.N.J. 1918); *Ex
parte Gerlach*, 247 F. 616, 617 (S.D.N.Y. 1917).

62. Melson, "Military Jurisdiction," 291–94.

63. House Subcommittee to Committee on Armed Services, *A Bill to Unify, Con-
solidate, Revise, and Codify the Articles of War, the Articles for the Government of the
Navy, and Disciplinary Laws of the Coast Guard, and to Enact and Establish a Uniform
Code of Military Justice: Hearings on H.R. 2498 Before the Subcomm. of the H. Comm.
on Armed Services*, 81st Cong. 565, 622–23 (1949) (statement of Felix Larkin, Assistant
General Counsel, Secretary of Defense).

64. In an article first written in 1954 by a major in the Judge Advocate General's
Corps who would later serve as the Judge Advocate General of the Army and reach the
rank of major general, then Major George Prugh, Jr., noted this dual purpose:

> Now, it seems apparent that any American code of military justice must serve
> a dual purpose: (1) it must establish a framework whereby offenders are appro-
> priately and promptly punished by means of an enlightened procedure fully in
> accord with the basic principles of American justice; (2) while at the same time,
> not only not impeding, but on the contrary, aiding the military commander in
> accomplishing his assigned mission.

George S. Prugh, Jr., "Observations on the Uniform Code of Military Justice: 1954
and 2000," *Mil. L. Rev.* 165 (2000): 23.

65. 10 U.S.C. §§ 801–946 (2000); Department of Army, "Contractor Deployment Guide," 1998, www.army.mil/usapa/epubs/pdf/p715_16.pdf. The MEJA Implementing Instruction published by the Department of Defense emphasizes the relationship between military discipline and civilian misconduct: "It is DoD policy that the requirement for order and discipline of the Armed Forces outside the United States extends to civilians employed by or accompanying the Armed Forces, and that such persons who engage in conduct constituting criminal offenses shall be held accountable for their actions, as appropriate" (Instruction No. 5525.11: 3).

66. 354 U.S. 1, 5 (1957).

8 Contractors' Wars and the Commission on Wartime Contracting

Allison Stanger

1. Introduction

Whenever America has gone to war, contractors have been part of the war effort. But they have never before featured so prominently in all aspects of the mission as they do in Iraq and Afghanistan today. Even at the height of the Vietnam War, contractors comprised just 14 percent of the American presence on the ground in Southeast Asia.[1] Today, contractors outnumber uniformed personnel on the ground in both Iraq and Afghanistan, and in the simplest of terms, the more than 40,000 armed security contractors deployed in Southwest Asia enable the United States to wage two wars simultaneously while avoiding the necessity of a draft. Contractors and contracting have thus become serious policy issues, and they will continue to be so wherever and whenever American power is projected abroad.

The explosion of what John Nagl and Richard Fontaine have called "Expeditionary Stabilization and Reconstruction" (ES&R) contracting—contracting in conflict environments—is a piece of a larger puzzle that amounts to a stealthy whole-scale paradigm shift in the core business of American foreign policy.[2] Contractors have quietly become prominent across the so-called three Ds of defense, diplomacy, and development, as well as in homeland security. In all of these realms, the majority of what used to be the exclusive work of government has been outsourced to private actors, both for-profit and not-for-profit. In the development realm, contracts and grants have become the principal vehicle for American efforts to help others help themselves. These changes are not the result of partisan politics; Democrats and Republicans alike have embraced the privatization imperative. Thus, while no one consciously planned it, much of the envisioning and execution of American objectives is today in private hands.[3]

The reinvention of government business has not been confined to US foreign policy institutions. To cite just one telling statistic, the federal government had the same number of full-time employees in 2008 as it had in 1963. Yet in real terms the federal budget more than tripled in that same period. That gap reflects the growing prominence of contractors, who have often been dispatched for reasons of expediency without any reflection on the unintended consequences of outsourcing particular functions. As Secretary Gates himself has aptly described it, "contracting in Iraq was done willy-nilly."[4] The longstanding debate over the size of government thus takes on different dimensions; government can be big in terms of the amount of money it spends, but small in terms of the number of people it directly employs to manage that spending.

That pattern is readily identifiable in Iraq and Afghanistan today. Faced with a mission that an all-volunteer force could not properly staff and America's allies were reluctant to embrace with the same degree of enthusiasm, the government deployed contractors to fill the gap between American ambitions and the degree of commitment the American people could muster for war on two fronts. In many ways, outsourcing proved an attractive path of least resistance, one that enabled American policy makers to throw money at the problem without having to rally the American people to fully support the enormous scale of operations.

But all of the potential problems that can accompany privatization are exacerbated when the work must be done beyond America's borders. Waste, fraud, and abuse are more difficult to contain in a war zone. Legal and regulatory challenges are daunting. Despite these risks, the new normal for policy is and will continue to involve a multi-sector workforce of public and private actors. ES&R contracting is here to stay. The challenge is to ensure that this blended workforce serves the interests of the American people rather than the interests of corporations.

This chapter demonstrates the glaring need for a contemporary Truman Committee and explores the work of the Commission on Wartime Contracting to date. The next section presents the politics surrounding the commission's creation. Section 3 delineates some of the moral and legal hazards that have arisen from ES&R contracting in Iraq and Afghanistan. The fourth reviews the scope of waste, fraud, and abuse that has already been exposed. Section 5 investigates the distinctive challenges associated with outsourcing security in war zones, especially at the subcontractor level. Section 6 considers the complex problems associated with counting and coordinating contractors in theater. The seventh concludes.

2. From the Truman Committee to the Commission on Wartime Contracting

Congress created the Commission on Wartime Contracting in Iraq and Afghanistan (CWC) as part of the National Defense Authorization Act for Fiscal Year 2008.[5] The commission "is required to study, assess and make recommendations concerning wartime contracting for the reconstruction, logistical support, and the performance of security functions in Iraq and Afghanistan. The Commission's major objectives include a thorough assessment of the systemic problems identified with interagency wartime contracting, the identification of instances of waste, fraud and abuse, and ensuring accountability for those responsible."[6]

The legislation was inspired by the legacy of the former Truman Committee (1941–1948), which was first led by Senator Harry S. Truman (D-MO), before he became FDR's running mate for the 1944 election. The Truman Committee investigated government waste during and after World War II and is said to have saved the US taxpayer some $178 billion in today's dollars ($15 billion in 1943 dollars).[7]

The story of the Truman Committee's genesis is instructive. As World War II began to engulf Europe, the United States began to prepare for war, appropriating $10 billion in defense contracts in 1940. Rumors of contract mismanagement and fraud subsequently began to multiply, and Senator Truman set off on a ten-thousand-mile tour of American military bases to investigate these allegations. On his tour, Truman discovered two things. First, he learned that many of the contracts that had been signed were cost-plus, with contractors being paid a fixed profit regardless of cost-effectiveness. Second, he learned that the vast majority of contracts exclusively benefited firms in the Northeast. The Truman Committee was Truman's idea for discouraging waste and fraud. By unanimous consent on March 1, 1941, the Senate created what is now widely perceived to have been one of the most productive investigating committees in congressional history.

Senior military officials opposed Truman's vision, believing it would only re-create the problems that President Lincoln had faced during the Civil War with the congressional Joint Committee on the Conduct of the War. Confederate General Robert E. Lee was said to have remarked that he considered the committee's relentless scrutiny of the Union war effort to be worth at least two Confederate divisions.[8] But the idea prevailed, just as it would more than 140 years later during the George W. Bush administration, despite the latter president's serious misgivings. In a signing statement, President Bush singled out the section that created a contemporary version of the Truman Commission in the 2008 Defense Authorization Bill, claiming that it could inhibit his constitutional obligations. The signing statement did not make clear whether the president objected to the creation of the commission or whether he was reserving the right to turn down its requests for information, or both.[9]

Like its predecessor, the CWC was tasked with a similarly broad mandate to research and investigate federal agency contracting for reconstruction, logistical support, and security functions in Iraq and Afghanistan. The law provides for eight appointed CWC commissioners, four of whom are appointed by Democrats and four by Republicans. The commissioners who have served to date have brought a wide range of experience to the table. They direct the CWC staff. While its work is ongoing, the CWC's ultimate aim is to "develop findings and recommendations on issues including the extent of reliance on contractors in wartime settings, contractor performance and accountability, federal contracting and management systems and practices, contractor use of force, and potential violations of law."[10]

The CWC held its first hearing on February 2, 2009. It issued an interim report in June 2009 and will deliver a final report to Congress in summer 2011. That final report was originally due in summer 2010, but the National Defense Authorization Act for Fiscal Year 2010 extended that deadline. This chapter of necessity went to press before the commission's work could be completed. However, the careful reader will surely note that much of the analysis that follows is informed by insights revealed at its hearings.

3. Moral and Legal Hazards of Wartime Contracting

The explosion of ES&R contracting has ushered in a wide array of moral and legal hazards. The moral hazards are as old as war itself. Since wartime needs are the most urgent imaginable, those who can provide for them stand to profit handsomely. There is nothing new in the idea of wartime profiteering. But what used to be an operation orchestrated by shadowy figures is today conducted by large corporations, whose stock is openly traded right alongside that of American icons Walt Disney and Apple. Because contractors outnumber uniformed personnel in Iraq and Afghanistan, the potential scope and scale of the money that can be legitimately made has also expanded exponentially. The pervasiveness and indispensability of contractors in the war effort have therefore legitimized wartime profiteering, rendering it both respectable and even patriotic. The moral temptations multiply concurrently when a contractor–industrial complex augments and further invigorates the military–industrial complex of whose perils President Eisenhower warned.[11]

Armed security contractors are a small subset of this much larger universe of activities and tasks performed by the ES&R workforce. Are armed security contractors currently performing inherently governmental functions in these conflict zones? While there is a consensus that there are activities so intrinsic to the nature of government that they should not be contracted out, there is little agreement on what those activities are. Both the White House Office of Management and Budget and Congress have repeatedly focused attention on the topic of inherently governmental functions, but to date have refrained from providing specific guidelines as to what particular activities must never be outsourced.

Restricting the focus to contractors able to deploy lethal force makes it easier to render a judgment. A leading advocate of minimal government, Milton Friedman, maintained "the basic functions of government are to defend the nation against foreign enemies, to prevent coercion of some individuals by others within the country, to provide a means of deciding on our rules, and to adjudicate disputes."[12] Using Friedman's minimalist definition, the use of contractors in the realms of security and justice demands the strictest scrutiny. Even under this leanest of definitions, moving security contractors are performing inherently governmental functions, since they are actively involved in defending the nation against foreign enemies.

Section 5 of the Federal Activities Inventory Reform Act defines an inherently governmental function in potentially broader terms as "a function that is so intimately related to the public interest as to require performance by Federal Government employees."[13] The Office of Federal Procurement Policy was expected to issue further guidance on this definition by late summer/ early fall 2010. Yet even without that additional guidance, it seems clear that taking up arms to defend the interests of the United States, whether remotely pulling triggers on drone flights or guarding government personnel as they travel in war zones, would seem to constitute active involvement in defending the nation against foreign enemies, hence clearing Milton Friedman's minimalist inherently governmental threshold. If anything at all is inherently governmental, armed security contractors deployed in war zones would seem to be it.

The legal implications of contractors' wars remain problematic, despite congressional efforts to address the challenge. The Military Extra-Territorial Jurisdiction Act (MEJA) allows contractors hired by DoD to be tried in US federal (civilian) courts for crimes committed overseas. In 2004, Congress extended MEJA to cover contractors hired by other government agencies that support DoD's mission overseas. That sounds good on paper for accountability—if MEJA clearly covered all contractors currently deployed in Iraq and Afghanistan. But MEJA's application turns on how DoD's mission is defined, and this can mean different things to different people. That is why in the aftermath of the Nisoor Square shooting, where Blackwater employees shot seventeen Iraqi civilians dead, the State Department for a time argued that MEJA did not apply to its contractors.[14] Consequently, relatively few contractors have been tried under MEJA since its promulgation in 2000 and its expansion in 2004. According to information obtained by Richard Fontaine from a DoD official, between March 2005 and March 2010, seventeen US national contractors were prosecuted or charged under MEJA, with an additional fifteen cases pending.[15] A potential solution would be for Congress to extend MEJA to cover unambiguously all contractors deployed in combat zones, but to date it has not done so.

Coming at the same problem from a different angle, Congress in 2007 extended the Uniform Code of Military Justice (UCMJ) or court-martial system to contractors operating in a contingency operation. Both MEJA and the UCMJ could therefore conceivably be deployed to prosecute contractor abuses. However, serious constitutional issues that flow from the very idea of trying civilians in military courts have yet to be properly resolved.

In short, MEJA provides a constitutionally sound basis for trying contractors, but the scope of its jurisdiction is ambiguous. The UCMJ is easier to apply, but its application to civilians is constitutionally questionable. The status of security contractors under international law is unclear, and their status under foreign law still more confusing, varying from country to country.[16]

The ultimate result is that armed contractors are an irreplaceable part of the mission in both Iraq and Afghanistan, yet they continue to operate in a legal and moral vacuum above and alongside the dictates of multifaceted and often competing legal considerations.

The challenges only multiply when subcontractors are added to the mix. The subcontracting of work to local nationals through the Afghan First program has the significant virtue of providing jobs for the people we are trying to help. But when corners are cut and prosecution is necessary, neither MEJA nor the UCMJ applies to local nationals, even when their paycheck is ultimately funded by the US taxpayer. Instead, jurisdiction lies with the Afghan criminal justice system, which remains underdeveloped and plagued with corruption.[17] More generally, problems of accountability are exacerbated by subcontracting, making it less likely that criminal offences will be detected. But even when they are, the means of prosecuting them remain highly unsatisfactory.

4. Waste, Fraud, and Abuse

The legal and moral hazards of wartime contracting make the potential for abuse large and the means for deterring corruption seemingly limited. With that as a backdrop, the outcomes in Iraq and Afghanistan have, in a certain basic sense, been utterly predictable. War is by definition an expensive endeavor, and when its execution becomes all the more complex, the costs grow commensurately. When the United States is heavily dependent on contractors and no American wants his or her country to fight war on the cheap, what was already a seller's market becomes even more so.

Training a spotlight on this dynamic, the CWC issued its first special report on September 21, 2009. It described a situation where billions of dollars were flowing out the door in contracts and grants without adequate accounting systems in place for tracking money flows or detecting contract cost errors. For example, the commission reviewed a collection of reports on contractor business systems that encompassed $43 billion of work and learned that fully half involving billing and compensation had been deemed inadequate by federal auditors.[18]

In addition, the commission found that the two primary government agencies overseeing these flows of funds, the Defense Contract Management Agency (DCMA) and the Defense Contract Audit Agency (DCAA), were not effectively working together to protect government interests. It recommended five priorities. First, DoD needs to ensure that the government speaks with one voice to contractors. Second, DoD should improve government accountability by moving decisively to resolve conflicts between the business systems of different agencies involved in wartime contracting. Third, the DCAA needs to refine its audit reports to move beyond rendering only a pass/fail verdict. Fourth, the DCMA needs to embrace aggressive compliance enforcement. Finally, both DCAA and DCMA need to make contingency-contractor oversight a top priority and request adequate resources to get the job done well.[19]

What are the majority of contingency contractors doing in Iraq and Afghanistan? The overwhelming majority are involved in the logistics of housing, clothing, and feeding American troops. The Logistics Civil Augmentation Program (LOGCAP) concept was developed in the mid-1980s and facilitates the outsourcing of goods and services needed to support military deployments. The first LOGCAP contract was awarded in 1992 to Brown and Root Services (today KBR). The company primarily supported both US and UN forces in Somalia and the Balkans. In 1997, LOGCAP II was awarded to DynCorp to support US armed forces in the Philippines, Latin America, and East Timor. KBR won the LOGCAP III contract in 2001. LOGCAP III supported operations in Iraq, Afghanistan, Kuwait, Djibouti, and Georgia and cost the US taxpayer some $31 billion between 2001 and 2009. LOGCAP IV was awarded in April 2008 to two of the more controversial companies involved in military logistics, DynCorp and KBR, as well as a new contributor to the cause, Fluor Intercontinental. LOGCAP IV involves a new approach. The three vendors are permitted to bid for individual task orders under the contract, the idea being that the enhanced competition will control costs and improve quality. It is estimated that its total price tag, when all is said and done, could reach $150 billion, for services including delivering food, water, fuel, and spare parts; operating dining and laundry facilities; providing housing and sanitation; moving personnel and supplies; engineering and constructing projects; and maintaining facilities.[20]

The State Department and DoD are not the only government agencies experiencing difficulties with contract management in war zones. The USAID inspector general has also been hard at work in Iraq and Afghanistan, where problems associated with subcontracts are common. In March 2009, the inspector general found that "USAID/Iraq's implementing partners could not detect deficiencies in security subcontractors' reporting of serious incidents because they had provided inadequate oversight of subcontractor practices in this area."[21] USAID is taking steps to address this deficiency. Through the Development Leadership Initiative, it has pledged to double the size of its Foreign Service Officer contingent by 2012.[22]

USAID has also embraced the Afghanization/Afghan First model in its programs. The aim is to increase local procurement and transfer responsibility for Afghan development to Afghans. This means moving away from large awards toward smaller and shorter-term grants and contracts and channeling more money through the Afghan government. According to the Special Inspector General for Afghan Reconstruction, "The United States and other donors have pledged to increase the proportion of development aid delivered through the Afghan government to about 50 percent in the next two years."[23] But much like the Host Nation Trucking contract, this strategy can only work as planned with reliable partners and scrupulous oversight. The former is difficult to muster in a country plagued by decades of war.[24] The latter cannot possibly be forthcoming without significant increases in USAID direct-hire staff. USAID has received staggering amounts of money through supplementals for development initiatives in Iraq and Afghanistan, going from a million dollar agency to a billion dollar one virtually overnight, without concurrent increases in staff to properly monitor those funds. For example, "Over the last five fiscal years, USAID managed resources for Afghanistan rose from over $700 million in Fiscal Year 2006 to enacted levels, estimated at $2.1 billion for 2010."[25]

The reconstruction experience in Iraq to date does not cause one to view the future of contracting in Afghanistan with optimism. Speaking before the CWC on May 24, 2010, Deputy Inspector General for Iraq Reconstruction Ginger Cruz summarized the results of the investigations of the Special Inspector General for Iraq Reconstruction (SIGIR) to date in worrisome terms:

> As of May 2010, SIGIR's investigations have led to 42 indictments, 32 convictions, and $72.4 million in fines, restitutions, and other monetary results. In addition, there exists one sealed indictment, one signed plea agreement, and at least 15 more draft indictments being prepared against other suspects at this time. Including cases with pending charges, we have more than 60 investigations where we expect judicial criminal action. Our caseload of 113 investigations is also steadily expanding, and the pool of subjects keeps growing. . . .
> The types of criminal activity and the programs looted vary. To date, SIGIR's

investigators have uncovered bribery and kickbacks between contract officials and contractors; extortion by contracting officials; embezzlements; thefts of cash and equipment by officials and contractor employees; bribery of Iraqi officials; and fraud by U.S. and allied contractors. Moreover, officials of the Departments of Defense (DoD) and State (DoS), as well as of non-governmental organizations, have all been found to have been involved in criminal activity. Both senior and junior officers and enlisted personnel in the U.S. military—up to the rank of full colonel—have been convicted of reconstruction-related crimes. Military personnel from coalition partner countries have also been convicted, as have the owners and employees of contracting firms, and civilian employees of the U.S. government.[26]

5. Outsourcing Security

When a mission is pursued in a war zone, security is often in scarce supply. Armed security contractors are deployed to bridge this gap between demand and supply. They may be further divided into two main categories: static security (guarding a particular location, such as an embassy or camp); and moving security (guarding personnel or convoys as they pursue work in different locations). Contractors providing static security do not venture out on missions. Those providing moving security often perform jobs indistinguishable from those of uniformed personnel and are more likely to end up using their weapons. The use of contractors to guard US embassies is a practice that began in the 1980s and has been a long-standing source of employment for local nationals. Although the use of privateers has a long history, contracting for moving security on land is largely a post–Cold War development, and our missions in Iraq and Afghanistan today are completely dependent on it.

America's current dependence on armed contractors in war zones is totally at odds with our stated intention to build state capacity in Iraq and Afghanistan, so that the Afghan and Iraqi governments might one day be capable of independently providing security for their own citizens. In Afghanistan, the Afghan First strategy aims to hire local nationals to provide private security, and it has been very successful. At least 90 percent of private security contractors in Afghanistan today are Afghans.[27] But in empowering these local privateers engaged in moving security, we are in turn forced to empower regional warlords, who are deeply involved in Afghan private security companies—precisely the opposite of building up Afghanistan's capacity to secure its own territory without massive infusions of US taxpayer money.[28] According to the UN, in Afghanistan drugs and bribes are the largest generators of income, amounting to about half the country's GDP.[29] In a country where per capita GDP is $425 per year and the average bribe is $160,[30] subcontracting chains are highly unlikely to resemble those of their Western counterparts.

Despite these worrisome hazards, in June 2010, a House Committee Majority Report found that DoD oversight of the multi-billion dollar Host Nation Trucking contract in Afghanistan was virtually non-existent. DoD essentially designed a contract that put responsibility for the security of US supply lines in the hands of wholly unaccountable Afghan subcontractors. "This arrangement has fueled a vast protection racket run by a shadowy network of warlords, strongmen, commanders, and corrupt Afghan officials. Not only does the system run afoul of the Department's own rules and regulations mandated by Congress, it also appears to risk undermining the U.S. strategy for achieving its goals in Afghanistan."[31] The Afghan First strategy actively encouraged the creation of local militias that are likely to be a destabilizing future presence for the security of the AfPak region. Since guns for hire, whether local or international, never pledge enduring allegiance to a particular state, America's rented allies today may very well become enemies tomorrow.

A March 2010 GAO study reported that in four of five cases, the United States government saved money by outsourcing static security in Iraq. The fifth case, the only one involving moving security, was a dramatically different story. The State Department's annual costs of using contractors for moving security in the Baghdad region was $380 million, compared to an estimated annual cost of $240 million for using diplomatic security to provide the same services.[32] To be sure, there are many different ways to estimate the relative costs of contracting for a service versus providing it in-house, and those estimates can be a matter for argument. The GAO's use of relative cost estimates that the State Department generated without any adjustment or investigation of State Department methodology was surprising. That said, one fact does seem indisputable given the publicly available evidence: hiring moving security is always likely to be more expensive than relying on state resources. Supplying the US military requires secure supply lines, so no price seems too high to pay to get the job done well and in a timely fashion. When qualified personnel for moving security are in short supply and demand is high, price adjusts to those market conditions. I know of no study that would disagree with this comparative assessment; the rationale for a standing army is in part built on this basic assumption.

But focusing on cost-effectiveness exclusively isn't a panacea either. The quality of the work matters as well. Consider the scandal surrounding the ArmorGroup North America (AGNA) contract to provide security for the US embassy in Kabul.[33] The State Department had repeatedly warned AGNA about deficiencies in its contract, yet none of these admonitions produced meaningful change. Despite these continuing problems, in July 2008 the State Department renewed AGNA's contract for another year. The saga of warnings and threats and noncompliance continued. At a June 2009 Senate hearing, State Department officials assured Congress that the problems with the AGNA contract had been addressed, and in July 2009 the State Department again renewed its contract for a year, with an option to extend until 2012.

When nearly 10 percent of the guards working under the AGNA contract had individually contacted the Project on Government Oversight (POGO) regarding what they perceived as a highly compromised security situation at the Kabul embassy, POGO sent a formal letter to Secretary Clinton. POGO's September 1, 2009, letter established a damning pattern of noncompliance, documented the specific nature of the deficiencies, and urged immediate action. Contractors were not only seriously overworked at the Kabul embassy, but the workforce was stitched together in highly impractical ways. For example, nearly two-thirds of the security contractors were Ghurkas, who spoke no English. But there was also a frat boy atmosphere at the embassy. There were hazing rituals, public urination, and heavy drinking in a Moslem country in which drinking alcohol is particularly offensive. These matters led whistleblowers to POGO.[34] POGO Executive Director Danielle Brian's September 2009 testimony before the CWC concluded, "What is truly obscene is that, practically from Day One, ArmorGroup North America (AGNA) knowingly underperformed in its mission in order to maximize its profits, endangering the diplomats and its own employees in the process—and the Department of State knew about it."[35]

Responding directly to this scandal involving armed security contractors, the CWC's second special report (October 1, 2009) argued that lowest-price security is simply inadequate for embassies in war zones. The State Department acknowledged that contractor performance had placed embassy personnel at risk.[36] The CWC urged the State Department to use a "best-value" rather than "lowest price" standard in the future.[37] Yet market realities continue to present a Faustian bargain; the United States government (USG) often has no choice but to return to firms that have failed it, precisely because the USG does not have the in-house capacity to perform the work itself, and viable alternative firms simply do not exist. This is the reason that the State Department kept renewing AGNA's contract.[38] It is the reason that the CIA continues to hire Blackwater (now Xe).

6. Who's In Charge? The Problem of Coordinating Contractors

It is not difficult to understand why waste, fraud, and abuse occur in a war zone; excess is embedded in the life or death choices that war presents. The USG is only beginning to be able to count the contractors it employs, let alone coordinate their efforts on the ground in any kind of systematic way. The Department of Defense's SPOT (Synchronized Predeployment and Operational Tracker) database now keeps accurate counts of DoD contractors, but there was no such tool in the early years of the wars in Afghanistan and Iraq. The SPOT system only recently began to include contractors working for the State Department and USAID.[39]

When contractors are so central to all aspects of the war effort, war profiteering is legitimized and corruption becomes business as usual. Containing corruption demands strict lines of accountability and command, but that is precisely what has been lacking to date in the execution of America's first contractors' wars. The coordination challenge has at least three dimensions. First, there is the day-to-day need to coordinate the activities of contractors on the ground. In Iraq, the USG appointed a contractor, AEGIS, to serve as its lead coordinator of armed contractors.[40] Second, there is the "who's in charge?" question of just who the point person for policy coordination within the government is. With the DoD drawdown in Iraq, roles previously filled by DoD will henceforth be the responsibility of the State Department. Until these twin challenges are met, accountability and hence effectiveness will continue to be elusive. In addition, there is the matter of allied coordination, but since what began as a NATO effort in Afghanistan has since been effectively Americanized, this particular aspect of the coordination issue is of lesser concern to us.

A closer look at police training in Iraq and Afghanistan sheds light on the contours of the coordination problem. In both places, albeit for differing reasons, the training of the police force was haphazard, with nobody clearly in charge. In Iraq, DoD was first in charge of police training, but with the draw-down, as of February 2010, the State Department has assumed responsibility for that task. Contractors were central to the training operation, regardless of who the ultimate overseer of a particular contract was. As Special Inspector General for Iraqi Reconstruction Stuart Bowen aptly summarized, "The bottom line is that no one person or entity controlled the resources, the contracts, and the requirements for Iraq police training. This fractured approach is no way to do business."[41]

Historically, the leadership for police training overseas had been the preserve of the Department of State and the Department of Justice, and the program was directly overseen by federal civilian employees. This was not the case in Iraq, where DoD was ostensibly in charge, working through the State Department, which outsourced the work to a contractor.[42] While the State Department is once more in charge in Iraq, ironically, in 2010 Afghanistan, DoD has again taken this responsibility from the State Department. The problems are very similar in both countries, but the oversight of police training contracts has been a moving target.[43] This is shocking, in that over half of all reconstruction dollars in Afghanistan have gone to training the Afghan police force.[44] A 2005 GAO report criticized both the State Department and Pentagon for not having a proper strategy for police training in place, even though the problem has been around for a long time.[45]

In a Senate hearing, General William B. Caldwell, currently in charge of training in Afghanistan, attributed the passing of eight years without training a proper police force in Afghanistan to a lack of appropriate contract oversight.[46] Control of the training exercise changed constantly, in part because the Afghanistan project began as a genuinely multinational effort. Police training was first the preserve of the Germans. It then shifted to the State Department under the DynCorp contract in 2003 and finally to DoD in 2005.[47] Ambassador Holbrooke is reported to have said in December 2009 that "we are seven years into this, $39 billion, and we are starting from scratch."[48] One particularly damning story comes from the DynCorp years, when Afghan trainees had gone for months without any significant improvement in their marksmanship, despite endless training. The Italians came in to look things over and discovered that the sights on the Afghan weapons were grossly misaligned as a consequence of poor maintenance, which explained why the Afghans could not seem to hit the side of a barn. Once the weapons were properly adjusted, scores dramatically improved. Senator Scott Brown, the newest ranking member of the Senate Committee on Homeland Security and Governmental Affairs, has called the situation an unparalleled financial mess, six billion dollars of taxpayer money that has delivered far too little.[49] Being nowhere after eight plus years and billions of dollars expended (cost estimates vary wildly—but they are all in the billions of dollars) raises the serious question as to whether any military or national police training should be delegated to contractors at all.

Multilateral initiatives by definition present significant coordination challenges. In Afghanistan, as the police training fiasco illustrates, there was no central hub to coordinate allied activities. NATO's International Security Assistance Force for Afghanistan now tracks many governance and reconstruction projects, but it is just getting started in this work.[50] But even when the United States goes it alone in ES&R contracting, the absence of a focal point within the government for supervising reconstruction and stabilization efforts is still keenly felt. It is understandable why this problem exists. Training police is work that spans the three Ds of diplomacy, development, and defense, so that the existing institutions, each designed to lead on one of the D's, are ill-equipped to deliver accountability for state-capacity-building projects. However, it is not evident why the problem persists, since everyone agrees that this coordination vacuum must be filled.

A variety of proposals have been floated to resolve the question of who is in charge of reconstruction and stabilization. Some have argued that the locus of coordination should reside in the National Security Council (NSC). Former National Security advisors, however, have countered that the NSC is not an operations body, so it is not the appropriate focal point for the coordination of ES&R contractors. It gives one pause to realize that the last individual who treated the NSC as an operations arm of the USG was Lieutenant-Colonel Oliver North. Others propose that the function reside within DoD, which currently has the in-house capacity and budget to do it competently. Still others believe that the appropriate authority already exists within the State Department in the relatively new Coordinator for Reconstruction and Stabilization (S/CRS). Ambassador John Herbst, the State Department's current Coordinator for Stabilization and Reconstruction, has argued that the existing office just needs to be granted the requisite resources to do its job.[51] S/CRS was created in 2004 but has not yet played a prominent role in coordinating reconstruction. It was denied authorization legislation three times, only receiving it in 2008. As of March 2010, it had a grand total of twenty employees in Afghanistan and none in Iraq. When asked why at a CWC hearing, Ambassador Herbst replied that it was because it had not been asked. Meanwhile, DoD is concurrently moving to source its civilian needs with its new Civilian Expeditionary Workforce (CEW), which will enable it to fill civilian jobs without having to depend on civilian agencies.[52]

SIGIR believes that the solution resides with the formation of a new agency, the US Office of Contingency Operations (USOCO), which would be the needed coordinating hub. Both DoD and the State Department politely disagreed, arguing that we should properly resource existing structures rather than build new ones. Within the State Department, USOCO would pose a potential challenge to State's regional bureaus. Once a country "went contingency," the entire policy leadership would of necessity shift from the relevant State regional bureau to USOCO, a highly problematic proposition for those interested in policy continuity and consistency.[53] Robert Zoellick has argued that multinational funds should be pooled through the World Bank. An alternative idea is to pool multinational funds through NATO.[54] In a letter dated December 15, 2009, to Secretary of State Clinton, Secretary of Defense Gates proposed the establishment of dual key Defense/State funds for security assistance, conflict prevention, and stabilization.[55] But that idea would do nothing to resolve coordination issues with allies and partners. With so many proposals vying for favor, it is clear that everyone realizes that there is a problem. But the absence of consensus practically guarantees that inertia and the status quo will carry the day without White House leadership on this issue.

The central coordination issue is intimately linked with the extensive use of contractors in stabilization and reconstruction. When the focal point for US authority is unclear, strong contract management and oversight is the first casualty, and the temptation to resolve the matter and move on to the next task by having contractors manage other contractors grows. Hiring more contractors is, in effect, an ephemeral "solution" to the problem of too many contractors and no clear lines of authority. That helps explain how we got into our present predicament. It is no excuse for staying there.

7. Conclusion

The shortcomings with ES&R contracting as it has been pursued to date are clear and indisputable. Why, then, do the same problems seem to keep recurring? It is worth identifying the obstacles to reform as a means of explaining the persistence of the status quo. The biggest obstacle resides in American aspirations, which were, in retrospect, over-sized. What many do not realize, however, is the extent to which ready access to contractors and wartime supplemental funding fueled this overly ambitious agenda. In crude terms, contractors provide a means of extending our armed forces and dispatching them on a mission that would otherwise have been called out sooner as unrealistic and overly ambitious. Contractors are a vehicle for throwing money at the problem of war so that only a minority of the population needs to be actively engaged in it. In this sense, over-reliance on contractors and the related dearth of transparency and accountability that accompany this addiction ultimately undermine democratic values.

But that is only part of the picture. The status quo endures because the status quo is perceived to benefit the people who would need to be part of any plan to overturn it. Wartime contracting is big business, and business has deep pockets that appeal to any elected official. Business has lobbies that keep its interests squarely in decision makers' minds. In this sense, the status quo undermines the public interest while serving the self-interest of many powerful forces. Changing the status quo will mean stepping on the toes of some very powerful and wealthy interests, always a significant impediment to meaningful change. But change we must if we do not want the principle of self-government to be a casualty of elite myopia and carelessness.

None of this is to suggest that contractors and business, or even a particular political party or administration, are principally to blame for the system that has developed. Contrary to the insinuations of America's extreme right and left, our current predicament is anything but a conspiracy. We are all to blame for the excesses of free market fundamentalism, which effectively caused government to lose its sense of those things that only government can do well.

Upholding the public interest in the future will require three things. We must demand leadership that does not shrink from drawing a clear line around those functions that should be exclusively performed by government. The oversight and management of contractors is an inherently governmental function. The task of providing moving security is as well. Second, Congress must deliver the legislation, and where necessary, the additional resources, for government to be able to in-source contractor management. Finally, and perhaps most importantly, we must insist on radical transparency in how US taxpayer money is used. Local security contractors in Afghanistan are hired through subcontracts, and information on subcontracts is currently unavailable to the public. The 2006 Federal Funding Transparency and Accountability Act, which created USAspending.gov (President Obama's "Google for Government"), required information on subcontracts and subgrants to be made available to the public by January 1, 2009; USAspending.gov has yet to deliver. The American people must insist that it do so.

Notes

1. Richard Fontaine and John Nagl, *Contracting in Conflicts: The Path to Reform* (Washington, DC: Center for a New American Security, 2010), 9.

2. Ibid., 7.

3. Allison Stanger, *One Nation under Contract: The Outsourcing of American Power and the Future of Foreign Policy* (New Haven, CT: Yale University Press, 2009), vii–viii.

4. Robert Gates, "Testimony before the Senate Armed Services Committee," Jan. 27, 2009.

5. Public Law 110-181. Section 841 of the law established the commission and delineated its duties. See www.wartimecontracting.gov/index.php/about/statute.

6. Commission on Wartime Contracting (CWC), *Background*, available at www.wartimecontracting.gov/index.php/about.

7. Ibid.

8. US Senate, *The Truman Committee*, available at www.senate.gov/artandhistory/history/minute/The_Truman_Committee.htm.

9. Charlie Savage, "Bush Asserts Authority to Bypass Defense Act," *Boston Globe*, Jan. 30, 2008, www.boston.com/news/nation/articles/2008/01/30/bush_asserts_authority_to_bypass_defense_act/.

10. CWC, "Inspectors General in the Spotlight at First Hearing of Commission on Wartime Contracting" (Jan. 28, 2009), http.wartimecontracting.gov/index.php/pressroom/pressreleases/48-cwc-nr-1.

11. Dwight D. Eisenhower, "Farewell Address to the American People" (1961); Thomas L. Friedman, "The Best Allies Money Can Buy," *New York Times*, Nov. 3, 2009, www.nytimes.com/2009/11/04/opinion/04friedman.html.

12. Milton Friedman, *Why Government Is the Problem* (Palo Alto, CA: Hoover Institution Press, 1993), 6.

13. *Federal Activities Inventory Reform Act of 1998* § 5.

14. Del Quentin Wilber and Karen DeYoung, "Justice Dept. Moves toward Charges against Contractors in Iraq Shooting," *Washington Post*, Aug. 17, 2008, http.washingtonpost.com/wp-dyn/content/article/2008/08/16/AR2008081601967.html.

15. Fontaine and Nagl, *Contracting in Conflicts*, 24.

16. Ibid., 24–25.

17. Raymond DiNunzio, "How Good Is Our System for Curbing Contract Waste, Fraud, and Abuse?" Testimony before the Commission on Wartime Contracting (May 24, 2010), 5. Mr. DiNunzio is Assistant Inspector General, Criminal Investigations Directorate, Special Inspector General for Afghanistan. http.wartimecontracting.gov/docs/hearing2010-05-24_statement-SIGAR-DiNunzio.pdf.

18. CWC, "Wartime Contracting Hearings Explore Contractor Business Systems and Linguist Support Services" (Aug. 6, 2009), http.wartimecontracting.gov/index.php/pressroom/pressreleases/90-cwc-nr-6.

19. CWC, "Defense Agencies Must Improve Their Oversight of Contractor Business Systems to Reduce Waste, Fraud, and Abuse," Special Report 1 (Sept. 21, 2009), http.wartimecontracting.gov/docs/CWC_SR1_business-systems_2009-09-21.pdf.

20. CWC, "Wartime Contracting Commission to Query Federal Officials" (April 28, 2009), http.wartimecontracting.gov/index.php/pressroom/pressreleases/65-cwc-nr-3.

21. Donald A. Gambatesa, "How Good Is Our System for Curbing Contract Fraud, Waste, and Abuse?" Testimony before the Commission on Wartime Contracting (May 24, 2010), 3. Mr. Gambatesa is the USAID Inspector General. http.wartimecontracting.gov/docs/hearing2010-05-24_statement-USAID-Gambatesa.pdf.

22. Ibid., 12.

23. Arnold Fields, "An Urgent Need: Coordinating Reconstruction and Stabilization in Contingency Operations," Transcript of Hearings before the Commission on Wartime Contracting (Feb. 22, 2010), 6. Mr. Fields is Special Inspector General for Afghanistan Reconstruction. http.wartimecontracting.gov/docs/hearing2010-02-22_transcript.pdf.

24. James Bever, "USAID Planning for Reconstruction in Iraq and Afghanistan," Testimony before the Commission on Wartime Contracting (Mar. 1, 2010), 1–5. Mr. Bever is the USAID Afghanistan-Pakistan Task Force Director. http.wartimecontracting.gov/docs/hearing2010-03-01_openingstatement-BeverJames.pdf.

25. Ibid., 1.

26. Ginger M. Cruz, "How Good Is Our System for Curbing Fraud, Waste, and Abuse?" Testimony before the Commission on Wartime Contracting (May 24, 2010), 2. Ms. Cruz is the Deputy Inspector General for Iraq Reconstruction. http.wartimecontracting.gov/docs/hearing2010-05-24_statement-SIGIR-Cruz.pdf.

27. Moshe Schwartz, *The Department of Defense's Use of Private Security Contractors in Iraq and Afghanistan: Background, Analysis, and Options for Congress* (Washington, DC: Congressional Research Service, 7-5700, Jan. 19, 2010), 9, www.fas.org/sgp/crs/natsec/R40835.pdf.

28. Dexter Filkins, "With US Aid, Warlord Builds Afghan Empire," *New York Times*, June 5, 2010, www.nytimes.com/2010/06/06/world/asia/06warlords.html?scp=9&sq=Dexter%20Filkins%20June%202010&st=cse. Citing their role in obstructing the development of the Afghan police and army, President Karzai announced in August 2010 that he wanted all security contractors out of the country by the end of the year.

29. United Nations Office on Drugs and Crime, *Corruption Widespread in Afghanistan, UNODC Survey Says*, http.unodc.org/unodc/en/frontpage/2010/January/corruption-widespread-in-afghanistan-unodc-survey-says.html.

30. Fields, "An Urgent Need," 18.

31. John F. Tierney, "Warlord, Inc.: Extortion and Corruption Along the U.S. Supply Chain in Afghanistan," Subcommittee on National Security and Foreign Affairs, Committee on Oversight and Government Reform, US House of Representatives. Report of the Majority Staff, John Tierney, Chair (June 2010), 1, http://oversight.house.gov/images/stories/subcommittees/NS_Subcommittee/6.22.10_HNT_HEARING/Warlord_Inc_compress.pdf.

32. GAO, *Warfighter Support: A Cost Comparison of Using State Department Employees Versus Contractors for Security Services in Iraq* (2010), 3.

33. AGNA is now owned by Wackenhut Services.

34. Danielle Brian, "POGO Letter to Secretary of State Hillary Clinton Regarding US Embassy in Kabul" (Sept. 1, 2009). Ms. Brian is Executive Director of the Project on Government Oversight (POGO).

35. Danielle Brian, "Oversight of Department of State Security Contracts," Testimony before the Commission on Wartime Contracting" (Sept. 14, 2009), 1, www.wartimecontracting.gov/images/download/documents/hearings/20090914/Ms_Danielle_Brian_POGO_Statement.pdf.

36. Letter dated July 19, 2007, from State Department to AGNA, Subject: Cure Notice Issued per FAR 49.402-3 /Contract No. S-AQMPD-07-C0054. See footnote 5, page 4 of CWC, "Lowest-Priced Security Not Good Enough for War-Zone Embassies," Special Report 2 (Oct. 1, 2009), http.wartimecontracting.gov/docs/CWC_SR2-2009-10-01.pdf.

37. CWC, "Lowest-Priced Security Not Good Enough for War-Zone Embassies," 1–6.

38. Brian, "Oversight of Department of State Security Contracts," 1–5.

39. Michael Thibault, Hearings on "Counting Contractors, Managing the Drawdown, and DCMA/DCAA Cooperation" (Nov. 2, 2009), Transcript of Panel 1, 1–5. Mr. Thibault is Co-Chair of the Commission on Wartime Contracting. http.wartimecontracting.gov/docs/hearing2009-11-02_transcript-panel1.pdf.

40. Stanger, *One Nation under Contract*, 100.

41. Stuart W. Bowen, Testimony before the Commission on Wartime Contracting on "An Urgent Need: Coordinating Reconstruction and Stabilization in Contingency Operations" (Feb. 22, 2010), 4. Mr. Bowen is the Special Inspector General for Iraq Reconstruction. http.wartimecontracting.gov/docs/hearing2010-02-22_testimony-BowenStuart.pdf.

42. Robert M. Perito, Transcript of Hearings before the Commission on Wartime Contracting on "An Urgent Need: Coordinating Reconstruction and Stabilization in Contingency Operations" (Feb. 22, 2010), 72, http.wartimecontracting.gov/docs/hearing2010-02-22_transcript.pdf.

43. Ibid., 72ff.

44. Arnold Fields, Testimony before the Commission on Wartime Contracting (Feb. 22, 2010), 3, http.sigar.mil/pdf/testimony/SIGAR-10-001T.pdf.

45. Senator McCaskill, Transcript of Senate Hearings on "Contracts for Afghan National Police Training," Committee on Homeland Security and Governmental Affairs, Ad Hoc Subcommittee on Contracting Oversight (April 15, 2010), 6, http://mccaskill.senate.gov/files/documents/pdf/0415HSGAC-SCO.pdf.

46. Ibid, 4.

47. Seth Jones, "Stabilization from the Bottom Up," Testimony before the Commission on Wartime Contracting in Iraq and Afghanistan (Feb. 5, 2010), 4. Mr. Jones is employed by the RAND Corporation. http.wartimecontracting.gov/docs/hearing2010-02-22_testimony-JonesSeth.pdf.

48. Bowen, Transcript of "An Urgent Need," 53.

49. Senator Brown, Transcript of Senate Hearings on "Contracts for Afghan National Police Training," Committee on Homeland Security and Governmental Affairs, Ad Hoc Subcommittee on Contracting Oversight (April 15, 2010), 8–11.

50. Christopher Shays, "An Urgent Need: Coordinating Reconstruction and Stabilization in Contingency Operations," Transcript of Hearings before the Commission on Wartime Contracting (Feb. 22, 2010), 2, http.wartimecontracting.gov/docs/hearing2010-02-22_Co-chairs_opener_Afg_coordination.pdf. Mr. Shays is Co-Chair of the Commission on Wartime Contracting.

51. John E. Herbst, Testimony before the Commission on Wartime Contracting (Mar. 1, 2010). Ambassador Herbst is Coordinator for Reconstruction and Stabilization, Department of State. http.wartimecontracting.gov/docs/hearing2010-03-01_openingstatement-HerbstJohn.pdf. See also Transcript of Hearings before the Commission on Wartime Contracting on "An Urgent Need," Part II (Mar. 1, 2010), http.wartimecontracting.gov/docs/hearing2010-03-01_transcript.pdf.

52. James Schear, Transcript of Hearings before the Commission on Wartime Contracting on "An Urgent Need: Coordinating Reconstruction and Coordinating Reconstruction and Stabilization in Contingency Operations," Part II (Mar. 1, 2010), 77–78. Mr. Schear is Deputy Assistant Secretary of Defense for Partnership Strategy and Stability Operations. http.wartimecontracting.gov/docs/hearing2010-03 01_transcript.pdf.

53. SIGIR, *Applying Iraq's Hard Lessons to the Reform of Stabilization and Reconstruction Operations* (Feb. 2010), www.sigir.mil/files/USOCO/ApplyingHardLessons.pdf#view=fit.

54. "An Urgent Need," Part II (Mar. 1, 2010), 91.

55. Secretary of Defense Robert Gates to Secretary of State Hillary Clinton, "Options for Remodeling Security Sector Assistance Authorities" (Dec. 15, 2009), http.washingtonpost.com/wp-srv/nation/documents/Gates_to_Clinton_121509.pdf (accessed Aug. 22, 2010).

9 Private Contractors, Public Consequences

The Need for an Effective Criminal Justice Framework

David E. Price

1. Introduction

Imagine the following scenario: one hot July day, three Americans and a man from the South Pacific island of Fiji are driving a sports utility vehicle through the streets of Baghdad. The four men work for a private company on a subcontract from another private company hired by the US Department of Defense (DoD) to provide security services in Iraq. Their job—protecting VIP convoys between the Baghdad airport and the "Green Zone" where US military and diplomatic operations are headquartered—requires them to bear arms and, if necessary, to use lethal force to defend their precious cargo.[1]

On their way to the airport to pick up a client, the four private security contractors (PSCs) are stopped at a checkpoint when they notice a white pickup truck creeping slowly toward the rear of their vehicle. They warn the driver of the truck to stop, but when the warning goes unheeded, one of the guards opens fire. The truck stops in its tracks and the four men proceed through the checkpoint. On their way back from the airport, they notice an ambulance and a good deal of commotion at the scene of the incident, but they do not stop to investigate.

Moments later, the men come upon a taxi driving slowly ahead of them along the airport highway. As their SUV overtakes the taxi, one of the four guards draws his pistol and opens fire directly into the vehicle's windshield, with no apparent provocation. The taxi veers off the road and comes to an abrupt stop, the fate of its driver unknown. As the four men speed away, one turns to another and says, "Nice shot."

For many people, accounts such as this have come to evoke a certain stereotype: the arrogant and trigger-happy contractor, wreaking havoc in a war zone and playing by a different set of rules than the military service member whose mission he ostensibly supports. From a criminal justice perspective, however, the real story is what happened *after* that fateful July day—or rather, what *didn't* happen. Only one of the four PSCs—the Fijian—submitted an incident report on the day of the shootings. Two of the men submitted nearly identical reports two days later, both of which blamed the misconduct on the fourth man. The fourth man had returned to the United States on leave the day after the shootings and filed a report only when one of his supervisors contacted him about the incident.

Based on these internal incident reports and a subsequent investigation, the company—Triple Canopy, a security services and risk management firm based in Reston, Virginia—decided to terminate the contracts of the three American employees (the Fijian employee reportedly quit on his own volition) and referred the case to the US Army officer in charge of security for the Green Zone. Despite the fact that Triple Canopy was a DoD subcontractor, however, neither DoD nor the US Department of Justice (DoJ) seemed interested in pursuing an investigation.[2] In fact, the incidents became public only when two of the men filed a wrongful termination lawsuit against Triple Canopy several months later. Contacted about the case by a reporter, a spokesperson for the US Central Command (CENTCOM) put it bluntly: "This is not a CENTCOM issue. It's whoever was running that contract. . . . We're fighting a war here."[3]

The Triple Canopy case offers a vivid illustration of the uncertain legal framework governing US government contractors overseas, including but not limited to PSCs. In the first instance, it demonstrates the need for clear and enforceable procedures for reporting potential misconduct by contractors as well as the considerable logistical and bureaucratic challenges involved in investigating such cases.

But suppose that DoD had investigated the incident and found the allegations of criminal misconduct to be credible. What legal options would be available? Could the military try the men directly under the Uniform Code of Military Justice (UCMJ)? Could DoJ try them under civilian laws, such as the Military Extraterritorial Jurisdiction Act (MEJA)? What about the Fijian man—could he be prosecuted under US law, or in his home country, or by the government of Iraq?[4] Moreover, what if Triple Canopy's contract had been with the State Department or another US agency instead of DoD? Would MEJA still apply? If not, could the men be prosecuted under other US laws, such as the War Crimes Act or the Special Maritime and Territorial Jurisdiction Act?

If the answers to these questions were known at the time, it was not by the four Triple Canopy employees. "We never knew if we fell under military law, American law, Iraqi law, or whatever," one of them told a reporter several months later.[5] "We were always told, from the very beginning, if for some reason something happened and the Iraqis were trying to prosecute us, they would put you in the back of a car and sneak you out of the country in the middle of the night."[6]

This chapter examines the legal framework governing private security contractors from the perspective of the United States Congress—or, more precisely, from the perspective of one member involved in recent efforts to promote greater transparency and accountability in the use of PSCs. Its goals are essentially threefold. First, it outlines the case for an effective criminal justice framework for PSCs, emphasizing that holding US personnel accountable for crimes committed overseas is both consistent with our core values and central to our national interests. Second, it offers a narrative account of recent congressional attempts to strengthen this framework, beginning in the spring of 2004 when two incidents in Iraq put the operations of PSCs squarely in the congressional spotlight for the first time. Third, it considers the current state of relevant laws and regulations, with an eye toward the evolving role of PSCs in global security operations.

By its nature, this is a narrative and somewhat impressionistic account that should not be considered an exhaustive reference on the full range of hearings, legislation, commissions, and other congressional actions surrounding this important policy issue, for which many of my colleagues deserve considerable credit.[7] By placing recent legislative efforts to improve the legal framework for PSCs in their historical and analytical context, however, this chapter attempts to bring into focus both the jurisprudential challenges underlying these efforts and the nature of the political debate that has accompanied them. It also intends to make a compelling case that, while significant progress has been made in recent years, there is still an urgent and essential need for a clear, comprehensive, and enforceable criminal justice framework that will close the "contractor loophole" once and for all.

2. The Case for Contractor Accountability

The United States government, like any government, has both a strategic interest and a legal responsibility to hold its personnel accountable for their conduct overseas.[8] When government personnel travel or live abroad for work—as diplomats, military service members, aid workers, intelligence agents, and those who support them—they serve as the public face of their country and the frontline implementers of its foreign and defense policies, and their conduct bears directly on the achievement of key strategic goals and the advancement of national interests. Any behavior that undermines these goals—including criminal misconduct—must be taken seriously and sanctioned appropriately in order to maintain discipline and unity of mission across the government.

In addition to this strategic interest, the US government has a legal responsibility to ensure that its official personnel are held accountable for crimes committed abroad. This responsibility inheres not just in our nation's rhetorical commitment to justice and the rule of law, but also in specific domestic statutes and international conventions (discussed at greater length below) that authorize—and in some cases require—prosecution for serious crimes such as murder, torture, or terrorism. Beyond the government's *positive* strategic interest and legal responsibility, there is also a strong *negative* motive at play: *failing* to hold government personnel accountable for crimes committed abroad can damage diplomatic relations, incite anti-American sentiment, and do lasting harm to our country's reputation as a champion of justice and the rule of law—a reputation that has already been dangerously eroded in recent years.

While this case for accountability applies broadly to all overseas government personnel, it is particularly pronounced for personnel operating in a war zone or in support of a contingency operation, for several reasons. First, the strategic imperative of ensuring that personnel conduct themselves in accordance with US goals and interests is even stronger, given the uniquely high stakes of their mission. Second, the government's legal responsibilities in armed conflict are clearly defined by core tenets of international humanitarian law—including the four Geneva Conventions and their additional protocols and treaties such as the Convention against Torture—many of which have been codified in US criminal law. Third, the consequences of failing to hold government personnel accountable for their misconduct are especially severe, often bearing directly on the success of the military's mission. Finally, armed conflict can render the host country's judicial system incapable of providing effective justice, leaving the "sending country" as the only viable option for pursuing legal accountability.

Up to this point, I have deliberately refrained from distinguishing between official government personnel and private contractors. This is in part because it is often, in practice, a distinction without a difference: for the insurgent in Iraq or Afghanistan, the private contractor guarding a base and the uniformed service member inside it are equally attractive targets; the fact that the Taliban has characterized its deadly attacks on US military personnel in Pakistan as "revenge for the blasts of Blackwater" testifies to this fact.[9] But there is also a firm legal basis for treating government contractors the same as government employees for purposes of criminal accountability.[10] If contractors are employed by the government, contractually bound to the government, and perceived by the local population as functionally equivalent to the government, then they should be treated as such under US and international law.

The problem, however, is that US and international laws have not kept pace with the evolution of global security operations over the past several decades in general, or with the rise of the PSC industry in particular. Historically, the US civilian criminal justice system has extended only as far as its borders. With notable but rare exceptions, American civilians who perpetrate or are victimized by crimes overseas must have their cases heard overseas. The military, by contrast, has operated under a separate justice system since the American Revolution, the purpose of which is to provide order and discipline as well as accountability for criminal misconduct.[11] In most cases, the military justice system has served as the court of first resort for crimes committed by service members, during peacetime and war and irrespective of the location of the crime.

By and large, these two systems of justice have been sufficient to provide jurisdictional coverage for the vast majority of criminal cases involving Americans abroad (either in foreign courts or in military courts-martial). But this coverage has not been airtight, and throughout US history Congress and the courts have recognized the need to "extend" US civilian jurisdiction to crimes committed abroad in certain cases. The US Special Maritime and Territorial Jurisdiction (SMTJ), for example, which has its origins in the attempts of the 1st Congress to combat piracy on the high seas, allows individuals to be tried domestically for crimes committed in international waters or on US-operated facilities abroad.[12]

For most of our nation's history, the exercise of extraterritorial jurisdiction by US courts was highly exceptional, and to an extent it still is. Since World War II, however, as the world has become more interconnected and American civilians have begun to live, work, and travel abroad in greater numbers, the cracks in the existing jurisdictional framework have widened. The challenges this trend has posed have been particularly acute in conflict situations, where civilians (both in and out of government) are performing an increasing number of tasks once reserved for the military, and where foreign courts are often unable to provide effective legal recourse. The rise of the PSC industry is one of the more visible manifestations of these challenges, but it must be understood in the context of the broader evolution of global security operations that has occurred in recent decades.[13]

In the early post–Cold War years, Congress enacted several laws designed to keep pace with this changing environment by broadening the reach of US extraterritorial jurisdiction, including the anti-torture statutes of 1994, the War Crimes Act of 1996, and the PATRIOT Act Amendments to SMTJ in 2001.[14] In 2000, Congress enacted the first law targeted directly at PSCs and other civilians accompanying the US military abroad: the Military Extraterritorial Jurisdiction Act (MEJA), which I discuss in greater detail below.[15]

While these laws have gone a long way toward ensuring that our jurisdictional framework keeps pace with today's global environment, the events of recent years have shown that the current patchwork of laws is insufficient to ensure that civilian personnel (and PSCs in particular) can be held accountable when they violate the law overseas. The US military campaigns in Iraq and Afghanistan have been punctuated by a series of high-profile incidents in which contractors have been implicated in murder, rape, torture, and other serious crimes; for reasons described below, the majority of these crimes have gone unresolved or unpunished. Our government's failure to hold these individuals accountable for their actions has threatened our national security and tarnished America's reputation as a champion of justice and the rule of law, and it is high time that Congress update our laws to account for this reality.

It should be noted that the case for contractor accountability is independent of the larger question of *when* and *how* contractors should be used in the first place—a debate that has not, in my view, been resolved satisfactorily. Which functions should be regarded, on legal or philosophical grounds, as "inherently governmental" and thus never delegated to the private sector? Beyond that, what do considerations of cost, practicality, and political viability dictate for the privatization of governmental functions under specific, real-world circumstances? Such questions are not always subject to hard-and-fast determinations, but Congress and the major federal contracting agencies have not devoted sufficient attention to answering them coherently.

Regardless of how one views the use of PSCs more broadly, however, as long as the US government is employing them, it has a responsibility both to establish a clear legal framework to govern their activities and to hold them accountable when they violate this framework. Philosophical and practical questions about whether and how PSCs should be used will no doubt persist, but all sides should be able to agree on the need to hold them accountable when they violate the law.

3. A Rude Awakening

On April 1, 2004, Americans awoke to the gruesome image on their morning news of four mutilated and badly burned corpses hanging from a bridge in Fallujah, Iraq. The dead men were employees of Blackwater USA (now Xe Services LLC), a North Carolina–based company that has come for many to epitomize the private security contracting industry. The men had been guarding a convoy delivering food and supplies when their vehicle was attacked by insurgents; the scenes of jubilant Iraqis celebrating their brutal deaths provoked an international outcry that contributed to the decision to launch a major military offensive against insurgents in Fallujah.[16]

Within Congress, the Fallujah attacks provided a rude awakening as to the extent of our country's dependence on the services of PSCs. Driven by several factors—the post–Cold War downsizing of the Active Duty force, the ideological preferences of some within the government, the entrepreneurialism of individual firms—the US government had been turning increasingly to private industry for security services since at least the 1990s.[17] Conflicts in the Balkans in the 1990s and the initial invasion of Afghanistan in 2001 had provided a glimpse of this new paradigm, but it was not until after the invasion of Iraq in 2003 and the events of early 2004 that the government's growing reliance on contractors began to penetrate the collective conscience of Congress.

Less than a month after the Fallujah incident, America received a second rude awakening when CBS aired the first public images of the shocking abuses that had occurred at Abu Ghraib prison, a US-run detention and interrogation facility on the outskirts of Baghdad.[18] A resulting investigation by the US Army found that at least one-third of the proven incidents of abuse had been committed by private contractors hired to assist US military and intelligence agencies with the interrogation of detainees.[19] Worse still, it soon became evident that the Abu Ghraib contractors had been operating in the legal equivalent of a black hole: the Coalition Provisional Authority (CPA) had granted contractors immunity from prosecution by Iraqi authorities, but the primary legal basis for prosecuting them in US courts (MEJA) had been called into question because their contract was with the Department of the Interior, not DoD.[20] Consequently, while several service members faced trial and punishment by the military justice system for their misconduct, none of the private contractors implicated in the scandal have ever been convicted for their involvement in the most significant prisoner abuse case in US history.[21]

The lack of a jurisdictional basis for prosecuting the Abu Ghraib contractors came as a shock to many within Congress. In the immediate wake of the scandal, I invited Peter Singer of the Brookings Institution, who recently had published a book on the subject, to present his research to a weekly discussion group that I co-chair (the Democratic Budget Group).[22] Shortly afterward, I drafted a letter to the Government Accountability Office requesting an investigation into the military's use and oversight of PSCs in Iraq, which attracted over 100 signatories in the House. The broad support for this letter made it clear that the lack of contractor accountability was an issue of growing concern in Congress, and I began to work with several outside organizations to identify an appropriate legislative fix.[23]

The logical starting point was MEJA, which was enacted specifically to ensure that civilians supporting the US military could be held accountable for criminal misconduct. The law had come about in the waning days of the Clinton administration as a result of a federal court case involving an Army sergeant's civilian husband, who had sexually abused his stepdaughter while their family was deployed in Germany. After being convicted of the crime initially, his conviction was overturned by a US Court of Appeals on the grounds that US civilian courts lacked jurisdiction over the military facility where the crime had occurred.[24] In an unorthodox move, the presiding judge referred the opinion to the Armed Services and Judiciary committees of the House and Senate in an effort to spur legislative action.[25] The measure received strong support from the Pentagon, which recognized that this legal loophole had, in the words of one DoD official, "undermined deterrence, lowered morale, and threatened good order and discipline."[26] Within a matter of months, MEJA had been approved overwhelmingly by both chambers and signed into law.

From a legislative perspective, MEJA's approach was elegantly simple: the law merely stipulated that any crime committed by a person "employed by or accompanying the Armed Forces outside the United States" could be prosecuted as if it had occurred domestically, provided the crime would be punishable by at least a year in prison and that no foreign government had pressed charges.[27] Covered persons were defined to include any DoD employee or contractor (including subcontractors at any tier) or any dependent of a military service member, DoD employee, or contractor, excepting citizens of the country in which the crime occurred.[28] MEJA designated DoD as the primary agency responsible for enforcing the law and included some minimal guidelines for the referral of cases to the civilian criminal justice system.[29]

As always, however, the devil was in the details. Because MEJA applied only to DoD contractors, it excluded a large number of US contractors abroad, including the Interior Department contractors working at Abu Ghraib.[30] There were questions about *which* US courts could be used to prosecute crimes under MEJA and the extent to which the law applied to foreign nationals working under contract to DoD. Additionally, the Pentagon was slow to issue implementing regulations, further complicating efforts to enforce the law.[31] By the time the Abu Ghraib revelations surfaced in 2004, MEJA had been invoked only once, in a case involving the alleged murder of an Air Force officer stationed in Turkey.[32]

The first opportunity to correct these deficiencies arose in the fiscal year 2005 National Defense Authorization Act (NDAA), the annual measure that sets funding levels and policy priorities for the military. Working with then-Rep. Christopher Shays (R-CT), I submitted an amendment to the NDAA clarifying that MEJA applied to any civilian employee or contractor working for any federal agency supporting the mission of DoD or present in an occupied territory. Our amendment also would have specified that DoD had the primary responsibility for arresting individuals and turning them over to the appropriate civilian authorities, removing the uncertainty that existed in the original statute. Unfortunately, despite its bipartisan sponsorship, our amendment was rejected by the House Republican leadership, so Rep. Shays and I introduced the measure as a stand-alone bill that we called the MEJA Clarification Act.[33]

The issue had also attracted the attention of several senators, including the original author of MEJA, Senator Jeff Sessions (R-AL). With little fanfare or debate, Senator Sessions offered an amendment to the Senate version of the NDAA that extended MEJA to any contractor employed by the US government "to the extent that such employment relates to supporting the mission of the Department of Defense," using language from the Price-Shays amendment.[34] Like the original MEJA, the so-called "MEJA amendments" were accepted unanimously in the Senate and maintained in the House-Senate conference; President Bush signed the measure into law in late October 2004. Since the MEJA amendments did not apply retroactively, the new law could not be used to prosecute the Abu Ghraib contractors whose actions had provided its impetus. Nevertheless, the 2005 NDAA, which also included several new reporting requirements for DoD contractors, represented the first concerted effort by Congress to clarify the legal framework governing PSCs in war zones, and was thus a significant step forward for the rule of law.

4. Contractors and Courts-Martial

With the MEJA amendments signed into law, Congress turned its attention to other matters, such as the need to ensure that DoD, the State Department, and other major contracting agencies were collecting sufficient data on their contract personnel and reporting this information to Congress in a timely manner. While I was one of several members to introduce legislation related to contractor management and coordination in the 109th Congress (2005–2006), no legislation related to contractor accountability was introduced in the House.

Across the Capitol, however, Senator Lindsey Graham (R-SC) had taken up the idea of using the Uniform Code of Military Justice (UCMJ) to try civilian contractors working in Iraq and Afghanistan. Enacted in the wake of World War II to codify the customary military justice system, UCMJ generally applied only to uniformed service members but had been extended during times of war to civilians "serving with or accompanying an armed force in the field."[35] However, since the US missions in Iraq and Afghanistan were technically "contingency operations" rather than declared wars, UCMJ could not be applied to civilians. To eliminate this distinction, Senator Graham sponsored a successful amendment to the FY 2007 NDAA that extended UCMJ's civilian coverage to "contingency operations," with the stated intent of applying it to PSCs.[36]

Extending military law to civilians whose operations are arguably "military" in nature has a certain intuitive appeal. Beyond the first blush, however, applying UCMJ to contractors raises serious issues—both constitutional and operational—that severely limit its viability as a solution to the problem of contractor accountability. The constitutionality of applying UCMJ to civilians has been the subject of a long and contentious debate that has yet to be resolved definitively. In a series of decisions in the wake of World War II, the US Supreme Court ruled that civilians could not be subjected to courts-martial during times of peace,[37] but this precedent has yet to be tested in the era of "contingency operations," when the very definition of war has lost the conceptual clarity it once possessed. Prior to being amended in 2006, UCMJ had not been used to try a civilian since 1968.[38]

Even if one believes that the application of military law to civilians is constitutional, the application of UCMJ to contractors suffers from an operational paradox: it is simultaneously too narrow in reach and too broad in scope. Since it applies only to civilians "serving with or accompanying an armed force in the field," the vast majority of contractors overseas (even, perhaps, in war zones) operate beyond its jurisdictional reach. Yet because UCMJ is designed fundamentally to maintain order and discipline within the military chain of command, it is a broad and incongruous fit even for those whom it clearly covers. How would one try a civilian contractor for insubordinate conduct, for example, or absence without leave?[39]

Given the serious constitutional and operational questions inherent in trying civilians under military law, UCMJ should not be considered a reliable basis for providing accountability to PSCs overseas. At best, it should be viewed as a supplement to the civilian legal system in certain exceptional cases in which an individual commits a crime that bears directly on the military's mission (such as treason or espionage). It is no surprise that the military has invoked its new UCMJ authority only once as of this writing.[40]

5. The Turning Point

In the midterm elections of 2006, the Democratic Party rode a wave of popular discontent with President George W. Bush into the congressional majority, gaining 31 seats in the House and a slight partisan edge in the Senate. Much of this discontent centered on the Iraq war, which a majority of Americans now viewed as an ill-advised adventure not worth its cost in blood and treasure.

While the reasons for Americans' growing questioning of the war were manifold, the presence and operations of private contractors in Iraq increasingly had become a focus of attention for many war opponents.

This negative publicity was due in part to the widespread (and largely justified) perception that contractors continued to operate with impunity despite continued reports of criminal misconduct. In one high-profile case, Jamie Leigh Jones, a young female contractor for Kellogg, Brown, and Root (a subsidiary of Halliburton), was allegedly gang-raped by her coworkers, but the Department of Justice never pressed charges due in part to an arbitration clause in her employment contract.[41] In another, a Blackwater employee shot and killed a member of the Iraqi vice president's security detail but never faced criminal charges, in part because of uncertainty over whether MEJA applied to State Department contractors.[42]

While the lack of accountability in these cases was largely attributable to the Bush administration's failure to pursue criminal charges, it also reflected the changing legal environment in Iraq. In June 2004, the CPA had transferred sovereignty to the Iraqi Interim Government, which in turn had transferred power to the Iraqi Transitional Government following parliamentary elections in January 2005. With this transition came a parallel transfer of the US mission "lead" from DoD to the State Department, which had the effect of placing many US contractors in Iraq (i.e., those not employed by DoD) under the nominal purview of the US embassy in Baghdad. In so doing, it reopened the loophole that had been closed temporarily by the MEJA amendments of 2004: the assertion that non-DoD contractors were "supporting the mission" of DoD in Iraq, already questionable, became even more tenuous with the State Department at the helm of the US mission.

Legislatively, the Democratic takeover of Congress also provided a fresh opportunity for members of the new majority to revive old initiatives that had been gathering dust under Republican leadership. The combination of the changing legal environment in Iraq and the changing political environment in Washington led me to introduce a new bill to expand and enhance MEJA, under the title of the MEJA Expansion and Enforcement Act (H.R. 2740).[43] Building on the earlier Price-Shays bill, the measure would have further expanded MEJA to include *all* US government employees and contractors operating in a war zone, regardless of whether they were "supporting the mission" of DoD.[44]

Additionally, the measure transferred primary responsibility for investigating and prosecuting crimes under MEJA to the Department of Justice. To fulfill this new mission, the legislation would establish new Theater Investigative Units, under the direction of the Federal Bureau of Investigation (FBI), which would be tasked with responding to allegations of contractor misconduct and coordinating with other federal agencies in the apprehension and investigation of suspects. This shift in focus from the Pentagon to DoJ aimed to consolidate responsibility for enforcing MEJA within the federal agency that was most qualified in law enforcement matters—rather than the agency that was already consumed with fighting the war—but it also reflected the growing impatience of many legislators with DoJ's apparent lack of interest in prosecuting extraterritorial cases under MEJA and other existing laws.

Across the Capitol, Senator Barack Obama, who had built a reputation for pursuing pragmatic, nonideological solutions to issues of good governance, introduced a virtually identical companion bill to H.R. 2740, which he called the Security Contractor Accountability Act of 2007.[45] Senator Obama's introduction of the measure marked the beginning of a productive working relationship at the staff level that would persist until the freshman senator from Illinois was elected president the following year.

Despite the heavy accumulation of unattended business facing the new Congress, I managed to secure support for H.R. 2740 from the leadership of the House Judiciary Committee, which reported the measure favorably out of committee in early August. As the House adjourned for its annual summer recess, I looked forward to continuing to nudge the effort forward with hopes of securing a floor vote by the end of 2007 or early 2008. To my surprise, the moment for action arrived much sooner.

On September 16, 2007, several Blackwater security guards employed by the State Department opened fire in a busy Baghdad intersection, leaving seventeen Iraqi civilians dead and several others wounded. The guards maintained that they were acting in self-defense, but both the Iraqi government and the US military concluded that the shootings were unprovoked.[46] The Nisoor Square shootings set off a firestorm of controversy in Iraq that spread quickly around the world, bringing the issue of contractor accountability into the legislative spotlight like never before.

It was immediately evident that the US government was almost totally unprepared to respond to the incident. The State Department—which, as the agency holding Blackwater's contract, bore primary responsibility for investigating the attacks—initially defended both the guards' actions and its own policies for contractor management and oversight.[47] State and the US Army (as well as the Iraqi police) eventually conducted separate investigations, but there appears to have been no systematic transfer of the case from State and military investigators to DoJ prosecutors. Moreover, the guards' initial incident reports, which had been compelled by State Department investigators in exchange for assurances that they would be inadmissible in court, soon leaked into the public domain and were accessed inappropriately by the DoJ prosecutors charged with building the eventual case against the guards—with fateful consequences, as I will describe below.

Beyond the uncoordinated and ad hoc nature of the government's response to Nisoor Square, it soon became clear that the uncertainty surrounding MEJA had never been resolved definitively. Because contractors still enjoyed immunity from Iraqi prosecution under the original CPA Order 17, the US government was the only authority that could prosecute the crimes; because the shootings occurred outside of the Green Zone, MEJA was the only basis available for such prosecution.[48] Yet whether State Department contractors in Iraq were employed "in support of the mission of the Department of Defense" was unclear at best, for reasons already stated. An internal State Department assessment drafted in the wake of the shootings found no "basis for holding non-DoD contractors accountable" for crimes committed in Iraq.[49] This conclusion was echoed by Secretary of State Condoleezza Rice in subsequent congressional testimony,[50] in a Memorandum of Agreement on contractor operations signed by State and DoD in December 2007,[51] and, to be sure, by the defense attorneys representing the Blackwater guards.[52]

As DoJ's eventual indictment in the Nisoor Square case demonstrated, the question of MEJA's applicability (or inapplicability) to non-DoD contractors is not as straightforward as these initial assessments portrayed it—but that is precisely the point. The law should leave no doubt about the US government's authority to hold its personnel accountable for criminal misconduct abroad, especially when it has granted them privileged legal status in a war zone. While the fate of DoJ's case remains uncertain as of this writing, this lack of certainty should itself be a call to action.

Fortunately, the leadership of the House of Representatives agreed: shortly after Congress returned from its summer recess, the House scheduled a vote on the MEJA Expansion and Enforcement Act. In the three intervening weeks since the Nisoor Square shootings, the measure had acquired the support of leading organizations within the PSC industry (including the International Peace Operations Association) and the human rights community (including

Human Rights First and Amnesty International, both of which have been leaders on this issue over the years). There had been no visible signs of opposition within the Congress, where the outrage at the lack of accountability for the Blackwater shootings appeared to be bipartisan.

In light of this broad internal and external support, it was somewhat puzzling when the Bush administration intervened shortly before the floor vote to oppose the legislation.[53] Rep. Randy Forbes (R-VA), the ranking Republican on the House Judiciary subcommittee with jurisdiction over the bill, was tapped to mount a late and half-hearted effort to kill the measure, but the White House provided neither a coherent rationale nor effective political support for his efforts. Prior to the final vote, Rep. Forbes offered a motion to recommit—a procedural tactic often used by the minority party to make a statement on legislation under consideration—stating that "nothing in this Act shall be construed to affect intelligence activities that are otherwise permissible" (a provision known as a "rule of construction" in legislative jargon). Since the rule of construction did not in any way alter the underlying bill, Judiciary Committee Chairman John Conyers (D-MI) and I accepted the motion, and the House approved H.R. 2740 by a broad bipartisan majority of 389 to 30.[54]

As it turned out, however, the motion to recommit was only the opening salvo of a debate that has inhibited the enactment of contractor accountability legislation ever since. Having intervened unsuccessfully during House consideration of H.R. 2740, the Bush administration ramped up its efforts in the Senate to include a "carve-out" in the legislation for the activities of the intelligence community. Senate Republicans, unwilling to break ranks with the president, refused to grant unanimous consent for the measure to proceed to a vote, despite the efforts of Sen. Obama and other supporters to achieve a bipartisan compromise. With the measure bogged down in the Senate, I successfully included it in the House version of the emergency supplemental appropriations bill for fiscal year 2008 (H.R. 2642), but it was stripped from the final version of the bill after President Bush threatened to veto the legislation (for this and other reasons).[55] The 110th Congress adjourned without enacting H.R. 2740 or any other measure to ensure that *all* PSCs employed by the US government could be held accountable for criminal misconduct.

I believed then—and continue to believe—that the Bush administration's opposition to H.R. 2740 was both mistaken in its assumptions and troubling in its implications. It was mistaken because the measure would not have restricted lawfully authorized intelligence activities in any way. Existing statutes and executive orders already prohibit US intelligence operatives from committing certain crimes such as assassination and torture, and MEJA already covers the activities of intelligence contractors operating in support of DoD missions. Effectively, H.R. 2740 would have extended this existing jurisdiction to intelligence contractors who (1) operate in a war zone but *not* in support of a DoD mission, and (2) commit a crime not otherwise proscribed by existing laws—a marginal impact at most.

Whether intelligence operatives should be granted greater leeway to take actions that might constitute lesser criminal offenses under US law (bribery, for example) is a legitimate question that is beyond the scope of this chapter. But even if one believes this to be so, two points must be kept in mind. First, covert operations are already governed by detailed legal agreements with the Justice Department and other executive branch authorities, which presumably could be modified to address the activities of contractors with minimal operational disruption. Second, unlike other legal bases for extraterritorial jurisdiction (the anti-torture statutes, for example), MEJA only authorizes prosecution—it does not require it. The Justice Department has the discretion to decide whether to prosecute based on the facts of the case as well as any mitigating circumstances, and the conduct of a duly authorized intelligence mission must surely be considered a mitigating circumstance.

This emphatically does *not* mean that intelligence community contractors should be exempt from prosecution under MEJA, however. The Bush administration's opposition to H.R. 2740 was troubling in its implications because it came at a time when the extent of the president's support for coercive interrogation techniques and other policies of questionable legality under US and international law had become increasingly clear. In light of this timing, one could justifiably conclude that the administration's effort to insert an intelligence "carve-out" in H.R. 2740 was a thinly veiled attempt to shield personnel engaged in coercive interrogations from legal accountability. While I was disappointed that the bill was never signed into law, if the price of enactment was to be officially sanctioned impunity for major violations of US and international law by American interrogators, it was not a price worth paying.

6. MEJA Tested?

As the 110th Congress and President Bush's second term drew to a close, the headlines were dominated by a presidential contest focused primarily on the flagging domestic economy.[56] It thus came as a surprise when DoJ announced in December 2008 that it had filed a 35-count indictment against five of the Blackwater employees implicated in the Nisoor Square shootings, charging them in relation to the deaths of fourteen unarmed civilians and the wounding of twenty others. (A sixth guard pleaded guilty, presumably agreeing to testify against his colleagues in exchange for leniency.) Announcing the charges, a senior DoJ official proclaimed: "Today's indictment and guilty plea demonstrate that those who engage in unprovoked and illegal attacks on civilians, whether during times of conflict or times of peace, will be held accountable."[57]

As the first prosecution of a non-DoD contractor under MEJA, the case represented a welcome, if belated, embrace by DoJ of its statutory authority to exercise extraterritorial jurisdiction over US personnel. The fact that the FBI had taken the lead role in investigating the case, in coordination with other US and Iraqi agencies, was also a significant development given the Bureau's previous reluctance to assume a prominent investigative role overseas.

Yet it was also immediately clear that the case rested on the argument that the Blackwater guards, who were on contract to the State Department, were working in support of a DoD mission—an assertion the State Department itself had previously questioned. If this argument held, then the continued uncertainty surrounding MEJA might be eliminated, at least in Iraq; if it didn't, then the case for legislative action would be even more urgent. In either instance, the Blackwater case would be a critical test of the government's ability to hold PSCs accountable.

Unfortunately, it was a test that would not come to pass—at least as of yet. On December 31, 2009, after a year of extensive pre-trial preparations and grand jury proceedings, the federal judge presiding over the case dismissed all charges against the guards, citing gross prosecutorial misconduct. In a strongly worded opinion, the judge accused DoJ of "reckless violations" of the defendants' constitutional rights and concluded that the case had been tainted irrevocably by the prosecutors' exposure to the incident reports that had been compelled by State Department investigators.[58]

Significantly, the opinion did not address whether MEJA applied to non-DoD contractors to begin with.[59] During a visit to Baghdad in late January 2010, Vice President Joseph Biden announced the government's intent to appeal the case, and a Notice of Appeal was filed by the Justice Department several days later.[60] Yet given the forcefulness of the judge's dismissal and the lingering questions over MEJA's applicability, many legal scholars believe the odds of a successful appeal are slim.[61] As of this writing, it appears that the most significant test of the government's authority to prosecute PSCs for crimes committed abroad may never see trial.

7. State of Play

Where does this leave us today? On the one hand, the United States has made considerable progress toward filling the legal and regulatory vacuum that existed when the first cases of contractor abuse in Iraq surfaced in early 2004. The MEJA amendments of 2004, the 2008 NDAA, and additional legislative initiatives have brought meaningful, if piecemeal, improvements to an area of policy in dire need of statutory clarity. Moreover, with a new president in office, the Bush administration's apparent aversion to the aggressive enforcement of extraterritorial jurisdiction may no longer be a concern.

On the other hand, the legal framework for PSCs continues to suffer from two enduring gaps that must be closed if the United States is to ensure that all government personnel can be held accountable for criminal misconduct. First, the *jurisdictional gap* in our domestic legal framework remains unclosed. Even if DoJ argues successfully that the State Department contractors charged in the Nisoor Square shootings were supporting DoD's mission, the need to establish a direct link to the military's mission will continue to make MEJA a tenuous basis for prosecution—especially as the US missions in Iraq, Afghanistan, and elsewhere transition increasingly from military occupation to civilian reconstruction. If we are to ensure that no representative of the US government is beyond the reach of the law, we must clarify that our extraterritorial laws apply to *any* US contractor overseas.

Second, even in cases where MEJA or other laws clearly apply there remains an *enforcement gap* that has allowed serious crimes to go unpunished. The Obama administration has demonstrated a greater willingness to invoke extraterritorial jurisdiction than the Bush administration, but even a well-intentioned administration requires adequate resources to investigate and prosecute alleged crimes overseas in a thorough and professional manner.[62] The dismissal of the Nisoor Square case resulted not from questions of jurisdiction but from mistakes made in the investigation and prosecution of the incident; while no law can rule out human error, a clearer and more consistent framework for the investigation and referral of the Blackwater case could have made the difference between justice and impunity.

Moreover, it has become increasingly evident that the jurisprudential challenges posed by private contractors are not limited to war zones. From Iraq and Afghanistan to the Horn of Africa and Haiti, hundreds of thousands of contractors currently operate overseas without a clear legal environment, rules of engagement, or coordination with local military and civilian officials.[63] Whether they are protecting private cargo ships against piracy, guarding humanitarian assistance missions, analyzing intelligence at forward operating bases, or supporting conventional military campaigns, private contractors are likely to play a prominent role in global security operations for the foreseeable future. This being the case, partial solutions focused only on Iraq and Afghanistan still leave a large portion of the total contractor workforce uncovered by US law.

Recent legislative efforts have reflected this evolution from a narrow approach focused on today's wars to a wider, global approach focused on all overseas contractors. In the 111th Congress, I have partnered with Senator Patrick Leahy (D-VT), the chairman of the Senate Judiciary Committee, to introduce an updated bill under the title of the Civilian Extraterritorial Jurisdiction Act (CEJA, or H.R. 4567 in the House).[64] Rather than attempting to amend MEJA to incorporate an ever-expanding number of civilian contractors, CEJA would establish a separate, freestanding jurisdiction that would apply to any US government contractor or employee working overseas who commits certain crimes that would otherwise be punishable under US law.[65] By establishing a permanent legal framework that is not limited to one conflict, one region, or one company, CEJA would serve as a sort of jurisdictional "safety net" that could be invoked when other laws, including MEJA, cannot.

As the fallout from the Blackwater case has demonstrated, closing the "contractor loophole" is not just a matter of upholding the basic American values of justice and the rule of law—it is also a matter of achieving key strategic goals and advancing essential national interests. With a president in office who once sponsored contractor accountability legislation, I am hopeful that the 111th Congress will act to close this loophole once and for all.

Epilogue—January 5, 2011

The 111th Congress adjourned in December 2010 without considering the Civilian Extraterritorial Jurisdiction Act or any other legislation to clarify the criminal justice framework governing the activities of private security contractors. This failure to act was due to several factors: delays in introduction of the legislation caused by the (ultimately fruitless) efforts of Senate Democrats to secure Republican cosponsorship; continued reservations about the legislation by some executive branch officials, despite the fact that the president sponsored similar legislation as a senator; and the absence of another major incident of contractor misconduct to galvanize the sort of public attention that prompted House action in 2007 in the wake of the Nisoor Square shootings.

Recent efforts to hold private security contractors accountable under the existing legal framework have also proved largely unsuccessful.[66] In October 2010, the Justice Department announced its decision not to prosecute a Blackwater security guard accused of killing a member of the Iraqi vice president's security detail in late 2006. There have been no further developments in the department's case against the guards implicated in the Nisoor Square shootings since their charges were dismissed in December 2009.

Despite its failure to consider contractor jurisdiction legislation, the 111th Congress did take several steps to strengthen federal oversight of the contracting industry before it adjourned. The Fiscal Year 2011 National Defense Authorization Act (H.R. 6523), enacted in late December 2010, included a provision sponsored by Reps. Price and John Spratt (D-SC) that extends the contractor oversight regime implemented in Iraq and Afghanistan to other areas with a significant contractor presence (Section 832). The measure also includes provisions to improve enforcement of contracts in combat areas (Section 831) and require the Department of Defense to explore options for third-party certification of security contractors (Section 833).

As of this publication, Representative Price and Senator Leahy are planning to reintroduce their legislation in the 112th Congress, though its prospects under Republican leadership in the House of Representatives are uncertain.

Notes

1. This account is based primarily on Human Rights First, *Private Security Contractors at War: Ending the Culture of Impunity* (New York: Human Rights First, 2008), Appendix E, 48; and Steve Fainaru, "Four Hired Guns in an Armored Truck, Bullets Flying, and a Pickup and a Taxi Brought to a Halt: Who Did the Shooting and Why?" *Washington Post*, April 15, 2007. As of this writing, the only official documentation of this episode is the incident reports filed by the Triple Canopy employees involved, so this account should be considered illustrative and not legally authoritative.

2. Fainaru, "Four Hired Guns in an Armored Truck."

3. Major David W. Small, quoted in ibid.

4. It should be noted that none of the Triple Canopy incident reports or media coverage of the incidents has implicated the Fijian employee, Isirel Nakamudi, in any criminal misconduct. Any suggestions to the contrary are intended purely for illustrative purposes.

5. Charles L. Sheppard III, quoted in Fainaru, "Four Hired Guns in an Armored Truck."

6. Ibid.

7. Among others, the following current or former members have shown a particular interest in the issue of contractor accountability: Reps. John Conyers, Rush Holt, Jan Schakowsky, Bobby Scott, Christopher Shays, Ike Skelton, and John Spratt; and Sens. Lindsay Graham, Ted Kaufman, Patrick Leahy, Barack Obama, and Jeff Sessions.

8. It could be argued that this strategic interest extends to all US citizens, whether or not they are employed by the government. For the sake of conceptual clarity, I have limited the focus here to official government personnel, for whom the government bears a legal responsibility that it does not bear for, say, American tourists or businessmen.

9. Hazrat Ali Bacha, "Bomb in Pakistan Kills 3 U.S. Soldiers, 3 Children," *Reuters*, Feb. 3, 2010, www.reuters.com/article/idUSTRE6120UH20100203 (accessed April 14, 2010).

10. For example, the doctrine of *respondeat superior* holds that employers— including the federal government—bear legal responsibility for criminal acts committed by their employees in the course of their duties. In many cases, private contractors are also contractually bound to abide by the law of the country in which they operate.

11. The Second Continental Congress on June 30, 1775, adopted 69 Articles of War to govern the conduct of the Continental Army. In 1806, using its constitutional authority to regulate the Armed Forces, the US Congress adopted 101 Articles of War, which were revised subsequently but continued to govern the Armed Forces until 1951, when they were formalized in the Uniform Code of Military Justice.

12. See 1st Congress, 2nd Sess., 1 Stat. 113 (1790) § 8.

13. For an excellent summary of the legal framework governing US contractors abroad, see Human Rights First, *Private Security Contractors at War*, 23–31. See also Jennifer Elsea, *Private Security Contractors in Iraq and Afghanistan: Legal Issues*, Congressional Research Service Report #R40991 (Jan. 7, 2010).

14. See *Foreign Relations Authorization Act, Fiscal Years 1994 and 1995*, Pub. L. No. 103-326 § 506, codified as amended at 18 U.S.C. § 2340 (2006); *War Crimes Act of 1996*, Pub. L. No. 104-192, codified as amended at 18 U.S.C. § 2441 (2006); and *Uniting and Strengthening America by Providing Appropriate Tools Required to Intercept and Obstruct Terrorism Act of 2001* (USA PATRIOT Act), Pub. L. No. 107-56 § 804, codified at 18 U.S.C. § 7 (2006).

15. *The Military Extraterritorial Jurisdiction Act of 2000*, Public Law 106-523, *U.S. Statutes at Large* 114 (2000): 2488, codified as amended at 18 U.S.C. § 3261 (2006).

16. Jane Arraf, "Marines, Iraqis Join Forces to Shut Down Fallujah," *CNN*, April 6, 2004, www.cnn.com/2004/WORLD/meast/04/05/iraq.main/index.html (accessed April 14, 2010).

17. See, e.g., Fred Schreier and Marina Caparini, *Privatising Security: Law, Practice, and Governance of Private Military and Security Companies* (Geneva: Geneva Centre for the Democratic Control of Armed Forces, 2005), www.dcaf.ch/_docs/occasional_6.pdf (accessed April 14, 2010). For contemporary statistics on the number of PSCs employed by the Department of Defense in Iraq and Afghanistan, see Moshe Schwartz, *The Department of Defense's Use of Private Security Contractors in Iraq and Afghanistan: Background, Analysis, and Options for Congress* (Washington, DC: Congressional Research Service Report, R40835, Jan. 19, 2010).

18. Rebecca Leung, "Abuse Of Iraqi POWs By GIs Probed," *60 Minutes II* (April 28, 2004), www.cbsnews.com/stories/2004/04/27/60II/main614063.shtml (accessed April 14, 2010).

19. P. W. Singer, "Outsourcing War," *Foreign Affairs* (Mar./April 2005): 5.

20. For a description of the legal status of the Abu Ghraib contractors, see Adam Liptak, "The Struggle for Iraq: The Law; Who Would Try Civilians from US? No One in Iraq," *New York Times*, May 26, 2004. It should be noted that other US statutes, such as the Anti-Torture Statute and the War Crimes Act, could potentially have been used to prosecute the contractors, but the Justice Department chose not to invoke them.

21. See Mark Benjamin and Michael Scherer, "'Big Steve' and Abu Ghraib," *Salon*, Mar. 31, 2006, www.salon.com/news/feature/2006/03/31/big_steve/ (accessed April 14, 2010). See also Adam Zagorin, "The Abu Ghraib Cases: Not Yet Over," *Time*, Aug. 29, 2007, www.time.com/time/politics/article/0,8599,1656906,00.html (accessed April 14, 2010).

22. P. W. Singer, *Corporate Warriors: The Rise of the Privatized Military Industry* (Ithaca, NY: Cornell University Press, updated 2007).

23. In addition to Peter Singer, I am grateful to Doug Brooks of the International Peace Operations Association and various individuals at Human Rights First, Amnesty International, the International Committee of the Red Cross, and several other organizations for their early and consistent interest in this effort. My former

staff member Eric Sapp also deserves considerable credit for his prescient work on this issue.

24. *United States v. Gatlin*, 216 F.3d 207 (2d Cir. 2000).

25. Glenn R. Schmitt, *Closing the Gap in Criminal Jurisdiction over Civilians Accompanying the Armed Forces Abroad: A First Person Account of the Creation of the Military Extraterritorial Jurisdiction Act of 2000*, 51 CATH. U. L. REV. 55 (2001).

26. House Subcommittee on Crime, *Military Extraterritorial Jurisdiction Act of 1999: Hearing on H.R. 3380 Before the H. Subcomm. On Crime*, 106th Cong., 2nd sess., 2000, 43 (statement of Robert E. Reed, associate deputy general counsel, United States Department of Defense).

27. See, generally, *The Military Extraterritorial Jurisdiction Act of 2000*, Public Law 106-523, *U.S. Statutes at Large* 114 (2000): 2488, codified as amended at 18 U.S.C. § 3261 (2006).

28. Ibid., § 3267.

29. Ibid., § 3266.

30. Glenn R. Schmitt, "Amending the Military Extraterritorial Jurisdiction Act of 2000: Rushing to Close an Unforeseen Loophole," *Army Lawyer* 41, 42 (June 2005).

31. The regulations finally were published in the Federal Register on February 2, 2004. See Proposed Rule, "Criminal Jurisdiction Over Civilians Employed By or Accompanying the Armed Forces Outside the United States, Certain Service Members, and Former Service Members," *Federal Register* 69, pt. 153 (Feb. 2, 2004): 4890 (to be codified at *Code of Federal Regulations* 32, pt. 153).

32. Liptak, "The Struggle for Iraq."

33. *MEJA Clarification Act*, H.R. 4390 108th Cong., 2nd sess., 2004.

34. S. Amdt. 3372, 108th Cong., 2nd sess., *Congressional Record* 150, no. 78, daily ed. (June 7, 2004): S6535.

35. *Uniform Code of Military Justice*, art. 2(10) (1951). Article 2(10) was later designated Article 2(a)(10); see *UCMJ*, 10 U.S.C. § 802(a)(10) (2000).

36. S. Amdt. 4226, 109th Cong., 2nd sess., *Congressional Record* 152, no. 80, daily ed. (June 20, 2006): S6119. Codified at 10 U.S.C. § 802(a) (2006).

37. See, e.g., *United States ex rel. Toth v. Quarles*, 350 U.S. 11, 22 (1955) ("There are dangers lurking in military trials which were sought to be avoided by the Bill of Rights and Article III of our Constitution. Free countries of the world have tried to restrict military tribunals to the narrowest jurisdiction deemed absolutely essential to maintaining discipline among troops in active service."). See also *Reid v. Covert*, 354 U.S. 1, 33 (1957) (A civilian woman convicted under the UCMJ of murdering her husband on an Air Force base had her conviction overturned because she was entitled to a civilian trial).

38. *Robb v. United* States, 456 F.2d 768 (Ct. Cl. 1972). *Also United States v. Averette*, 19 C.M.A. 363 (C.M.A. 1970). Note that Article 2(a)(10) is not the only UCMJ provision that covers civilians; see, e.g., *Willenbring v. Neurauter*, 48 M.J.152 (1998). However, these additional sections do not necessarily apply in contingency operations and are beyond the scope of this chapter.

39. See, e.g., *Parker v. Levy*, 417 U.S. 733, 749–50 (1974) ("While a civilian criminal code carves out a relatively small segment of potential conduct and declares it criminal, the Uniform Code of Military Justice essays more varied regulation of a much larger segment of the activities of the more tightly knit military community.").

40. The case involved a dual Iraqi-Canadian citizen, Alaa Mohammad Ali, who was charged in the stabbing of another contractor on a military facility in Iraq. See, e.g., Dean Yates, "First Contractor Convicted under U.S. Military Law in Iraq," *Reuters*, June 24, 2008, http://uk.reuters.com/article/idUKL243864420080624 (accessed April 14, 2010).

41. John R. Parkinson, "Naked, Sore, Bruised, and Bleeding: Alleged U.S. Contractor Victim Fights for Day in Court," *ABC News*, Oct. 7, 2009, http://abcnews.go.com/Blotter/halliburton-employee-jamie-leigh-jones-testifies-senate-rape/story?id=8775641&page=1 (accessed April 14, 2010).

42. John M. Broder, "Suspect in Iraq Killing Keeps Lips Sealed," *New York Times*, Sept. 22, 2009. Blackwater eventually reached a civil settlement with the victim's family.

43. *MEJA Expansion and Enforcement Act of 2007*, H.R. 2740, 110th Cong., 1st sess., *Congressional Record* 153, no. 149, daily ed. (Oct. 3, 2007): H11221–11223.

44. Ibid. at § 2(a). See also House Committee on the Judiciary, *MEJA Expansion and Enforcement Act of 2007*, 110th Cong., 1st sess., 2007, H.R. REP. 352 § 2. The tradeoff inherent in H.R. 2740—expanding MEJA to cover all government agencies but restricting it to current war zones or contingency operations—was intended to preserve the original intent of the law (prosecuting civilians deployed in support of military operations) while removing any remaining uncertainty as to which federal agencies were covered by the law.

45. S.2147, 110th Cong., 1st sess., 2007.

46. Sudarsan Raghavan, "Blackwater Faulted in Military Reports From Shooting Scene," *Washington Post*, Oct. 5, 2007; James Glanz and Sabrina Tavernise, "Blackwater Case Will Go to Iraqi Courts," *New York Times*, Sept. 22, 2007.

47. Brian Bennett and Adam Zagorin, "Bush and Maliki to Talk Blackwater," *Time*, Sept. 19, 2007, www.time.com/time/world/article/0,8599,1663306,00.html (accessed April 14, 2010).

48. Had the shootings occurred in the Green Zone or on another US military facility, the case could be tried under the Special Maritime and Territorial Jurisdiction of the United States, as amended by the USA PATRIOT Act. Public Law 107-56, *U.S. Statutes at Large* 115 (2001): 275, § 804, codified at 18 U.S.C. § 7 (2006).

49. Report of the Secretary of State's Panel on Personal Protective Services in Iraq 5 (2007).

50. House Committee on Oversight and Government Reform, *The State Department and the Iraq War*, 110th Cong., 1st Sess. 93-105, Oct. 25, 2007 (testimony of Secretary Condoleezza Rice), quoted in "Private Security Contractors at War: Ending the Culture of Impunity," 20.

51. John Negroponte and Gordon England, *Memorandum of Agreement between the Department of Defense and the Department of State on USG Private Security Contractors*, Dec. 5, 2007.

52. Def.'s Mot. to Bifurcate Trial and for a Bench Trial on Extraterritorial Jurisdiction 2, *United States v. Slough, et al.* (2009). *See also* Gov.'s Mot. to Exclude Out-Of-Court Legal Opinions Regarding Applicability of MEJA to Private Security Contractors in Iraq, *United States v. Slough et al.* (2009).

53. See Statement of Administration Policy at www.presidency.ucsb.edu/ws/index.php?pid=75852 (accessed April 14, 2010).

54. During floor consideration, the House also approved three amendments to refine and improve the measure: an amendment by Rep. John Conyers (D-MI) requiring the Justice Department to investigate any fatalities resulting from the potentially unlawful use of force and allowing it to request material assistance and personnel from other federal agencies in the conduct of its investigations; an amendment by Rep. Jan Schakowsky (D-IL) requiring the Justice Department to report to Congress on all legal actions taken against contractors in Iraq and Afghanistan; and an amendment by Rep. Baron Hill (D-IN) requiring the FBI to report annually to Congress on the activities and resources needs of its Theater Investigative Units.

55. *Supplemental Appropriations Act, 2008*, Engrossed Amendment as Agreed to by House, § 11301, 2nd sess., *Congressional Record* 154, daily ed. (May 15, 2008): H3919–H3920

56. It should be noted that during the Democratic primary campaign, Sens. Clinton and Obama disagreed on the right approach to PSC regulation. See Jeremy Scahill, "Blackwater Seeps into the Campaign," *The Nation* online edition, Mar. 18, 2008, www.thenation.com/doc/20080331/scahill (accessed April 14, 2010).

57. US Department of Justice Press Release, "Five Blackwater Employees Indicted on Manslaughter and Weapons Charges for Fatal Nisur Square Shooting in Iraq" (Dec. 8, 2008), http.justice.gov/opa/pr/2008/December/08-nsd-1068.html (accessed April 14, 2010).

58. Memorandum Opinion: Granting the Defendants' Motion to Dismiss the Indictment; Denying as Moot the Government's Motion to Dismiss the Indictment against Defendant Slatten Without Prejudice at 2, *United States v. Slough* (2009). Available at http://documents.nytimes.com/memorandum-of-dismissal-of-charges-against-blackwater-guards#document/p1 (accessed April 14, 2010).

59. See, e.g., Alissa J. Rubin and Paul von Zielbauer, "Blackwater Case Highlights Legal Uncertainties," *New York Times*, Oct. 11, 2007, www.nytimes.com/2007/10/11/world/middleeast/11legal.html (accessed April 14, 2010).

60. Notice of Appeal, *United States v. Slough* (2010); available at http.scribd.com/doc/26058192/Notice-of-Appeal (accessed April 14, 2010).

61. See, e.g., Del Quentin Wilber, "Charges Dismissed against Blackwater Guards in Iraq Deaths," *Washington Post*, Jan. 1, 2010, http.washingtonpost.com/wp-dyn/content/article/2009/12/31/AR2009123101936.html?sid=ST2009123102027 (accessed April 14, 2010) ("The Justice Department can appeal the ruling. But legal experts said it will have a difficult time because Urbina wrote such a detailed opinion and held such long hearings. Prosecutors can also seek a fresh indictment but would be precluded from using any evidence that Urbina ruled was tainted. That would be another tough task because Urbina eviscerated much of the government's case. He also found that many

of its key witnesses were badly tainted by the guards' statements, which they had read or heard about in the news media.").

62. As a possible indication of this greater willingness, in January 2010 the Department of Justice invoked MEJA to charge two DoD contractors working in Afghanistan with the shooting deaths of two Afghan nationals. See Department of Justice Press Release, "Two Individuals Charged with Murder and Other Offenses Related to Shooting Death of Two Afghan Nationals in Kabul, Afghanistan" (Jan. 7, 2010), http://washingtondc.fbi.gov/dojpressrel/pressrel10/wfo010710.htm (accessed April 14, 2010).

63. See, e.g., Paul McLeary, "Contractor UAVs in the Skies over Haiti (Updated)," *Aviation Week*, Jan. 19, 2010; Mark Bowden, "Flight Risk," *The Atlantic* (July/Aug. 2009), http.theatlantic.com/magazine/archive/2009/07/flight-risk/7492/ (accessed April 14, 2010); Tristan McConnell, "Security Guards Shoot Dead Somali Pirate in Attack on MV Almezaan Cargo Ship," *The Times* (UK), Mar. 25, 2010, www.timesonline.co.uk/tol/news/world/africa/article7074160.ece (accessed April 14, 2010).

64. *Civilian Extraterritorial Jurisdiction Act (CEJA) of 2010*, H.R. 4567, 111th Cong., 2nd sess.; *Civilian Extraterritorial Jurisdiction Act (CEJA) of 2010*, S.2979, 111th Cong., 2nd sess., *Congressional Record* 156, no. 15, daily ed. (Feb. 2, 2010): S 442–45.

65. Ibid., H.R. 4567 § 2. Covered crimes include arson; assault, resisting, or maiming if such offense would be punishable by more than one year in prison; bribery; forgery of various official badges, decorations, and documents; extortion and threats punishable by more than three years in prison; extortionate credit transactions; use of a firearm in a violent or drug trafficking crime; genocide; murder; manslaughter; kidnapping; obstruction of justice and witness tampering; racketeering; hijacking; money laundering; robbery; burglary; sexual abuse; terrorism; torture; treason, sedition, and subversive activities; war crimes; manufacture, distribution, or possession of controlled substances if the offense is punishable by twenty years or more in prison.

66. See, for example, James Risen, "Efforts to Prosecute Blackwater Are Collapsing," *New York Times*, Oct. 20, 2010, www.nytimes.com/2010/10/21/world/21contractors.html?pagewanted=1&ref=blackwaterusa (accessed Jan. 4, 2011).

IV US ADMINISTRATIVE STRUCTURES REQUIRED TO SUSTAIN CONTRACTOR OPERATIONS

10 How to Decide When a Contractor Source Is Better to Use Than a Government Source[1]

Frank Camm

1. Introduction

During the 1990s, several distinct trends came together to encourage the outsourcing of government activities—that is, the substitution of contractor sources for government sources—particularly in the Department of Defense (DoD).[2] A wave of outsourcing under way in the private sector suggested that government agencies could better focus on their inherently governmental core competencies by pushing activities that were not inherently governmental to external sources. Efforts to downsize the government workforce under the National Performance Review led to outsourcing of individual positions and then whole organizations to get the number of government positions down. As DoD purchases of weapon systems plummeted with the end of the Cold War, defense contractors pushed for expanded support contracts to sustain their revenue flows, creating a large and well-placed constituency in support of outsourcing logistics support services. And over all these trends hung a renewed appreciation that "the long-standing policy of the federal government has been to rely on the private sector for needed commercial services"[3] and a broader belief among many Americans that the private sector is inherently a better source of services than any government agency could hope to be.[4]

All of these trends carried over into arguments favoring expanded use of contractors in deployed operations, first in the First Gulf War of 1990–1991, and then in a series of operations around the world. To date, few attempts have been made to compare the actual costs or performance levels of government and contractor sources when they provide similar services to deployed military forces. The most reliable effort to date is that by the Congressional Budget Office, which found that, because contractor and government sources of troop support provide this service in similar ways, their costs are similar for the actual work.[5] But government policy requires that government "sources" (units, teams, or even individuals) rotate in and out of deployment and be paid whether they are deployed or not. The government pays contractor sources only while they are deployed. This gives contractor sources an inherent cost advantage. This is not the inherent advantage that privatization advocates initially attributed to private-sector sources, but it is an important inherent advantage of using contractor sources.

No firm empirical basis exists to make broad statements about the relative desirability of government and private-sector sources to support deployed forces. But DoD's standard approach to managing risk can be used to compare the risks associated with using government and private-sector sources to provide a particular service. This chapter explains how to apply this standard approach by treating each alternative source as a different course of action, mitigating the risks associated with each course of action, and then comparing the "residual risk"—the risk that remains after all practical mitigations have been applied—associated with each source.[6]

As we apply this framework, we must be ever cognizant that the time scale for a decision heavily shapes our options. If a contingency arises today, the United States can draw only on sources that exist today to address that contingency; choices today are heavily shaped—and limited—by force structure choices made in the past, choices that typically take many years to change. Broader choices are available only when the United States weighs the relative desirability of different sources that, with investments today, it can make available to decision makers who must address future contingencies. That is, as we approach some contingency in the future, we gain more information about what mix of sources might best address it, but the closer we get, the harder it is to get the mix we want in place. On balance, when we ask whether a government or private-sector source is more likely to be appropriate, a longer-term perspective is usually the most useful. Guidelines on choosing among different sources should focus on the future, so there will be time to change the basic mix of sources, and not on constraining any current combatant commander, who has available only the forces at hand and so must rely on contractors when suitable government sources are not available.

Section 2 of this chapter briefly reviews a number of concepts and policy issues relevant to any comparison of government and contractor sources. Section 3 explains how to use DoD's standard risk management framework to compare alternative sources. Section 4 explains how this framework treats command and control, which can be thought of as an explicit set of mitigation measures to limit risks associated with each type of source. Section 5 illustrates how to use the framework to examine the relative desirability of using government and contractor sources to provide three different kinds of services for deployed forces that have been much in the news. The chapter closes with a brief conclusion.

2. Some Basic Concepts and Policy Issues

A number of concepts and policy issues arise repeatedly in any discussion of DoD sourcing policy. This section reviews them in preparation for our discussion of the risk framework.

Standard DoD sourcing guidance conceives the sourcing decision in terms of a series of screens.[7] When considering the appropriate source for any activity, the first screen asks if the position is *inherently military*. If it is, comparison stops; only a military occupant is appropriate. Despite years of attempting to define the meaning of inherently military, though, DoD lacks clear guidelines, giving considerable latitude to those responsible for choosing the appropriate source for any position. As a result, the concept of what is inherently military is not consistent across the armed services or even within any of the services.

If an activity is not inherently military, the guidance then asks whether it is *inherently governmental*. Government policy provides clearer guidelines to help decide if a position is inherently governmental, but even these allow much discretion. Federal policy defines an "inherently governmental function" as

> so intimately related to the public interest as to mandate performance by Government employees. . . . The term includes activities that require either the exercise of discretion in applying Federal Government authority or the making of value judgments in making decisions for the Federal Government, including judgments relating to monetary transactions and entitlements. An inherently governmental function involves, among other things, the interpretation

and execution of the laws of the United States so as . . . to significantly affect the life, liberty, or property of private persons.[8]

If an activity is inherently governmental, analysis stops; only a government source is appropriate. Next, the guidance asks if the activity is required to provide a *rotation base* for deployed forces or to *build human capital* in individuals who will, later in their careers, serve as government supervisors or managers. The rotation base provides government jobs for government personnel to occupy between periods of deployment. For example, if deployment policy expects each deployed person to spend two years in a nondeployed setting for every year deployed, the rotation base should provide two nondeployed positions for every position deployed. Similarly, because the US government tends to promote from within to build its nonpolitical senior leadership, it must sustain junior government positions for its personnel to occupy as they accumulate the skills and experience required to perform government tasks later in their careers, even if those junior government positions are not inherently governmental. If an activity is required for the rotation base or to build human capital, only governmental provision is appropriate.

Next, the guidance asks if *esprit de corps* depends heavily on using a military source. Examples include military bands and military color guards. If so, such positions are automatically classified as military.

Any activity that survives these screens is available to compare with a contractor source. In practice, the vast majority of positions in the armed services fail to survive all of these screens and thus must be military or government civilian. The annual Inherently Governmental and Commercial Activity (IGCA) process, which is explicitly designed to identify the positions available for comparison, year in and year out identifies only a small fraction of DoD's total government work force—typically ten percent or less—that is suitable for comparison with a contractor alternative under these rules. During the 2000s, senior defense officials routinely asked why DoD should rely so heavily on military personnel when DoD cost accounts made it clear to them that contractor sources would be much less expensive. Even if those accounts were correct—we will return to this question below—DoD's process of choosing sources exempts the vast majority of government positions from direct cost comparison, making it impossible to justify greater reliance on contractor sources. Of course, these screens do not even address contractor positions for potential in-sourcing; almost no comparisons of these positions occur.

In the end, cost is literally irrelevant to the vast majority of positions in DoD sources.

In any effort to choose an optimal mix of sources, we can usefully think of the screens listed above—inherently military, inherently governmental, rotation base, development of human capital, and esprit de corps—as *constraints* on the optimization. They in effect define the bounds within which optimization occurs. All of these bounds apply when we think about choosing sources for support of deployed forces. In fact, given the nature of military deployment activities, they apply more to deployed activities than to the rest of DoD.

Other constraints that are not relevant to sourcing decisions in the rest of DoD also apply. Status of forces agreements can limit the types of contractors that the United States can use in a specific country or theater or affect their cost to DoD by affecting the taxes and tariffs relevant to their use in theater. Host nations, Congress, and various political and diplomatic considerations can dictate end-strength constraints on numbers of US military and/or government civilians. Use of contractors—especially host-nation nationals—in a deployed setting can provide a simple way to extend US capabilities beyond those available from only US government sources when such end-strength constraints apply.

In any contingency, the most important constraints may be the shape of US force structure, the time it takes to change that structure, the pace of the contingency's expansion, and the capability of civilian government agencies when the contingency arises. The US government simply cannot deploy government capabilities that do not exist or that cannot be acquired quickly. For most noncombat activities, US and non-US contractor sources typically offer large opportunities to rapidly extend US government capabilities—much more rapidly than the force can be expanded. Even when that occurs—and perhaps especially when that rapid expansion can and does occur—DoD can still typically benefit from giving close attention to the relative desirability of using government and contractor sources for specific activities. For example, if a combatant commander has a strong preference for military over contractor sources, it may be appropriate to strip nondeployed activities of military personnel and use contractor sources to backfill these nondeployed activities; that is, use contractors to augment the deployed force by filling in at nondeployed locations so that those locations can release their military capabilities for deployment.

Any effort to decide whether the government or a contractor is the more desirable source for a particular activity must frame that decision with all these constraints in mind. Over the long term, potential opportunities exist to ease many of these constraints by changing rotation policies, career management policies, and the structure of the DoD itself. Unfortunately, like the proverbial farmer who decides not to patch his roof because it isn't raining and can't patch his roof when it is raining, DoD may have difficulty looking beyond its immediate concerns to change the mix of government and contractor capabilities it will have available in the future.[9] If DoD delays the investments required to make desirable changes in this mix, its options will remain limited when it addresses each new contingency. The next section offers a way to treat alternative sources as alternative courses of action *when the constraints that DoD faces in any situation allow a real choice.*

3. Comparing the Risks of Alternative Sources as Alternative Courses of Action

The standard DoD approach to assessing risk starts with a threat, which we can usefully think of as some external source of danger, such as a potential attack on a friendly military force or on vulnerable civilian targets.[10] This threat imposes risks; the military planner seeks to reduce those risks or have plans in place to manage the threat if it materializes. The standard DoD approach states that the risks associated with a threat increases as (1) the probability of a bad outcome increases or (2) the magnitude of harm associated with a bad outcome increases.[11] When faced with a set of risks, a planner seeks alternative ways to reduce the probability and/or magnitude of harm associated with these risks. S/he does this by constructing a set of alternative courses of action (COAs), each of which provides a different way to mitigate the risks associated with a standing threat. DoD has a standard template for characterizing the quality of information about the risks and ultimately comparing the risks that remain in each COA after each has applied its mitigations. These "residual risks" provide a basis for choosing among COAs. The decision maker whom the planner supports considers the residual risks associated with each COA before choosing a final COA to implement.

One can think of the choice among different types of sources as a choice among alternative COAs for addressing a threat on the battlefield.[12] This choice is one among many that a military commander must make when structuring and employing a deployed force and, ideally, could be made as a part of a seamless, integrated planning process for the total deployed force. The risks that a military planner normally considers include those associated with the likely degree of military success of an operation, the cost of that operation in terms of loss of friendly personnel and other combat assets, and collateral effects of the operation that have political or diplomatic implications.

Additional risks become relevant when a planner compares alternative sources of support services. Four types of risks arise repeatedly in military discussions of the use of contractors on the battlefield:[13]

(a) Likely level of operational success, which encompasses all the factors listed in the paragraph above.

(b) Likely level of contractor casualties and loss of other contractor assets.

(c) Likely monetary or resource cost to the government.

(d) Likely effects of broader considerations, such as compliance with the international laws of war, compliance with acquisition regulations, effects on total force development, and so on.

In each dimension, risk rises as the probability or the magnitude of a bad outcome increases.

The relative importance of these dimensions of risk typically differs from one situation to another.[14] In any particular situation, the relevant commander must weigh these dimensions of risk when comparing the relative desirability of different sources of any particular support service. As in many other aspects of force planning, this comparison is highly subjective and depends on the professional military judgment of the commander and her or his staff. As direct military experience with the use of contractor sources to support deployed forces increases over time, the quality and sophistication of this judgment should increase, yielding better sourcing decisions. The framework offered here seeks to inform that application of professional military judgment by clarifying the nature of the risks relevant to the sourcing decisions.[15]

For example, the military often uses a contractor source to maintain sophisticated equipment because, as the result of acquisition program decisions and personnel policies, contractors often have better qualified personnel and more advanced methods to do this than military sources do, particularly when the equipment is newly fielded. But contractor personnel may not be trained and able to defend themselves if attacked. As a result, when the military chooses a contractor source to maintain equipment, that source may increase the likelihood of operational success by bringing better technical personnel to the task than a military source could. But the military might also feel a need to commit some military forces to the defense of this contractor source, diluting the military capability available to support operations and so reducing the likelihood of operational success. On net, which course of action enhances the likelihood of operational success while limiting risks to contractor personnel to an acceptable level? Inherently subjective trade-offs of this kind are pervasive in force planning; they are as relevant to comparing the courses of action associated with sourcing decisions as they are to comparing all other courses of action on the battlefield.

Similarly, the use of contractors always requires the presence of dual chains of command. Although DoD policy now places all deployed contractors under the purview of the Uniform Code of Military Justice (UCMJ), which governs the oversight of military personnel, DoD acquisition regulations still prevent a commander from circumventing the contracting chain of command when demanding performance from a contractor source when such performance would be outside the bounds of a contract already in place. This second chain of command adds complexity to the already complex challenge of sustaining unified command and control in a potentially chaotic battle space. Unless a commander and his or her command staff are familiar with the use of contractors, this added complexity can reduce the likelihood of operational success even when contractor sources are substantially better qualified to perform support services, like the maintenance of high-technology defense electronics, than military sources. Trade-offs between a commander's control of a source and its inherent capabilities are pervasive and differ from one situation to another as the relevant commander's familiarity with using contractor sources differs.

4. The Role of Command and Control in a Sourcing Decision

The role of command and control deserves special attention in any discussion of alternative sources. The discussion of outsourcing during the 1990s, described at the opening of this chapter, gave almost no attention to command and control. Few participants in the public policy debate at the time recognized that outsourcing could increase in the private sector precisely because new governance arrangements were emerging there that gave a buyer more effective control over an external source. DoD (and the rest of the government) are still learning how to do what exemplar outsourcers were doing to improve their own performance during the 1990s. Outsourcing to reduce levels of government staffing gave no attention to effects on and need for command and control, even though, as this trend continued, the contractor personnel providing services to the government became increasingly more senior and experienced than the government personnel charged with overseeing these contractor sources.

Personnel who converted in place—that is, moved from the government workforce to being a contractor employee, sometimes without even changing desks—often found themselves in the delicate position of now reporting to the personnel who had reported to them the week before and who had remained government employees. Logistics support contracts that left the contractors with ownership of technical data on the weapon and information systems that DoD uses have severely limited DoD's ability to control the behavior of these contractors because they limit DoD's ability to seek alternative sources—public or private. OMB Circular A-76, the dominant vehicle for comparing government and contractor sources for particular services during the 1990s, never explicitly mentions command and control as a factor to consider.

Experience with outsourcing services in the United Kingdom during the 1980s revealed the danger of neglecting the role of command and control in sourcing decisions.[16] The academic literature on the relative performance of public and private sources before that time indicated that privately owned sources of services such as airlines, railways, electric power, and heavy manufacturing industries tended to have lower costs than publicly owned sources of the same products. This literature gave little attention to sources that provided services directly to the government. The UK experience revealed that, even though privatizing industrial activities tended to reduce their production costs, the government's cost of overseeing the companies that continued to provide services to the government increased over the level in place when the government provided these services in-house. This increase in cost tended to offset reductions in production costs, leaving the government with no net savings.

Without claiming that DoD's oversight of its external providers imposes a cost of similar magnitude, it is still reasonable to recognize the potential of such a cost and to consider it explicitly when DoD chooses between government and private-sector sources. The cost need not be only a monetary cost.

It can also be a loss in quality or responsiveness due to limitations in effective control. Although this concern is relevant when comparing government and private-sector sources for any service provided to DoD, it is doubly important when considering the provision of services to support deployed forces. This is true for several reasons.[17]

First and most important, despite massive and unprecedented DoD dependence on contractor sources in recent operations in Iraq and Afghanistan, military commanders and their command staffs still have more formal training and experience in using traditional command and control mechanisms, built to oversee in-house sources under the complete aegis of the UCMJ, than in using contractor sources.[18] Recent experience is changing this situation quickly, at least for the services that commanders have come to expect from contractor sources when the commanders arrive in the theater of operations. That experience may give these commanders and their staffs the confidence to use contractor sources in new applications. The key point here is that the effective command and control of contractor sources that support deployed forces depends fundamentally on the capabilities of the commander and staff responsible for integrating these sources into the total force in theater. The relative inherent production capability or cost of government and contractor sources has almost no bearing on this observation.

Second, even for commanders and staffs skilled in the oversight of contractors, command and control of contractor sources is inherently more difficult than the command and control of government sources, because government acquisition regulations require that any commander direct any contractor through the appropriate contracting officer, a specialist trained to understand these acquisition regulations and the limitations they impose on government control over any contractor or its personnel. Skilled commanders and their staffs learn to integrate appropriate contracting personnel into their command and control mechanisms to allow smooth oversight. But the language of the underlying contracts themselves limits what commanders can ask for in ways that simply would not arise if a commander were addressing an in-house government source. The government is learning to write more flexible and responsive contracts. But again, the relative inherent production capability and cost of government and contractor sources have almost no bearing on a commander's effective use of the contracting community's chain of command or on a government program manager's ability to value and write an effective contract.

Third, the US expeditionary approach to applying deployed force complicates the issues discussed in the two preceding paragraphs.[19] This approach basically asks military units to fall in on standing contractual arrangements in theater for six to fifteen months or so and then return to home station. For example, the structure of the Logistics Capability Augmentation Program (LOGCAP) contracts, which have been the largest contract vehicles to provide support to deployed forces over the last two decades, was originally created and administered in a small Army Corps of Engineers office located in downstate Virginia. Responsibility for these contracts has since migrated to the Army Sustainment Command, located in Illinois. When they arrive in theater, individual Army units are supported through these contracts, which provide resources that provide a significant portion of the logistics support.

The commanders and staffs that provide logistics support, using both government and contract sources, also rotate through theater and access these contracts through their own contracting officers or officials in the theater with the Joint Contracting Command (JCC).[20] They do not use LOGCAP contracts until they arrive in theater. So their operations at home station do not naturally prepare them to integrate with or exercise command and control over resources provided through the LOGCAP contracts. Meanwhile, the Defense Contract Management Agency (DCMA) sends contracting officers to theater for six-month tours to help oversee the overall execution of the LOGCAP contracts. Each DCMA official arriving new in theater must learn quickly how LOGCAP works. Finally, the primary mechanism to motivate LOGCAP performance, its award fee process, draws input from the home command office, local oversight, individual units supported during the six-month period of performance on which the award is based, and DCMA personnel to reach a judgment.

All of this occurs outside the standard channels of military command and control in theater. Even if a particular commander effectively integrates LOGCAP providers to sustain unity of command during a particular operation, no one military commander has effective oversight of the contractor for more than a short time. This limits each commander's ability to shape LOGCAP providers in the same way that he or she can shape the military sources attached to a deployed unit. The relative inherent production capability and cost of government and contractor sources are irrelevant to the effective functioning of this complex approach to DoD governance of contractor sources.[21]

In sum, analytic comparisons of government and contractor sources of services have traditionally ignored the role that command and control plays in integrating any particular source with the broader goals of a government agency. This neglect is particularly troublesome, for the reasons described above, when comparing government and contractor sources that provide support services to deployed military forces.[22] If anything, in a deployed setting, a contractor's understanding of the expeditionary approach to contract governance may be more important than its inherent production capabilities and costs when making such a comparison. But such a consideration would not even arise in traditional analytic approaches to comparing government and contractor sources.

5. Comparing Military and Contractor Sources for Specific Activities

As explained elsewhere in this volume, in-theater contractor sources provide a broad range of services to support deployed forces.[23] Is this use appropriate? The discussion so far in this chapter suggests that it depends. A military source might be appropriate for one type of service in a particular set of circumstances; a contractor source might make more sense for another type of service in other circumstances. This section brings the ideas discussed above together into a simple set of accounts to compare the relative desirability of using government and contractor sources to provide three qualitatively different types of services to deployed forces that have received significant attention in Iraq:

(a) *Troop support* services provide a broad range of services to support personnel, but not their weapons or security. Examples are housing and food services and maintenance of noncombat vehicles and other equipment. The LOGCAP contracts are the best examples of these; as noted above, they account for more DoD spending than any other type of contractor-provided service.

(b) *System support* services maintain weapons and information technology (IT)-based systems. Maintenance of helicopters, tanks, and headquarters IT systems are examples. Original equipment manufacturers often provide such support within deployed military units. Others, like ITT's global maintenance support and services (GMASS) activity at Camp Arifjan in Kuwait, work in depot-like settings farther from combat operations.[24]

(c) *Security protection* services provide armed security (sometimes heavily armed) for convoys, facilities, high-profile individuals, and contractor activities. Blackwater (now Xe) has been the most publicized of these contractors. But most contractor security protection involves routine protection of buildings and other facilities by low-skilled foreign nationals serving as guards.

We can use DoD's standard risk assessment methods to treat military and contractor sources as alternative courses of actions for dealing with the risks associated with each of these types of services. As noted above, four types of risks are relevant: risks associated with operational success, injury to contractors, cost, and the success of broader policies. Table 1 summarizes the application of this approach by placing each type of service in a different column and listing attributes relevant to these risks in separate rows. The last row in the table offers a summary assessment of the relative desirability of using military and contractor sources for each type of service, based on a qualitative but informed consideration of the sources of risk and the government's ability to apply its command and control system to mitigate them.[25] The particulars of specific circumstances, of course, could change these assessments; the discussion below explains how.

Space limitations do not allow a detailed discussion of the contents of this table. But a quick summary of the contents can illustrate how to use information of this kind to compare government and contractor sources.

For troop support, government decisions about limits on the size of the force structure have not provided enough capacity to support large, long-term deployments. When a new contingency requires additional capacity for troop support, contractors are able to hire and train the personnel needed for that specific contingency more quickly than the government can. These circumstances drive heavy reliance on contractors today. The government has the option of changing these circumstances over the longer run. The capabilities required to provide troop support are not technologically demanding. In all likelihood, either a contractor or the government could manage such services to yield similar performance; in the larger scheme of things, a difference of 10 percent in performance or cost to the government or even more is not enough to suggest a strong preference.

TABLE 1. A Comparison of Sources for Three Types of Support Services

Service type attribute	Troop support services	System support services in theater	Security protection services
Risk 1. Skills, experience required for **operational success**	Contractor sources more available	Contractor dominates on new systems, many older systems	Government, contractors both have capabilities; contractors take government-trained personnel
Risk 2. **Injury to contractors**	Importance depends on location of service	Importance depends on location of service	High-risk for contractors, but contractors are able to defend themselves
Risk 3. **Relative cost**	Comparable during deployment	Comparable during deployment	Both high; linked by contractor hiring of government personnel
Risk 4. Achievement of **broader priorities**			
Inherently military or governmental	Not an issue	For practical purposes, a minor issue	A significant issue
Rotation base or human capital development	Rotation base favors contractor	Rotation base favors contractor; human capital concerns are growing	Rotation base favors contractor
Mitigation of risk via effective **command and control**			
Contractual vehicles available	Well framed	Varies	Requirements definition remains problematic
Integration with current operations	Typically not demanding	Typically more demanding	Highly demanding; not well done
Effective administration of contracts	Remains a challenge	Remains a challenge	Remains a challenge
Similarity to non-deployed experience	Preparation of commanders is limited	Preparation of commanders is typically better	Little preparation for commanders
Bottom line	Easiest to justify use of contractor	Depends heavily on quality of contractor	Specification of requirements, integration, and strategic ramifications make contractor use problematic

Potential injury to contractors favors a government source here, as it almost always does.[26] But if contractors work on well-protected reservations and are not subject to indirect fire such as rocket attacks, the probability of injury is small. This risk has not been an impediment to the use of contractors in Iraq. It is more problematic if contractor support requires movement along poorly secured roads. If the government manages a contractor properly, the concerns about inherently governmental activity discussed above do not arise here. The Congressional Budget Office (CBO) study mentioned above suggests that costs would be similar for deployed contractor or government services if there is not a rotational requirement. However, in terms of cost, the CBO study found that broader rotational policies favor use of a contractor here, as they always do.

The most serious risks associated with troop support services arise from their command and control. LOGCAP has developed effective, flexible contractual vehicles that facilitate command and control. Integration with military operations is less demanding for troop support than for other activities in a theater unless the theater is especially chaotic. Despite this, a shortage of skilled government contract personnel has led to persistent difficulties in administering troop support contracts. The flexibility built into the LOGCAP contracts works only if government contracting officials state clear contract requirements based on real operational requirements and systematically and persistently push back against contractors' efforts to exploit flexibility to their own advantage. Publicly reported failures to provide effective contractor troop support more often than not result from slips in contract administration. Commanders are growing more knowledgeable about troop support contracts as they spend more time deployed, but the command and control associated with these contracts differs fundamentally from that which commanders apply at home station. In effect, in the case of troop support contracts, the Army does not train the way it fights.

Under these conditions, when a real choice exists, contractors are preferable to government sources of troop support services when the circumstances in theater are not too chaotic and when the concerned commanders and their staffs and contracting specialists know how to ensure effective command and control of contractor sources.

As in troop support, contractors have more capability and capacity for system support than the government, because past government decisions about personnel and acquisition policies have induced this outcome. Government policy does not support the development and sustainment of highly skilled and experienced system support technicians in the same way that it has supported skilled and experienced military surgeons. If it had, DoD would not have to rely on contractors for the support of its newest systems and, increasingly, the support of older systems that are modified to add new capabilities. As a consequence, in many circumstances, contractors can offer a better likelihood of operational success in the support of systems in theater than government sources can. The decision to rely more heavily on contractor support for new systems and to sustain contractor support for a longer portion of a system's life cycle will likely expand the contractor advantage.

As above, the risk of potential injury to contractors tends to favor the use of a government source. But this is more important when system support occurs close to the fight—for example, at the battalion level—than if it occurs in a depot in Kuwait, in theater, but in a more secure location. No systematic empirical evidence is available on the relative cost of government and contractor sources of system support in theater, but if the government has the ability to provide support, it will probably do so much as a contractor would, achieving similar costs.

Properly managed, contractor system support raises none of the concerns about inherently governmental functions discussed above. But some lawyers worry that contractor support of weapon systems that contribute directly to war-fighting capability may compromise the protection that contractors accompanying the force receive under the international laws of war. This concern has not shaped practical decisions about US use of contractors in deployed operations. Concerns about the rotation base favor contractors, as above. Persistent contractor support of newer systems may be preventing the development of the technical knowledge that government leaders need to oversee such contracts in theater. This problem has not resulted in any well-publicized serious failures to date in system support, but such failures could become more likely.

As with troop support, the risks relevant to system support derive more from command and control than from the factors considered above. In general, system support contracts have not been as well framed as troop support contracts, although some are much better written than others. Integration with military operations is more important than for troop support activities, especially when DoD employs inventory management policies that assume rapid repair of spare parts following their failure in systems. A lack of knowledgeable contract administrators in theater and limits on reach-back support by specialists at home continue to complicate oversight of contracts. But commanders and their staffs often use the same system support contractors at home station that they use in theater. When this occurs, they are probably better prepared to use those contractors effectively when deployed.

In sum, given current DoD personnel and acquisition policies, it will be hard for the government even to offer effective system support in many circumstances. When it can, government provision becomes relatively more attractive in less secure areas, when a deploying unit must fall in on a support capability in theater rather than bringing its own contractors, and when a commander and staff have less experience working with contractors to get system support. In general, use of contractors becomes relatively more attractive as the government can field a more effective contract oversight infrastructure in a deployed theater.

Similar arguments apply for security protection services. The biggest differences probably concern the small share of security protection services that use highly skilled, heavily armed personnel to protect high-priority activities. Unlike its treatment of the service types reviewed above, DoD actively develops and sustains a government capability to provide such services. With a few very exceptional circumstances, the effectiveness of government sources is probably at least as good as that of contractor sources. But allowing a market for such services encourages contractors to compete for the personnel the government has paid to train. This competition creates a kind of self-fulfilling prophecy—when DoD deals with a shortage of government capabilities to provide security protection services by hiring contractors, those contractors hire the personnel the government has trained, sustaining and aggravating the shortage. The decision to use contractor sources in itself helps create this problem.

In addition, serious concerns about inherently governmental activities can arise in security protection services. Such activities are likely to be inherently governmental as they have effects on the life, liberty, or property of individual members of the public and as they make use of deadly force initiated at the discretion of the security protection service, with—as we have seen—significant political and even strategic implications. Government policy makes it clear that it is often difficult to determine whether a function is inherently governmental. The answer "depends upon an analysis of the factors of the case . . . and the presence or absence of any one is not in itself determinative of the issue."[27] Nonetheless, concerns about inherently government activity are far more likely to yield a preference for a government source here than in troop support or system support services.

In sum, given all the factors in the table, concerns about contractor competition for government-trained personnel and about discretionary application of deadly force when many innocents are present suggest that the government should prefer a government source of high-profile security protection service to a contractor source. A contractor source of security protection of buildings and facilities is much easier to justify, especially if the local citizenry do not have ready access to the property protected.

6. Conclusion

Is a contractor source likely to be better in a deployed setting than a government source? The answer depends first and foremost on what options are available. If past and ongoing decisions about force structure or current constraints on operations in theater prevent use of a government source, the answer is easy. Since a government source is not available, which is better is irrelevant. This situation helps explain a large portion of America's reliance on contractors to support deployed forces over its history.

If a real choice is available, the answer depends. This chapter has presented a simple way to apply DoD's standard approach to risk management to an assessment of four sources of risk and the government's mitigation of these risks. This adaptation can help force planners decide which type of source is better in any particular case. Specific circumstances matter, but the analysis suggests that the answer depends most on the type of service produced, the threat to contractors in the portion of the contingency in which the service occurs, and the government's ability to provide effective command and control of the contractor service when and where it is needed. Small differences between government and contractor costs or effectiveness are less likely to be relevant to the answer than any of these three factors. And the relative importance of these factors will vary from one situation to another. When a contract source allows the government to avoid the need for maintaining a rotation base, of course, the contractor source can offer much lower costs than a government source. This cost advantage can favor the contractor source, even if a government source offers significant advantages in the other dimensions of risk.

Notes

1. This chapter draws on Frank Camm, "Using Contractors Effectively to Support Stability Operations," Briefing given at a conference, "Are We Outsourcing Our National Security?" Ft. McNair, Washington, DC, June 18, 2008, and benefits from the discussion that accompanied that briefing. It has also benefited from discussions in the "Senior Manager Course on National Security," Elliott School of International Affairs, George Washington University, Washington, DC, 2007; "Princeton Problem-Solving Workshop Series in Law and Security: A New Legal Framework for Military Contractors?" Woodrow Wilson School of Public and International Affairs, Princeton University, Princeton, NJ, 2007–2008; "Panel on Outsourcing Sovereignty," Cardozo School of Law, Yeshiva University, New York (Nov. 26, 2007); and Stanford–Harvard Universities Preventive Defense Project workshop on "Defense Management Challenges: The Role of Contractors in DoD Operations," Washington, DC, Oct. 7, 2008. I thank John A. Ausink, Frank A. Camm (USA, retired), Carl J. Dahlman, Susan M. Gates, W. Michael Hix, Henry A. Leonard, Eric Peltz, Ellen M. Pint, and Albert A. Robbert for comments on earlier drafts.

2. For a more detailed discussion of these trends, see Frank Camm, *Expanding Private Production of Defense Services*, MR-734-CRMAF (Santa Monica, CA: RAND Corporation, 1996).

3. This is how the Office of Management and Budget (OMB)'s Circular A-76, which the Clinton administration chose to give renewed emphasis, opens the statement of its purpose; see Office of Management and Budget, "Performance of Commercial Activities," Circular A-76 (Washington, DC: Office of Management and Budget, May 29, 2003), section 4.

4. Some equated private-sector sources with competition. As OMB Circular A-76 states, "commercial activities should be subject to the forces of competition"; see ibid. Many others simply felt that any private-sector source was likely to be inherently more capable than a government source.

5. Congressional Budget Office, *Logistics Support for Deployed Military Forces* (Washington, DC: Congressional Budget Office, Oct. 2005); Congressional Budget Office, *Contractors' Support of U.S. Operations in Iraq* (Washington, DC: Congressional Budget Office, Aug. 2008).

6. In principle, we could use this framework to compare any alternative sources—for example, US military, allied military, US government civilian, host-nation civilian, US contractor, foreign contractor, and so on—of services to support deployed forces. See, for example, Frank Camm, "Policy Issues Relevant to Civilianizing Billets in the Department of Defense," unpublished research (Santa Monica, CA: RAND Corporation, 2005), for an application to US military and US government civilians. Ideally, a comparison of government and contractor sources should fall out of a broader strategic consideration of all potential sources. Neither the federal government nor even DoD has an integrated strategic policy on this broader sourcing issue. (I thank Carl Dahlman for this important insight.) Given the focus and space limitations of this

book, this chapter mainly uses a simple choice between contractor and US military sources to illustrate the comparison of sources.

7. Department of Defense, "Guidance for Determining Workforce Mix," DoD Instruction 1100.22, Office of the Under Secretary for Personnel and Readiness (Washington, DC: Department of Defense, April 2007), provides the guidance for these screens. The DoD Inherently Governmental and Commercial Activity (IGCA) inventory program updates and refines this guidance annually. See, for example, Department of Defense, "DoD Inventory of Commercial and Inherently Governmental Activities, Guide to Inventory Submission 2009" (Washington, DC: Department of Defense, Office of the Under Secretary for Personnel and Readiness, Oct. 2008). The discussion in the text abstracts from this guidance to present the concepts underlying the guidance as simply as possible.

8. *Federal Activities Inventory Reform Act of 1998* § 5.

9. DoD's current budgeting process and the way it translates changing sourcing priorities into qualitatively new sourcing mixes make this difficult. Describing the sources of that difficulty lies outside the scope of this chapter.

10. Headquarters, Department of the Army, *Risk Management—Multiservice Tactics, Techniques, and Procedures for Risk Management*, FM 3-100.12 (Washington, DC: Department of the Army, Jan. 2006), explains the standard DoD approach. The other armed services use the same manual but apply different document numbers to it.

11. DoD does not define the level of risk as the mathematical product of the probability and magnitude of loss. The operational assessment of risk is more subjective than this. That said, this approach is compatible with the threat-vulnerability-consequences (TVC) approach used more broadly in the risk assessment community and, in particular, in the homeland security community. Under the TVC approach, risk rises when the probability that a threat will manifest itself increases, our ability to counter this threat when it manifests itself falls, or the magnitude of harm that occurs when we cannot counter the threat rises. The TVC approach simply unpacks the factors considered in the DoD approach in a slightly different way. For a discussion of the TVC approach, see for example, Department of Homeland Security, *National Infrastructure Protection Plan* (Washington, DC: Department of Homeland Security, 2009).

12. Frank Camm and Victoria A. Greenfield, *How Should the Army Use Contractors on the Battlefield? Assessing Comparative Risk in Sourcing Decisions*, MG-296-A (Santa Monica, CA: RAND Corporation, 2005), explains in detail how to apply the standard DoD approach to such a sourcing decision.

13. For a detailed discussion of these four dimensions of risk and their relevance to sourcing decisions, see ibid.

14. For an assessment of the risks associated with the use of a contractor source that clarifies the relevance of local circumstances, see Victoria A. Greenfield and Frank Camm, *Risk Management and Performance in the Balkans Support Contract*, MG-282-A (Santa Monica, CA: RAND Corporation, 2005); Victoria A. Greenfield and Frank Camm, "Contractors on the Battlefield: When and How? Using the US Military's Risk Management Framework to Learn from the Balkans Support Contract,"

Proceedings of the Fourth Annual Acquisition Research Symposium, Naval Post Graduate School, Monterey, CA (May 16, 2007), 190–204.

15. For a deeper discussion of the practical integration of professional military judgment and formal analysis in force planning, see Frank Camm et al., *Managing Risk in USAF Force Planning*, MG-827-AF (Santa Monica, CA: RAND Corporation, 2009).

16. For more details on the discussion in this paragraph, see Camm, *Expanding Private Production of Defense Services*.

17. The discussion that follows draws heavily on Greenfield and Camm, *Risk Management and Performance in the Balkans Support Contract*.

18. Formal doctrine and guidance are not the problem, at least in the Army. Over the last two decades, the Army has developed relatively sophisticated guidance on the use of contractors accompanying the force. Key documents include U.S. Department of Defense, *Contractor Personnel Authorized to Accompany the U.S. Armed Forces*, DoD Instruction 3020.41 (Washington, DC, Oct. 3, 2005), http.dtic.mil/whs/directives/corres/pdf/302041p.pdf; U.S. Department of Defense, *Operational Contract Support OSC)*, DoD Instruction 3020.41 (Washington, DC, Dec. 20, 2011), http.dtic.mil/whs/directives/corres/pdf/302041p.pdf (accessed Jan. 20, 2012); Headquarters, Department of the Army, *Contractors Accompanying the Force*, Regulation AR 715-9 (Washington, DC: Department of the Army, Oct. 1999); Headquarters, Department of the Army, *Contractors on the Battlefield*, Field Manual FM 3-100.21 (Washington, DC: Department of the Army, Jan. 3, 2003). See also Chairman of the Joint Chiefs of Staff, *Operational Contract Support*, Joint Publication 4-10 (Washington, DC: Department of Defense, Oct. 17, 2008); Defense Acquisition University, "Overview of Contingency Contracting Operations and Contractors Accompanying the Force," Briefing (Ft. Belvoir, VA: Defense Acquisition University, n.d.); Office of the Deputy Assistant, Secretary of the Army (Policy & Procurement), *Contingency Contracting Handbook* (Arlington, VA: Dept. of Defense, Sept. 2006); and U.S. Army Procurement and Industrial Base Policy Office, *Army Contractors Accompanying the Force (CAF) (AKA Contractors on the Battlefield) Guidebook* (Arlington, VA: Office of the Deputy Assistant Secretary of the Army [Policy & Procurement], Sept. 8, 2003). In recent congressional testimony, the comptroller general noted that

> With regard to contractor support for deployed forces, DOD's primary challenges have been to provide effective management and oversight. These challenges include *failure to follow planning guidance* [emphasis added], an inadequate number of contract oversight personnel, failure to systematically capture and distribute lessons learned, and a lack of comprehensive training for military commanders and contract oversight personnel. These challenges have led to negative operational and monetary impacts at deployed locations. (See David M. Walker, "DoD Needs to Reexamine Its Extensive Reliance on Contractors and Continue to Improve Management and Oversight," Testimony before the Subcommittee on Readiness, Committee on Armed Services, House of Representatives, GAO-08-

572T, U.S. Government Accountability Office, Washington, DC, Mar. 11, 2008, 3, www.gao.gov/new.items/d08572t.pdf [accessed Feb. 21, 2011].)

19. For more detail and useful citations on the challenges of "expeditionary contracting," see Moshe Schwartz, *Training the Military to Manage Contractors during Expeditionary Operations: Overview and Options for Congress*, R40057 (Washington, DC: Congressional Research Service, Dec. 2008).

20. I thank John Ausink for information from his unpublished analysis of the JCC. For more information, see Special Inspector General for Iraq Reconstruction, *Iraq Reconstruction: Lessons in Contracting and Procurement*, Report #2 of the Special Inspector General for Iraq Reconstruction (July 2006), www.sigir.mil/reports/pdf/Lessons_Learned_July 21.pdf (accessed Jan. 25, 2010).

21. That is not to say that, historically, delivery of support services has in fact been any worse because the military relied on contractor rather than government sources. For example, control of nonmilitary government sources presents its own problems. Our intent is simply to highlight the extra challenge that effective command and control of contractor sources poses—a challenge that sourcing decisions should reflect.

22. Even the CBO studies, which offer the most detailed empirical comparisons of government and contractor sources to support deployed forces, have little to say about this issue.

23. See, for example, Lawrence K. Grubbs (Col., U.S. Air Force), Patrick M. Shaw (Col., U.S. Air Force), Timothy A. Vuono (LTC(P), U.S. Army), et al., *Privatized Military Operations Industry Study*, Final Report (Fort McNair, Washington, DC: Industrial College of the Armed Forces, National Defense University, Spring 2007), http. google.com/search?q=grubbs+vuono+shaw&rls=com.microsoft:en-us&ie=UTF-8&oe=UTF-8&startIndex=&startPage=1 (accessed Feb. 21, 2011).

24. See, for example, Government Accountability Office, *Defense Logistics: The Army Needs to Implement an Effective Management and Oversight Plan for the Equipment Maintenance Contract in Kuwait*, GAO-08-316R (Washington, DC: Government Accountability Office, Jan. 22, 2008).

25. To my knowledge, no formal empirical analysis is available to test the observations offered here. Such analysis would be highly desirable.

26. If a contract source is entirely out of harm's way, there is no difference. However, as a contractor faces increasing levels of danger, the government's advantage rises.

27. Office of Management and Budget (OMB), "Inherently Governmental Functions," Policy Letter 92-1 (Washington, DC: Office of Management and Budget, Sept. 1992), Sec. 7.

11 Reforming the US Approach to Stabilization and Reconstruction Operations

Stuart W. Bowen, Jr.

1. Introduction: Lessons Unlearned

"The absence of the ability to plan, execute, and lead stability and reconstruction operations was painfully apparent."[1] The author of this pointed criticism of the US-led rebuilding program in post-Saddam Iraq was referring to his own experience on a civilian–military Provincial Reconstruction Team (PRT) in southern Baghdad. His observation, however, generally applies to many aspects of the 8-year, $56 billion[2] US stabilization and reconstruction operation (SRO) in Iraq. The broad truth contained at the heart of his criticism underscores the compelling need for a coherent and complete reform of the US approach to SROs.

Over the past seven years, my office, the Special Inspector General for Iraq Reconstruction (SIGIR) developed an extensive catalogue of hard lessons learned derived from our oversight reporting on the Iraq reconstruction experience.[3] Among other things, we found that US relief and reconstruction efforts too often were commenced with insufficient regard for or input from local authorities, that coordination between the military and civilian elements was frequently weak, and that a lack of unity of effort between and among the lead operational agencies kept the program from achieving its ambitious goals.

The hardest lesson from Iraq, though, was the fact that no US office had full responsibility for planning, executing, or being held accountable for the rebuilding program.[4] Within the SRO management vacuum that existed in

2003 (when the Iraq reconstruction program was conceived and begun), an "adhocracy" evolved that, in toto, failed to realize sufficient value for the United States' massive rebuilding investment in Iraq, the largest foreign reconstruction program funded by US taxpayers since the Marshall Plan (NB: the US investment in Afghanistan's reconstruction will pass investment in Iraq in 2011). The US tendency toward taking ad hoc approaches to manage SROs is not a new problem. Current Under Secretary of Defense for Policy Michèle Flournoy noted in a report on SRO reform that she co-authored prior to joining the Obama administration:

> *Ad hoc* or relationship-based practices, although sometimes temporarily effective, do not hold up over time. Indeed, they often blur chains of command and responsibility. Instead, institutional solutions should be based on best practices and lessons learned, and . . . passed from administration to administration to be used (or not) as the President sees fit.[5]

"Ad hoc" is the operative phrase here. Improvising the management of an SRO needlessly exposes the program to fraud, waste, and abuse. Notwithstanding the reform initiatives undertaken in response to the discontinuities encountered during the ad hoc Iraq program, the US approach to managing SROs has not significantly improved. Almost a decade after the 9/11 attacks, the American system for executing contingency reconstruction operations remains plagued by problems in coordination, integration, management, and oversight. Operational responsibility for planning and executing contingency stabilization operations remains diffused across a raft of agencies, with at least twenty-six different federal departments ostensibly designated to play roles in SRO efforts.[6] Lines of responsibility and accountability are poorly defined, leaving the question of who is in charge and who is accountable unanswered—and unanswerable. These hard realities are painfully evident today in Afghanistan.

Since the end of the Cold War, the United States has engaged in more than ten overseas contingency operations, stretching from Panama to Iraq. While divergent in scope, most of these engagements entailed notable stabilization and reconstruction components. Yet the lessons learned from these operations failed to lead to an integrated approach for planning and executing SROs. Indubitably, the United States will again find itself engaged in complex contingencies in the coming decade. But if these future operations are to succeed, much must be done to apply the lessons learned from recent

SRO experience. This chapter proposes a way forward toward success. It first reviews the efforts to improve the US approach to SROs, then highlights the minimum essential reforms necessary to avoid repeating past mistakes, and finally proposes an innovative and economical approach that could make success in SROs consistently achievable.

2. Recapitulating Reconstructing Iraq

On January 20, 2003—just sixty days before invading Iraq—President George W. Bush issued National Security Presidential Directive 24, addressing the management of postwar relief and reconstruction operations. Breaking with tradition, NSPD-24 put DoD in exclusive charge of managing Iraq's reconstruction.[7] It established an Office of Reconstruction and Humanitarian Assistance (ORHA), under the Pentagon's aegis, to execute rebuilding and relief operations. The president's directive contained within it the very seeds of disunity that would burden reconstruction efforts for years to come. A news article stated that USAID, traditionally the lead US foreign assistance agency, "would handle much of the humanitarian and reconstruction work, *but ORHA would control the funding*" (emphasis added).[8] This management dichotomy—defense in charge of funding but civilians in charge of policy—would recur repeatedly in subsequent ad hoc iterations of reconstruction management in Iraq over the next eight years.

The negative effects of an ad hoc approach to reconstruction management became evident early in Iraq. Just three weeks after the fall of Baghdad and barely having begun its work, ORHA was peremptorily supplanted by another improvised structure—the Coalition Provisional Authority (CPA). The CPA was led by former diplomat Ambassador L. Paul Bremer III, who quickly took charge of the rebuilding program in May 2003, transforming it from "liberate and leave" to "occupy and reconstruct." Immediately upon CPA's creation, Secretary of Defense Donald Rumsfeld directed Ambassador Bremer to exercise responsibility "for the temporary governance of Iraq" and to "coordinate all executive, legislative, and judicial functions necessary to carry out this responsibility, including humanitarian relief and reconstruction and assisting in the formation of an Iraqi interim authority."[9]

The CPA's quickly cobbled together structure suffered from a reporting dichotomy that hobbled overall program direction. Ambassador Bremer was the CPA administrator reporting to Secretary Rumsfeld, but he also was commissioned as the president's envoy to Iraq. Possessing two charters, he took direction from DoD and the White House; those directions occasionally collided, sometimes in spirit, sometimes in letter. The ad hoc segmenting of the chain of command exposed weaknesses in the US structure for managing the Iraq SRO.

The CPA bore responsibility for a wide range of relief and reconstruction duties that traditionally fell within the ambit of DoS and USAID. As a start-up, Ambassador Bremer's new organization had neither the time nor resources to plan sufficiently for and execute effectively the largest overseas rebuilding program in history. Crucially, it did not possess the necessary trained staff with the applicable expertise required to implement so grand and ambitious an effort as that envisioned by Ambassador Bremer. Staffed primarily with temporary employees quickly drawn from federal agencies, the CPA operated against the backdrop of a rapidly deteriorating security situation. Decisions were driven by ever-changing circumstances, and security breakdowns impeded progress on every front.

Many of the CPA's adversities were perhaps beyond its capacity to control. Nevertheless, a well-developed SRO plan implemented by an existing interagency management office could have brought a better-organized capacity to bear on the many problems that erupted in Iraq in 2003–2004. Moreover, it would have had an established resource base from which to implement timely and effective adjustments. Had such an entity existed at the outset of the Iraq program, the United States could have averted some of the significant waste that occurred. Ultimately, ORHA and then the CPA became necessary because nothing else existed in 2003 that was capable of executing the kind of stabilization and reconstruction mission demanded at that moment. And, unfortunately, no such office exists today.

3. Provincial Reconstruction Teams: A Case Study in the Need to Integrate Stability and Reconstruction Operations

The post-CPA reconstruction program struggled to gain footing in the face of a rising insurgency that enveloped Iraq in late 2004 and early 2005. Innovation was needed, and it came in October 2005, when the US ambassador to Iraq Zalmay Khalilzad, in conjunction with General George Casey, the commanding general of Multi-National Forces–Iraq, established the Provincial

Reconstruction Team (PRT) program in Iraq.[10] Ambassador Khalilzad modeled the new effort in Iraq on a similar program he had established in Afghanistan, where he served as ambassador from 2003 to 2005. The PRTs would provide integrated multidisciplinary teams of US and coalition personnel to teach, coach, and mentor provincial and local government officials in the core competencies of governance and economic development. At the program's peak, reached early in 2009, there were eighteen PRTs (and ten smaller embedded PRTs) operating across Iraq.[11]

The PRT program undoubtedly helped move local capacity building forward, but it too was burdened by the fact that it was ad hoc. From October 2006 to April 2009, SIGIR issued five audits focusing on the PRTs, finding that the challenges inherent in the Iraq SRO were exacerbated by the improvisational nature of the overall program. SIGIR found that:

- Clearly defined objectives and performances measures to guide the PRTs were not formally established until several years into the program.[12]
- The embassy office charged with managing the latter stages of the program—the Office of Provincial Affairs (OPA)—did not consistently require the PRTs to develop and submit written work plans that identified planned activities to address areas of weakness identified in their areas of operations.[13]
- Projects funded by the military's Commander's Emergency Response Program (CERP) often conflicted with PRT activities in the same area.[14]
- US agencies had no requirement to capture PRT costs, so those costs were not routinely tracked.[15]

Many of SIGIR's findings resonated in a recent report by Blake Stone, a Naval War College professor who spent eighteen months with the Baghdad PRT between 2008 and 2010.[16] His observations are particularly persuasive, derived as they are from events witnessed firsthand several years after the program's establishment. Mr. Stone wrote that neither the embassy nor OPA ever issued "guidance to the field that was of any benefit" to the PRT's stabilization and reconstruction operations.[17] For instance, projects were often undertaken without coordinating with the local Government of Iraq (GOI) representatives.[18] Further, there appeared to be little or no linkage between the strategic

and tactical levels of reconstruction operations, resulting in a yawning disconnect between "projects and other reconstruction efforts executed at the
local level and the achievement of [the US] strategic end state."[19]

Mr. Stone's report further criticizes DoS and DoD for failing to coordinate reconstruction efforts, noting that PRT attempts to focus on developing
local capacities were repeatedly undercut by US commanders "who evaluated
relative 'success' by the amount of CERP money obligated."[20] In Stone's esti-
mation, there was an "almost complete lack of unity and effort" between the
PRTs and local unit commanders that hampered both the nominally civilian-
lead reconstruction effort and the military's kinetic operations.[21]

The UK-led PRT in Basra, the southernmost province in Iraq, encountered
similar challenges. In a declassified lessons-learned report on the activities of
the Basra PRT, the UK government concluded that the failure to integrate the
efforts of the various British ministries involved in stabilization and reconstruction operations caused "substantial administrative difficulty," and that
the program "failed to achieve its potential."[22] Several key findings from this
report buttress the argument for an integrated approach to planning and executing SROs:[23]

- When conducting SROs, integrated planning is as important as
  integrated execution.
- Integration is not divisible, and neither can it be imposed. The civil–
  military relationship is particularly important, and cannot easily be
  fashioned ad hoc.
- Where integrated bodies such as the PRT are raised in the future, they
  should be recruited by a single authority. Ideally such groups would
  train together and deploy as a formed body, with that single authority
  financially and administratively responsible for the operating requirements of the group.
- A whole-of-government approach requires procedural and structural
  change *at all levels of government* if it is to be successfully undertaken.
  (Emphasis added)

4. Recent Reform Initiatives: Right
Reaction, Wrong Solution

The early shortfalls in US reconstruction efforts in Iraq catalyzed a response
toward reforming the US government's management approach. A series of

laudably motivated initiatives arose from the recognized need to improve the systems governing the Iraq reconstruction program, signifying that the US government was willing to pursue reform of weak SRO management systems. The various reforms and their limited success suggest, however, that the inter-agency community has yet to arrive at a comprehensive solution. Thus, the time for more ambitious remedial actions by the Congress appears ripe.

In pursuing one area requiring significant strengthening—the need for more trained civilian SRO personnel—the Department of State created the Office of the Coordinator for Reconstruction and Stabilization (S/CRS) in July 2005 to "lead, coordinate, and institutionalize U.S. government civilian capacity to prevent or prepare for post-conflict situations."[24] But the fledgling S/CRS struggled to find its footing, first failing to receive the funding it needed to be effective and then finding itself marginalized within State's turf-conscious bureaucracy. S/CRS cannot today be characterized as a successful SRO reform effort.

The Pentagon's pursuit of reform—unsurprisingly—has been more robust. In November 2005, DoD issued Directive 3000.05, *Military Support for Stability, Security, Transition, and Reconstruction (SSTR) Operations*, thereby committing DoD to developing and expanding its capacities to support SROs.[25] The directive defined "stability operations" as military and civilian activities conducted across the spectrum from peace to war activities to establish or maintain order, further stating that stability operations are a "core U.S. military mission" that should be given priority comparable to combat operations and be explicitly addressed in all DoD activities.[26] In 2009, DoD reissued 3000.05 as an "Instruction," emphasizing that the military must be ready to support civilian agencies leading stability operations, as well as to support foreign governments and nongovernmental and international entities. Despite recognizing the centrality of stability and reconstruction operations—necessarily a civilian-driven solution—to contemporary national security policy, DoD has made limited headway in integrating civilian agencies into its approach to SROs.

In December 2005, President George W. Bush signed Presidential Directive 44 (NSPD-44), *Management of Interagency Efforts Concerning Reconstruction and Stabilization*, which stated that "reconstruction and stabilization are more closely tied to foreign policy leadership and diplomacy than to military operations."[27] NSPD-44 aimed at improving the coordination, planning, and implementation of US government reconstruction and stabilization missions in states and regions at risk of, in, or in transition from conflict or civil strife.[28] But the NSPD, though rightly seeking to respond to evident SRO weaknesses, failed to promote much progress in the areas it targeted.

Pursuant to NSPD-44, the Coordinator for S/CRS was charged with leading the development of a strong stability and reconstruction response mechanism. DoS and DoD were required to "integrate stabilization and reconstruction contingency plans with military contingency plans when relevant and appropriate."[29] To date, S/CRS has deployed no one to Iraq and has intermittently deployed several handfuls of staff to Afghanistan with limited effect.[30] Ultimately, NSPD-44 represents a well-intentioned effort to marry civilian expertise in the fields of stabilization and reconstruction with the US military's unsurpassed ability to deploy massive resources to remote contingency environments. But the marriage did not take, at least under these auspices.

Near the close of his administration, President Bush signed the Duncan Hunter National Defense Authorization Act for Fiscal Year 2009, Title XVI of which contained the Reconstruction and Stabilization Civilian Management Act of 2008 (RSCMA).[31] Effectively codifying S/CRS into law, RSCMA assigned chief responsibility for planning and managing the civilian response to overseas contingencies to the Department of State, requiring DoS and USAID to develop an interagency strategy for reconstruction and stabilization engagements. Since its passage, however, implementation of this critically important provision has been limited; and the funding for RSCMA's various authorizations fell far short of the act's legislative vision.

Implicitly recognizing that S/CRS is not the solution to SRO management, DoS's November 2010 Draft Quadrennial Diplomacy and Development Review (QDDR) proposed the creation of a new Bureau for Crisis and Conflict Operations (CCO), which would absorb S/CRS into a broader management structure.[32] The QDDR indicated that USAID's Office of Transition Initiatives—which works on the ground to provide short-term assistance targeted at key political transition and stabilization needs in fragile or failed states—would be relocated from USAID to the CCO.[33] If eventually established, the CCO would take several years before being capable of making substantial contributions to the management of SROs. Moreover, creating the CCO does not resolve the fundamental cross-jurisdictional problems that inhibit current SRO management.

5. Core Functional Reforms: What Must Be Done Now

Since 2004, SIGIR has published more than 350 reports covering a diverse array of topics, including interagency reconstruction decision making, program and project execution, and government contract administration. Although some matters addressed by SIGIR are unique to Iraq and, as such, may not facilitate systemic solutions, most of the recurring problems identified in our work mark out a clear path pointing toward the need for comprehensive SRO reform. Regardless of the particular coordinating mechanism ultimately decided upon, enacting certain fundamental reforms that address chronic SRO problems is the sine qua non to improving the protection of US national security interests in overseas contingency operations. Meaningful functional reform requires the following actions:

(a) Draft Joint Doctrine

The relevant operational agencies—DoD, DoS, USAID, the Department of Justice, the Department of Treasury, inter alia—should develop joint interagency doctrine and policies for SROs, with the National Security Council (NSC) defining the requirements and the agencies developing the implementing mechanisms. Each agency would draft programmatic details, focusing on how it would operationally integrate into a complex contingency event. The agencies then would define the basic concept of operations and identify the applicable roles, responsibilities, operating procedures, and structures for participants. The NSC would guide this heuristic process to conclusion, clarifying doctrine and policies on planning and implementation questions and resolving the inevitable ambiguities that will arise regarding agency roles and responsibilities. The existing Interagency Management System (IMS) has not sufficiently met the need for a clear joint SRO doctrine. While the Integration Planning Cell (part of the IMS) provides a forum for exchange, coordination, and decision making, it has not led to the creation and implementation of the kind of joint doctrine necessary to achieve integrated operations in SROs.

(b) Integrate Planning

All relevant agencies should work together to develop integrated operational planning capabilities for SROs. Currently, there is "no systemic effort at strategic planning [for SROs] that is inclusive, deliberate, or integrative."[34] Given their relatively limited funding (when compared to DoD), US civilian agencies tend to approach planning with resource constraints at the forefront, thereby fiscally foreshortening the vision they may have for effective contingency planning. Civilian agencies thus have developed a culture of planning driven chiefly by available appropriations; i.e., planning to the money as opposed to funding a truly joint operational plan. Promoting integrative planning would open up access to more resources, resulting in better programs and improved project execution. Regular planning exercises could develop familiarity and understanding among the agencies and prepare them to work together during contingency operations. The current relatively limited support for and commitment to realistic SRO training constrains success in the field.

(c) Revise the Budget Process

The NSC and the Office of Management and Budget (OMB) should work with the relevant agencies to develop advance budget requirements for potential overseas contingency engagements. The Project on National Security Reform (PNSR), led by James Locher, has issued multiple reports wisely urging the United States to link resources to national security goals through mission-based analysis and budgeting. An August 2009 PNSR report highlighted several major problems with the way budgets of civilian agencies with SRO responsibilities are currently formulated:[35]

- There is "no established process for moving resources between agencies with national security responsibilities; such trades are *ad hoc* and rare."
- There is "no agreement on which parts of each agency budget should be included in an overall national security budget, and no current process for making this determination."
- There are "significant discrepancies across national security agencies in terms of program/budget calendars, resource displays/formats, and planning horizons."
- The committee structure in Congress is "not attuned to a comprehensive, cross-agency review of national security strategy, programs and budgets."

This PNSR report underscored the many difficulties entailed in reforming the current budget process for complex overseas contingency events:

[Reform] will require participation by agency personnel who: 1) know their agency's structure, missions, programs and information systems very well; and 2) are willing to consider themselves part of the larger national security enterprise for this purpose. In addition to providing strong leadership, OMB will have to ensure that workable guidelines are developed and applied consistently across all agencies.[36]

Developing detailed budgetary requirements serves several purposes. First, it fiscally forces strategic estimates regarding mission capacity, which critically influence second-order decision making regarding mission, objectives, and possible alternative courses of action. Second, it provides policy makers with a preview of the budget implications inherent in a possible contingency. Finally, early fiscal forecasting shapes mission orientation, allowing budget demands to inform mission requirements.

The November 2010 Draft Quadrennial Diplomacy and Development Review (QDDR) underscores the desire for progress in reforming the budgeting and contracting processes. The QDDR recommends that DoS apply joint planning and budgeting processes to establish an overseas contingency operations title in DoS/USAID's annual budget. This will reflect the extraordinary costs to civilian agencies endemic to most contingency operations.[37] This recommendation suggests a growing realization on the part of US policy makers that budgeting for the mission is more economically coherent than simply resourcing multiple "stovepipes" that are separate and apart from any unified mission authority.

(d) Incentivize Civilian Personnel

Existing federal personnel regulations should be adjusted to provide stronger incentives to encourage civilian employees to accept temporary deployments in support of SROs. Incumbent employees who deploy on such operations must be able to return to their home agencies upon the completion of their mission. This is not always the case. In fact, existing personnel rules and long-held institutional prejudices militate against rewarding federal employees for participating in SROs. Modifying long-established federal employment laws to incentivize greater interagency participation in overseas contingency engagements is essential to ensuring that the best federal employees step forward to support their country's national security interests in time of need.

Upon taking office in 2009, President Obama—continuing the Bush administration's approach to Iraq—placed renewed emphasis on a "civilian surge" for Afghanistan. As of late 2010, DoS "has largely met the goals *it set for itself* in matching the military surge" with an enhanced presence of about 1,200 civilian reconstruction experts, but it remains "unclear what factors were taken into consideration when determining the size of the civilian uplift."[38] Moreover, in the words of the US military's former liaison officer to Embassy Kabul's Office of Interagency Provincial Affairs, "many of the civilian 'experts' who have been hired for the uplift are too fat, frail and/or flaky to undertake their responsibilities . . . [while] others are not taken seriously and do not know how to represent the agency they speak for and thus are quickly marginalized by the military."[39] Most strikingly, because of the inherently ad hoc nature of the Afghanistan civilian surge, "it is already becoming clear that [it] can be sustained only for the next year or two as it is currently organized."[40]

(e) Institutionalize Interagency Training Programs

The Congress or the administration should consolidate existing SRO training initiatives by establishing an interagency training center and a joint curriculum modeled on the US Army Training and Doctrine Command's (TRADOC) Interagency Fellowship Program or the interagency training programs now conducted by the National Defense University. An interagency educational and training center could help create a cadre of cross-trained professionals that the US government could call upon to plan and manage future SROs. Moreover, such an integrated interagency training culture for SROs would inculcate a lingua franca for overseas contingencies, creating cross-jurisdictional connections that could further consonant thinking and build greater unity of effort for SROs.

(f) Reform Contracting and Program Management

As discussed in Parts I and II of this volume, private-sector contractors increasingly play essential roles in supporting the military in stabilization and reconstruction missions. Their roles are crucial, because, axiomatically, the success of post-conflict stabilization efforts depends on delivering services, materials, and their supporting systems where and when needed. Many of these standing capabilities exist largely in the private sector, but it is imperative that they be employed efficiently and managed effectively by the government. Only a well-structured contracting and procurement process can optimize the use of private-sector providers during contingency situations. Therefore, the Congress or the administration should create a set of simple and accessible contingency contracting procedures, expand the US government's contingency contracting capacity and ensure more thorough, uninterrupted, accountable program management by government personnel. SIGIR's lessons-learned report on contracting and procurement in Iraq makes several key recommendations applicable to contracting in other contingency operations. For example:[41]

- Include contracting and procurement personnel in all planning stages for post-conflict reconstruction operations.
- Clearly define, properly allocate, and effectively communicate essential contracting and procurement roles and responsibilities to all participating agencies.
- Avoid using sole-source and limited-competition contracting actions, except where unavoidable. These exceptional contracting actions should be used as necessary, but the emphasis must always be on full transparency in contracting and procurement.
- Establish a single set of simple contracting regulations and procedures that provide uniform direction to all contracting personnel in contingency environments.
- Develop deployable contracting and procurement systems before mobilizing for post-conflict efforts and test them to ensure that they can be effectively implemented in contingency situations.
- Ensure sufficient data collection and integration before developing contract or task-order requirements.
- Designate a single unified contracting entity to coordinate all contracting activity in theater.

If implemented, these measures would help the US government more fully take advantage of civilian-sector SRO capacities, while mitigating the inevitable waste that occurs during contingencies.

(g) Coordinate US Government Efforts with the Contractor Community

SIGIR has published a raft of audits detailing the US government's evolving relationship with government contractors. These reports often identified serious management and oversight gaps on the part of the government. For example, in 2009, SIGIR looked at the coordination and management of private security contractors (PSCs) in Iraq, finding that US government agencies lacked uniform policies and procedures to manage, oversee, and report on PSC operations.[42] Acting on SIGIR's recommendations, the oversight, coordination, and control of PSC activities in Iraq was strengthened, albeit in an ad hoc fashion. But the creation of an integrated entity responsible for managing SROs would provide contractors operating in a contingency environment with a single point of contact, thereby simplifying reporting responsibilities and improving coordination.

(h) Integrate Information Systems

Civilian agencies participating in SROs need to use a single interoperable—or at least integrated—information technology system that is capable of tracking all relief and reconstruction projects in theater. In Iraq, SIGIR found that different agencies stored their program and project data on different information management systems that could not interface with one another. The resulting inability of the US government to accurately and quickly compile and sort disparate project data caused the inefficient allocation of resources and gross redundancies. Ensuring improved mission-wide project and program information would significantly improve timely decision making and coordination. Mandating commonality of information management systems' output formats and data-update cycles would increase the knowledge level of decision makers operating in the fast-paced, often-chaotic contingency environment.

(i) Provide for Uninterrupted Oversight

When time is short and dollars must be spent quickly, waste, fraud, and abuse become serious threats. In Iraq, the US government spent huge sums of reconstruction money without basic accounting procedures in place. SIGIR's review of the Iraq rebuilding effort, *Hard Lessons: The Iraq Reconstruction Experience*, points out that no oversight plan accompanied either Lieutenant General Jay Garner or Ambassador Jerry Bremer when they first went to Iraq to head ORHA and CPA, respectively.

The unique nature of contingency operations means that multiple agencies may sometimes share funding responsibilities for discrete aspects of a larger program or project. To assess the efficacy of a joint DoD–DoS program, it is not sufficient for the DoD Office of the Inspector General to conduct an audit because any such evaluation would be unable to fully assess DoS's performance. Thus, because contingency operations are necessarily interagency, the body charged with overseeing them should posses a mandate enabling it to audit and inspect programs and projects conducted by all agencies present in theater. Absent that, oversight will be fragmented and incomplete. Consequently, the Congress should create a permanent inspector general (IG) charged with providing timely and comprehensive audit, inspection, and investigation services for SROs. An independent IG for contingency operations would possess the necessary jurisdiction and resources to focus on all agencies involved in an SRO.

(j) Anticipate International Involvement
Management systems, planning paradigms, and preparatory exercises should be structured in anticipation of international participation in SROs. In developing curricula, programs, and system requirements, there should be a conscious recognition that international participation may be highly desirable—if not inevitable—in most contingency operations. This is not simply a matter of money, although international assets might be more than welcome in the current budget environment. Rather, the political support embodied by an international coalition, as well as the input and expertise of other nations, is crucial to the success of complex overseas contingency operations. Within the SRO context, the United States previously has not taken sufficient advantage of existing international capacities.

6. Integrating the Interagency: The Calculus of Effective Coordination

With regard to SRO reform, the past eight years of experience and responses thereto provide an important, if painful prologue. Real reform awaits further action. According to DoS, there are currently thirty-six active conflicts across the globe and fifty-five so-called "fragile states."[43] This means that the next SRO will begin sooner than anyone might wish. Its demands will tax an already resource-weak system that still lacks an effective integrated management structure.

To meet these inevitable challenges, the US government must, in the words of Secretary of State Hillary Clinton, "harness all three Ds—diplomacy, development and defense."[44] The government's "3-D" strategy for SROs recognizes that defense, diplomacy and development all play a role in such operations and nominally treats the three Ds as equal in value and power.[45] But SROs constitute something beyond the three Ds. Although they embrace elements of each—defense, development, and diplomacy—none of these necessarily predominates. SROs conceptually constitute a "fourth D," a hybrid of the capacities provided by State, Defense, and USAID (diplomacy/defense/

development). A new structure is needed to harness this new "fourth D" effectively.

7. Options for Reform: Expanding the Art of the Possible

Some urge that the best way to address the perceived "militarization" of SROs is to revitalize and resource USAID, providing it with the authorities needed to manage all operational aspects of an SRO. This approach has been championed by, among others, Ambassador James Dobbins, the Bush administration's first senior envoy to Afghanistan, and James "Spike" Stephenson, the first USAID Mission Director in post-Saddam Iraq.[46] Their position is buttressed by the truth that USAID possesses substantial experience in operating in fragile states (38 percent of USAID personnel currently work in high-risk or unstable states), and its Office of Transition Initiatives has experience in more than thirty countries.[47] USAID, however, is a shell of its former self. It was dramatically downsized after its Vietnam-era apogee, its workforce declining by 38 percent between 1990 and 2007.[48] Today, most USAID-funded programs are implemented by contractors or "implementing partners."[49] Furthermore, USAID's institutional culture is focused primarily on long-term development projects, not on post-conflict stabilization and reconstruction. Absent a massive augmentation of its budget, staff, and logistical capabilities, USAID lacks the capacities to manage large-scale SROs.[50]

A second potential solution to managing SROs is to create a new "Civil Affairs Interagency Command" (CAIC). This idea is championed by former Commander of US Central Command General Anthony Zinni, who believes that DoD should serve as the administrative backbone for SROs, with civilian agencies plugging into the management structure. DoD would provide planning, logistics, administrative, and communications capabilities, while the civil side would provide subject-matter expertise. The CAIC would be headed by a civilian and include permanent representatives from DoS and USAID. Relevant civilian agencies' personnel would also participate in regular training exercises that would be orchestrated, planned, and managed by CAIC, enabling an enhanced degree of pre-deployment coordination between its military and the civilian SRO elements.[51] The CAIC's advantages lie in its ability to draw upon DoD's vast resources. As demonstrated in contingency events as diverse as the Indonesian tsunami of 2004 and the Haitian earthquake of 2010, DoD has a quick-response capability unmatched by any other federal agency. Having a civilian in charge of CAIC would mitigate the perceived "militarization" aspects of this approach.

The CAIC would not be truly independent, however, because, as a DoD embedded organization, it would be necessarily dependant on the Pentagon for all manner of support. Moreover, it would be functionally subordinate to the ranking military officer in theater. While such an arrangement potentially could function effectively, success would significantly depend on the personal relationships between CAIC leadership and the rest of DoD. Lacking its own autonomous support structure, the CAIC would be at risk of marginalization and thus being pushed to the periphery of the Department of Defense whose top priorities naturally lie in war-fighting.

8. Create an Independent Agency to Manage SROs: Occam's Razor Economically Applied

The third approach to SRO reform—and the one that SIGIR supports—is the creation of a new, quasi-independent office to manage SROs—the US Office of Contingency Operations (USOCO). Right now, there is no single agency that devotes its entire mission to SROs. For DoS, USAID, and DoD, SROs are but a limited aspect of those departments' much larger missions—"additional duties," if you will. No entity has SRO management as its primary mission.

To resolve the ongoing diffusion of SRO duties among the agencies, USOCO would unify the existing SRO mission elements under one roof, including S/CRS, the various DoD stabilization and reconstruction pro-grams, the Department of Justice's international police-training office, the Department of the Treasury's Office of Technical Assistance, and USAID's Office of Transition Initiatives. USOCO would consolidate existing structures into a unified operation, rather than layer another level of management upon scattered SRO operational pieces. Its efficiencies would ensure that the office would quickly pay for itself many times over. Interestingly, this approach resembles one proposed by Under Secretary of Defense for Policy Michèle Flournoy in a 2005 report she co-authored for the Center for Strategic and International Studies.[52]

Upon its creation by the Congress, USOCO would become the locus for planning, funding, staffing, and managing SROs, replacing the fragmented process that now exists and providing a single office whose sole mission is to ensure that the United States is prepared for the next contingency operation. It would also solve the so-called "lead agency" dilemma. In the words of one former senior NSC official, "*lead agency* really means *sole agency*, as no one will follow the lead agency if its direction substantially affects their organizational equities."[53] When a lead agency is put in charge, issues are too narrowly defined as military, diplomatic, or foreign-assistance challenges. By establishing an office that would be explicitly charged with managing SROs—and focused on the "fourth D"—the question of which agency to put in charge of the next contingency operation need never be asked. Proposed key senior leadership and staff positions within USOCO would include:

- Director: the director would be a presidential appointment requiring Senate confirmation. The proposed nominee would be jointly recommended to the president by the secretaries of state and defense. The director would report to both secretaries (as is the case with SIGIR).
- Three Deputy Directors: the three deputy directors, one each appointed by DoD, DoS, and USAID.
- Permanent Staff: the director and the three deputies would determine staffing levels, with persons detailed from other civilian agencies supplementing the permanent staff.
- Surge Personnel: in the event of a declared SRO, pre-positioned field cells would immediately be reinforced with deployable elements drawn from permanent USOCO personnel, as well as trained "ready reserve" experts from other federal departments and contractors.

At the outset of an SRO, USOCO would deploy, and the USOCO director would manage all stabilization and reconstruction assets in theater, reporting directly to the secretaries of state and defense. On-the-ground management authority would begin when the president declared an SRO effective and would end upon presidential declaration of its conclusion (in a manner similar to how the Federal Emergency Management Agency obtains its management control during a presidentially declared disaster). The director would bear complete accountability and responsibility for the SRO's reconstruction budget, contracting, expenditures, and outcomes. Further, the director would possess authority over all program and project decision making, while coordinating closely on needs and requirements with the commanding general, the chief of mission, and the USAID mission director.

An organization like USOCO already exists in the United Kingdom. The Stabilisation Unit coordinates and supports the UK's inter-ministry SRO planning and execution. It reports to the Ministry of Defence, the Foreign Office, and the Department for International Development, and includes staff from all three agencies. The SU has developed a Civilian Stabilisation Group (CSG) comprising more than 1,000 professionals trained to conduct a wide variety of SRO missions and ready to deploy overseas on short notice. When not deployed, these experts train together on a regular basis and work with the private sector and international community to refine their approach to SROs. With experience on the ground in Pakistan, Sudan, Palestine, Kosovo, Iraq, and Afghanistan, the SU has demonstrated the value of an integrated approach to SROs that brings together under a single authority experts from across the government.[54]

When briefed on the USOCO concept, former National Security Advisor Lieutenant General Brent Scowcroft concluded that an integrated management office like USOCO could help solve the chronic problem of poorly managed SROs.[55] Former Ambassador to Iraq Ryan Crocker also found the concept worthy of implementation.[56] The views of General Scowcroft and Ambassador Crocker are particularly compelling because of their lengthy governmental service in this area and their firsthand knowledge of the difficulties involved in getting the interagency community to work together to implement US national security strategy.

9. Conclusion: From Options to Operational Capabilities

The US approach to SROs requires reform. Hard lessons from Iraq—and from Afghanistan—make compellingly clear that the current structure is not adequate to the task. SRO responsibilities remain scattered among agencies whose capacity to carry out contingency operations varies greatly. Each has a piece of SRO management, but none is in charge, and their operations are far from integrated. The existing system does not promote unity of effort. No office is exclusively responsible for preparing and executing SROs; and none is accountable for their results. This approach creates a disabling lack of accountability.

Something new is necessary. Key stakeholders in the US interagency community generally agree on the need for more substantial SRO reform, and some believe that establishing an office explicitly charged with planning and executing contingency relief and reconstruction operations makes the most sense. But strong disagreement remains over whether such an organization should be quasi-independent or embedded within an existing agency, such as USAID, DoS, or DoD.

Housing a new SRO management office within USAID or DoD would leverage extant capacities, but neither option would resolve the "stovepiping" problem that daunts SRO management today. Those stovepipes can only be knocked down by creating a new entity whose sole mission is to plan and manage contingency reconstruction operations. Academics and policy makers concur that "unity of effort in interagency operations is a necessity."[57] An independent USOCO would provide that urgently needed unity of effort, consolidating overlapping missions and amalgamating imbalanced resources. By bringing all the SRO mission elements under a single roof, USOCO would achieve management integration.

The SRO experiences in Iraq and Afghanistan exposed systemic weaknesses in the US system. The lessons learned therefrom must shape further reform. To its credit, the interagency community has awakened to the need for improving SRO management. Succeeding in this effort will be critical to ensuring that US national security interests are sufficiently protected in future overseas stabilization and reconstruction operations.

Notes

1. Blake Stone, "Blind Ambition: Lessons Learned and Not Learned in an Embedded PRT," *PRISM* 1, 4 (2010): 152.

2. SIGIR, Quarterly Report (Oct. 30, 2010), 3, http.sigir.mil/files/quarterlyreports/October2010/Section1_-_October_2010.pdf#view=fit.

3. The US Congress created the Office of the Special Inspector General for Iraq Reconstruction, an independent federal agency, in 2004. SIGIR has oversight of the more than $50 billion in US funds committed thus far to the reconstruction of Iraq. To date, SIGIR has produced a total of 177 audits, 170 inspections, 27 quarterly reports, 1 evaluation, and 5 lessons-learned reports. This chapter is based on SIGIR's most recent lessons-learned report: *Applying Iraq's Hard Lessons to the Reform of Stabilization and Reconstruction Operations*, which recommends an innovative solution to the persistent problem of integrating civilian agencies' efforts with those of the military during overseas stability and reconstruction operations. To read the complete report, see SIGIR's website: www.sigir.mil/applyinghardlessons/index.html.

4. For a detailed analysis of the US reconstruction effort in Iraq, see SIGIR's *Hard Lessons: The Iraq Reconstruction Experience* (Feb. 2009), www.sigir.mil/files/Hard Lessons/Hard_Lessons_Report.pdf#view=fit.

5. Clark A. Murdock and Michèle Flournoy (Lead Investigators), *Beyond Goldwater-Nichols: U.S. Government and Defense Reform for a New Strategic Era*, Phase 2 Report (Washington, DC: Center for Strategic and International Studies, July 2005), 21.

6. Todd Moss, "Too Big to Succeed? Why (W)Hole-of-Government Cannot Work for U.S. Development Policy," Global Development: Views from the Center (Oct. 5, 2010), http://blogs.cgdev.org (accessed Dec. 9, 2010).

7. *In the Wake of War: Improving U.S. Post-Conflict Capabilities*, Report of an Independent Task Force sponsored by the Council on Foreign Relations, 2005, 11, http.cfr.org/content/publications/attachments/Post-Conflict_Capabilities_final.pdf (accessed Dec. 5, 2010).

8. E. Elaine Halchin, *The Coalition Provisional Authority (CPA): Origin, Characteristics, and Institutional Authorities* CRS-2 (Washington, DC: Congressional Research Service, April 29, 2004), www.fas.org/man/crs/RL32370.pdf (accessed Nov. 27, 2010).

9. Donald Rumsfeld, Secretary of Defense, memorandum to L. Paul Bremer, Presidential Envoy to Iraq, "Designation as Administrator of the Coalition Provisional Authority" (May 13, 2003).

10. SIGIR, 06-034, *Status of the Provincial Reconstruction Team Program in Iraq* (Oct. 29, 2006), http.sigir.mil/files/audits/06-034.pdf#view=fit.

11. SIGIR, 09-020, *Provincial Reconstruction Teams: Developing a Cost-Tracking Process Will Enhance Decision-Making* (April 28, 2009), http.sigir.mil/files/audits/09-020.pdf#view=fit.

12. SIGIR, 06-034, *Status of the Provincial Reconstruction Team Program in Iraq*.

13. SIGIR, 09-013, *Provincial Reconstruction Teams' Performance Measurement Process Has Improved* (Jan. 28, 2009), http.sigir.mil/files/audits/09-013.pdf#view=fit.

14. SIGIR, 07-015, *Review of the Effectiveness of the Provincial Reconstruction Team Program in Iraq* (Oct. 18, 2007), http.sigir.mil/files/audits/07-015.pdf#view=fit.

15. SIGIR, 09-020, *Provincial Reconstruction Teams: Developing a Cost-Tracking Process Will Enhance Decision-Making*.

16. Stone, "Blind Ambition."

17. Ibid., 151.

18. Ibid., 152.

19. Ibid.

20. Ibid., 157.

21. Ibid., 154.

22. Post Conflict Reconstruction Unit (UK), *The Establishment and Operation of the Basra Provincial Reconstruction Team (PRT), April 2006–January 2007; Lessons Identified* (Mar. 26, 2007), 10, 13, http.iraqinquiry.org.uk/media/47317/lessons-identified-basraprt-06-07.pdf (accessed Dec. 13, 2010).

23. Ibid., 1–2.

24. *Consolidated Appropriations Act*, 2005, Public Law 108-447 (2004), § 408.

25. DoD 300.05, *Military Support for Stability, Security, Transition and Reconstruction (SSTR) Operations* (Washington, DC: Department of Defense, Nov. 28, 2005).

26. Ibid., 2.

27. Dane Smith, *An Expanded Mandate for Peace Building: The State Department Role in Peace Diplomacy, Reconstruction, and Stabilization* (Washington, DC: Center for Strategic and International Studies [CSIS], April 30, 2009), 39.

28. In March 2004, CSIS president John Hamre endorsed legislation that would have institutionalized stabilization policy within the NSC. Instead, President George W. Bush signed NSPD-44.

29. HQ Department of the Army, *Stability Operations FM 3-07* (Washington, DC: US Department of the Army, Oct. 2008), chap. 1: 13.

30. Special Inspector General for Afghanistan Reconstruction (SIGAR), *Quarterly Report* (Oct. 30, 2010), 3, www.sigar.mil/pdf/quarterlyreports/Oct2010/Lores /SIGAR4Q_2010Book.pdf.

31. RSCMA was included as Title XVI of the *Duncan Hunter National Defense Authorization Act* of FY 2009, which was signed into law on Oct. 14, 2008, as Public Law 110-417. It is similar to an earlier bill proposed by Senator Richard Lugar and then-Senator Joseph Biden, which passed the Senate Foreign Relations Committee, but did not go further.

32. Department of State, *Leading through Civilian Power*, 2010 Quadrennial Diplomacy & Development Review (Nov. 2010).

33. Ibid.

34. Michèle A. Flournoy and Shawn W. Brimley, "Strategic Planning for National Security," *Joint Force Quarterly* (2nd Quarter 2006): 80–81.

35. Michael Leonard, *Matching Policy and Strategy with Resources* (Washington, DC: Project on National Security Reform, Aug. 10, 2009).

36. Ibid.

37. Department of State, *Leading through Civilian Power*, slide 24.

38. Dan Green, "The Other Surge," *Armed Forces Journal* (Oct. 2010), www .armedforcesjournal.com/2010/10/4771231 (accessed Dec. 10, 2010).

39. Ibid.

40. Ibid.

41. SIGIR, *Lessons Learned in Contracting and Procurement* (July 2006), www.sigir .mil/files/lessonslearned/Lessons_Learned_July21.pdf#view=fit.

42. SIGIR, 09-019, *Opportunities to Improve Processes for Reporting, Investigating, and Remediating Serious Incidents Involving Private Security Contractors in Iraq* (April 30, 2009), http.sigir.mil/files/audits/09-019.pdf#view=fit.

43. Department of State, *Leading through Civilian Power*.

44. Secretary of State Hillary Clinton, Testimony on the 2010 DoS budget request, Senate Foreign Relations Committee (May 20, 2009).

45. Secretary of State Hillary Clinton, Speech to the Peterson Institute, Jan. 6, 2010.

46. Ambassador James Dobbins and James "Spike" Stephenson, separate interviews with SIGIR, 2009–2010.

47. USAID, "Transition Initiatives," http.usaid.gov/our_work/cross-cutting_programs/transition_initiatives/ (accessed Dec. 2, 2010).

48. Department of State, *Leading through Civilian Power*.

49. See, e.g., U.S. General Accounting Office (now known as the U.S. Government Accountability Office), *Foreign Assistance: USAID's Operating Expense Account Does Not Fully Reflect the Cost of Delivering Foreign Assistance* (Sept. 30, 2003), http://pdf. usaid.gov/pdf_docs/PCAAB138.pdf (accessed Nov. 30, 2010).

50. The QDDR recommends increasing the annual number of mid-level USAID staff hired each year by a mere 65 individuals. See Department of State, *Leading through Civilian Power*, slide 16.

51. General Anthony Zinni (ret.), interview with SIGIR, Aug. 24, 2010.

52. "In the longer term, however, Congress may want to consider consolidating S/CRS and parts of USAID into a new agency for Stability and Reconstruction Operations reporting to the Secretary of State. Establishing a new independent agency under the Secretary of State would facilitate the creation of the operations-oriented culture so critical to the success of any civilian rapid response capability—a culture that is largely absent from mainstream State Department and mainstream USAID. It would also create an institutional home and a more viable set of career paths for civilian professionals who want to become true experts in planning and conducting various aspects of interagency operations" (Murdock and Flournoy, *Beyond Goldwater-Nichols*, 63).

53. Hans Binnendijk and Patrick Cronin (eds.), *Civilian Surge: Key to Complex Operations* (Washington, DC: National Defense University, July 2, 2009), 48.

54. Foreign and Commonwealth Office, Stabilisation Unit, www.stabilisationunit.gov.uk/ (accessed Dec. 11, 2010).

55. General Brent Scowcroft (ret.), interview with SIGIR, 2009.

56. Ambassador Ryan Crocker, interviews with SIGIR, 2009–2010.

57. Murdock and Flournoy, *Beyond Goldwater-Nichols*, 17.

12 Contractors Supporting Military Operations

Many Challenges Remain

Jacques S. Gansler and William Lucyshyn

1. Introduction

The United States military has always depended on the support of contractors during times of war. Civilian wagon drivers hauled supplies for General Washington's troops. Sutlers (civilian merchants that sold provisions to an army in the field or in camp) supplied Union troops during the Civil War. By World War II, civilian workers hired either individually or through firms provided support services in all the theaters of war. And, in some cases, such as the Flying Tigers, were hired to engage enemy forces in combat operations. During the Korean War, contractors provided services ranging from stevedoring, road and rail maintenance, to transportation. The Vietnam War saw the expansion of the contractor's role in support of logistics, supporting a variety of tasks including construction, base operations, water and ground transportation, maintenance, and other technical support for high-tech military systems.

After the Cold War, DoD significantly reduced active duty troop levels from 2.1 million at their peak, to less than 1.4 million in 2000. The remaining forces were focused on core war-fighting activities, with a major share of the drawdown coming from support units. At the same time the services continued to introduce higher and higher technology systems—and these often required high levels of contractor support. The restructuring of the active and reserve forces, coupled with the increased support requirements, created an increased need for contractors to support deployed military forces.

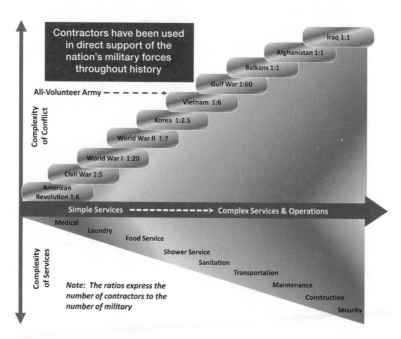

FIGURE 1. Historical Perspective

SOURCE: Commission on Wartime Contracting in Iraq and Afghanistan, *At What Cost? Contingency Contracting in Iraq and Afghanistan*, Interim Report, June 2009.

In the past, contractors have made up a small percentage of in-theater support personnel, but in recent wars the ratio has been approximately 1:1 (see Figure 1). These contractors provide many essential services, which include base operations support, construction, logistics, and translation support. These categories are very general, but if one really wants to understand the role of contractors, looking at Bosnia and Kosovo gives us a better picture of the function they performed. In fiscal year 1999, contractors performed 100 percent of the maintenance, food service, laundry, sewage, hazardous material handling, and mail; and they performed over 70 percent of the construction, water, fuel and heavy equipment transportation.[1]

With the nation's involvement in Iraq and Afghanistan, America's reliance on contractors for those operations has grown to unparalleled proportions. The Department of Defense currently has more than 240,000 contractor employees working to support its efforts in Iraq and Afghanistan (see Table 1) managing dining facilities, maintaining equipment, providing security for bases and individuals, transporting supplies, and constructing facilities.

TABLE 1. Comparison of Contractor Personnel
to Troop Levels (as of September 2009)

	Contractors	Troops	Ratio
Iraq only	119,706	134,571	.89:1
Afghanistan only	73,968	55,107	1.34:1
CENTCOM AOR	243,735	282,000	.87:1

SOURCE: CENTCOM *4th Quarter Contractor Census Report,* cited in Moshe Schwartz, *Department of Defense Contractors in Iraq and Afghanistan: Background and Analysis,* Congressional Research Service Report (Dec. 14, 2009), 5.

Of these large numbers, only a small percentage (under 10,000 of the contractors) are actually involved in "security" functions, and a very small percentage of those are involved in personal protection (i.e., the "bodyguards" used to protect senior government officials when they go out into the field). Most of the "security" functions are at fixed government installations (e.g., at guard posts). Although they are armed, they are limited to self-defense roles. The need for contractors to perform these functions was partially recognized by the Congress in the 2003 Defense Authorization Act, which allowed contractors to be used in guarding military bases.[2] Other functions, not previously observed, but now being performed by contractors, are training of the police and military of the countries in which the United States is involved, and the support of intelligence—not as "spies" but, rather, as analysts. A critical function in stability operations is the analysis of the large volume of data being received from multiple sensors (both airborne and ground-based). This is highly skilled and sensitive work, and is a compliment to the work being done by the military and government-civilian security analysts.[3]

2. The Issues

Using contractors to perform noncombat activities provides several benefits: when a requirement arises, contractors can be hired and deployed quickly, they can provide expertise in specialized fields (e.g., language capabilities), and they can be let go when their services are no longer needed. In the long run, using contractors only when needed costs significantly less than maintaining a permanent organic capability.

The challenge was that this increased dependence on contractor support, and the "battlefield" environment in which the contractors would be operating, was not adequately recognized or addressed by the DoD. This fact was highlighted by the GAO as early as 2003, when it reported that "as the defense industry boosts its staff overseas, companies are increasingly concerned about their workers' safety. The government's responsibility to contractors, in the event of hostilities, is not clear; causing confusion and complicating management of the civilians."[4] Further, the Army and the Joint Chiefs of Staff had conflicting notions of who was responsible for contractor security: the local military commander or the contractors themselves.[5] Moreover, after the operation in Iraq had been underway for five years, the deputy undersecretary of defense, Jack Bell, speaking before the Senate Homeland Security Subcommittee, said, "Faced with this unprecedented scale of our dependence on contractors, we have confronted major challenges associated with the visibility, integration, oversight and management of a large contractor force working alongside our deployed military personnel that, frankly, we were not adequately prepared to address."[6] At that same hearing, the special inspector general for Iraq reconstruction, Stuart Bowen, testified that "the contracting process in Iraq suffered from a tapestry of regulations applied by diverse agencies, which caused inconsistencies and inefficiencies that inhibited management and oversight." Finally, the US Army, based on the hard lessons learned in Iraq and Afghanistan (where initial military successes were followed by long, grueling struggles to establish control), released a new operations manual putting stability operations (or nation-building) on an equal footing with defeating adversaries on the battlefield.[7]

Needless to say, the very large size of the contractor population (equal to, or greater than, that of the military forces) operating in the Iraq/Afghanistan theaters raised a significant number of issues that would require major changes to mitigate. Many, however, did not want to accept that the types of activities being undertaken in Iraq and Afghanistan were representative of future military engagements, and much of the military organizations' culture, doctrine, and practices were still geared to much more traditional military operations. This resulted in significant institutional resistance. We have categorized these issues into three major categories: human capital; policies, processes, and procedures; and information technology. These are discussed in detail below.

3. Human Capital

(a) Acquisition Workforce

The DoD acquisition workforce (both military and civilian) has not kept pace with the enormous growth in the number and value of contingency contracts, and, as a result, is under-resourced to respond effectively to wartime requirements. From fiscal years 2001 through 2008, DoD's reported obligations on all contracts for services, measured in real-dollar terms, more than doubled—from roughly $92 billion to slightly over $200 billion. And, for fiscal year 2008, this figure included more than $25 billion for services to support contingency operations in Iraq and Afghanistan.[8] While the numbers and value of service contracts in Iraq and Afghanistan have risen dramatically, agencies have not increased the trained and skilled acquisition workforce in numbers sufficient to ensure that contractors are performing as required. Moreover, these service contracts (where the department purchases services rather than hardware) are generally more complex than is widely appreciated. But, the overall acquisition workforce (especially the military component) is weapon-systems oriented and is generally not prepared, without additional training, to transition from their stateside home-base peacetime perspective to one that can respond to the accelerated operational tempo demands of expeditionary operations.

When the defense procurement budget plummeted at the end of the Cold War, it was only natural that the acquisition workforce in the Department of Defense would correspondingly be reduced significantly. As the procurement budget flattened out in the mid-nineties, the DoD Authorization Act for fiscal year 1996 required the DoD to further reduce its acquisition workforce, by 25 percent, by the end of fiscal year 2000—even as the budget started to turn around. As a result of these cumulative reductions, between 1990 and 2000, DoD reduced its number of acquisition personnel by approximately 65 percent. Then, as defense acquisition expenditures grew rapidly, to compensate for the "procurement holiday" and the response to 9/11/2001, the acquisition workload increased significantly, but the acquisition workforce continued to decline.[9] This caused a huge gap between the work to be done and the people to do it. This problem was compounded by the fact that a significant share of the added work was in the difficult contracting area of "services" (rather than the traditional equipment procurements, for which the acquisition workforce had been trained).

A complicating factor is that, in the contracting area, the vast majority of the DoD's contracting specialists are government civilians—only a small percentage are active-duty military (in the US Army, for example, about three percent of the contracting personnel are regular Army). When the requirement for contracting personnel spiked in the war-zones, civilian employees were asked to "volunteer" to deploy. Since those that volunteered and deployed left unfilled positions in their organizations, there was actually a perverse incentive for supervisors to discourage them from going, since they would not be back-filled. As a result, many of the in-theater positions were not filled.

In 2008, DoD began to take some corrective actions. The Army, for example, established a new Army Contracting Command[10] and has authorized five new General Officers to oversee the contracting activities. (In 1990, there had been five, but by 2007 there were none.)[11] There was also a decision to increase the number of acquisition personnel in the Defense Department, but the competition for people with the relevant experience across the overall federal government (as well as in industry) became intense, especially since, for the DoD, the greatest need was to hire people willing to go into the war zone to do contracting and acquisition management. Thus, incentive bonuses for sign-up, as well as extensive internship programs and other benefits were being used to recruit these key people. But changes of the magnitude and nature required will clearly take significant effort and time. In the Iraq–Afghanistan theaters, for example, a large percentage of the requisitions for contracting people were still not filled. Of those that were filled, only 35 percent were certified for the positions they were in—and there were actually no people there to do independent pricing or contract closeouts.[12]

In May 2009, the secretary of defense announced a plan to reduce acquisition staffing shortages. The department's fiscal year 2010 budget request contained funding to hire approximately 13,800 government employees to reduce reliance on contractor employees. This figure included 2,500 acquisition specialists. In addition, the department will increase the acquisition workforce by another 1,580 government employees, for a total of 4,080 in fiscal 2010. By 2015, the acquisition workforce will grow by about 20,000 people.

This plan should reduce some of the understaffing and improve support to the contingency contracting mission. Senior leaders must track the progress and ensure that high standards are developed and maintained; this must not become a quota exercise. To compliment these civilian employees, the military services, particularly the Army, must increase their number of military acquisition personnel, so there will be a cadre of immediately deployable specialists to support contingency operations.

(b) Contracting Officer's Representatives

In addition to contracting officers, contracting officer's representatives (CORs) are key members of the acquisition workforce. The CORs are appointed in writing by a contracting officer to perform a number of contract administration and oversight duties, and can be especially important in a contingency environment, where the risk of failure has great consequences. Yet, in Iraq and Afghanistan the COR role is usually performed as an additional duty, in conjunction with the primary job function (often defined as an "extra duty") that required no experience.[13] Moreover, since this was an extra duty, and the CORs' evaluations are based on their performance of their primary function, they naturally focused on those. This may work satisfactorily for simple, low-dollar service contracts, but clearly more complex, high-value, long-term service contracts may demand a full-time COR. Clearly, simple and complex service contracts demand different levels of COR commitment and training.

Finally, in addition to the heavy workload, in Iraq and Afghanistan, CORs often lacked the necessary training and skills to perform their critical function. Although CORs are required to complete the COR training before appointment, troop rotation schedules and other operational considerations often meant that inexperienced and untrained individuals were appointed. There are online training courses available, but information technology infrastructure constraints created frustratingly long training periods.[14] In the future, commanders of appropriate units must designate certain positions as COR capable, and those individuals should be trained on a recurring basis while in garrison.

(c) Compensation for Deployed Civilian Employees

As noted above, since the vast majority of DoD's contracting people are government civilians, and when contracting is required in the "combat zone," civilians are asked to "volunteer" to go. The volunteers, however, face several personal hardships. First, in many cases their personal life insurance does not cover a loss of life resulting from an act of war (most civilian policies have a "war exclusion" clause). Second, if they happen to be severely injured, they would not receive long-term medical coverage (as the military members do through the Department of Veterans Administration). Third, their total compensation is limited by Congress, even though in many cases they are expected to work continuous, long hours on almost a 24/7 basis. Finally, all of this work must often be done under extremely hazardous and austere conditions. Thus, these issues act to make the volunteering for these critical positions even less attractive.

Clearly, this is an area that needs to get congressional attention to resolve compensation and health-care issues. Moreover, the DoD must change its procedures, so that there would be a set of "pre-volunteered" government civilian personnel, who would go to the battlefield when needed (in a sense like the military's "ready reserve"). An alternative approach may be to have these civilians be members of military reserve units, and then, when necessary they could be mobilized and deployed. Under this scenario a cadre of personnel, trained to do expeditionary contracting, would be available for deployment worldwide, on a "stand-by" basis.

(d) Culture

The military culture in general does not sufficiently value or recognize the importance of contracting, contract management and, more generally, contractors in expeditionary operations. And, even though contractors are providing essential battlefield services, combatant commanders are not trained to appreciate or to understand contracting. Contracting personnel have, for example, been called "shoppers" by members of Congress, rather than being viewed as a critical element of the "total force." This is despite the length of time and extent that combat-support contracting has been going on, particularly in the current military operations. To a large extent, military personnel still do not appreciate the issues and complexities involved in writing and managing these service contracts. And, as a result, this devaluing of skills has resulted in a lack of a clear career path for army officers with contracting skills, with a corresponding lack of advancement for these personnel.[15]

The military services in general, and the Army specifically, must transform their culture with regard to contracting. They must develop career paths and improve promotion potential, so that they can attract some of the "best and brightest" into these critical support functions.

4. Policies, Procedures, and Processes

(a) Expeditionary Contracting Procedures

Virtually all of the government contracting people involved in supporting expeditionary operations have been trained in performing conventional weapons procurement, using the Federal Acquisition Regulation (FAR), and the other required procurement practices. There was a natural tension when these individuals were faced with the requirement to support combat operations, where service requirements arose rapidly and changed quickly, and the combatant commander needed support "immediately." Peacetime business processes are ill-suited to support contingency operations. In many cases, there is no time for market surveys, draft requests for proposals, contractors to respond, or detailed source selection and contract negotiation. Peacetime cycles of six months or more are just unacceptable. Needless to say, this has caused significant problems. Furthermore, the complete set of other mandated requirements include the "Buy American Act," socioeconomic contracting goals (to include small and minority businesses), the specialized cost-accounting requirements, the "instant" audit requirements, the security issues, the occupational safety requirements, the need to comply with export control requirements, the use of domestic specialty metals, and the list goes on. All of these have presented significant barriers to the speed and effectiveness required. There are also the requirements of having to do business in a war zone. These include dealing with the "cash economy," and the unavailability or high cost of life and medical insurance for personnel operating in close proximity to combat operations. Perhaps the most important was the fact that the contracts in most cases were being administered back in the United States, while the people writing the requirements and those doing the work were in the war zone. What was clearly required (and was finally done in 2008) was the issuance of a manual on "expeditionary contracting," which took all of the "special clauses" in the FAR that allowed for exceptions under wartime conditions, and put them all into one manual. Then, of course, the contracting people who were going to go to the war zone needed to be trained on these clauses.

Based on the many lessons learned from current operations, the Department of Defense needs to develop and gain the necessary approval for a clear, concise, and well-understood expeditionary contracting manual. This manual should provide the guidance necessary to enable the timely procurement of supplies and services required to support expeditionary operations. This

guidance would eliminate the need for the many organizations to individually interpret the Federal Acquisition Regulation (in many cases they arrive
at different interpretations), and as a result they would use consistent procedures and processes. Furthermore, the manual should distinguish between
the various phases of an operation, recognizing that, for example, early stages
may require a quicker, more immediate, response, than latter stages.

Other factors that should be addressed include: socioeconomic contract
requirements that are difficult or impossible to implement overseas; procedures to proceed with mission-essential contracts even in light of acknowledged administrative errors; and a review of the audit function—recognizing
that, especially for fast-paced operations, applying peacetime standards may
be inappropriate. Finally, consideration should be given to continue to raise
dollar limits for the various forms of simplified contracting methods, to enable
their greater use for the support of in-theater contingency contracting.[16]

(b) Lines of Authority

The military identifies "unity of command"[17] as a key principle of war. However, when using routine contracting processes, to modify or add a new task
to a contract requires the contract to be modified by the contracting officer;
however, today, multiple commands have responsibility for contracting. In
many cases, with expeditionary contracts, the contracting officer resides back
in the United States. Further, the current Army policy clearly states "contractor employees are *not* under the direct supervision of military personnel in the
chain-of-command."[18] As a result, there are multiple actors and interactions,
which often results in varying policy interpretations. And, unfortunately,
in the expeditionary environment, with its increased contracting workload,
complexity, and tempo, this can slow and otherwise hinder performance.

Clearly, there is an opportunity here for considerable ambiguity, particularly when contactors are providing critical support in a fluid battlefield
environment. Under these extreme circumstances, it may be difficult, if not
impossible, when something is needed immediately, to go back to the United
States (which, of course, is also in a different time zone) and get a contract
modification. With the current organization, no single contracting command
has responsibility to synchronize all aspects of contracting below the service
secretary level.

Thus, clarification of the chain-of-command issues must be addressed,
i.e., the battlefield commander's command and control of contractors must
be aligned with his/her command authority. To accomplish this will require

passing as many lines of contract authority through the in-theater joint command as is feasible; this may involve transferring contracting authority from an outside agency to the joint command. If this is not possible, developing procedures that increase the joint command's visibility and ability to coordinate and influence the contracts may be sufficient. The theater contracting authority should be centralized at the level of the joint commander, to ensure proper coordination of operational support throughout the theater.[19]

(c) Contractors Performing Inherently Governmental Functions

Inherently governmental functions are defined as those that are so closely related to the public interest that they must be performed by federal employees or service members and should not be contracted. These include direct or active participation in combat operations, awarding contracts, and the supervision of military members and DoD civilians. Most theater combat support and sustainment functions, however, are not inherently governmental and can be partially or fully contracted out.[20] Further, although contractors are precluded from performing inherently governmental functions, they can provide support to those functions. With the current shortages of qualified government contracting personnel, for example, as long as there were no conflicts of interests (personal or corporate) contractors could assist in the process, with the government employee there to review and sign the contract.

With the large numbers of contractors involved in the current operations in Iraq and Afghanistan, and the urgency under which many of the activities take place, it is very important for the government personnel supervising these activities to ensure that there are no conflicts of interests, and that the contractors are not doing "inherently governmental" work. Complicating this issue are the various definitions of "inherently governmental" functions. These still fail to provide a crisp boundary, along with the expediency often required when supporting combat operations. Clear guidance must be provided by the DoD so that the narrow band of work that is truly "inherently governmental" can unambiguously be identified. This work must be reserved for government civilians or military personnel.

(d) Funding Flexibility

A major problem, particular during the initial phases of an expedited expeditionary operation, is the pace of funding. In many cases in Iraq, contractors were asked to do work before funding was available. In an effort to be responsive to the combatant commander's tasking, contractors often put up large amounts of their firm's funds so that they could complete the tasks. As a result, they were at risk while waiting for the contracts to be modified and the funds to be released. Congress recognized this problem during the Balkans operation, when it approved an "overseas contingency operation transfer fund" that allowed, for example, shifting of appropriated funds from "procurement" to "operations and maintenance," providing the necessary flexibility. Of course, there was a requirement after the fact to report to Congress on the actual use of the funds. This flexibility was not extended to the large contracts in Iraq and Afghanistan. This lack of flexibility creates both legal and financial barriers to operating effectively and efficiently under wartime conditions. Congress should address this issue, and ensure the necessary flexibility is available for future contingency military operations.

(e) Comparing Costs

An ongoing challenge is comparing the cost of contracting-out required support to the cost of maintaining the required capability organically. The Congressional Budget Office analyzed specific contracted functions in Iraq and found that "the cost of a private security contract is comparable to those of a U.S. military unit performing similar functions. During peacetime, however, the private security contract would not have to be renewed, whereas the military unit would remain in the force structure."[21] Many mistakenly assume that because military personnel have a low hourly rate as compared to the "billed rate" for a private contractor, it would be much cheaper to use military personnel for these functions. The cost of the contractor, however, includes all overhead costs, along with all training and equipment costs, all other indirect costs, and they are hired only for the required time frame.

On the other hand, military salaries do not include all of these costs. Even if one includes the costs for medical care, retirement, hostile-fire pay, life insurance, family separation allowances, there are still the costs for equipment and administrative support in theater, post-service veterans benefits, in-service education, mid-tour or home leave, training leave, and the overhead cost associated with their management. Most importantly, the military figures excludes the rotation base; ideally the Army needs to maintain two units stateside for each deployed unit. That means for each soldier in theater the Army needs approximately two more soldiers stateside. And, as noted, perhaps the big advantage of contractors is that when they are no longer needed, the contract can be terminated, eliminating the cost. The DoD should develop a more rigorous methodology for capturing all the costs associated with deploying military personnel so that more informed comparisons and decisions can be made.

5. Roles and Responsibilities

(a) Contractor Reliability in a High-Threat Environment

Military personnel can be ordered to stay on the battlefield and court-martialed for leaving it. This, of course, is not the case with contractors. Many believed that contractors would have a tendency to "run, if under fire," since from their perspective, the worst that could happen is they would not get paid for not providing the contracted-for service. However, based on recent experiences in both Iraq and Afghanistan, this has not yet proved to be a significant problem, on either the individual or company level. There were almost no reported incidences, even under extreme conditions, in which contractors did not perform their assigned duties.

In one case, a corporation decided not to renew its contract because of the hazardous environment. When initially awarded a contract in 2003, Bechtel was "assured" the company would have a safe environment for its workers. But after three years, as Iraq dissolved into insurgency and sectarian violence, fifty-two of its employees had been killed, and much of their work had been sabotaged. Additionally, some of Bechtel's employees and subcontractors had been kidnapped, others were marched out of their office and shot, and a significant number had been wounded. So Bechtel chose not to renew its contract.[22] Needless to say, having already received $2.3 billion for its work (rebuilding roads, power plants, and waterworks, and other construction activities), over that three-year period, and since this was typical of the business it does on a worldwide basis, it was not easy for Bechtel to walk away from a follow-on contract of this sort. However, the conditions differed greatly from those that the government represented, and Bechtel believed the "working conditions" warranted its action. Of course, there were other contractors willing to step in to do that work on the next contract. After all, it was huge business.

There are several factors, however, that could make contingency contracting unattractive for basic, business-risk reasons. For example, the political pressure to use more fixed-price contracting or difficulty in finding required insurance at reasonable rates (or the government refusing to reimburse the contractor for the full cost of this insurance) can increase the business risk to an unacceptable range. The federal government and the DoD must resist contractor-bashing political opportunism with accompanying, ill-advised policies, to ensure that contractors have the appropriate incentives to continue to support military operations.

(b) Laws Governing Contractors

Several aspects of law remain unclear. One is the classification of modern contractors in international humanitarian law particularly with regard to their status and conduct. US legislation that clarifies the federal government's grasp of changes in this field would be a valuable development for American companies, their employees, agents, and subcontractors.

Another area of confusion is in determining who has jurisdiction over the criminal activity of contractors, especially when operating in a country without an existing status of forces agreement (SOFA). Although authorities existed for applying US law (under the Military Extra-Territorial Jurisdiction Act [MEJA]), these were often not exercised in Iraq or Afghanistan. In some cases, the only remedy seemed to be to fire the contractor employees who committed a crime and ship them out of theater.[23] Congress also has amended the Uniform Code of Military Justice (UCMJ) to clearly cover civilians who support military operations, and the DoD issued the necessary implementation guidelines. Thus legal action against contractors can now be taken—by either the Department of Justice, under MEJA, or by DoD, under the UCMJ. This area needs clarification, both to ensure that criminal activity is appropriately punished, but also to protect civilians from host-country laws that may impose punishments much more severe than US laws would allow.

(c) Armed Contractors

Operations in both Iraq and Afghanistan have demonstrated that large numbers of contractors are capable of operating in a theater of operations without creating an undue burden for the deployed military forces. In most cases, contractors use private security firms to provide protection for their workers. As a result, there are many contractors armed with weapons for their self-defense. This is an area of great ambiguity, especially (as previously discussed), if a contractor is captured with a gun. Will he/she be viewed as having taken part in combat? This raises legitimate questions of, among others, who is allowed to carry a gun for self-defense and the nature of rules of engagement. These issues not only apply to the contractors performing security functions, but also to the far larger number of contractors who may be "in harm's way."

There are many contractors in this latter category, such as truck drivers subject to ambush, interpreters in direct support of combat troops, and workers involved in reconstruction in dangerous areas.

In an effort to clarify some of these questions, the DoD issued instructions in October 2005.[24] The new instructions gave the theater military commander the responsibility to authorize contractors to be armed with either government-issued or privately owned weapons and to wear military clothing. That is, contractors must have the express permission of a combatant commander to be armed, if the military forces cannot adequately protect the contractor personnel. Furthermore, contractors performing private security functions are specifically prohibited from engaging in any offensive military operations, and are subject to more restrictive "rules of the use of force," as opposed to the "rules of engagement" that govern military forces. Contractors authorized to be armed for personal security are limited to carrying government-approved weapons. For the Iraq and Afghanistan theaters, the Beretta M9 pistol (or equivalent) is the accepted standard, unless another weapon is specifically requested and approved.[25] With the large numbers of contractors, there is still a need to improve the combatant commander's visibility of the numbers and locations of support contractors in theater, so that s/he can make informed decisions concerning their security.

6. Information Technology

Expeditionary forces need improved information technology with improved business tools. Expeditionary contracting personnel are working in an environment where the operational tempo demands the support of automated tools. They are, however, often limited in terms of the tools available. DoD has not developed and deployed systems required for this level of contractor battlefield support.

> Contract writing systems are insufficient and not standardized, negatively impacting the ability to accomplish the mission. Information systems to track contractor personnel, assets, and performance are critical but lacking. Commanders need a common, relevant picture of contractors in the battle space, for operational planning, logistics planning, and situational awareness.[26]

Deployed contracting personnel would greatly benefit from electronic business tools and sample documents such as statements of work, model contracts, etc., that would leverage technology to act as an in-theater force multiplier for contracting specialists.

Additionally, since many of the contractors are supporting logistics operations, the DoD's non-integrated, non-interoperable logistics systems create another significant challenge. In-theater logisticians lack asset visibility, preventing them from efficiently managing and optimizing their logistics enterprise. As a result, forces in the field routinely stock too many parts, and because they do not trust that they will receive what they need, they order needed parts multiple times—contributing to large inventories and increasing the requirement for yet more contractors. To overcome this inefficiency and waste, DoD must work toward implementing a world-class logistics information system that extends from "factory to foxhole," to replace its current set of more than 1,000 different logistics information systems. This will significantly reduce the overall cost, and will also greatly improve the efficiency and effectiveness of theater operations, reducing the need for as many support contractors.

7. Conclusion

It is important to recognize, as Defense Secretary Gates has done in his article in the January–February 2009 issue of *Foreign Affairs*, that future military operations will very likely resemble the environment the United States found itself in during the Iraq and Afghanistan conflicts.[27] If this type of scenario is realistic for the future, then DoD must also accept that there will continue to be a significant need for contractor support—up to 50 percent of the total force. If these are valid assumptions, as we believe they are, then it is essential that DoD's organization, culture, doctrine, planning, and exercises all change to accept these levels of contractor support as "the norm."

DoD has already initiated several actions in response to some of the difficult lessons learned. One response concerned the recommendations made by the Commission on Army Acquisition and Program Management in Expeditionary Operations. In January 2008 the Army established the U.S. Army Contracting Command "to provide a more effective structure through which to execute expeditionary contracting efforts."[28] Further, with the passage of section 849 of the National Defense Authorization Act for Fiscal Year 2008, Congress directed implementation of many of the above-noted commission's recommendations. But much more needs to be done to improve the expeditionary operations of the public–private total force—military, civilian employees, and contractors.

Notes

1. Government Accountability Office, *Contingency Operations: Army Should Do More to Control Contract Costs in the Balkans*, GAO/NSIAD-00-225 (Sept. 2000).

2. Jason Peckenpaugh, "Law Allows Contractors to Help Guard Military Bases," *Government Executive* (Dec. 5, 2002), www.govexec.com/dailyfed/1202/120502p1.htm.

3. Steve Fainaru and Alec Klein, "In Iraq, A Private Realm of Intelligence-Gathering: Firm Extends US Government's Reach," *Washington Post*, July 1, 2007, A-20.

4. Government Accountability Office, *Military Operations: Contractors Provide Vital Services to Deployed Forces But Are Not Adequately Addressed in DoD Plans*, GAO-03-695 (June 2003).

5. Renae Merle, "No Protection Policy for Overseas Contractors: Oversight 'Inconsistent' Report Says," *Washington Post*, June 26, 2003.

6. Robert Brodsky, "New Direction Charted for Wartime Contracting," *Government Executive*, Jan. 25, 2008.

7. Michael R. Gordon, "U.S. Army Shifts Focus to Nation-building," *New York Times*, Feb. 8, 2008, http.nytimes.com/2008/02/08/world/americas/08iht-military.1.9863829.html.

8. Government Accountability Office, *Defense Acquisitions: Actions Needed to Ensure Value for Service Contracts*, testimony before the Defense Acquisition Reform Panel, Committee on Armed Services, US House of Representatives, GAO-09-643-T (April 23, 2009).

9. Commission on Wartime Contracting in Iraq and Afghanistan, *At What Cost? Contingency Contracting in Iraq and Afghanistan*, Interim Report (June 2009).

10. Elise Castelli, "Army Shaping Civilian Role in New Contracting Command," *Federal Times*, Mar. 17, 2008, 6.

11. Richard Lardner, "Army Adding Five Generals to Oversee Purchasing, Contractors," *Boston Globe*, July 3, 2008, A-11.

12. Commission on Wartime Contracting in Iraq and Afghanistan, *At What Cost?*.

13. Commission on Army Acquisition and Program Management in Expeditionary Operations, *Urgent Reform Required: Army Expeditionary Contracting* (Oct. 31, 2007), www.Army.mil/docs/gansler_commission_report_final_071031.pdf.

14. Commission on Wartime Contracting in Iraq and Afghanistan, *At What Cost?*.

15. Commission on Army Acquisition and Program Management in Expeditionary Operations, *Urgent Reform Required*.

16. Richard L. Dunn, *Contractors Supporting Combat Operations: Developing the Vision to Fill Gaps in Policy* (College Park: University of Maryland, Center for Public Policy and Private Enterprise, Jan. 2008).

17. The Army Field Manual 3-0 definition for unity of command: "For every objective, ensure unity of effort under one responsible commander." It further states, "Unity of command means that a single commander directs and coordinates the actions of all forces toward a common objective. Cooperation may produce coordination, but giving a single commander the required authority unifies action."

18. Army Regulation 715-9, *Contractors Accompanying the Force* (Oc. 29, 1999), 13.

19. Dunn, *Contractors Supporting Combat Operations.*

20. U.S. Joint Chiefs of Staff, Joint Publication 4-10, *Operational Contract Support*, Final Coordination (Washington, DC: JCS, Nov. 1, 2007), I-12.

21. Congressional Budget Office, *Contractors' Support of U.S. Operations in Iraq* (Aug. 2008), 2.

22. "Bechtel Pulling Out after Three Rough Years of Rebuilding Work," *San Francisco Chronicle*, Nov. 1, 2006, 2.

23. Mark Lindemann, "Civilian Contractors under Military Law," *Parameters* 37 (Autumn 2007): 83–94.

24. Department of Defense, Instruction No. 3020.41, issued by the Undersecretary of Defense (Acquisition, Technology and Logistics), Oct. 3, 2005.

25. CENTCOM Message, *Modification to USCENTCOM Civilian and Contractor Arming Policy and Delegation of Authority for Iraq and Afghanistan* (Nov. 7, 2006), http.dla.mil/j-3/j-3311/dlad/CENTCOM%20Message%20DTG%20070902Z%20Nov%2006.pdf.

26. Commission on Wartime Contracting in Iraq and Afghanistan, *At What Cost?.*

27. Robert M. Gates, "A Balanced Strategy: Reprogramming the Pentagon for a New Age," *Foreign Affairs* (Jan./Feb. 2009): 28–40.

28. Department of the Army, *Realignment of ACA and Establishment of ACC* (Jan. 30, 2008).

Conclusion

Christopher Kinsey and Malcolm Hugh Patterson

[Since 1955] . . . all DoD support services [have] been contracted out to private vendors except those functions which are inherently governmental or directly impact war-fighting capability, or for which no adequate private sector capability exists or can be expected to be established.

Defense Science Board, 1996[1]

THE SELF-SUFFICIENT MILITARY DID NOT EXIST FOR MOST OF THE TWENtieth century. Nor has the delivery of defense support services been the sole responsibility of the US Department of Defense (DoD). However, the level of military outsourcing at the start of the twenty-first century is unparalleled and will eventually transform the military structure. In this transformation contractors are changing the character of modern warfare and the way governments understand military power. These suppliers of goods and services are now a key component in expeditionary deployments. They play a prominent role in all operations, including the reconstruction and stabilization of failing and failed states. This extensive and growing role is not without problems.

These difficulties concern the US legislature and executive, military personnel, civil servants and the directors, managers, and employees within contractor firms. They also carry consequences for populations within states in which the United States conducts operations. Nor is the US military the only force undergoing change as a consequence of the market assuming support services that were once the responsibility of the military. The British, French, and German militaries are undergoing similar changes. However, the US military is unique in the extent of its reliance on contractors in the operational space. The American government also faces important choices in reform of legal and administrative structures required to deliver the expertise contractors can offer expeditionary operations.

The authors have demonstrated that the ability of industry to support military operations is a key factor in the decision to deploy military force and how that force will be applied. As part of a transformation to a force centered on war-fighting capabilities, contractors have become part of the larger geostrategic environment that determines whether and how to deploy military force in a crisis. The editors believe this process should be accelerated and extended, so that contractors become further integrated into operational planning and management.

Another strategic consideration is the need for an administration to consider the time taken by industry to organize support of a military operation. Speed of technological change may carry the assurance of superior equipment, but this may not be ready for imminent deployment. For example, companies that supply technical support to weapons platforms may require time to organize their production lines to deliver spare parts or up-grade software programs. Technicians may require fresh training before they are competent to repair and maintain a new piece of equipment.[2] Even locating sufficient qualified staff to support equipment in theater may add to an already complicated geostrategic and operational environment. By contrast, companies that supply and maintain other forms of support will not hold these concerns. For instance, a firm that supplies messing facilities is likely to draw on global supply chains that will readily provide its needs in theater.

Despite their shortcomings, contractors have become invaluable to US policy makers. They provide expert knowledge and commercial experience that may be unavailable within the government. They offer theater commanders the flexibility to carry out tasks in a manner different from past approaches. Contractors create an adaptable and agile supply chain through local, national, and international actors that contribute simultaneously to the same environment. This adoption of a multilayered approach is fundamentally different from the way US troops were supplied during the Cold War. Academic interest in the subject has been stirred by the changing mix of resources and shifting balance of responsibilities within public and private sectors.

Part I: The Nature of Contractor Support
in Future US Military Operations

Robert Mandel's opening chapter provides the reader with an overview of the role of private contractors in support of US expeditionary operations. He outlines several issues associated with military reliance on contractors: a shortage of civilian and military personnel, casualty aversion, large numbers of demobilized military (many of whom are from economically depressed states and who seek work); a rising number of threats to US interests abroad; reasons to limit the use of US military force and a simultaneous unease over growing dependence on private companies that carry out what were public responsibilities. Mandel identifies dangers to the United States from foreign domestic insurgencies, internal civil wars, and failing states. These are complemented by the "spread of weapons of mass destruction, transnational organized crime, and violent acts perpetrated by transnational terrorists."

He also refers to controversies arising from contractor deployments. These concern corruption, loyalty, moral standards, policy alternatives, inadequate management by a depleted DoD civilian workforce; retribution inflicted on US counterinsurgency forces as a consequence of contractor misbehavior; tensions between contractors and the military; moral, legal, and public responsibility issues arising from the legitimacy of contractor acts of violence; and a desirable balance between public and private support. He also identifies the highly polemical nature of debate on contractors and implicitly, the need for methodical evaluation of evidence of misconduct. He then summarizes arguments for and against reliance on contractors, concluding with comments on their future engagement by the US government (USG). These include an acknowledgment that contractor influence is likely to grow to a point where it will shape the strategic planning of future American expeditionary operations.

At present there are unresolved issues of cost efficiency, task suitability, and corruption—the last in Iraq in particular. In that light, his message emphasizes the need to identify specific conditions under which the United States should or should not use contractors. Mandel emphasizes the requirement for "sustained systematic data on the conditions most conducive to private contractor usage [and] the differing projected outcomes from different types of private contractor usage." A sound choice will avoid unwelcome impact on expeditionary operations and wider US foreign policy objectives. Making prudent decisions will require astute political judgment and better understanding of why and how functions should be divided between government and the market. On that aspect, the most important conundrum is determining what is or is not an inherently governmental task. Resolving that entails grappling with political and legal challenges, but the matter demands an answer. Otherwise, the issue may be manipulated by the increasingly pervasive influence of the market. Mandel does not explicitly describe which tasks should be set aside for the government and its military; but he does identify sources of federal intentions—most prominently, in the Federal Acquisition Regulation.[3]

The Regulation prescribes government employees rather than private contractors to undertake tasks that involve either the exercise of discretion in applying government authority or value judgments when making decisions for government. Mandel acknowledges that most matters of security necessitate the exercise of discretion and value judgments; but the key appears to be the scale of consequences and the better positioning of government to withstand the political costs of misadventure. It is difficult to disagree with his view, yet the government has yet to clarify this issue unambiguously. If left unresolved, the matter may undermine the morale of uniformed personnel. This is a concern investigated in the next chapter, by Ryan Kelty and Darcy Schnack.

Chapter Two begins with some remarks on the nature of military identity, then a discussion of the civilianization of the military. Kelty and Schnack follow with the effects of contractor integration on service members and conclude with an evaluation of the meaning of these changes. One strength of the chapter is that the authors rely on two of their own surveys as well as the research of others. Early in their writing they observe that military employment and culture are often seen by civilian society as separate and distinct from civilian life. This is in part because many military tasks have until recently differed from those performed by civilians. Some remain. But because outsourcing is eroding this exclusive military responsibility, it is not difficult to understand why civilianization leads to some resistance within the military. Kelty and Schnack echo Mandel's concern in Chapter One over the absence of a clear distinction between jobs that constitute inherently military work and nonmilitary tasks that support the military.

The military is uncertain of the span of its future tasks if the government develops a "total defense workforce" mix of military, government civilians, and contractor personnel. Kelty and Schnack also cite research that suggests that integration of contractors has a negative effect on retention attitudes of service personnel. It is understandable that the military seeks to protect a nucleus of inherently governmental functions in the face of encroaching competition. The more general attitude toward contracts seems to be one of ambivalence, something identified toward the end of the chapter. That mixed response may spring from a very different cause identified by Moskos over thirty years ago. An institutional military is one in which soldiers are bound by traditional values and norms such as duty and honor. These are traditionally viewed as indispensable when building a collective identity and shaping a loyal and cohesive group. In an occupational military, soldiers are more likely to see military life as simply one occupation among others.[4]

It seems that the latter view is more common today—and may make it easier to accept contractors into military company. Contemporary soldiers appear more likely to attach importance to motives more commonly valued by civilians, like monetary compensation and training in skills transferable to civilian life. If so, that shift suggests that soldiers' motives combine a desire to serve with a more pronounced intention to secure their own interests. This orientation to military life has been fostered to some extent by the ideologically driven Office of Management and Budget Circular A-76. The circular has been promoted with varying degrees of enthusiasm by succeeding administrations and guided outsourcing in federal government departments including Defense since 1966. Nonetheless, Kelty and Schnack also identify remaining differences between civilian and military attitudes to risk and a willingness to accept a rigid employment structure.

They cite Moskos's view of a shift toward the occupational model and implied changes to the US military's structure and functions.[5] This change has occurred with increasing speed over the last decade, during which military reliance on contractors has increased significantly. In particular, Operation Iraqi Freedom (OIF) marked a transformation away from the Cold War self-sufficiency model to dependence on contractors for mission support.[6] The US military is now close to adopting a core-competency model of organization. Once again, the question remains how the military's core competencies or inherently military functions might be defined. Explanations from classic texts tend to be very general and axiomatic, like Huntington's succinct explanation that "[the] distinct sphere of military competence . . . is . . . the management of violence."[7] The logical corollary to Huntington's premise is support of military management of violence through various auxiliary functions. But this is equally abstract and without the manifest and practical form sought by readers concerned with evolving US policy.

Kelty and Schnack attach importance to at least four forces that propel structural and functional changes facing the US military: a lack of political will to retain a military on the scale required by the Cold War, military ambivalence toward growing contractor numbers and the expanding roles of contractors; considerable changes to the character of armed conflict; and the more complex social and political environment of the twenty-first century. Collectively, these shifts demand a new force structure that is capable of responding to the uncertainties arising from the sometimes nebulous threats that now face the United States. This last point is partly the subject of Renée de Nevers' chapter, in which she scrutinizes the role of contractors in US global operations.

She examines some of the lessons from Iraq since 2003, before evaluating American reliance on contractors in attempts at achieving long-term stability in Afghanistan, Africa, and South America. De Nevers emphasizes the need for competent management and adequate criminal laws to ensure that contractors are employed in a disciplined work culture and within the boundaries of a functional criminal justice system. In Iraq the former was unreliable and the latter did not exist. Contractors instead contributed to a broader failure to plan and conduct operations competently after the invasion. She also asserts a need for the military to possess authority to control contractors—private military and security companies in particular—operating in conflict zones.

De Nevers emphasizes that without adequate management and control of contractors, their actions may undermine the objectives of a military mission. Today these objectives are often associated with winning a hearts-and-minds campaign (something further explored by Carmola in Chapter Six.) She contends that responsibilities within and outside former US military roles have been contracted to the market with insufficient consideration of the consequences for long-term goals. She believes greater attention should be paid to how contractors perform their tasks, their influence on US military objectives, and the policies of host nations. She also provides an example of how poor performance by contractors erodes military objectives. US contractors have played a major role in training the Afghan police and army. This training program is seriously defective and has failed to build an Afghan police force capable of guaranteeing internal security for the citizenry. Afghan National Army (ANA) training has also produced very mixed results. As a consequence, the United States may not be in a position to reduce its military presence as rapidly as the Obama administration would wish. In Africa the principal US military presence is Africa Command (AFRICOM) and the State Department Africa Peacekeeping Program (AFRICAP). Both are serviced by contractors in a region where there remains considerable sensitivity to privatized military training and support, and wariness of a policy emphasis on military rather than civilian tasks. In South America contractor police and military training in Plan Colombia has led to security improvements, but contractor tasks and numbers are less than clear. The Merida Initiative is an anti-drug program directed mostly at Mexico that also employs contractors. Both programs have permitted the US government more options in response to a demand for low-intensity operations. De Nevers remains concerned that in both cases contractors may be the emerging face of a foreign policy that has become both heavily militarized and extensively outsourced.

Of the various issues broached in Part I, three matters in particular attract comment. The first is a need to clarify what is inherently governmental and what is not, and what tasks contractors should and should not carry out. The second is the indispensability of a reliable criminal justice system installed at the center of broader concepts of contractor governance. The third is that for the present, no USG agency other than DoD possesses the resources and self-interest to capably manage contractors in the field.

Various options for change pose demanding questions. How should military responsibilities be more competently managed in the short term? How and to what extent should contractor management and supervision be dispersed in the future? Among which organs of state should these duties be distributed? Should fresh responsibilities be conferred on existing agencies or should a new and specialized agency be created for these purposes? Responsibility for resolving each of these challenges is not confined to politicians. The US legislature and executive will require the support of American citizens to bring about political and legal changes that keep contractors within the bounds of appropriate tasks, remove the criminal impunity that became notorious in Iraq, and establish civilian and military administrative structures that effectively supervise contractor operations. In all of these ambitions the military and other USG agencies still have to function without shouldering onerous or unsuitable responsibilities.

Part II: Reconstruction and Stabilization Operations

The three chapters in this part focus on the conduct of stability and reconstruction operations (SROs) at the strategic and operational level. The authors examine ways and means with which the US military, US nongovernmental organizations (NGOs), and contractors manage practical problems when working alongside one another. The first chapter concerns the US military and its relations with contractors on expeditionary operations. Colonel Flavin begins with an overview of the contemporary operational environment, emphasizing the need for adequate government and private-sector resources. Both will be required to address the wide range of challenges US forces will face. Flavin argues that US civilian and military structures lack the full spectrum of skills needed to succeed in stability operations. He also points out that it is not feasible to expect the government to recruit or maintain such a wide range of expertise. This is particularly so when a valuable skill has a narrow application, such as in-depth knowledge of a certain culture. He believes that the way for civilian and military agencies to overcome their skills gap is to contract from the private sector. This seems reasonable, as many of those with appropriate skills are no longer found in the military, academia, or government agencies. They have moved to the for-profit private sector.

Another of Flavin's concerns is that military commanders should focus on the effects contractors exert on the operational environment. Which contractor is to be responsible for a task intended to achieve a particular effect and how it should be performed are both key to the success of an operation. He points to two types of contracting effects: direct and indirect. Indirect effects are those he describes as "coincidental to the purpose of the contract." Examples of contractors who exercise an indirect effect are those that support the force. Their effect on the operational environment frees soldiers to engage in combat or mission planning.

By contrast, direct contracting affects the host government, elites, and the population within a state. It can exert a prompt and long-term impact, resulting in an outcome that supports mission accomplishment. Examples include training, educating, and mentoring host-nation security forces and government ministries; conducting security sector reform, intelligence operations, static and mobile security; and creating command, control, and communication centers. Flavin qualifies his support for direct contracting with a note of caution. He warns that this type of contracting should not necessarily be seen as a replacement for existing deficiencies in US military or other government capacity or capability. Instead, contractors should augment improved US government resources. This brings to mind the preceding chapter, where De Nevers refers to contractors who did a conspicuously poor job of training the Afghan police and army over an extensive period of time and at considerable expense. In that example, if contractors had supplemented US military personnel it seems likely that fewer mistakes would have occurred. Flavin is mindful that—as in this case—firms driven by profit will attempt to maintain their contracts, even if these prove unsatisfactory and do not meet the needs of the client.

He also contends that contracting should in the future be "nested in operational and strategic frameworks." This will create a higher likelihood of operational success once contractors have been fully integrated into "the military decision-making process and interagency planning framework." He identifies this framework as consisting of five areas: assessment and understanding of the drivers of conflict and underlying grievances; achievement of a comprehensive approach to building unity of effort; ensuring legitimacy of the operation; strengthening the host nation through capacity building; and conducting all of these aspects under the rule of law. Contractors can easily undermine these areas if they are not properly integrated into the complete framework. That integration should lower the risk of contractor miscalculation and enhance unity of purpose within an operation. This argument is consistent with Flavin's acknowledgment that Department of State postconflict reconstruction goals and the US military both identify the primary reconstruction actors as civilians, with the military in support. His proposal for centralized organization also endorses aspects of Stuart Bowen's proposal in Chapter Eleven. Last, it seems apparent that to ignore the need for greater integration of contractors and centralization of their management risks undermining US government objectives. This will also put at risk the goals of US NGOs, which is Samuel Worthington's concern in Chapter Five.

His primary concern is the growing tension between NGOs and local communities as a consequence of the conduct of the US military and its contractors. The chapter begins with an explanation of a widely accepted NGO approach to working in difficult places, and then moves to problems when NGOs share space with the US military and its contractors. For example, sometimes the military engages in relief and development projects designed to support a counterinsurgency strategy. The idea is to win over the hearts and minds of the local population. These quick-fix projects address some symptoms of insecurity but not underlying causes. This can hamper the efforts of well-informed NGOs, which instead focus on long-term welfare and development needs.

Equally importantly, NGOs ensure the security of their personnel by seeking acceptance in a local community, often after years of diligent effort. They pursue this through conduct based on principles of impartiality and independence. Becoming a part of the community they assist in this fashion is very different from the approach applied by the military and some of its contractors, whose actions can undermine these principles. Because local communities often associate armed foreigners with other foreigners who work in their area, misbehavior by private security contractors is likely to have been one cause of a rise in recent attacks on staff at humanitarian NGOs. This makes it very difficult or even impossible for US and other NGOs to do their work.

Another concern for Worthington is the growing militarization of US foreign assistance as resources have been transferred from other agencies to the DoD. Stanger and Bowen raise similar concerns in their chapters. Since the US military established the first Provincial Reconstruction Teams (PRTs) in Afghanistan in late 2001, there has been a noticeable growth in defense spending on relief, reconstruction, and development projects in coordination with private contractors. Worthington and other US NGO leaders would prefer to see money for these projects sourced from international assistance funds and not the defense budget. He believes that civilian agencies should be responsible for administering these projects, as there is ample evidence to conclude that the effectiveness of the DoD as a development actor is very doubtful. At a fundamental level, DoD philosophy and purposes toward development work are irreconcilable with those held by successful NGOs.

Worthington's point here is that NGOs are independent actors with their own purposes. US NGOs in particular are not instruments of the US military and their independence from US foreign policy is often vital to their ability to carry out their programs unhindered. Worthington stresses that the US military and its contractors should consider creating a strategy that takes account of this independence and avoids undermining US NGOs in the long-term. His apprehension may be well-founded. There is a move afoot to further maneuver NGOs through two new data collection systems that will identify NGOs more closely with US military and intelligence agencies. The Partner Vetting System (PVS) and the Synchronized Pre-Deployment and Operational

Tracker (SPOT) will almost certainly carry objectionable consequences for NGO staff who already face escalating risks in difficult environments.

In the third chapter of Part II Kateri Carmola explains an entirely different problem. Her interest lies in the organizational risk cultures of private military and security companies (PMSCs). Her premise is that these cultures undermine US military operations because they do not align with the US military's own organizational risk culture. There are four components to this concept: a cultural attitude toward risk in general, the type of organization used to carry out the task, the environment in which the task will be carried out, and the overall mission. She offers the example of the military culture supporting a counterinsurgency strategy that emphasizes support for a host government. This support is crucial for building legitimacy, security, and trust within a population. Carmola explains that by contrast, PMSCs hold a risk posture that is likely to damage this support.

The crux of this argument is that some risks are transferred to the market because the military is less suited to accommodate them and PMSCs are notably risk-tolerant. Carmola makes the familiar point that the political risk attached to contractor casualties is significantly reduced because unlike military casualties, they are not reported publicly. She focuses on three types of security contractor: bodyguards, convoy security guards, and CIA field contractors. Although the bodyguard segment carries the greatest likelihood of violent misconduct, she argues that each of these groups carries out inherently governmental tasks, and exacerbates an already difficult situation for the US military because of their different perceptions of risk and different approaches to security and regulation.

She is on firm ground when arguing that present COIN strategy is dogged by complexity and a lack of transparency about the end state of a successful operation. There is also a persistent absence of clarity regarding the criminal justice regime(s) that govern PMSCs and their staffs. This has created a situation that is both volatile and opaque; and she asserts that this will permit PMSCs to create additional chaos in an already chaotic counterinsurgency environment. For Carmola, this takes the form of heightened hazards attached to three areas: operational risk, legal risk, and reputational risk. While operational risk can be reduced with careful planning, the legal and reputational risks associated with deploying PMSCs present more intractable challenges. In the wake of excessively violent PMSC behavior in Iraq, the US military was attacked in retribution. This occurred because guerillas within the local population did not distinguish between the US military and PMSCs. In other words, the US military reputation suffered with very tangible consequences. If establishing then maintaining the rule of law is central to creating peace and stability, tolerating delinquent behavior by armed contractors by letting them go unpunished sends precisely the wrong message to a local population: that there is one rule for the inhabitants and another for the foreigners.[8]

Counterinsurgency operations are likely to be successful only with the support of a local population. Carmola observes that this will only result as a consequence of a partnership based on trust. Yet contractor deployments raise persistent issues of weak controls, poor US government management, and an inadequate criminal justice regime. These are likely to undermine the chances of success. Strengthening appropriate laws to ensure that some of these risks are averted or at least diminished will resolve one aspect of this problem. An improved legal regime is in large measure the subject of Part III.

Part III: Legal Aspects of Future US Operations

This part is concerned with legal issues arising from a contractor presence on operations, a legislative response to unsatisfactory legal and bureaucratic structures, and reforms needed to establish a reliable criminal justice regime. Geoffrey Corn opens the first chapter with a very modern premise: that what occurs on the battlefield is now subject to a degree of public and political examination that would have been inconceivable in the past. He holds that this scrutiny is in large measure driven by an assessment of legality, which has become the primary criterion for defining the legitimacy of military action. Legality is certainly an important criterion, and there is little doubt that there exists an increasing tendency to scrutinize the role and behavior of civilian contractors through a legal lens. He identifies three issues that commonly emerge in legal debate on contractors: their legal status while operating alongside US forces; the ambit of tasks that are inherently governmental functions (IGFs) properly undertaken by government employees rather than contractors; and the as yet incomplete aspiration to construct a reliable criminal justice regime that extends jurisdiction to contractors on deployed operations.

Establishing the status of contractors on expeditionary operations is the first step in determining permissible tasks and conduct. With expanding numbers of contractors supporting the military, clarity as to contractors' status has been pressing for some time. Corn considers this status within the law of armed conflict (LOAC) through the frailties of a "direct participation test," something which lacks certainty as contractors move steadily toward the sharp end of military power projection. He then assesses the ambit of inherently governmental functions in the "Burman Letter" test, which is another broad description. The latter test attracts a larger point. Administrations since 9/11 appear to have accepted a state of perpetual warfare, in which conformity with the principles of the LOAC carries secondary importance behind administrative developments within the US government. This is evident in Corn's section on "authorized functions."

In one of his examples, armed security contractors defend themselves and others against "threats that are presumptively unlawful." If defending say, a US base against attack by criminals, this will be so—although even then a *presumptive* claim is weak, as the attackers' identity is unlikely to have been confirmed beforehand. However, his assertion is weaker still when confronted with a far more likely scenario—that insurgents attack the same base. To enemy belligerents, a US military base is a legitimate target and mounting an assault would be lawful in terms of the LOAC. Corn emphasizes government policy on IGFs and armed contractors, something that carries a purpose other than LOAC compliance. More generally, over the last decade US policy has led a steady retreat from the LOAC. Under the Bush administrations in particular, the consequences attracted widespread, uncomplimentary and mostly accurate comment.[9]

He exposes another dilemma when he refers to the separation of contractors from the "kill chain" of IGF functions that results in engagement of the enemy via unmanned aerial vehicles (UAVs). Corn's reference to contractors having a purely technical role is not convincing. The problem is that UAVs are operated by both the US military and—in a separate chain of authority—by the CIA from within Pakistan. Philip Alston is an eminent human rights lawyer and the UN Special Rapporteur on Extra-Judicial Killings. He has pointed out that unlike the military, the CIA operates in complete secrecy and pursues classified purposes that may or may not pay regard to the LOAC.[10] Second, and highly pertinent for present purposes, the bulk of the workforce serving CIA's National Clandestine Service now comprises outsourced contractors, according to investigative journalist Tim Shorrock.[11] Put another way, it is not possible to test Corn's claims on UAVs in light of what is publicly known.

The remainder of his chapter concerns disciplinary options to address contractor misconduct. Here Corn provides an incisive and detailed explanation of legal changes through which there has been a resurrection of military jurisdiction over civilians in a theater of operations. The result is yet more uncertainty as to the scope of persons who accompany the force (and perhaps others) and the constitutional validity of trials of civilians in military courts. It is quite likely that these matters will be resolved in the US Supreme Court in several years' time. In the meantime, present uncertainties and US policy invite further outsourcing where there is profit and a willingness to embrace risk—something Carmola described in the preceding chapter. Without decisive legislative and executive government willingness to address the criminal justice issue, there remains, as Corn observes, a risk to the effectiveness of contract support and belief in the legitimacy of US operations.

In Chapter Eight, Allison Stanger delivers a commentary on the Commission on Wartime Contracting (CWC). She begins by reminding the reader that contractors are now an integral part of defense, diplomacy, development, and homeland security. She refers to the former three as "the three Ds" and extensive contracting within them has proved an attractive option for executive government. This is because contracting allows US policy makers to purchase a degree of support for foreign policy objectives, rather than having to earn the political favor of the American people and their elected representatives. This path of lesser resistance has nonetheless supplied its own disadvantages: widespread criminal misconduct and massive fraud in Iraq in particular. Her message is twofold: first, that responsibilities will continue to be outsourced to the private sector in future reconstruction and stabilization operations; and second, the US government should ensure that its workforce mix of military personnel, government employees, and contract staff serves the interests of the American people rather than a corporate agenda.

She follows with a brief discussion of the Truman Committee investigations during and after the Second World War and explains why a similarly broad authorization was required to investigate recent government contracting. Stanger then remarks on the moral and legal hazards of wartime contracting. Somewhat contentiously, she argues that the pervasiveness and indispensability of contractors on the modern battlefield has legitimized profiteering. She goes further, asserting that profiteering has become "both respectable and even patriotic." An absence of exactitude in the meaning of "profiteering" and a fondness for rhetoric aside, Stanger then makes three points that are more persuasive and shared by several authors in this book. First, she refers to the imprecision of government direction as to what is (and more importantly is not) an inherently governmental function. Second, she identifies elements of an unsatisfactory criminal justice regime (adding that the widespread practice of subcontracting greatly aggravates already formidable difficulties in law enforcement). Third, and several pages further on, she raises the now familiar case of Afghan police training as an example of how not to deploy and manage contractor support.

In the next section, she lists several CWC achievements, such as identifying the enormous sums of money that have disappeared and exposing shortcomings in relevant supervisory agencies and statutory sources of US taxpayer monies. She also cites particular examples of alarmingly widespread misconduct. However, she contributes her most damning remarks in the following section on security contractors. Stanger believes that they perform inherently governmental functions. Unencumbered by legal rigor, she adopts a broad test loosely founded in political philosophy. Armed contractors perform an IGF because they are "defending the nation against foreign enemies." This kind of dogma is less than helpful, but her case is stronger when referring to serious flaws in contractor security in Afghanistan.

Afghan warlords have been given the responsibility for securing US military supply lines. This has proved to be a protection racket subsidized by the American taxpayer. She observes that it is not unusual for local warlords to work against the objectives of US counterinsurgency operations if it is in their financial or other interests to do so. Logically enough, warlords also view attempts at state capacity building as threats to their powerbases. It is therefore in their interests to undermine fundamental planks of counterinsurgency policy. Corruption of this and other kinds could be prevented by stringent mechanisms to manage and to some extent control contractor behavior. Yet there is no organization with overall responsibility for these functions. Instead, she points out that duties are spread among agencies rather than centralized in a single organ. Here she echoes Flavin's earlier remarks and Stuart Bowen's message in Chapter Eleven.

Finally, Stanger sets out two obstacles to reform and three objectives. The former include the need to reduce foreign policy ambitions—which seems plausible—and overcoming an entrenched status quo of business interests. The latter appears to be another less than entirely helpful statement of ideological conviction. Her three objectives are to stop contractors carrying out

IGFs; influence Congress to deliver legislation and resources to "in-source" contractor management—both of which are sound in principle; and radical transparency on how US taxpayer money is used. This is another notion that sounds desirable, but even the most receptive reader requires some explanation in support of the premise that Stanger presents.

Congressman David Price has written the final chapter in Part III. In common with other contributors, he is concerned with inadequate legislative effort directed to inherently governmental tasks, and the roles of cost, practicality, and political viability in contractor deployment. But these topics are not investigated here. He is instead concerned with the legal framework governing private security contractors from the perspective of a member of the US Congress. In the first of three parts of the chapter, he outlines the need for an effective criminal justice framework for contractors. Second, he offers a narrative account of congressional attempts to strengthen the existing framework. Third, he evaluates the current state of American laws that regulate contractors working in overseas deployments. Price is well aware that contractors have escaped trial after involvement in a range of serious crimes. He is also sensitive to the consequences of an absence of criminal justice: diplomatic damage, incitement of anti-Americanism, and further harm to the US reputation of what he describes as a "champion of justice and the rule of law." His goal is to establish a comprehensive criminal justice system. This he sees as both a strategic and legal responsibility of the US state. This responsibility takes the form of a federal governmental obligation to supply adequate law and—as he later argues—sufficient resources for enforcement. He is well-qualified to comment. Price has been active in support of improved management, transparency, and the introduction of effective criminal laws since 2004 in the wake of the Abu Ghraib incident.

He identifies sources of obligation that include a rhetorical commitment to the rule of law as well as US and international laws that bind the US government. Price then provides the reader with informative details of the legislative evolution of several statutes over the last few years. These include a valuable explanation of weaknesses in changes to the Uniform Code of Military Justice and the Military Extraterritorial Jurisdiction Act; the curious lack of will evinced by the Department of Justice, which for some time resisted utilizing MEJA or other laws to prosecute several of the more egregious examples of contractor criminality; and a disturbing intervention by the Bush administration in an attempt to stop the (then) widely supported MEJA Expansion and

Enforcement Act in the House. This took place a few weeks after the notorious Nisoor Square killings by members of Blackwater. That skirmish with the White House was the beginning of lengthy resistance exerted in both the Senate and House. Price finds the president's conduct particularly "troubling," as Mr. Bush opposed an effective criminal justice framework at a time when he also supported policies of doubtful legality while enthusiastically promoting what Price euphemistically terms "coercive interrogation techniques."[12]

Although there have been recent failures in the prosecution of various Blackwater personnel, Price charts some progress. In 2010, he allied with Senator Patrick Leahy to introduce a new bill titled the *Civilian Extraterritorial Jurisdiction Act*. Instead of trying to amend MEJA, this bill was to establish a separate basis of jurisdiction applicable to any US government contractor or employer working outside of America. For various reasons, the 111th Congress adjourned without considering the act. Although Price and Leahy planned to reintroduce it in the 112th Congress in 2011, Republican leadership in the House at that time suggested an uncertain response. He nonetheless retains a clear imperative: that his government should leave no legislative doubt as to its authority to prosecute civilians who act in its name beyond US borders.

Part IV: US Administrative Structures Required to Sustain Contractor Operations

In this part Frank Camm begins by querying the existence of criteria that adequately determine whether a contractor rather than a government source is preferable for DoD purposes. In the second chapter, Bowen grapples with reform to the management of American stabilization and reconstruction operations (SROs). The final chapter illustrates how changes in today's operations have met with some institutional resistance. Jacques Gansler and William Lucyshyn identify a range of problems and the means by which some of them are addressed.

Camm grapples with the bases on which DoD decides how and why it chooses a government or private-sector provider of goods or services. His opening message is that there is no strong empirical basis on which to make broad observations about the relative desirability of government or contractor support to deployed forces. In his view, suitability depends on an existing ability to manage risks associated with deploying a government or contractor source that has undertaken a specific task. To address this matter, he applies a standardized DoD approach to managing risks associated with both government and commercial sources of goods and services. Each source is treated separately, its risks mitigated and residual risks compared before a private or public source is chosen. He presents his argument in five steps: a review of concepts and policy issues; an explanation of the use of the DoD risk management framework; a description of how the framework treats command and control (which is itself a risk-mitigation measure); a means of applying the framework to assess government/contractor sources of three specified services: troop support, system support, and security protection; and a conclusion.

Another factor is the time it would take each source to deploy. For example, if the military is ordered to mobilize immediately, it may only be possible to draw on goods or services that are to hand at this moment. If so, a particular item or service is more likely to be of military or at least government origin, since contractors usually require a lead time in which to organize before responding. The British writer Caldicott makes a similar point concerning the necessity for sufficient time in which to organize an optimum mix of sources for military operations: "Contractors need notice of what they are expected to provide in order to assure the military and themselves of their ability to generate, prepare, deploy and operate capabilities to a mutually satisfactory standard."[13]

Camm emphasizes that guidelines on choice among different sources should focus on future requirements. This is likely to mean procuring the most favorable mix of sources for DoD deployments in contingency operations. Nonetheless, he believes the US military struggles to improve prospective combinations of military and contractor capability. Changing the mix of government/contractor capabilities in the future is complicated by the DoD budgeting process and the way it deals with new sourcing priorities. If DoD continues to delay the investment necessary to create desirable changes to this mixture, Camm maintains that the department will exacerbate existing restrictions on support of future contingency operations.

In his conclusion, he offers several guiding principles. If various reasons prevent government sources from deploying, then a private source will be chosen. In this circumstance, whichever choice might have been superior in the job becomes irrelevant. Where there is genuine choice, applied risk analysis suggests that the choice will depend on three variables: the type of service produced; the threat to contractors in the portion of the contingency in which the service occurs; and the government's ability to provide effective command and control of the contractor service where and when it is required.

Bowen's chapter examines the failure by the US government to competently plan, execute, and then manage stability and reconstruction operations. His contribution distills the lessons of his eight years as SIGIR, during which he acquired extensive experience of the consequences of government mismanagement. Bowen reviews efforts to improve stability and reconstruction operations and considers the nature of reforms required to avoid repeating costly mistakes of the recent past. In an era when the combined three Ds of diplomacy, development, and defense carry increased importance, he argues the necessity for improved and centralized SRO management.

Early in his chapter, Bowen lists several fundamental mistakes during military operations in Iraq. The durability of these shortcomings suggests that the military has been preoccupied with more conventional forms of armed conflict. For example, there was a failure to pay sufficient regard to opinions voiced by Iraqi authorities; there was weak coordination between US military and civilian elements of the occupation; and there was a lack of liaison between different USG agencies. These factors reduced the effectiveness of the recovery program. At the same time, the military continues to resist attempts to shift responsibility for the management of SROs elsewhere. This has been the case even where other agencies have been better placed to assume this role.

The other major problem that Bowen raises is the tendency toward an ad hoc or "adhocracy" approach to the management of SROs. If conventional warfare is to be displaced by more SROs in the future, then this newer type of operation will demand more of the military's attention and implies a vital need to address the ad hoc approach. The US military's key role in these operations should include managing contractors as efficiently as possible while preventing the widespread dishonesty witnessed in Iraq. In the eyes of both Bowen and Stanger, poor administration has contributed to contractor fraud and corruption, and undermined the interests of the American people while benefiting corporate purposes.

Evidence of adhocracy is found in the Provincial Reconstruction Team (PRT) program, which is mostly staffed by a mixture of US military/government and contractor personnel. PRTs did not establish their objectives until sometime after the invasion of Iraq, nor did they have to create work plans; and projects were launched without coordination with the interim Iraq government. This suggests a need for superior organization to avoid compromising NGO relationships with the local community, undermining the work of local unit commanders, and irritating the Iraqi administration. As Flavin argues in a similar vein in Chapter Four, both contractors and PRTs should be embedded in operational and strategic frameworks to ensure a better chance of success. Bowen has a strong point in arguing for an integrated approach to planning and executing SROs. Among other virtues, this advance would effectively reform the way PRTs are devised and managed.

However, attempts at restructuring planning and execution of SROs have so far met with limited success. It appears that US government agencies involved in these operations have tended to resist a comprehensive solution. Nonetheless, Bowen identifies three alternative models for reform. The first is a revitalized and more heavily resourced USAID, replete with the authority to manage all aspects of an operation; the second is the establishment of a Civil Affairs Interagency Command (CAIC) with the DoD acting as the administrative backbone for an operation with other US government agencies having a role in the management structure; and the third is a new quasi-independent office to manage SROs called the "US Office for Contingency Operations" (USOCO). At present, responsibility for SROs is scattered across several government agencies, the capabilities of which differ considerably. Each is responsible for managing some aspects, but none has overall authority. Bowen delivers a compelling case for comprehensive change in the form of the USOCO model.

The last chapter examines the military and its bureaucracy. Gansler and Lucyshyn explain why uniformed and civilian branches of DoD rely on so many contractors and what this means for organization, culture, doctrine, planning, and exercises. The authors begin by identifying several causes of the military's increasing reliance on contractors and some of the problems this has caused. The latter include shortages in acquisition staff at DoD; inadequate contract training for military personnel; unsuitable pay and conditions for deployed DoD civilians; a necessity for further work on expeditionary contracting procedures; and shortcomings in existing information technology. They then discuss the US military acquisition workforce and examine the policies, procedures, and processes associated with expeditionary contracts.

In common with several other authors, Gansler and Lucyshyn start by outlining the benefits and risks associated with contractors. They highlight the challenges of integration and the management of contractors who work alongside the military on SROs. They also raise a challenge in military culture. As Kelty and Schnack observed in Chapter Two, although more soldiers now accept contractors as part of the military force structure, there are still those who are not inclined to recognize that the functions performed by contractors in Afghanistan and Iraq will eventually become normal practice elsewhere. Much like Bowen, Gansler and Lucyshyn find the military mentality still preoccupied with traditional operations and insufficiently attuned to SROs. This creates an institutional resistance that obstructs desirable change. This tension may become more pointed if the US military is tasked with more SROs.

Their major criticism concerns management of the US military acquisition workforce. Several writers in this book and elsewhere have echoed the Gansler and Lucyshyn view that a major challenge facing the US military lies in preventing contractor dishonesty and waste. Yet improvement is possible only if the acquisition workforce expands in line with the growth of SRO-related contracts. The Gansler Commission Final Report concluded that this has not occurred. Instead, "the number of Army civilian and military in the contracting workforce is stagnant or declining."[14] Plainly, the acquisition workforce is at present insufficiently resourced to react efficiently to contingency contracting demands. Now that contractors are a part of the military force structure, the armed forces will have to increase the number of civilians, officers, and non-commissioned officers who are trained to staff acquisition roles. Without their presence, contractor compliance will continue to fall short of reasonable expectations. However, attracting new people into the acquisition workforce may prove a struggle as long as the military culture undervalues the importance of this responsibility. To resolve this problem, the stature of the acquisition workforce will have to be raised to the point that it is seen as a critical element of the total force. A first step should be improvements in the career development of contracting staff and especially those sent on expeditionary operations.

Gansler and Lucyshyn also argue that the acquisition contracting workforce needs restructuring so that it can more ably manage SRO contracts. Acquisition workforce members who support SROs are trained to carry out general or mainstream procurement tasks, such as weapons system procurement. Yet business processes integral to mainstream procurement in peacetime are largely out of place when supporting SROs. Conflict zones are fluid environments. Their continually changing nature requires the military and its support elements to adapt accordingly. That presents contractors with challenges, the most crucial of which is to sustain reliability in the event of erratic and unpredictable volatility in hostilities. Evidence to date suggests that contractors have performed well, even under difficult conditions. Even so, the concern that they could fail at a critical moment in an SRO (where a military unit may not) remains a risk of uncertain dimension and nature. Contracting still has some distance to travel before government and corporations will confidently deliver support to US military deployments without inefficiency, waste, and corruption—particularly in arduous and dangerous circumstances.

Conclusion: Policy Implications of Contractor Support of Contingency Operations

Future American security is likely to involve armed conflict within the plentiful and complex intrastate struggles of the twenty-first century. More broadly, wherever the United States is involved in expeditionary operations, operational support will involve an increasing dependence on private-sector contractors. Whether this reliance will be assisted or inhibited depends principally on choices exercised by the executive and legislative branches of government. Cultural acceptance of the consequences by the civilian bureaucracy and military will be another objective. If government evaluates matters examined in this book in a timely and comprehensive fashion, this will assist the delivery of improved operational support. If ignored or denied, persistent risks and chronic problems will probably impede well-intentioned changes for the better. Tangible advantages should include enhanced operational efficiency, heightened effectiveness, and an overall increase in the probability of mission success. However, these prospects will not be wholly realized until those who wield authority eliminate existing sources of ambiguity, corruption, waste, incompetence, bureaucratic resistance, and ideological myopia. If sufficient resolve is given form in legislative and administrative reform, this will permit shifts in fundamental concepts and practical details. This book provides examples of new thinking that might be contained in both.

Prudent changes would include contractor legislation consistent with the law of armed conflict and a reinvigorated embrace of international legal principles more generally. This step will benefit operations conducted in America's strategic interests in at least three ways: clarification of the legal status of both armed and unarmed contractors who accompany US forces in conventional and contingency operations; reassurance of friends and allies of a shift to a more internationally defensible legal posture; and assistance in the evolution of US military and civilian laws.

The exercise of philosophical and legal precision through legislation and administrative developments would also address several quite different matters. In particular, the creation of a coherent and practical extension of the US criminal justice system will provide certainty in functionally effective process; clarity in the partition between military and civilian criminal justice systems; and good faith in the application of substantive principles, which will reassure Americans, host state populaces, and third-party nationals. Another task is to comprehensively clarify the ambit of inherently governmental functions and their corollary: the explicit nature of those tasks that may properly be discharged by contractors and those that may not. The key here is by now familiar to the reader: practical cooperation between the legislature and executive government. This collaboration will be necessary to deliver other benefits: a degree of certainty in agency principles, fairness in contracts among the various parties, and practical means of securing realistic remedies across transnational boundaries. Last, the creation of a statutory basis for an organization along the lines of Stuart Bowen's US Office for Contingency Operations (USOCO) appears a desirable and effective step for administrative management of contractors deployed in SROs.

Another matter concerns the nature of research. An informed decision to opt for greater or lesser contractor involvement should not be determined by received wisdom or anecdote and the fallacies that tend to accompany both. Equally, one does not expect a contractor deployment to be cynically contrived to serve political convenience, to pay back corporate favors supplied earlier to a political party, or to serve unsophisticated ideological conviction. Convincing research and modeling on whether to base a sourcing decision on contractor or government remains less than comprehensive and more work is necessary to ensure that choices rest on sound bases. Satisfactory outcomes are likely to be derived from a mix of sufficient analytical skill directed to economics and social science analyses. In time, one expects these and other fields to generate increasingly reliable quantitative and qualitative criteria.

The future appears likely to exhibit a more formalized relationship between contractors, DoD, and other branches of government. One reason for this is that various non-lethal capabilities found largely outside the military are sought in counterinsurgencies and SROs. This trend is likely to expand. Whether in future contingency operations or conventional military campaigns, the US government seems likely to integrate contractors within organization and management at an earlier phase and in higher levels of pre-deployment planning. The sense in this is logical enough: a cooperative unity of effort; shared goals widely understood by the participants; and transparency in the methods and means employed.

Finally, the purposes in creating *Contractors and War* have been two-fold. The first has been to select and arrange in a coherent fashion perceptive analyses of several prominent issues in contractor support of US expeditionary operations. The second has been to generate constructive discussion as to how the US government might better serve the national interest by evaluating uncertainties posed by ongoing changes in the nature of expeditionary engagements. These changes extend to growth in civilian armed security; training police, military, and other personnel within foreign states; and augmenting a growing civilian presence in and around the battlefield more generally. Both purposes will be realized if the authors and editors' collective efforts stimulate further debate and research among readers from government, business, and the academies.

Notes

1. Defense Science Board, *Task Force Report* (1996), 6A, cited in Molly Dunigan, *Victory for Hire* (Stanford, CA: Stanford University Press, 2011), 11.

2. Trevor Taylor, "Contractors on Deployed Operations and Equipment Support," *Defence Studies Journal* 4, 2 (2004): 184.

3. Cited in David M. Walker, *DOD Needs to Reexamine Its Extensive Reliance on Contractors and Continue to Improve Management and Oversight* (Washington, DC: Government Accountability Office, Mar. 11, 2008), www.gao.gov/new.items/d08572t .pdf at 5. See also Flavin at Chapter Four for further reference to DoD and the FAR.

4. See Charles C. Moskos, "From Institution to Occupation: Trends in Military Organization," *Armed Forces and Society* 4, 1 (1977): 41–50, at 42–44.

5. Ibid., 45.

6. Christopher Kinsey, *Private Contractors and the Reconstruction of Iraq: Transforming Military Logistics* (Oxford: Routledge, 2009), 54–55.

7. Samuel Huntington, *The Soldier and the State* (Cambridge, MA: Belknap Press, Harvard University Press, 1957), 11–12.

8. For a detailed discussion on the failure to prosecute contractors during the Iraq conflict, see Human Rights First, *Private Security Contractors at War: Ending the Culture of Impunity* (New York: Human Rights First, 2008).

9. Some consequences of the US retreat from LOAC and other international obligations are explained in Philippe Sands, *Torture Team: Rumsfeld's Memo and the Betrayal of American Values* (London: Palgrave Macmillan, 2008).

10. ABC Radio National, *The Law Report*, May 25, 2010, www.abc.net.au/rn/lawreport/stories/2010/2907797.htm (accessed July 14, 2011).

11. Tim Shorrock, *Spies for Hire: The Secret World of Intelligence Outsourcing* (New York: Simon and Shuster, 2008), 14.

12. For an informed discussion of problems in defining torture explained by a psychiatrist who treats torture victims, see Philippe Sands, "The Green Light," *Vanity Fair* (May 2008).

13. M. E. G. Caldicott, *To What Extent Should Contractors Contribute to Future British Military Contingencies Overseas?* Defence Research Paper (UK: Joint Services Command and Staff College, 2011), 33.

14. Commission on Army Acquisition and Program Management in Expeditionary Operations, *Urgent Reform Required: Army Expeditionary Contacting* (Oct. 2007), 4.

Contributors

Stuart W. Bowen, Jr., is Special Inspector General for Iraq Reconstruction. He was appointed Inspector General for the Coalition Provisional Authority in January 2004. Mr. Bowen is the primary author of *Hard Lessons: The Iraq Reconstruction Experience.* Prior to his appointment as Inspector General, he served in the White House as Deputy Assistant to the President, Deputy Staff Secretary, Special Assistant to the President, and Associate Counsel. He holds a B.A. from the University of the South and a J.D. from St. Mary's Law School.

Frank Camm is a Senior Economist at the RAND Corporation, where he has spent most of his career since 1976. He is the author of numerous books on managing risk in the military. His recent publications include *How Should the Army Use Contractors on the Battlefield? Assessing Comparative Risk in Sourcing Decisions* (with Victoria A. Greenfield, 2005); *Risk Management and Performance in the Balkans Support Contract* (with Victoria A. Greenfield, 2005); *Analyzing the Operation of Performance-Based Accountability Systems for Public Services* (with Brian Stecher, 2010).

Kateri Carmola is an Associate Professor of Political Science at Middlebury College, Vermont. She is the author of *Private Security Contractors and New Wars: Risk, Law, and Ethics* (Routledge, 2010). Dr. Carmola has participated in forums on private security contracting hosted by the American Bar Association, the Princeton Project on National Security, and Harvard University Law

School. Her opinions have been sought by the UN Working Group on Mercenaries, National Public Radio, and the *New York Times*.

Geoffrey S. Corn is a Professor of Law at South Texas College of Law in Houston, Texas, a retired US Army Lieutenant Colonel, and formerly the Special Assistant to the US Army Judge Advocate General for Law of War Matters. He is the lead author of *The Laws of War and the War on Terror*, published by Oxford University Press; and a co-author of *Principles of Counter-Terrorism Law*, published by Thompson-West.

Renée de Nevers is Associate Professor in the Department of Public Administration and International Affairs in the Maxwell School at Syracuse University. Her previous books include *Combating Terrorism* (with William C. Banks and Mitchel Wallerstein, Congressional Quarterly Press, 2008) and *Comrades No More: The Seeds of Change in Eastern Europe* (MIT Press, 2003).

Colonel William J. Flavin (ret'd) is Directing Professor in the Doctrine, Concepts, Training and Education Division, Peacekeeping and Stability Operations Institute, U.S. Army War College, Carlisle, Pennsylvania. He is a past senior fellow at the Center for Strategic and International Studies (CSIS), and a senior foreign affairs analyst with Booz Allen and Hamilton. He holds a BA in History from VMI and an MA in History from Emory University. His most recent publication is *Finding the Balance: U.S. Military and Future Operations* (PKSOI, 2011).

The Honorable *Jacques S. Gansler* is a former Under Secretary of Defense for Acquisition, Technology, and Logistics. He holds the Roger C. Lipitz Chair in Public Policy and Private Enterprise in the School of Public Policy, and is the Director of the Center for Public Policy and Private Enterprise at the University of Maryland. Before joining the Clinton administration, he held a variety of senior positions in government and the private sector. He is the author of *The Defense Industry* (1980), *Affording Defense* (1989), *Defense Conversion* (1995), *Democracy's Arsenal* (2011) [all MIT Press]; and *Ballistic Missile Defense* (2010, NDU Press). Professor Gansler has contributed 25 book chapters and authored over 100 papers.

Ryan Kelty is Associate Professor of Sociology in the Department of Sociology and Anthropology at Washington College. He teaches courses on Armed Forces and Society, Social Inequalities, Death and Dying, and Environmental Sociology. He is co-editor, with Morten Ender and Lynn Woehrle, of *Teaching the Sociology of Peace, War, and Military Institutions* (American Sociological

Association, 2007). Dr. Kelty's research interests include civilianization of the military, diversity in the military, social identity, and environmental sociology.

Christopher Kinsey is a Senior Lecturer in International Security with King's College London. Based in the Defence Studies Department at the Joint Services Command and Staff College, he teaches military officers from around the world. His research interest is the role of contractors in war. Dr. Kinsey has published widely on this subject in leading academic journals and his previous books include *Corporate Soldiers and International Security* (Routledge, 2006), and *Private Contractors and the Reconstruction of Iraq: Transforming Military Logistics* (Routledge, 2009).

William Lucyshyn is the Director of Research and Senior Research Scholar at the Center for Public Policy and Private Enterprise in the School of Public Policy at the University of Maryland. He is responsible for directing research on public sector management and operations, and how government works with private enterprise. He has authored numerous reports, book chapters, and journal articles. Mr. Lucyshyn is a past research director, program manager, and the principal technical advisor to the Director of the Defense Advanced Research Projects Agency (DARPA).

Robert Mandel is Chair and Professor of International Affairs at Lewis & Clark College in Portland, Oregon. He is the author of ten books and over forty articles and book chapters on security and conflict issues. His latest book is *Dark Logic: Transnational Criminal Tactics and Global Security* (Stanford University Press, 2011). He has just finished another book manuscript, titled *Global Security Upheaval: Armed Non-State Groups Usurping State Stability Functions*. He has testified before the United States Congress and worked for several government intelligence agencies.

Malcolm Hugh Patterson is an Australian lawyer who teaches international law and international relations. Since the award of his PhD from the University of Cambridge in 2008 he has taught at the University of New South Wales and Macquarie University in Sydney. He is the author of *Privatising Peace: A Corporate Adjunct to United Nations Peacekeeping and Humanitarian Operations* (Palgrave, 2009), and has published in the *Journal of Conflict and Security Law* and contributed a chapter to *The Global Arms Trade: A Handbook*.

Congressman David E. Price represents the Fourth District of North Carolina. Prior to entering Congress in 1987, he was a professor of political science and public policy at Duke University. He has authored four books on Congress and the American political system and currently serves on the House Appropriations Committee and is the ranking member of the Homeland Security Appropriations Subcommittee. Dr. Price is a recognized leader in foreign policy and co-chairs the House Democracy Partnership, which he initiated to strengthen parliaments in emerging democracies.

Darcy Schnack is a logistics Major in the US Army and currently attends the Army Command and General Staff College at Ft. Leavenworth, Kansas. Major Schnack graduated from West Point in 1996 and since then has been on active duty, serving two tours in Iraq in addition to several stateside locations. Major Schnack earned her MA in Sociology from Boston College, where she will begin her PhD studies in January 2012, examining civil–military relations and military sociology.

Allison Stanger is the Russell Leng '60 Professor of International Politics and Economics and Chair of the Political Science Department at Middlebury College. Her most recent book, *One Nation Under Contract: The Outsourcing of American Power and the Future of Foreign Policy*, was published by Yale University Press in fall 2009 (with a paperback edition in January 2011). In 2010, Stanger testified on contracting issues before the Commission on Wartime Contracting, the Senate Budget Committee, and the Congressional Oversight Panel. From 2009 to 2011, she served as an advisor to the Secretary's Policy Planning Staff, US Department of State. Stanger received her PhD in Political Science from Harvard University.

Since his arrival, *Samuel Worthington* has led InterAction to renewed prominence as a vibrant and vital force advocating globally on behalf of the world's poor and vulnerable, protecting NGO and civil society space, and promoting partnership with multiple actors as a means of addressing poverty, environmental impact and food security, human rights and more. He is a member of the Council on Foreign Relations, serves on USAID's Advisory Committee for Voluntary Foreign Assistance (ACVFA) and the Inter-Agency Standing Committee (IASC) at the United Nations. Additionally, he sits on the boards of the U.S. Global Leadership Campaign and the Alliance to End Hunger, and is an International Trustee of Religions for Peace. Previous leadership roles include chairing the global NGO Impact Initiative on behalf of the office of the UN Special Envoy for Tsunami Recovery (President Clinton) and co-founding the Hope for African Children Initiative (HACI), a partnership of NGOs working to address the impact of AIDS on children.

Index